Middle School 2-2

중간고사 완벽대비

적중 100

영어 기출 문제집

중**2**

동아 | 이병민

Best Collection

구성과 특징

교과서의 주요 학습 내용을 중심으로 학습 영역별 특성에 맞춰 단계별로 다양한 학습 기회를 제공하여 단원별 학습능력 평가는 물론 중간 및 기말고사 시험 등에 완벽하게 대비할 수 있도록 내용을 구성

Words & Expressions

Step1   Key Words 단원별 핵심 단어 설명 및 풀이
          Key Expression 단원별 핵심 숙어 및 관용어 설명
          Word Power 반대 또는 비슷한 뜻 단어 배우기
          English Dictionary 영어로 배우는 영어 단어

Step2   실력평가 단원별 수시평가 대비 주관식, 객관식 문제풀이

Step3   서술형 대비 학업성취도 및 수행능력평가 대비 서술형 문제풀이

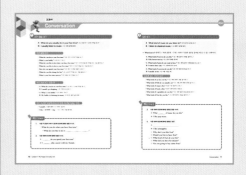

Conversation

Step1   핵심 의사소통 의사소통에 필요한 주요 표현 방법 요약
          핵심 Check 기본적인 표현 방법 및 활용능력 확인

Step2   대화문 익히기 상황에 따른 대화문 활용 및 연습

Step3   기본평가 시험대비 기초 학습 능력 평가

Step4   실력평가 단원별 수시평가 대비 주관식, 객관식 문제풀이

Step5   서술형 대비 학업성취도 및 수행능력평가 대비 서술형 문제풀이

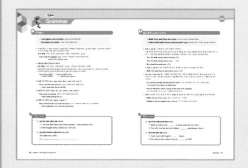

Grammar

Step1   주요 문법 단원별 주요 문법 사항과 예문을 알기 쉽게 설명
          핵심 Check 기본 문법사항에 대한 이해 여부 확인

Step2   기본평가 시험대비 기초 학습 능력 평가

Step3   실력평가 단원별 수시평가 대비 주관식, 객관식 문제풀이

Step4   서술형 대비 학업성취도 및 수행능력평가 대비 서술형 문제풀이

Reading

Step1   구문 분석 단원별로 제시된 문장에 대한 구문별 분석과 내용 설명
          확인문제 문장에 대한 기본적인 이해와 인지능력 확인

Step2   확인학습A 빈칸 채우기를 통한 문장 완성 능력 확인

Step3   확인학습B 제시된 우리말을 영어로 완성하여 작문 능력 키우기

Step4   실력평가 단원별 수시평가 대비 주관식, 객관식 문제풀이

Step5   서술형 대비 학업성취도 및 수행능력평가 대비 서술형 문제풀이
          교과서 구석구석 교과서에 나오는 기타 문장까지 완벽 학습

Composition

   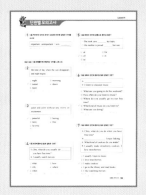

|영역별 핵심문제|

단어 및 어휘, 대화문, 문법, 독해 등 각 영역별 기출문제의 출제 유형을 분석하여 실전에 대비하고 연습할 수 있도록 문제를 배열

|서술형 실전 및 창의사고력 문제|

학교 시험에서 점차 늘어나는 서술형 시험에 집중 대비하고 고득점을 취득하는데 만전을 기하기 위한 학습 코너

|단원별 예상문제|

기출문제를 분석한 후 새로운 시험 출제 경향을 더하여 새롭게 출제될 수 있는 문제를 포함하여 시험에 완벽하게 대비할 수 있도록 준비

|단원별 모의고사|

영역별, 단계별 학습을 모두 마친 후 실전 연습을 위한 모의고사

on the textbook   교과서 파헤치기

- **단어Test1~2** 영어 단어 우리말 쓰기와 우리말을 영어 단어로 쓰기

- **대화문Test1~2** 대화문 빈칸 완성 및 전체 대화문 쓰기

- **본문Test1~5** 빈칸 완성, 우리말 쓰기, 문장 배열연습, 영어 작문하기 복습 등 단계별 반복 학습을 통해 교과서 지문에 대한 완벽한 습득

- **구석구석지문Test1~2** 지문 빈칸 완성 및 전문 영어로 쓰기

이책의 차례 Contents

Lesson 5

Come One, Come All

🎤 **의사소통 기능**

- 길 묻고 답하기
  A: How can I get to the post office?
  B: Go straight to 1st Street and make a right.

- 소요 시간 말하기
  A: How long will it take to make the sandwiches?
  B: Maybe it will take about an hour.

🎤 **언어 형식**

- 가주어 It
  It is a lot of fun **to throw** colorful powder at everyone.

- 지각동사
  You can **hear** musicians **playing** beautiful live music.

교과서
Words & Expressions

Key Words

- **adult** [ədʌ́lt] 명 성인, 어른
- **advertise** [ǽdvərtàiz] 동 광고하다
- **almost** [ɔ́ːlmoust] 부 거의
- **amazing** [əméiziŋ] 형 놀라운
- **appear** [əpíər] 동 나타나다
- **arrow** [ǽrou] 명 화살
- **artwork** [áːrtwərk] 명 예술 작품
- **bakery** [béikəri] 명 빵집, 제과점
- **block** [blɑk] 명 블록, 구획
- **boat** [bout] 명 배, 선박
- **celebrate** [séləbrèit] 동 축하하다, 기념하다
- **chase** [tʃeis] 동 뒤쫓다
- **colorful** [kʌ́lərfəl] 형 형형색색의
- **competition** [kàmpətíʃən] 명 대회, 시합, 경쟁
- **completely** [kəmplíːtli] 부 완전히
- **cross** [krɔːs] 동 가로지르다, 가로질러 건너다
- **dark** [dɑːrk] 형 어두운
- **decorate** [dékərèit] 동 장식하다
- **during** [djúəriŋ] 전 ~ 동안
- **far** [fɑːər] 형 먼 부 멀리
- **festival** [féstəvəl] 명 축제

- **firework** [fáiərwərk] 명 폭죽, 불꽃놀이
- **follow** [fálou] 동 따르다
- **gather** [gǽðər] 동 모이다, 모으다
- **hold** [hould] 동 개최하다
- **hometown** [hóumtaun] 명 고향
- **huge** [hjuːdʒ] 형 거대한
- **last** [læst] 동 지속하다
- **live** [laiv] 형 라이브의, 실황인
- **musician** [mjuːzíʃən] 명 음악가
- **near** [niər] 형 가까운, 가까이에 있는
- **neighborhood** [néibərhùd] 명 근처, 이웃, 인근
- **outdoor** [áutdɔːr] 형 야외의
- **parade** [pəréid] 명 퍼레이드, 행진
- **pile** [pail] 명 더미
- **post** [poust] 동 게시하다
- **powder** [páudər] 명 가루
- **sail** [seil] 명 돛
- **shape** [ʃeip] 명 형태 동 ~ 모양으로 만들다
- **sled** [sled] 명 썰매
- **solve** [sɑlv] 동 해결하다
- **take** [teik] 동 (시간이) 걸리다, (탈 것을) 타다
- **throw** [θrou] 동 던지다

Key Expressions

- **because of** ~ 때문에
- **between A and B** A와 B 사이에
- **come out** 나오다
- **each other** 서로
- **from beginning to end** 처음부터 끝까지
- **get off** 내리다
- **go on** 지속되다, 계속되다

- **go straight** 앞으로 곧장 가다
- **in front of** ~ 앞에
- **make a left[right]** 왼쪽[오른쪽]으로 돌다
- **more and more** 더욱 더
- **next to** ~ ~ 옆에
- **on one's right** ~의 오른편에
- **out of hand** 손을 쓸 수 없는

Word Power

※ 서로 반대되는 뜻을 가진 단어

- [ ] **far** 먼 ↔ **near** 가까운
- [ ] **dark** 어두운 ↔ **bright** 밝은
- [ ] **outdoor** 야외의 ↔ **indoor** 실내의
- [ ] **complete** 완전한 ↔ **incomplete** 불완전한
- [ ] **huge** 거대한 ↔ **tiny** 작은
- [ ] **get on** (탈 것을) 타다 ↔ **get off** 내리다

- [ ] **appear** 나타나다 ↔ **disappear** 사라지다
- [ ] **adult** 어른, 성인 ↔ **child** 아이, 어린이
- [ ] **live** 살아 있는 ↔ **dead** 죽은
- [ ] **follow** 뒤따르다 ↔ **precede** 선행하다, 앞서다
- [ ] **compete** 경쟁하다 ↔ **cooperate** 협력하다, 협동하다
- [ ] **throw** 던지다 ↔ **receive** 받다

English Dictionary

- [ ] **adult** 어른
  - → a fully grown person
  - 완전히 자란 사람

- [ ] **advertise** 광고하다
  - → to tell the public about goods to make people buy them
  - 사람들이 물건을 사게 만들도록 물건에 대해 대중에게 이야기하다

- [ ] **artwork** 예술 작품
  - → objects produced by artists
  - 예술가들에 의해 만들어진 물체

- [ ] **celebrate** 축하하다
  - → to do something special for an important event, holiday, etc.
  - 중요한 행사나 휴일 등을 위해 특별한 무언가를 하다

- [ ] **chase** 뒤쫓다
  - → to follow and try to catch
  - 따라가서 잡으려고 노력하다

- [ ] **competition** 대회, 경쟁
  - → an event or contest in which people compete
  - 사람들이 경쟁하는 행사 또는 대회

- [ ] **completely** 완전히
  - → totally, fully
  - 완전히

- [ ] **decorate** 장식하다
  - → to make something look more beautiful by putting things on it
  - 위에 물건들을 올려놓음으로써 더 아름답게 보이도록 만들다

- [ ] **festival** 축제
  - → a day or period of celebration
  - 축하하는 날이나 기간

- [ ] **gather** 모이다
  - → to come together to form a group
  - 모임을 형성하기 위해 함께 모이다

- [ ] **hold** 개최하다
  - → to have a meeting, competition, conversation, etc.
  - 만남, 경쟁, 대화 등을 갖다

- [ ] **hometown** 고향
  - → the city or town where you were born or grew up
  - 당신이 태어나거나 자란 도시나 마을

- [ ] **last** 지속하다
  - → to continue in time
  - 시간에 있어서 계속되다

- [ ] **lift** 들어올리다
  - → to move something or someone to a higher position
  - 어떤 것이나 어떤 사람을 높은 위치로 옮기다

- [ ] **live** 라이브의, 실황인
  - → given or made when people are watching, not pre-recorded
  - 미리 녹화되지 않고 사람들이 보고 시청하고 있을 때 주어지거나 만들어진

- [ ] **pile** 더미
  - → a mass of something that has been placed somewhere
  - 어딘가에 놓여진 무언가의 덩어리

- [ ] **shape** ~ 모양으로 만들다
  - → to make something into a particular shape
  - 무언가를 특정한 모양으로 만들다

- [ ] **sled** 썰매
  - → a small vehicle used for sliding over snow
  - 눈 위에서 미끄러지기 위해 사용된 작은 탈 것

서답형

01 다음 짝지어진 단어의 관계가 같도록 빈칸에 알맞은 말을 쓰시오.

> heavy: light = _____ : near

서답형

02 다음 영영풀이가 가리키는 말을 쓰시오.

> the city or town where you were born or grew up

➡ _____

03 다음 중 밑줄 친 부분의 뜻풀이가 바르지 <u>않은</u> 것은?

① That yacht with white <u>sails</u> is my dad's. 항해하다
② He raked the leaves into <u>piles</u>. 더미
③ I heard the band playing <u>live</u> music. 라이브의, 실황의
④ This movie <u>lasts</u> two hours. 지속하다
⑤ The technique is <u>completely</u> new. 완전히

서답형

04 다음 문장의 빈칸에 들어갈 말을 〈보기〉에서 골라 쓰시오.

> ┌─ 보기 ─┐
> parade / neighborhood / pile / advertise / regularly

(1) Is there a bakery in this _____ ?
(2) The band is marching in a _____ .
(3) We made a plan to _____ our new product.
(4) He is looking at a _____ of newspapers.
(5) She attended church _____ .

중요

05 다음 주어진 문장의 밑줄 친 live와 같은 의미로 쓰인 것은?

> Musicians played beautiful <u>live</u> music.

① This program is <u>live</u> from Time Square.
② We used to <u>live</u> in Jeju-do.
③ Mike needs to find somewhere to <u>live</u>.
④ This moment will <u>live</u> in our memory for a long time.
⑤ Bears can <u>live</u> for several days without food.

06 다음 문장에 공통으로 들어갈 말을 고르시오.

> • You should _____ the sea to get to the island.
> • My brother is waiting to _____ the street.
> • I put a _____ on the map to show where the hotel is.

① follow　　　② chase
③ parade　　　④ shape
⑤ cross

서답형

07 다음 우리말에 맞게 빈칸에 알맞은 말을 쓰시오.

(1) 그들은 개 썰매로 이동하곤 했다.
➡ They used to travel by dog _____ .
(2) 사진 속의 형형색색의 꽃들을 보세요.
➡ Look at the _____ flowers in the picture.
(3) 시간이 화살처럼 지나갔다.
➡ Time flew like an _____ .

01 다음 짝지어진 단어의 관계가 같도록 빈칸에 알맞은 말을 쓰시오.

> complete : incomplete = appear : _____

02 다음 문장의 빈칸에 들어갈 말을 〈보기〉에서 골라 쓰시오.

> ┤ 보기 ├
> almost / live / artwork / fireworks

(1) I'm looking forward to the _____ music performance.

(2) They celebrate the festival with _____.

(3) It's been _____ 5 years since I moved to Korea.

(4) His _____ is going to be displayed in a gallery.

03 다음 우리말에 맞게 주어진 빈칸을 완성하시오.

(1) 나는 이 책을 처음부터 끝까지 읽을 거야.
➡ I'll read this book from beginning _____ _____.

(2) 경쟁이 더욱 더 심해졌다.
➡ The competition became _____ _____ _____ severe.

(3) 언제 그 책이 나왔습니까?
➡ When did the book _____ _____?

(4) 일이 아주 엉망이 되었다.
➡ Things really got _____ _____ _____.

04 다음 우리말을 주어진 단어를 이용하여 영작하시오.

(1) 음악 축제가 언제 열리나요? (will, held)
➡ _____

(2) 나는 크리스마스 트리 장식하는 것을 즐겼다. (enjoyed)
➡ _____

(3) 사람들이 그 가수를 보기 위해 함께 모였다. (gathered)
➡ _____

05 다음 우리말과 일치하도록 주어진 어구를 배열하여 완성하시오.

(1) 사람들이 이틀 동안 여기저기서 축제를 기념한다.
(two / everywhere / days / people / the festival / celebrate / for)
➡ _____

(2) 내가 가장 좋아하는 가수를 직접 본 것은 정말 놀라웠다.
(singer / in / amazing / it / to / see / favorite / person / my / was)
➡ _____

(3) 사람들은 미술가들이 그들의 작품을 만드는 것을 처음부터 끝까지 지켜본다.
(watch / the / shaping / artists / from / end / works / beginning / to / their / people)
➡ _____

Conversation

1 길 묻고 답하기

A How can I get to the post office? 우체국에 어떻게 가나요?

B Go straight to 1st Street and make a right. 1가로 곧장 간 후 오른쪽으로 도세요.

■ 'How can I get to + 장소 명사?'는 '~에 어떻게 갈 수 있나요?'라는 뜻으로 길을 묻는 표현이다. 'How can I go to ~?'로 물을 수도 있다. 대답으로 길을 안내할 때는 보통 'Go straight.'처럼 명령문의 형태로 대답한다.

길 묻고 답하기

- Where can I find the police station? 경찰서가 어디에 있나요?
- Do you know where the library is? 도서관이 어디에 있는지 아세요?
- Is there a bakery around here? 이곳 주위에 빵집이 있나요?
- Walk straight ahead. 앞쪽으로 곧장 걸어가세요.
- You can't miss it. 쉽게 찾을 수 있을 거야.
- It's just around the corner. 그것은 바로 모퉁이를 돌면 있어.
- It's across from the museum. 그것은 박물관 건너편에 있어.

핵심 Check

1. 다음 우리말과 일치하도록 빈칸에 알맞은 말을 쓰시오.

(1) **A:** _____ _____ _____ _____ _____ the museum?

(박물관에 어떻게 가나요?)

   B: Come out from the school and go straight one block.

(학교에서 나와서 한 구역 곧장 가세요.)

(2) **A:** Where can I find the theater? (극장이 어디에 있나요?)

   B: _____ _____ _____ and _____ _____ two blocks.

(길을 건너서 두 구역을 곧장 가세요.)

(3) **A:** _____ _____ _____ _____ around here? (이곳 주위에 병원이 있나요?)

   B: Yes, it's _____ _____ the corner. (네, 그것은 바로 모퉁이를 돌면 있어요.)

2 소요 시간 말하기

A How long will it take to make the sandwiches? 샌드위치를 만드는 데 시간이 얼마나 걸릴까?

B Maybe it will take about an hour. 아마도 약 한 시간 정도 걸릴 거야.

■ 'How long will it take to ~?'는 '~하는 데 시간이 얼마가 걸릴까?'라는 뜻으로, 소요 시간을 묻는 표현이다. 대답으로 '(시간이) ~ 걸리다'의 뜻을 나타내는 동사 take를 사용하여 소요 시간을 말한다. 대답할 때는 소요 시간을 구체적으로 말하는 것이 보통이다.

- How long will it take to finish your work? 일을 마치는 데 얼마나 걸리겠어요?
- How long will it take to go to London? 런던까지 가는 데는 얼마나 걸립니까?
- It will take more than an hour. 한 시간 이상 걸릴 것이다.
- It will take about ten minutes on foot. 걸어서 10분 정도 걸립니다.

핵심 Check

2. 다음 우리말과 일치하도록 빈칸에 알맞은 말을 쓰시오.

(1) **A:** How long will it take to clean the classroom? (교실을 청소하는 데 얼마나 걸릴까?)

   B: It'll _____ _____ _____ _____ _____ . (약 30분 정도 걸릴 거야.)

(2) **A:** _____ _____ _____ _____ _____ get to the theater?

   (영화관까지 가는 데 시간이 얼마가 걸릴까?)

   B: It'll take about 15 minutes _____ _____ . (버스로 약 15분 정도 걸릴 거야.)

(3) **A:** _____ _____ _____ _____ _____ _____ _____

   _____? (교실을 장식하는 데 얼마나 걸릴까?)

   B: It'll _____ _____ _____ _____ . (약 두 시간 정도 걸릴 거야.)

🎤 **Listen and Speak 1-B**

(*A phone rings.*)
Minsu: Hi, Emma. What's up?
Emma: Hey, Minsu. Are you free this Saturday?
Minsu: Yes. Why do you ask?
Emma: Well, ❶how about having lunch together?
Minsu: Sure.
Emma: Let's try the new Chinese restaurant, Ming's. ❷It's near the school.
Minsu: Okay. ❸How can I get there from the school?
Emma: ❹Come out from the school and go straight to Green Street. ❺Make a left, and the restaurant will be on your left.
Minsu: All right. Let's meet at 12 o'clock.
Emma: Wonderful. See you then.

(전화벨이 울린다.)
Minsu: 안녕, Emma. 잘 지내니?
Emma: 안녕, 민수야. 이번 토요일에 한가하니?
Minsu: 응. 왜 묻는 거니?
Emma: 그럼, 함께 점심 먹는 게 어떠니?
Minsu: 좋아.
Emma: Ming's라는 새로 생긴 중국 음식점에 가 보자. 학교 근처에 있어.
Minsu: 좋아. 학교에서 거기까지 어떻게 가니?
Emma: 학교에서 나와서 Green Street까지 곧장 가. 왼쪽으로 돌면 음식점이 네 왼쪽에 있을 거야.
Minsu: 알겠어. 12시에 만나자.
Emma: 좋아. 그때 보자.

❶ 'How about ~?'은 '~하는 게 어때?'라고 제안하는 표현으로 'Why don't we ~?' 또는 'What about ~?'으로 바꾸어 쓸 수 있다.
❷ be near ~: ~와 가깝다
❸ How can I get ~?은 '~에 어떻게 가니?'라고 길을 묻는 표현이다.
❹ 동사원형으로 시작하는 명령문이다.
❺ make a left: 왼쪽으로 돌다(= turn left)

Check(√) True or False

(1) Minsu and Emma will have lunch together. T ☐ F ☐

(2) The Chinese restaurant is far from the school. T ☐ F ☐

🎤 **Real Life Talk**

Man: Excuse me. How can I get to Suwon Hwaseong from here?
Mina: It's easy. Do you see the bus stop over there?
Man: Yes, I do.
Mina: Take the No. 11 bus and ❶get off at the sixth stop.
Man: ❷How long will it take to get there?
Mina: It will take ❸about 20 minutes.
Man: Thank you very much.
Mina: No problem. ❹Are you going there for the festival?
Man: Yes. I heard it's a lot of fun.
Mina: I hope you have a great time.

Man: 실례합니다. 여기에서 수원 화성까지 어떻게 가나요?
Mina: 쉬워요. 저쪽에 버스 정류장 보이세요?
Man: 네, 보여요.
Mina: 11번 버스를 타서 여섯 번째 정류장에서 내리세요.
Man: 그곳까지 가는 데 시간이 얼마나 걸릴까요?
Mina: 대략 20분 정도 걸릴 거에요.
Man: 정말 고마워요.
Mina: 별말씀을요. 그곳에 축제 때문에 가시는 건가요?
Man: 네. 그 축제가 무척 재미있다고 들었어요.
Mina: 즐거운 시간 보내길 바라요.

❶ get off: 내리다 ↔ get on: 타다
❷ How long will it take to get there?: '그곳에 가는 데 얼마나 걸리나요?'라는 의미로 소요 시간을 묻는 표현이다.
❸ about: 대략
❹ 수원 화성에 가는 목적을 묻고 있다.

Check(√) True or False

(3) It'll take about 20 minutes for the man to go to Suwon Hwaseong by bus. T ☐ F ☐

(4) Mina wants to visit the festival in Suwon Hwaseong. T ☐ F ☐

Listen and Speak 1-A

Sora: Excuse me. ❶How can I get to the library?

Tom: Oh, the library? ❷Cross the street and go straight two blocks. Then ❸make a left.

Sora: Thank you very much.

❶ 도서관에 가는 법을 묻는 표현이다.
❷ cross: 건너다
❸ make a left: 왼쪽으로 돌다(= turn left)

Listen and Speak 1-C

A: Excuse me. How can I get to the post office?

B: Go straight to 1st Street and make a right. It will be ❶on your right.

A: Is it ❷far from here?

B: No, it's not.

A: Thank you very much.

❶ on one's right: ~의 오른편에
❷ far: 먼; 멀리

Listen and Speak 2-A

Amy: Jinho, hurry up. We're going to be late for the movie.

Jinho: Okay. ❶How long will it take to get to the theater?

Amy: It will take about 15 minutes ❷by bus.

Jinho: All right. I'm ❸almost ready.

❶ 극장에 가는 소요 시간을 묻고 있다.
❷ by bus: 버스로
❸ almost: 거의

Listen and Speak 2-B

Andy: I'm so excited about the school festival this Friday.

Mike: ❶Me, too. What can we do to advertise ❷it, Andy?

Andy: How about making posters?

Mike: Great idea. We can post ❸them in our neighborhood.

Andy: Right. ❹How long will it take to make them?

Mike: Well, it will take about three hours.

Andy: Okay, I hope many people come to the festival.

❶ '나도 그래.'라는 의미로 'So am I.'와 바꾸어 쓸 수 있다.
❷ it은 the school festival을 가리킨다.
❸ them은 posters를 가리킨다.
❹ 포스터를 제작하는 데 걸리는 소요 시간을 묻고 있다.

Listen and Speak 2-C

Rachel: Chris, what will you do for the class party?

Chris: I'll make sandwiches.

Rachel: Great idea. How long will it take to make ❶them?

Chris: Maybe it'll take ❷about an hour.

❶ them은 sandwiches를 가리킨다.
❷ about: 약, 대략

● 다음 우리말과 일치하도록 빈칸에 알맞은 말을 쓰시오.

Listen and Speak 1-A

Sora: Excuse me. _____ _____ _____ _____ _____
_____ _____?

Tom: Oh, the library? _____ the street and _____ _____ two
blocks. Then _____ a left.

Sora: Thank you very much.

해석

Sora: 실례합니다. 도서관까지 어떻게 가나요?

Tom: 아, 도서관이요? 길을 건너서 두 구역을 곧장 가세요. 그런 다음 왼쪽으로 도세요.

Sora: 정말 고마워요.

Listen and Speak 1-B

(*A phone rings.*)

Minsu: Hi, Emma. _____ _____?

Emma: Hey, Minsu. Are you _____ this Saturday?

Minsu: Yes. _____ do you _____?

Emma: Well, how about _____ lunch together?

Minsu: Sure.

Emma: _____ try the new Chinese restaurant, Ming's. It's _____
the school.

Minsu: Okay. _____ _____ _____ _____ _____
_____ _____?

Emma: _____ _____ from the school and _____ _____ to
Green Street. _____ _____ _____, and the restaurant
will be _____ _____ _____.

Minsu: All right. _____ _____ at 12 o'clock.

Emma: Wonderful. _____ you _____.

(전화벨이 울린다.)

Minsu: 안녕, Emma. 잘 지내니?

Emma: 안녕, 민수야. 이번 토요일에 한가하니?

Minsu: 응. 왜 묻는 거니?

Emma: 음, 함께 점심 먹는 게 어떠니?

Minsu: 좋아.

Emma: Ming's라는 새로 생긴 중국 음식점에 가 보자. 학교 근처에 있어.

Minsu: 좋아. 학교에서 거기까지 어떻게 가니?

Emma: 학교에서 나와서 Green Street까지 곧장 가. 왼쪽으로 돌면 음식점이 네 왼쪽에 있을 거야.

Minsu: 알겠어. 12시에 만나자.

Emma: 좋아. 그때 보자.

Listen and Speak 1-C

A: Excuse me. _____ _____ I _____ _____ the post office?

B: _____ _____ to 1st Street and _____ a right. It will _____
_____ _____ _____.

A: Is it _____ _____ here?

B: No, it's _____.

A: Thank you very much.

A: 실례합니다. 우체국에 어떻게 갈 수 있나요?

B: 1st Street까지 곧장 가서 오른쪽으로 도세요. 그것은 오른쪽에 있을 거예요.

A: 여기서 먼가요?

B: 아니요, 멀지 않아요.

A: 정말 고마워요.

Listen and Speak 2-A

Amy: Jinho, hurry up. We're going to _____ _____ _____ the movie.

Jinho: Okay. _____ _____ _____ _____ _____ _____ _____ _____ _____ _____ _____ ?

Amy: It will _____ _____ 15 minutes _____ _____ .

Jinho: All right. I'm _____ ready.

Listen and Speak 2-B

Andy: I'm so _____ about the school festival this Friday.

Mike: _____ , _____ . What can we do to _____ it, Andy?

Andy: How _____ _____ posters?

Mike: Great idea. We can _____ _____ in our _____ .

Andy: Right. _____ _____ _____ _____ _____ _____ _____ make them?

Mike: Well, it will _____ _____ three hours.

Andy: Okay, I hope many people _____ _____ the festival.

Real Life Talk

Man: Excuse me. How can I _____ _____ Suwon Hwaseong from here?

Mina: It's easy. Do you see the bus stop _____ _____ ?

Man: Yes, I do.

Mina: _____ the No. 11 bus and _____ _____ at the sixth stop.

Man: _____ _____ _____ _____ _____ _____ _____ _____ ?

Mina: It will _____ _____ 20 minutes.

Man: Thank you very much.

Mina: No problem. Are you going there for _____ _____ ?

Man: Yes. I heard _____ _____ _____ _____ _____ .

Mina: I hope you _____ _____ _____ _____ .

해석

Amy: 진호야, 서둘러. 우리 영화 시간에 늦겠어.
Jinho: 응. 영화관까지 가는 데 시간이 얼마나 걸릴까?
Amy: 버스로 대략 15분 정도 걸릴 거야.
Jinho: 알겠어. 나 거의 준비됐어.

Andy: 나는 이번 금요일 학교 축제가 정말 기대돼.
Mike: 나도. 축제를 광고하기 위해 무엇을 할 수 있을까, Andy?
Andy: 포스터를 만들면 어떨까?
Mike: 좋은 생각이야. 이 근방에 포스터를 붙일 수 있겠다.
Andy: 맞아. 포스터를 만드는 데 시간이 얼마나 걸릴까?
Mike: 음, 대략 세 시간 정도 걸릴 거야.
Andy: 좋아, 많은 사람들이 축제에 왔으면 좋겠다.

Man: 실례합니다. 여기에서 수원 화성까지 어떻게 가나요?
Mina: 쉬워요. 저쪽에 버스 정류장 보이세요?
Man: 네, 보여요.
Mina: 11번 버스를 타서 여섯 번째 정류장에서 내리세요.
Man: 그곳까지 가는 데 시간이 얼마나 걸릴까요?
Mina: 대략 20분 정도 걸릴 거예요.
Man: 정말 고마워요.
Mina: 별말씀을요. 그곳에 축제 때문에 가시는 건가요?
Man: 네. 그 축제가 무척 재미있다고 들었어요.
Mina: 즐거운 시간 보내길 바라요.

01 다음 대화의 빈칸에 들어갈 말을 〈보기〉에 주어진 단어를 배열하여 완성하시오.

> A: How long will it take to get to the pharmacy?
>
> B: _____

> ┤ 보기 ├
>
> by / car / about / take / it / 5 minutes / will

➡ _____

02 다음 대화가 자연스럽게 이어지도록 순서대로 배열하시오.

> (A) Thank you very much.
> (B) Excuse me. How can I get to the post office?
> (C) Is it far from here?
> (D) No, it's not.
> (E) Go straight to 1st Street and make a right. It will be on your right.

➡ _____

[03~04] 다음 대화를 읽고 물음에 답하시오.

> A: Excuse me. How can I get ⓐto the police station?
> B: Go straight to Green Street. ⓑCross the street. Then make a right. The police station is between the flower shop ⓒor the bakery.
> A: How ⓓlong will it take to get there?
> B: It will take ⓔabout 5 minutes.
> A: Thank you very much.

03 위 대화의 밑줄 친 ⓐ~ⓔ 중 어법상 바르지 <u>않은</u> 것을 찾아 바르게 고치시오.

➡ _____

04 위 대화의 내용과 일치하지 <u>않는</u> 것은?
① A는 경찰서를 찾고 있다.
② 경찰서는 꽃가게와 빵집 사이에 위치해 있다.
③ 경찰서까지 5분 정도 걸릴 것이다.
④ 경찰서에 가기 위해 Green Street까지 직진해서 길을 건넌 후 오른쪽으로 돌아야 한다.
⑤ B는 A에게 버스를 타고 경찰서 가는 법을 설명하고 있다.

[01~02] 다음 대화를 읽고 물음에 답하시오.

Amy: Jinho, hurry up. We're going to be late for the movie.

Jinho: Okay. _____(A)_____?

Amy: It will take about 15 minutes ___(B)___ bus.

Jinho: All right. I'm almost ready.

01 위 대화의 빈칸 (A)에 들어갈 말을 〈보기〉의 단어를 배열하여 완성하시오.

┌─── 보기 ───┐
take / get / it / the / to / to / theater / how / will / long
└───────────┘

➡ _____

02 위 대화의 빈칸 (B)에 들어갈 말로 적절한 것은?

① by   ② at   ③ from
④ on   ⑤ for

[03~04] 다음 대화를 읽고 물음에 답하시오.

Minsu: Hi, Emma. What's up?

Emma: Hey, Minsu. Are you free this Saturday?

Minsu: Yes. Why do you ask?

Emma: Well, (A)how about having lunch together?

Minsu: Sure.

Emma: Let's try the new Chinese restaurant, Ming's. It's near the school.

Minsu: Okay. How can I get there from the school?

Emma: Come out from the school and go straight to Green Street. Make a left, and the restaurant will be on your left.

Minsu: All right. Let's meet at 12 o'clock.

Emma: Wonderful. See you then.

서답형

03 위 대화의 밑줄 친 (A)와 의미가 같도록 why를 사용하여 다시 쓰시오.

➡ _____

04 위 대화를 읽고 대답할 수 <u>없는</u> 것은?

① What are Emma and Minsu going to do this Saturday?
② What restaurant are Emma and Minsu going to try?
③ How can Minsu get to Ming's?
④ What time are Emma and Minsu going to meet?
⑤ How long does it take for Emma to go to Ming's?

[05~07] 다음 대화를 읽고 물음에 답하시오.

Andy: I'm so excited about the school festival this Friday.

Mike: Me, too. What can we do to advertise ⓐit, Andy?

Andy: How about making posters?

Mike: Great idea. We can post them in our neighborhood.

Andy: Right. How long will it take to make ⓑ them?

Mike: Well, it will take about three hours.

Andy: Okay, I hope many people come to the festival.

서답형

05 위 대화에서 다음 영영풀이가 나타내는 말을 찾아 쓰시오.

> to tell the public about goods to make people buy them

➡ _____

서답형

06 위 대화의 밑줄 친 ⓐ와 ⓑ가 각각 가리키는 것을 쓰시오.

➡ ⓐ _____ ⓑ _____

07 위 대화의 내용과 일치하지 <u>않는</u> 것은?

① Andy and Mike are excited about the school festival.
② The school festival is going to be held this Friday.
③ Andy and Mike are going to make posters to advertise the school festival.
④ It will take about three hours to make the posters.
⑤ Andy and Mike are going to post the posters with their neighbors.

서답형

[08~10] 다음 대화를 읽고 물음에 답하시오.

Man: Excuse me. How can I get to Suwon Hwaseong from here?
Mina: It's easy. Do you see the bus stop over there?
Man: Yes, I do.
Mina: Take the No. 11 bus and get off at the sixth stop.
Man: How long will it take to get there?
Mina: It will take about 20 minutes.
Man: Thank you very much.

Mina: No problem. Are you going there for the festival?
Man: Yes. I heard it's a lot of fun.
Mina: I hope you have a great time.

08 How will the man go to Suwon Hwaseong?

➡ _____

09 Why does the man want to join the festival?

➡ _____

10 Which bus should the man take to go to Suwon Hwaseong?

➡ _____

서답형

11 다음 대화에 알맞은 말을 〈보기〉에서 골라 쓰시오.

> ┤ 보기 ├
> a right / front / get / one block / go straight

A: Excuse me. How can I ___(A)___ to the market?
B: ___(B)___ to Green Street. Make ___(C)___ . Go straight ___(D)___ and cross the street. The market will be in ___(E)___ of you.
A: Thank you very much.

➡ (A) _____
(B) _____
(C) _____
(D) _____
(E) _____

[01~02] 다음 대화를 읽고 물음에 답하시오.

Sora: Excuse me. _____(A)_____?
Tom: Oh, the library? Cross the street and go straight two blocks. Then ____(B)____.
Sora: Thank you very much.

중요

01 다음 대화의 빈칸 (A)에 들어갈 말을 〈보기〉에 주어진 단어를 배열하여 완성하시오.

┌─ 보기 ─┐
get / how / I / to / library / can / the

➡ _____

02 다음 표지판의 내용과 일치하도록 빈칸 (B)를 완성하시오.

➡ _____

[03~05] 다음 대화를 읽고 물음에 답하시오.

Andy: I'm so ⓐexciting about the school festival this Friday.
Mike: Me, too. What can we do ⓑto advertise it, Andy?
Andy: How about ⓒmaking posters?
Mike: Great idea. We can post them in our neighborhood.
Andy: Right. How long will it take to make them?
Mike: Well, it will take ⓓabout three hours.
Andy: Okay, I hope many people ⓔcome to the festival.

03 위 대화의 ⓐ~ⓔ 중 어법상 바르지 않은 것을 찾아 바르게 고치시오.

➡ _____

04 What are Andy and Mike going to advertise?

➡ _____

05 What are Andy and Mike going to make?

➡ _____

중요

06 다음 그림의 내용과 일치하도록 빈칸 (A)와 (B)를 완성하시오.

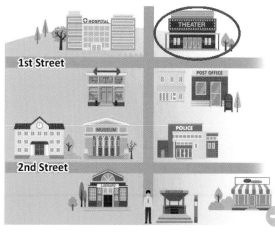

Aram: Excuse me. How can I get to the theater?
Brian: _____(A)_____. It will be on your ____(B)____.
Aram: Thank you so much.

➡ (A) _____
(B) _____

Grammar

① 가주어 It

> * **It** is a pleasure **to talk** with you. 너와 대화하는 것은 즐거워.
> * **It** was difficult **to stop** my bad habit. 나의 나쁜 습관을 멈추는 것은 어려웠다.

■ to부정사구가 문장의 주어로 쓰여 주어가 길어진 경우, 주어부를 문장의 맨 뒤로 보내고 이 자리에 It을 쓰는 것이 가주어 It이다.

　• **To exercise** regularly is very important.

　= **It** is very important **to exercise** regularly. 규칙적으로 운동하는 것은 매우 중요하다.

■ 가주어 It은 따로 해석하지 않으며 to부정사구를 주어로 해석해야 한다. to부정사구의 부정은 'not+to V'로 나타낸다.

　• **It** is fun **to learn** a foreign language. 외국어를 배우는 것은 재미있다.

　• **It** was hard **to say** sorry to you. 너에게 미안하다고 말하는 것은 힘들었어.

　• **It** is good **to know** how to say hello. 인사하는 방법을 아는 것은 좋다.

　• **It** is important **not to use** your phone while walking. 걷는 동안 휴대 전화기를 사용하지 않는 것이 중요하다.

핵심 Check

1. 다음 우리말과 일치하도록 빈칸에 알맞은 말을 쓰시오.

(1) 아침 일찍 운동하는 것은 좋다.

➡ _____ is good _____ _____ early in the morning.

(2) 부주의하게 운전하는 것은 위험하다.

➡ _____ is dangerous _____ _____ carelessly.

(3) 너의 친구에게 거짓말하는 것은 옳지 않아.

➡ It is wrong _____ _____ to your friend.

② 지각동사

- **I heard** her **crying**. 나는 그녀가 우는 소리를 들었어.
- **They saw** the boy **playing** the piano. 그들은 그 소년이 피아노를 연주하는 것을 보았다.

■ 지각동사란 신체 감각과 관련된 동사로 보고, 듣고, 느끼는 동사인 see, watch, hear, feel 등이 이에 해당한다. 5형식 동사에 해당하여 목적어와 목적격보어를 취한다.

　• June **heard** the dog **barking** at someone. June은 그 개가 누군가를 향해 짖는 소리를 들었다.

■ '지각동사+목적어+V(ing)'로 쓰이는 경우, 목적어와 목적격보어는 능동 관계가 된다. 동작이 진행 중인 것을 강조하고 싶을 때에는 보통 현재분사를 쓴다. '지각동사+목적어+p.p.'로 쓰이는 경우 목적어와 목적격보어의 관계는 수동이다.

　• We **watched** our children **singing** songs. 우리는 우리 아이들이 노래 부르는 것을 지켜보았다.

　• Did you **see** the glass **broken**? 너는 그 유리잔이 깨어진 것을 봤니?

■ 사역동사의 쓰임과 혼동하지 않도록 한다. 사역동사 make, have, let 역시 5형식 동사로 목적어와 목적격보어를 취하지만, 사역동사의 목적격보어는 원형부정사이며 '목적어가 ~하게 시키다'라는 의미이다.

　• Mom **makes** me **eat** carrots. 엄마는 내가 당근을 먹게 하신다.

　• The teacher **had** us **do** some homework. 그 선생님은 우리가 약간의 숙제를 하도록 시키셨다.

핵심 Check

2. 다음 우리말과 일치하도록 빈칸에 알맞은 말을 쓰시오.

(1) 그 사냥꾼은 누군가가 그를 따라오는 것을 느꼈다.

➡ The hunter _____ someone _____ him.

(2) 우리는 그가 집으로 들어가는 것을 보았다.

➡ We _____ him _____ the house.

(3) 아빠는 내가 내 방 청소를 하도록 시키셨다.

➡ Dad _____ me _____ my room.

01 다음 문장에서 어법상 <u>어색한</u> 부분을 바르게 고쳐 쓰시오.

(1) It is natural for you get angry.

_____ ➡ _____

(2) It was impossible to changing the plan.

_____ ➡ _____

(3) Didn't you hear him said he was busy?

_____ ➡ _____

(4) We watched Jane to dance on the stage.

_____ ➡ _____

02 주어진 단어를 어법에 맞게 빈칸에 쓰시오.

(1) Perry saw her friend _____ off the stairs. (fall)

(2) It is really exciting _____ on a picnic. (go)

(3) I saw the boy _____ the window. (break)

(4) It was fun _____ with your sisters. (play)

03 주어진 단어를 바르게 배열하여 다음 우리말을 영어로 쓰시오. 필요하다면 단어를 추가하거나 변형하시오.

(2) wake up: 일어나다
(3) island: 섬

(1) 나는 그 아기가 우는 소리를 들었어. (cry / the baby / heard / I)

➡ _____

(2) 너가 일찍 일어나는 것은 좋은 생각이야. (early / it / a good idea / for / you / wake up / is)

➡ _____

(3) Emma는 그들이 섬 주변에서 수영하는 것을 보았다. (the island / Emma / them / swim / saw / around)

➡ _____

(4) 사람들은 미술가들이 그들의 작품을 만드는 것을 처음부터 끝까지 지켜본다. (from beginning to end / the artists / people / their / create / watch / works)

➡ _____

01 다음 중 밑줄 친 부분의 쓰임이 <u>다른</u> 하나는?

① <u>It</u> is nice to clean your room by yourself.

② <u>It</u> is not that difficult to speak Korean well.

③ <u>It</u> is under the sofa in the living room.

④ <u>It</u> was hard to tell the truth to her.

⑤ <u>It</u> was easy to find the way to get there.

02 중요 다음 빈칸에 들어갈 말로 가장 적절한 것은?

James saw his friends _____ football on the playground.

① to play   ② play   ③ played

④ plays   ⑤ to playing

03 다음 우리말을 영어로 바르게 옮긴 것은?

이 책을 읽는 것은 어려웠다.

① It is difficult to read this book.

② I was difficult to read this book.

③ It was difficult read this book.

④ It was difficult to read this book.

⑤ It is difficult to reading this book.

서답형

04 주어진 단어를 이용하여 다음 우리말을 영어로 쓰시오.

거짓말을 하는 것은 잘못된 일이다.
(it / wrong)

➡ _____

05 중요 다음 중 어법상 바르지 <u>않은</u> 것은?

① It is good to do your job on your own.

② David saw his brother wearing his cap.

③ It is important to help others.

④ Wendy saw the bus leaving right in front of her eyes.

⑤ Mom made me to wash my clothes every day.

06 다음 빈칸에 들어갈 말이 바르게 짝지어진 것은?

• I heard the couple _____ last night.
• Did you feel the house _____ ?

① to fight – to shake

② fight – shaken

③ fighting – shake

④ fight – to shake

⑤ fighting – shaken

07 다음 중 어법상 바르지 <u>않은</u> 것은?

I like ①<u>to listen</u> ②<u>to</u> ③<u>the birds</u> ④ <u>to sing</u> when I ⑤<u>get up</u> early in the morning.

①   ②   ③   ④   ⑤

서답형

08 주어진 단어를 바르게 배열하여 다음 우리말을 영어로 쓰시오. 필요하다면 단어를 추가하시오.

헬멧을 쓰지 않고 오토바이를 타는 것은 위험해. (dangerous / a helmet / without / a motorcycle / is / it / ride)

➡ _____

_____

09 다음 우리말을 영어로 바르게 옮긴 것을 고르시오.

> 최선을 다하는 것은 중요해.

① It was important to do best.
② It is important to doing your best.
③ It is important do your best.
④ It is important to do your best.
⑤ It is important for doing your best.

10 다음 중 어법상 바르지 않은 것은?

① I saw the man got into the car alone.
② Julia heard Bill talking with someone.
③ It is fun to live in a dormitory.
④ It was careless of you to fall asleep while you were driving.
⑤ It is not easy to learn how to swim.

11 다음 중 쓰임이 다른 하나는?

① It is wrong to say like that to your friend.
② I am so happy to hear the news from you.
③ To see is to believe.
④ It is easy to solve the problem.
⑤ Is it difficult to write a poem?

서답형
12 다음 대화의 빈칸에 알맞은 말을 세 단어로 쓰시오.

> A: Did anybody go out?
> B: I don't think so. I didn't see _____.

➡ _____

13 다음 빈칸에 들어갈 말로 가장 적절한 것은?

> I didn't hear you _____ in. You must have been very quiet.

① will come
② come
③ came
④ to come
⑤ to coming

14 다음 중 (A)~(C)에서 어법상 옳은 것끼리 바르게 짝지은 것은?

> • I saw my friend (A)[running / to run] down the street.
> • It was thoughtful of you (B)[to give / give] her a present.
> • Jason heard somebody (C)[say / to say] something to her.

① to run – give – to say
② to run – to give – to say
③ running – to give – say
④ running – give – say
⑤ running – to give – to say

15 다음 중 주어진 문장의 It과 쓰임이 같은 것은?

> It is kind of you to help your mom.

① It is time to go to bed now.
② It was too dark outside.
③ It was made of 100 blocks of stone.
④ It makes me nervous.
⑤ It is not easy to plant a tree.

서답형
16 주어진 단어를 활용하여 다음 우리말을 영어로 쓰시오.

> 말을 타는 것은 매우 재미있어. (it / lot / of / fun)

➡ _____

17 다음 상황을 읽고 빈칸에 들어갈 말로 가장 적절한 것을 고르시오.

> Brad was walking along the street. I saw that when I drove past in my car.
> → I _____.

① saw Brad driving past

② heard Brad drive my car

③ saw Brad in my car

④ saw Brad walking along the street

⑤ heard Brad walking with someone

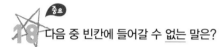

18 다음 중 빈칸에 들어갈 수 <u>없는</u> 말은?

> We _____ the boys playing the guitars.

① watched   ② listened to   ③ saw

④ heard   ⑤ made

19 다음 빈칸에 알맞은 말은?

> A: Did I close the window when I went out?
> B: Yes, you did. I _____.

① saw you go out

② heard you go out

③ saw you closing the window

④ heard you closed the window

⑤ heard you going out through the window

서답형

20 다음 대화의 밑줄 친 우리말을 영어로 옮기시오.

> A: What was Jane doing then?
> B: <u>나는 그녀가 누군가에게 전화하고 있는 것을 보았어.</u>

➡ _____

21 빈칸에 알맞은 말이 바르게 짝지어진 것을 <u>모두</u> 고르시오.

> It is fun _____ someone _____ comedy.

① seeing – doing   ② see – doing

③ seeing – to do   ④ to see – do

⑤ see – do

22 다음 중 밑줄 친 부분이 어법상 <u>틀린</u> 것은?

① It is really fun <u>to play</u> tennis with you.

② I want <u>to play</u> computer games.

③ It is exciting <u>to play</u> basketball.

④ Tom was tired of <u>playing</u> alone.

⑤ It is dangerous <u>to playing</u> with a knife.

서답형

23 다음 두 문장을 하나의 문장으로 쓰시오.

> • The boy fell off the tree yesterday.
> • I saw that.

➡ _____

서답형

24 다음 대화를 읽고 빈칸에 알맞은 말을 쓰시오.

> Kelly: What is Jimmy doing over there?
> Amelia: He is using his phone.

➡ Amelia sees Jimmy _____.

서답형

25 주어진 단어를 활용하여 다음 우리말을 7 단어로 이루어진 한 문장으로 쓰시오.

> 여기에 머무는 것은 안전하지 않아.
> (safe / stay)

➡ _____

01 다음 대화의 빈칸에 알맞은 말을 쓰시오.

> A: How do you know I rode a bike yesterday?
> B: I know because I saw _____ .

➡ _____

02 가주어 It을 이용하여 다음 우리말을 영어로 쓰시오.

> 계단에서 뛰는 것은 나쁘다.

➡ _____

03 다음 두 문장을 하나의 문장으로 쓰시오.

> • The accident happened.
> • Did you see that?

➡ _____

04 다음 빈칸에 알맞은 말을 쓰시오.

> To hear you say that was good.
> = _____ to hear you say that.

➡ _____

05 주어진 단어를 바르게 배열하여 다음 우리말을 영어로 쓰시오. 한 단어는 두 번 쓰시오.

> 학생들이 학교에서 휴대전화를 이용하도록 허락하는 것은 좋은 생각이 아니다.
> (in school / a good idea / students / allow / cell phones / to / it / not / is / use)

➡ _____

_____

06 주어진 단어를 이용하여 다음 대화의 빈칸에 알맞은 말을 쓰시오.

> A: Did Susan cross the street?
> B: Yes, she did. I _____ .(see)

➡ _____

07 주어진 단어를 이용하여 다음 우리말을 9 단어로 이루어진 한 문장으로 쓰시오.

> 네가 예의 바르게 인사하지 않는 것은 무례하다.
> (it / bow / politely / of)

➡ _____

08 주어진 문장을 지시에 맞게 영어로 쓰시오.

> 물을 절약하는 것은 중요합니다.

(1) to부정사 주어를 써서 작문할 것

➡ _____

(2) 가주어를 써서 작문할 것

➡ _____

09 다음 빈칸에 알맞은 말을 쓰시오.

> A: Who opened the window?
> B: I saw a man _____ but I don't know who he was.

➡ _____

10 다음 우리말을 영어로 쓰시오.

> 화살을 쏘는 것은 어렵다.

➡ _____

11 다음 대화의 빈칸에 알맞은 말을 7 단어로 쓰시오.

> A: I heard that you carried out a campaign to reduce food waste in school cafeteria. Did it work?
> B: It was a little hard _____ , but the campaign turned out to be successful.

➡ _____

12 다음 상황을 읽고 빈칸에 알맞은 말을 쓰시오.

> There are many people in the park. Musicians play beautiful live music. Children play catch. Couples sing a song.

➡ In the park, you can hear _____ _____ . Also, you can see children _____ and couples _____ .

13 밑줄 친 말의 반의어를 이용하여 빈칸에 알맞은 말을 쓰시오.

> A: Brian, isn't it difficult to look up a word in a dictionary?
> B: No. _____

➡ _____

14 다음 우리말을 영어로 쓰시오.

> 나는 누군가가 피아노를 연주하는 소리를 들었다.

➡ _____

15 주어진 문장과 같은 의미의 문장을 쓰시오.

> To be honest and fair is important.

➡ _____

16 다음 중 어법상 어색한 것을 골라 바르게 고치고, 그렇게 고친 이유를 서술하시오.

> Brady saw Clara to do something and wondered what she was doing.

➡ 잘못된 곳: _____ ➡ _____
고친 이유: _____
_____

17 주어진 단어를 활용하여 다음 우리말을 영어로 쓰시오.

> 의사가 되는 것은 쉽지 않아. (It)

➡ _____

18 다음 우리말에 맞게 빈칸에 알맞은 말을 쓰시오.

> 그들이 그 탁자를 옮기는 것을 지켜보는 것은 아주 재미있었다.
> It was a lot of fun _____ .

➡ _____

19 다음 우리말을 영어로 쓰시오.

> 나는 어제 누군가가 나를 따라오는 것을 느꼈다.

➡ _____

교과서

Let's Party!

Holi, the Festival of Colors

Amala from Delhi, India
출신을 나타내는 전치사 from

Holi is the most popular festival in my country. It is usually in March.
가장 인기 있는(최상급)　　　　　　= Holi　　　연도 앞에

During the festival, we say goodbye to cold winter and hello to warm
전치사(~ 동안)　　　　~에게 작별 인사를 하다

spring. We celebrate the festival everywhere for two days. On the first
　　　　　　　　　　　　　　　전치사(~ 동안)+구체적인 기간　　특정 날짜 앞에

day, people gather around a big fire at night and sing and dance. The
　　　　　　　　　　　　　　　　　　　　　등위접속사: sing과 dance를 대등하게 연결

main event begins the next day. Children and adults chase each other
　　　　　　　그 다음 날　　　　　　　　　　　　　　서로(chase의 목적어)

with *gulal*. What is *gulal*? It is blue, yellow, green and pink powder.

It's a lot of fun to run around and throw colorful powder at everyone.
가주어 It　　　진주어 to부정사　　　　　　　　　throw A at B: B를 향해 A를 던지다

We also join street parades!

White Nights Festival

Victor from St. Petersburg, Russia

Have you heard of the *White Nights*? Every summer, this amazing
~에 대해 들어봤니?(경험을 묻는 현재완료)　　　every+단수명사: 모든 ~, 매 ~　　　the White

thing happens in my hometown. The night sky does not get completely
Nights를 지칭　　　　　　　　　　　　　　get+형용사: (어떤 상태가) 되다

dark.

| usually 주로 |
| celebrate 축하하다, 기념하다 |
| gather 모이다, 모으다 |
| adult 어른 |
| chase 뒤쫓다 |
| throw 던지다 |
| parade 퍼레이드, 행진 |
| happen 발생하다 |
| completely 완전히 |

 확인문제

● 다음 문장이 본문의 내용과 일치하면 T, 일치하지 않으면 F를 쓰시오.

1　Holi is held in India. ⬜

2　People in India celebrate Holi for two weeks. ⬜

3　There is a big fire at night on the second day of Holi. ⬜

4　We can see white nights in Victor's hometown every summer. ⬜

During that time, we hold the White Nights Festival. It usually starts
= the White Nights   = the White Nights Festival

in May and lasts for about a month. During the festival, there is a
약

ballet or an opera almost every night. The most popular event is the
거의   가장 인기 있는

Scarlet Sails celebration. A boat with red sails slowly appears on the
전치사(~가 부착된, ~가 달린)   자동사(수동태 안 됨)

river. Soon, fireworks begin and a water show follows. You can also
(시간, 순서상으로) 뒤를 잇다

hear musicians playing beautiful live music.
지각동사+목적어+현재분사

Kiruna Snow Festival

Ebba from Kiruna, Sweden

Winter is my favorite season because of the Kiruna Snow Festival.
~ 때문에

The festival starts in the last week of January and goes on for five or
마지막 주   진행되다

six days. The largest event is the snow design competition. The artists
가장 큰(최상급)

shape huge piles of snow into animals, buildings, and other beautiful
shape A into B: A를 B의 형태로 만들다

artworks. People watch the artists shaping their works from beginning
지각동사+목적어+현재분사   처음부터 끝까지(= from start to finish)

to end. My favorite activity is the dog sled ride. It is amazing to fly
타기, 타는 것(명사)   가주어 It   진주어 to부정사

through a world of snow on a dog sled.

last 지속하다
celebration 축하, 기념, 축하 행사
appear 나타나다
follow 따라가다, 따라오다
fireworks 불꽃놀이
live 라이브의, 실황인
musician 음악가
favorite 가장 좋아하는
competition 대회, 시합, 경쟁
other 다른
from A to B A부터 B까지
sled 썰매

📎 **확인문제**

● 다음 문장이 본문의 내용과 일치하면 T, 일치하지 <u>않으면</u> F를 쓰시오.

1 The White Nights Festival continues for about a month. ☐

2 A boat with no sails appears on the river during the Scarlet Sails celebration. ☐

3 The Kiruna Snow Festival is held in Kiruna. ☐

4 The Kiruna Snow Festival starts in the first week of January. ☐

5 At the Kiruna Snow Festival, artists shape huge piles of snow into animals, buildings, and other artworks. ☐

● 우리말을 참고하여 빈칸에 알맞은 말을 쓰시오.

1   Holi, the _____ of Colors

2   Amala _____ Delhi, India

3   Holi is _____ _____ _____ festival in my country.

4   It _____ _____ in March.

5   During the festival, we _____ _____ to cold winter and _____ to warm spring.

6   We _____ the festival everywhere _____ two days.

7   _____ the first day, people _____ _____ a big fire _____ _____ and sing and dance.

8   The main event _____ _____ _____ _____ .

9   Children and adults _____ _____ _____ with *gulal*.

10   _____ is *gulal*? It is blue, yellow, green and pink _____ .

11   It's a lot of fun _____ _____ _____ and _____ colorful powder _____ everyone.

12   We also _____ _____ _____ !

13   _____ _____ Festival

14   Victor _____ St. Petersburg, Russia

15   _____ you _____ _____ the *White Nights*?

16   Every summer, this _____ thing _____ in my hometown.

1   홀리, 색의 축제

2   인도, 델리의 Amala

3   '홀리'는 우리나라에서 가장 인기 있는 축제예요.

4   그것은 보통 3월에 있어요.

5   축제 기간 동안에, 우리는 추운 겨울에게 작별 인사를 하고 따뜻한 봄을 맞는 인사를 해요.

6   우리는 이틀 동안 어디서든 축제를 기념해요.

7   첫째 날, 사람들은 밤에 큰 모닥불 주변에 모여 노래하고 춤을 춰요.

8   주요 행사는 다음 날에 시작돼요.

9   어린이들과 어른들이 'gulal'을 지니고 서로를 쫓아다녀요.

10   'gulal'이 무엇이냐고요? 그것은 파랑, 노랑, 초록, 분홍의 가루예요.

11   주변을 뛰어다니며 형형색색의 가루를 모든 사람들에게 던지는 것은 정말 재미있어요.

12   우리는 거리 행진에도 참가해요!

13   백야 축제

14   러시아, 상트페테르부르크의 Victor

15   '백야'에 대해 들어 봤나요?

16   매년 여름, 이 놀라운 일이 나의 고향에서 벌어져요.

17 The night sky _____ _____ _____ _____ dark.

18 _____ that time, we _____ the White Nights Festival.

19 It usually _____ _____ May and _____ for _____ a month.

20 During the festival, _____ _____ a ballet or an opera _____ _____ _____.

21 The most _____ event is the Scarlet Sails _____.

22 A boat with red sails slowly _____ _____ _____ _____.

23 Soon, fireworks _____ and a water show _____.

24 You can also _____ musicians _____ beautiful live music.

25 Kiruna _____ _____

26 Ebba _____ Kiruna, Sweden

27 Winter is _____ _____ _____ _____ _____ the Kiruna Snow Festival.

28 The festival _____ _____ _____ _____ of January and _____ _____ for five or six days.

29 _____ _____ _____ is the snow design competition.

30 The artists _____ huge piles of snow _____ animals, buildings, and _____ beautiful artworks.

31 People _____ the artists _____ their works _____ beginning _____ end.

32 My _____ _____ is the dog sled ride.

33 It is amazing _____ _____ _____ a world of snow _____ a dog sled.

---

17 밤하늘이 완전히 어두워지지 않아요.

18 그 시기 동안, 우리는 백야 축제를 열어요.

19 축제는 보통 5월에 시작되고 약 한 달 동안 지속돼요.

20 축제 기간 동안 거의 매일 밤 발레나 오페라 공연이 있어요.

21 가장 인기 있는 행사는 '붉은 돛 축하 행사'예요.

22 빨간 돛을 단 배가 강 위에 서서히 나타나요.

23 곧 불꽃놀이가 시작되고 물 쇼가 이어져요.

24 또한 여러분은 음악가들이 아름다운 라이브 음악을 연주하는 것을 들을 수 있어요.

25 키루나 눈 축제

26 스웨덴, 키루나의 Ebba

27 겨울은 키루나 눈 축제 때문에 내가 가장 좋아하는 계절이에요.

28 축제는 1월 마지막 주에 시작해서 5일이나 6일 동안 계속돼요.

29 가장 큰 행사는 '눈 디자인 대회'예요.

30 미술가들이 거대한 눈 덩어리를 동물, 건물, 다른 아름다운 작품의 모양으로 만들어요.

31 사람들은 미술가들이 그들의 작품을 만드는 것을 처음부터 끝까지 지켜봐요.

32 내가 가장 좋아하는 활동은 개썰매 타기예요.

33 개썰매를 타고 눈 세상을 날아가는 것은 정말 놀라워요.

● 우리말을 참고하여 본문을 영작하시오.

1 홀리, 색의 축제

➡ _____

2 인도, 델리의 Amala

➡ _____

3 '홀리'는 우리나라에서 가장 인기 있는 축제예요.

➡ _____

4 그것은 보통 3월에 있어요.

➡ _____

5 축제 기간 동안에, 우리는 추운 겨울에게 작별 인사를 하고 따뜻한 봄을 맞는 인사를 해요.

➡ _____

6 우리는 이틀 동안 어디서든 축제를 기념해요.

➡ _____

7 첫째 날, 사람들은 밤에 큰 모닥불 주변에 모여 노래하고 춤을 춰요.

➡ _____

8 주요 행사는 다음 날에 시작돼요.

➡ _____

9 어린이들과 어른들이 'gulal'을 지니고 서로를 쫓아다녀요.

➡ _____

10 'gulal'이 무엇이냐고요? 그것은 파랑, 노랑, 초록, 분홍의 가루예요.

➡ _____

11 주변을 뛰어다니며 형형색색의 가루를 모든 사람들에게 던지는 것은 정말 재미있어요.

➡ _____

12 우리는 거리 행진에도 참가해요!

➡ _____

13 백야 축제

➡ _____

14 러시아, 상트페테르부르크의 Victor

➡ _____

15 '백야'에 대해 들어 봤나요?

➡ _____

16 매년 여름, 이 놀라운 일이 나의 고향에서 벌어져요.

➡ _____

17 밤하늘이 완전히 어두워지지 않아요.

➡ _____

18 그 시기 동안, 우리는 백야 축제를 열어요.

➡ _____

19 축제는 보통 5월에 시작되고 약 한 달 동안 지속돼요.

➡ _____

20 축제 기간 동안 거의 매일 밤 발레나 오페라 공연이 있어요.

➡ _____

21 가장 인기 있는 행사는 '붉은 돛 축하 행사'예요.

➡ _____

22 빨간 돛을 단 배가 강 위에 서서히 나타나요.

➡ _____

23 곧 불꽃놀이가 시작되고 물 쇼가 이어져요.

➡ _____

24 또한 여러분은 음악가들이 아름다운 라이브 음악을 연주하는 것을 들을 수 있어요.

➡ _____

25 키루나 눈 축제

➡ _____

26 스웨덴, 키루나의 Ebba

➡ _____

27 겨울은 키루나 눈 축제 때문에 내가 가장 좋아하는 계절이에요.

➡ _____

28 축제는 1월 마지막 주에 시작해서 5일이나 6일 동안 계속돼요.

➡ _____

29 가장 큰 행사는 '눈 디자인 대회'예요.

➡ _____

30 미술가들이 거대한 눈 덩어리를 동물, 건물, 다른 아름다운 작품의 모양으로 만들어요.

➡ _____

31 사람들은 미술가들이 그들의 작품을 만드는 것을 처음부터 끝까지 지켜봐요.

➡ _____

32 내가 가장 좋아하는 활동은 개썰매 타기예요.

➡ _____

33 개썰매를 타고 눈 세상을 날아가는 것은 정말 놀라워요.

➡ _____

[01~06] 다음 글을 읽고 물음에 답하시오.

Holi, the Festival of Colors

Amala from Delhi, India

Holi is the most popular festival in my country. It is usually in March. During the festival, we say goodbye to cold winter and hello to warm spring. We celebrate the festival everywhere for two days. On the first day, people gather around a big fire _____ⓐ_____ night and sing and dance. The main event begins the next day. Children and adults chase each other with *gulal*. What is *gulal*? It is blue, yellow, green and pink powder. It's a lot of fun ___ⓑ___ around and throw colorful powder ___ⓒ___ everyone. We also join street parades!

01 빈칸 ⓐ와 ⓒ에 공통으로 들어갈 말로 가장 적절한 것은?

① by   ② on   ③ to
④ at   ⑤ in

서답형

02 빈칸 ⓑ에 동사 run을 어법에 맞게 쓰시오.

➡ _____

중요

03 다음 중 위 글의 내용과 일치하지 <u>않는</u> 것은?

① Holi is usually in March.
② The festival lasts for two days.
③ There is the main event on the first day.
④ *Gulal* is colorful powder.
⑤ There are street parades at the festival.

서답형

04 According to the passage, what is the most popular festival in India?

➡ _____

서답형

05 다음 빈칸에 들어갈 말을 위 글에서 찾아 쓰시오.

> If people _____ somewhere, they come together in a group.

➡ _____

06 다음 중 홀리 축제 기간에 볼 수 <u>없는</u> 것은?

① people gathering around a big fire
② people singing and dancing at night
③ street parades
④ adults and children chasing each other with *gulal*
⑤ children throwing colorful balls

[07~10] 다음 글을 읽고 물음에 답하시오.

White Nights Festival

Victor from St. Petersburg, Russia

(A)Have you heard of the *White Nights*? Every summer, (B)this amazing thing happens in my hometown. The night sky does not get completely dark. During that time, we (C)hold the White Nights Festival. It usually starts in May and lasts for about a month. During the festival, there is a ballet or an opera almost every night. The most popular event is the Scarlet Sails celebration. A boat with red sails slowly appears on the river. Soon, fireworks begin and a water show follows. You can also hear musicians playing beautiful live music.

07 밑줄 친 (A)와 현재완료의 용법이 같은 것은?

① We have known each other for ten years.
② Nora has been to Vietnam three times.
③ The employer has just arrived at the airport.
④ David has lost his car key.
⑤ Karen has played the guitar since she was twelve years old.

서답형
08 밑줄 친 (B)가 의미하는 것을 위 글에서 찾아 쓰시오.

➡ _____

09 다음 중 밑줄 친 (C)와 같은 의미로 쓰인 것은?

① Janet held her head because of headache.
② The chair is strong enough to hold your weight.
③ Tom held his girl friend's hand tightly.
④ Can you hold a minute, please?
⑤ We hold our class meeting every Monday.

서답형
10 During the festival, what can you see almost every night? Answer the question with a full sentence.

➡ _____

[11~14] 다음 글을 읽고 물음에 답하시오.

Kiruna Snow Festival
Ebba from Kiruna, Sweden
Winter is my favorite season (A)[because / because of] the Kiruna Snow Festival. The festival starts in the last week of January and goes on for five or six days. The largest event is the snow design competition. The artists shape huge piles of snow into animals, buildings, and (B)[other / another] beautiful artworks. People watch the artists ⓐ _____ their works from beginning to end. My favorite activity is the dog sled ride. It is (C)[amazing / amazed] to fly through a world of snow on a dog sled.

서답형
11 동사 shape를 어법에 맞게 활용하여 빈칸 ⓐ에 쓰시오.

➡ _____

12 (A)~(C)에서 어법상 옳은 것끼리 바르게 묶은 것은?

① because of – another – amazed
② because of – other – amazing
③ because – other – amazed
④ because – other – amazing
⑤ because – another – amazed

13 다음 중 위 글을 읽고 답할 수 없는 것은?

① When does the festival start?
② What is the largest event of the festival?
③ What do the artists do at the festival?
④ What is Ebba's favorite activity?
⑤ How many artists take part in the snow design competition?

서답형
14 How long does the festival last? Answer in English with a full sentence.

➡ _____

[15~19] 다음 글을 읽고 물음에 답하시오.

Holi, the Festival of Colors

Amala ___(A)___ Delhi, India

Holi is ①the most popular festival in my country. It is usually ___(B)___ March. ___(C)___ the festival, we say goodbye to cold winter and hello to warm spring. We celebrate the festival everywhere ②for two days. ③On the first day, people gather around a big fire at night and sing and dance. The main event begins the next day. Children and adults chase each other with *gulal*. What is *gulal*? It is blue, yellow, green and pink powder. It's ④a lot of fun to run around and throw colorful powder at everyone. We also ⑤join with street parades!

중요

15 빈칸 (A)~(C)에 들어갈 말이 바르게 짝지어진 것은?

① from – at – While
② from – in – During
③ at – on – For
④ in – about – At
⑤ in – by – About

16 다음 중 위 글의 내용과 일치하는 것은?

① Holi is not a famous festival in India.
② Holi is held in summer.
③ People celebrate the festival at a special place.
④ People dance and sing on the first night of the festival.
⑤ Amala doesn't like throwing *gulal* at the festival.

17 밑줄 친 ①~⑤ 중 어법상 옳지 않은 것은?

①   ②   ③   ④   ⑤

서답형

18 위 글의 내용에 맞게 빈칸에 알맞은 말을 쓰시오.

On the last day of the festival, we can see children and adults _____.

➡ _____

서답형

19 If you want to see only the main event of the festival, when should you go to the festival?

➡ _____

[20~23] 다음 글을 읽고 물음에 답하시오.

White Nights Festival

Victor from St. Petersburg, Russia

Have you heard of the *White Nights*? Every summer, this amazing thing happens in my hometown. The night sky does not get completely dark. During that time, we hold the White Nights Festival. It usually starts in May and lasts for about a month. During the festival, there is a ballet or an opera almost every night. The most popular event is the Scarlet Sails celebration. A boat with red sails slowly appears on the river. Soon, fireworks begin and a water show follows. You can also hear musicians ___(A)___ beautiful live music.

서답형

20 play를 어법에 맞게 빈칸 (A)에 쓰시오.

➡ _____

서답형

21 위 글의 내용에 맞게 빈칸에 알맞은 말을 쓰시오.

The White Nights Festival is held in Victor's hometown _____ _____.

22 다음 중 위 글을 읽고 답할 수 없는 것은?

① Where is Victor from?

② What is Victor mainly talking about?

③ When is the White Nights Festival held?

④ How long does the festival last?

⑤ Where does the boat come from?

23 다음 중 백야 축제에 관한 내용으로 바르지 않은 것은?

① It is held in St. Petersburg in Russia.

② Scarlet Sails celebration is more popular than any other event.

③ There is a boat with red sails.

④ The boat moves really fast on the river.

⑤ After the boat appears, fireworks begin.

[24~28] 다음 글을 읽고 물음에 답하시오.

Kiruna Snow Festival

Ebba from Kiruna, Sweden

Winter is my favorite season because of the Kiruna Snow Festival. The festival starts in ①the last week of January and ②goes on for five or six days. ③The largest event is the snow design competition. The artists shape huge piles of snow into animals, buildings, and other beautiful artworks. People watch the artists shaping their works ④from beginning to end. My favorite activity is the dog sled ride. (A)It is amazing to fly through ⑤a world of snow on a dog sled.

24 다음 중 ①~⑤의 뜻풀이로 바르지 않은 것은?

① 1월 마지막 주 ② 나아가다

③ 가장 큰 행사 ④ 처음부터 끝까지

⑤ 눈 세상

25 Which is NOT true about Ebba?

① She is from Sweden.

② Her favorite season is winter.

③ She likes the dog sled ride.

④ She thinks flying through a world of snow on a dog sled is amazing.

⑤ She can shape huge piles of snow into animals.

26 위 글의 내용에 맞게 빈칸에 알맞은 말을 세 단어로 쓰시오.

> At the Kiruna Snow Festival, you can see the artists _____ from beginning to end.

➡ _____

27 다음 중 위 글의 내용을 잘못 이해한 사람은?

① Kelly: The Kiruna Snow Festival lasts five or six days.

② Susan: I will be able to see many artists in the snow design competition.

③ Jason: Many artists make their works in front of people.

④ Brian: The artists have to make only animals and buildings with snow.

⑤ David: I will ride the dog sled at the festival.

28 다음 중 밑줄 친 (A)와 쓰임이 같은 것을 모두 고르시오.

① It made Jenny upset.

② It is hot and humid outside.

③ It is surprising to meet you here.

④ It was found under the sofa.

⑤ It was difficult for me to study hard.

[01~05] 다음 글을 읽고 물음에 답하시오.

Holi, the Festival of Colors

Amala from Delhi, India

Holi is the most popular festival in my country. It is usually in March. During the festival, we say goodbye to cold winter and hello to warm spring. We celebrate the festival everywhere for two days. On the first day, people gather around a big fire at night and sing and dance. The main event begins the next day. Children and adults chase each other with *gulal*. What is *gulal*? It is blue, yellow, green and pink powder. (A) To run around and throw colorful powder at everyone is a lot of fun. We also join street parades!

01 How long do Indians celebrate the festival? Answer the question with seven words.

➡ _____

02 글의 내용에 맞게 대화의 빈칸에 알맞은 말을 쓰시오.

> A: I heard about a festival, Holi.
> B: What is it?
> A: It is the festival of colors. On the first day of the festival, we can see people _____ a big fire at night and _____ .

➡ _____ , _____

03 주어진 단어를 주어로 하여 밑줄 친 문장 (A)를 다시 쓰시오.

➡ It _____

04 글의 내용에 맞게 빈칸에 알맞은 말을 세 단어로 쓰시오.

> A: I want to see the festival, Holi.
> B: Oh, then you have to go to _____ . It is usually held then.

➡ _____

05 What is *gulal*? Answer in English with a full sentence.

➡ _____

[06~11] 다음 글을 읽고 물음에 답하시오.

White Nights Festival

Victor from St. Petersburg, Russia

Have you heard of the *White Nights*? Every summer, this amazing thing happens in (A) my hometown. The night sky does not get completely dark. During that time, we hold the White Nights Festival. (B)It starts in May and lasts for about a month. During the festival, there is a ballet or an opera almost every night. The most popular event is the Scarlet Sails celebration. A boat with red sails slowly appears on the river. Soon, fireworks begin and a water show follows. You can also hear musicians playing beautiful live music.

06 밑줄 친 (A)를 구체적으로 쓰시오.

➡ _____

07 단어 usually를 넣어 밑줄 친 문장 (B)를 다시 쓰시오.

➡ _____

08 위 글에서 백야를 설명하는 문장을 찾아 쓰시오.

➡ _____

09 According to the passage, what kinds of events are at the White Nights Festival?

➡ _____

10 다음은 백야 축제를 다녀온 학생이 쓴 일기의 일부이다. 빈칸에 알맞은 말을 다섯 단어로 쓰시오.

> ... I saw a boat _____. It had red sails. Shortly, fireworks began. ...

➡ _____

[11~15] 다음 글을 읽고 물음에 답하시오.

Kiruna Snow Festival

Ebba from Kiruna, Sweden

Winter is my favorite season because of the Kiruna Snow Festival. The festival starts in the last week of January and goes on for five or six days. The largest event is the snow design competition. The artists shape huge piles of snow into animals, buildings, and other beautiful artworks. People watch the artists shaping their works from beginning to end. My favorite activity is the dog sled ride. It is amazing   (A)   through a world of snow on a dog sled.

11 동사 fly를 어법에 맞게 빈칸 (A)에 쓰시오.

➡ _____

12 Write the reason why winter is Ebba's favorite season.

➡ _____

13 다음 대화의 빈칸에 알맞은 말을 쓰시오.

> A: I heard that you will visit _____ to see the Kiruna Snow Festival.
> B: Yes. I'm so excited.
> A: Then you should see _____. It is the largest event at the festival.

➡ _____, _____

14 According to the passage, how long does the Kiruna Snow Festival last? Answer in English with a full sentence.

➡ _____

15 다음은 축제를 방문한 두 사람의 대화이다. 우리말에 맞게 주어진 어구를 바르게 배열하시오.

> A: What are you watching?
> B: 나는 저 미술가가 하나의 거대한 눈 덩어리를 코끼리 모양으로 바꾸는 것을 보고 있어.
> (a huge pile of / an elephant / I / shaping / watching / snow / am / into / the artist)

➡ _____

_____

Listen and Speak 2-C

A: Chris, what will you do for the class party?

B: I'll make sandwiches.

A: Great idea. How long will it take to make them?
= sandwiches

B: Maybe it'll take about an hour.
= Perhaps   대략, ~ 정도

구문해설 • take: (시간이) 걸리다

해석

A: Chris, 학급 파티를 위해 무엇을 할 거니?
B: 나는 샌드위치를 만들 거야.
A: 좋은 생각이야. 그것들을 만드는 데 얼마가 걸릴까?
B: 아마도 약 한 시간 정도 걸릴 거야.

Think and Write

I Love Gangneung

I live in Gangneung. There are beautiful beaches in my neighborhood. It's a
~이 있다 (뒤에 있는 명사에 수의 일치)   나의 이웃에   가주어 It

lot of fun to swim at the beach. There is a famous hanok in Gangneung. It is
진주어(to부정사)

called Ojukheon. Yulgok was born there. The most famous food in Gangneung
수동태   in Ojukheon

is potato tteok. It is soft and sweet. Come and enjoy Gangneung!
= Potato tteok

구문해설 • beach: 해변 • neighborhood: 이웃 • be born: 태어나다

강릉이 정말 좋아요

저는 강릉에 살아요. 나의 이웃에는 아름다운 해변들이 있어요. 해변에서 수영하는 것은 정말 재미있어요. 강릉에는 유명한 한옥이 있어요. 그것은 오죽헌이라고 불려요. 율곡이 거기에서 태어났어요. 강릉에서 가장 유명한 음식은 감자떡이에요. 그것은 부드럽고 달콤해요. 와서 강릉을 즐기세요!

Project Culture

I want to introduce Boryeong Mud Festival. It is held in Daecheon Beach
to부정사를 목적어로 취하는 동사   수동태

in July. There are many interesting events in the festival. First, you can
월, 연도 앞에 쓰는 전치사   흥미를 유발할 때 쓰는 현재분사형 형용사

see people do Ssireum in mud. Also it is fun to do colorful mud body painting
지각동사+목적어+동사원형   가주어   진주어

on your body. Lastly, there is an outdoor concert. You can hear musicians play
지각동사+목적어+동사원형

beautiful musics.

구문해설 • introduce: 소개하다 • mud: 진흙 • festival: 축제 • interesting: 흥미로운
• event: 행사

나는 보령 진흙 축제를 소개하고 싶어요. 그것은 7월에 대천 해수욕장에서 열립니다. 그 축제에는 많은 흥미로운 행사가 있습니다. 우선, 당신은 사람들이 진흙 속에서 씨름하는 것을 볼 수 있어요. 또한 당신의 몸에 형형색색의 진흙을 바르는 것은 재미있어요. 마지막으로, 실외 콘서트가 있습니다. 당신은 음악가들이 아름다운 음악을 연주하는 것을 들을 수 있습니다.

영역별 핵심문제

Words & Expressions

01 다음 짝지어진 단어의 관계가 같도록 빈칸에 알맞은 말을 쓰시오.

> _____ : bright = give : receive

02 다음 영영풀이가 가리키는 것을 고르시오.

> to follow and try to catch

① chase   ② advertise
③ decorate   ④ hold
⑤ gather

03 다음 중 밑줄 친 부분의 뜻풀이가 바르지 않은 것은?

① Time goes by and you will become an adult soon. 어른
② The painting is my son's latest artwork. 예술 작품
③ We made a poster to advertise our school festival. 광고하다
④ The police officers chased the thief. 체포하다
⑤ There is a competition between players. 경쟁

04 다음 우리말에 맞게 빈칸에 알맞은 말을 쓰시오.

(1) 한 블록 곧장 간 후 왼쪽으로 도세요.
➡ _____ _____ one block and _____ a left.
(2) 우리는 서로 너무 다르다.
➡ We are too different from _____ _____.
(3) 어느 버스 정류장에서 내려야 하나요?
➡ Which bus stop should I _____ _____ at?

05 다음 주어진 문장의 밑줄 친 sail과 같은 의미로 쓰인 것은?

> A boat with a red sail appeared on the river.

① After retirement, I want to sail around the world.
② The navigator extended the sail on the boat.
③ The sailors couldn't sail against the wind.
④ The ferry will sail to the Atlantic.
⑤ We are ready to sail to New York.

06 다음 주어진 우리말을 영작하시오.

(1) 당신의 고향은 어디입니까?
➡ _____
(2) 그것은 박물관 건너편에 있어요.
➡ _____
(3) 내 친구들이 내 생일을 축하해 주기 위해 모였다.
➡ _____

Conversation

[07~08] 다음 대화를 읽고 물음에 답하시오.

Minsu: Hi, Emma. What's up?
Emma: Hey, Minsu. Are you free this Saturday?
Minsu: Yes. Why do you ask?
Emma: Well, how about having lunch together?
Minsu: Sure.
Emma: Let's try the new Chinese restaurant, Ming's. It's near the school.
Minsu: Okay. _____(A)

Emma: Come out from the school and go straight to Green Street. Make a left, and the restaurant will be on your left.

Minsu: All right. Let's meet at 12 o'clock.

Emma: Wonderful. See you then.

07 위 대화의 빈칸 (A)에 들어갈 말을 〈보기〉에 주어진 단어를 배열하여 완성하시오.

┌─── 보기 ───┐
the / how / school / from / I / get / there / can
└──────────┘

➡ _____

08 위 대화의 내용과 일치하지 않는 것은?

① Emma and Minsu are going to have lunch together this Saturday.
② Emma and Minsu are going to visit Ming's, the new Chinese restaurant.
③ Ming's is located near the school.
④ Minsu should make a left in the front of the school and go straight to Green Street to get to Ming's.
⑤ Emma and Minsu are going to meet at 12 o'clock this Saturday.

[09~10] 다음 대화를 읽고 물음에 답하시오.

Andy: I'm so excited about the school festival this Friday.

Mike: Me, too. What can we do to advertise it, Andy?

Andy: How about making posters?

Mike: Great idea. We can post them in our neighborhood.

Andy: Right. How long will it take to make them?

Mike: Well, it will take about three hours.

Andy: Okay, _____ (A)

09 위 대화의 빈칸 (A)에 들어갈 말을 주어진 단어를 배열하여 완성하시오.

┌─── 보기 ───┐
hope / many / the / to / festival / come / I / people
└──────────┘

➡ _____

10 위 대화를 읽고 대답할 수 없는 것은?

① What are Andy and Mike looking forward to?
② What do Andy and Mike want to advertise?
③ What do Andy and Mike decide to make?
④ How long will it take to make the poster?
⑤ Where will Andy and Mike make the posters?

[11~13] 다음 대화를 읽고 물음에 답하시오.

Man: Excuse me. How can I (A)[take / get] to Suwon Hwaseong from here?

Mina: It's easy. Do you see the bus stop over there?

Man: Yes, I do.

Mina: Take the No. 11 bus and get (B)[on / off] at the sixth stop.

Man: How (C)[long / far] will it take to get there?

Mina: It will take about 20 minutes.

Man: Thank you very much.

Mina: _____ⓐ_____ Are you going there for the festival?

Man: Yes. I heard it's a lot of fun.

Mina: I hope you have a great time.

11 위 대화의 빈칸 ⓐ에 들어갈 말로 적절하지 않은 것은?

① No problem.　　② You're welcome.
③ Don't mention it.　④ It's my pleasure.
⑤ Of course not.

12 위 대화의 (A)~(C)에 알맞은 것으로 짝지어진 것은?

	(A)	(B)	(C)
①	take	on	long
②	take	off	far
③	get	off	far
④	get	off	long
⑤	get	on	long

13 위 대화를 읽고 대답할 수 <u>없는</u> 것은?

① What does the man want?

② How can the man get to Suwon Hwaseong?

③ How long will it take to get to Suwon Hwaseong?

④ Why does the man want to visit Suwon Hwaseong?

⑤ Has Mina ever visited the festival of Suwon Hwaseong?

Grammar

14 다음 빈칸에 들어갈 수 <u>없는</u> 것은?

> It is good to _____ you laugh.

① see   ② hear   ③ watch

④ make   ⑤ encourage

15 다음 중 밑줄 친 부분의 쓰임이 <u>다른</u> 하나는?

① <u>It</u> is five miles from here to the beach.

② Is <u>it</u> possible to get there in time?

③ Was <u>it</u> cloudy this afternoon?

④ <u>It</u> is five past three.

⑤ <u>It</u> is not dark in this cave.

16 다음 우리말을 영어로 바르게 옮긴 것은?

> 나는 누군가가 문을 열고 나가는 소리를 들었어.

① I heard someone opened the door and went out.

② I heard someone opened the door and go out.

③ I heard someone open the door and went out.

④ I heard someone open the door and go out.

⑤ I heard someone opening the door and went out.

17 다음 대화의 빈칸에 알맞은 말을 쓰시오.

> A: Did you see Tom shouting at someone?
>
> B: Yes, I did. It was surprising _____ _____ _____ _____ _____ because he is known to us as a kind and quiet man.

18 다음 중 어법상 바르지 <u>않은</u> 것은?

① I felt someone pulling my hair.

② It was my fault to believe such a thing.

③ Did you see the boys kicked the ball?

④ To make you laugh is my job.

⑤ The situation made me tell a lot of lies.

19 다음 중 주어진 문장의 밑줄 친 부분과 쓰임이 같은 것은?

> It is necessary for you <u>to buy</u> a concert ticket now.

① My brother wanted you <u>to call</u> him.

② <u>To eat</u> lunch alone, Karen went out.

③ Do you have a chair <u>to sit</u> on?

④ I didn't plan <u>to do</u> it.

⑤ It is good <u>to hear</u> from you.

20 다음 문장에서 어법상 바르지 <u>않은</u> 것을 찾아 바르게 고치시오.

> It is very boring to hearing someone talking constantly.

_____ ➡ _____

21 주어진 단어를 활용하여 다음 우리말을 영어로 쓰시오.

> 영어를 배우는 것은 흥미롭다. (it / excite)

➡ _____

22 다음 중 어법상 <u>틀린</u> 문장의 개수는?

> ⓐ It is impossible to understand her.
> ⓑ Is it possible for me to visit your office?
> ⓒ We listened to the old man told his story from beginning to end.
> ⓓ Yesterday, I saw Kate to wait for a bus alone.
> ⓔ It was not easy to find your house.

① 1개 ② 2개 ③ 3개 ④ 4개 ⑤ 5개

23 빈칸에 들어갈 말이 바르게 짝지어진 것은?

> • It is dangerous _____ the mountain alone.
> • Did you see the man _____ the mountain alone?

① climb – climb
② to climb – climbed
③ to climb – climbing
④ to climb – to climb
⑤ to climbing – climbing

24 다음 우리말을 영어로 쓰시오.

> 나는 누군가가 내 어깨를 만지는 것을 느꼈다.

➡ _____

Reading

[25~28] 다음 글을 읽고 물음에 답하시오.

Holi, the Festival of Colors

Amala from Delhi, India

Holi is the most popular festival in my country. ① It is usually in March. During the festival, we say goodbye to cold winter and hello to warm spring. ② We __ⓐ__ the festival everywhere for two days. On the first day, people gather around a big fire at night and sing and dance. ③ The main event begins the next day. ④ What is *gulal*? It is blue, yellow, green and pink powder. It's a lot of fun ⓑto run around and throw colorful powder at everyone. ⑤ We also join street parades!

25 다음과 같이 풀이되는 단어를 빈칸 ⓐ에 쓰시오.

> to do something special for an important event, holiday, etc.

➡ _____

26 ①~⑤ 중 주어진 문장이 들어가기에 가장 적절한 곳은?

> Children and adults chase each other with *gulal*.

①   ②   ③   ④   ⑤

27 위 글의 밑줄 친 ⓑ와 쓰임이 같은 것은?

① Tim went to Rome to see his girlfriend.
② Sarah was sad to hear the news.
③ To see her crying was painful for me.
④ I need something warm to wear.
⑤ The problem was very difficult to solve.

28 다음 중 위 글을 읽고 답할 수 없는 것은?

① What is Holi?
② What do people in India do during the festival?
③ How long does the festival last?
④ When does the main event begin?
⑤ How much *gulal* do people have at the festival?

[29~33] 다음 글을 읽고 물음에 답하시오.

Kiruna Snow Festival
Ebba from Kiruna, Sweden
Winter is my favorite season because of the Kiruna Snow Festival. The festival starts in the last week of January and (A)goes on for five or six days. The largest event is the snow design competition. The artists shape huge piles of snow into animals, buildings, and other beautiful artworks. People watch the artists shaping their works from beginning to end. My favorite activity is the dog sled ride. It is amazing to fly through a world of snow on a dog sled.

29 다음 중 밑줄 친 (A) 대신에 쓰일 수 있는 것은?

① quits   ② goes by
③ continues   ④ increases
⑤ expects

30 위 글의 내용에 맞게 다음 물음에 완전한 문장의 영어로 답하시오.

Q: What can we see at the snow design competition?

➡ _____

_____

31 다음 대화에서 위 글의 내용과 일치하지 않는 것은?

A: ①As we are here in Sweden, I want to visit Kiruna.
B: ②Oh, there is the snow festival in Kiruna, right?
A: ③Yes. I heard it starts in the last week of January, so we can see the festival.
B: That's nice. ④I'm so excited to see the largest event, the dog sled ride.
A: Me, too. ⑤I will also see how huge piles of snow are turned into various artworks.

①   ②   ③   ④   ⑤

32 위 글의 표현을 이용하여 다음 우리말을 영어로 쓰시오. 주어진 단어를 사용하시오.

미술가들이 그들의 작품을 만드는 것을 처음부터 끝까지 지켜보는 것은 흥미롭다.
(it / interesting)

➡ _____

_____

33 다음과 같이 풀이되는 단어를 위 글에서 찾아 쓰시오.

a small vehicle used for sliding over snow

➡ _____

단원별 예상문제

[01~02] 다음 그림을 보고 물음에 답하시오.

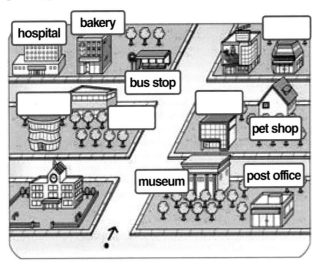

✏️ 출제율 90%

01 다음 대화를 읽고 bank의 위치를 그림에 표시하시오.

> A: Excuse me. Is there a bank around here?
> B: Yes, there is. It's not far from here.
> A: How can I get there?
> B: Go straight two blocks and make a right. It's across from the pet shop. You can't miss it.
> A: Thank you so much.

✏️ 출제율 95%

02 위 그림의 내용과 일치하도록 대화의 빈칸을 완성하시오.

> A: Excuse me. How can I get to the bakery?
> B: _____
> A: Is it far from here?
> B: No, it's not.
> A: Thank you.

➡️ _____

✏️ 출제율 100%

03 다음 짝지어진 대화가 <u>어색한</u> 것을 고르시오.

① A: How can I get to the post office?
　 B: Go straight to 1st Street and make a right.
② A: How long will it take to make the sandwiches?
　 B: Maybe it will take about an hour.
③ A: Do you know where the subway station is?
　 B: Sure. Walk straight ahead.
④ A: Is there a pet shop around here?
　 B: It's just around the corner.
⑤ A: Where can I find a museum?
　 B: It will take about 15 minutes by taxi.

[04~05] 다음 대화를 읽고 물음에 답하시오.

> Man: Excuse me. How can I get to Suwon Hwaseong from here?
> Mina: It's easy. Do you see the bus stop over there?
> Man: Yes, I do.
> Mina: Take the No. 11 bus and get off at the sixth stop.
> Man: (A)그곳까지 가는 데 시간이 얼마나 걸릴까요?
> Mina: It will take about 20 minutes.
> Man: Thank you very much.
> Mina: No problem. Are you going there for the festival?
> Man: Yes. I heard it's a lot of fun.
> Mina: I hope you have a great time.

✏️ 출제율 85%

04 위 대화의 밑줄 친 (A)의 우리말을 주어진 단어를 써서 영어로 옮기시오.

(long, it, get)

➡️ _____

05 위 대화의 내용과 일치하지 <u>않는</u> 것은?

① The man wants to visit Suwon Hwaseong on foot.

② Mina tells the man how to get to Suwon Hwaseong.

③ The man should take the No. 11 bus and get off at the sixth stop to get to Suwon Hwaseong.

④ It will take about 20 minutes for the man to get to Suwon Hwaseong by bus.

⑤ The festival is being held in Suwon Hwaseong.

06 다음 대화의 내용과 일치하도록 빈칸을 완성하시오.

> Andy: I'm so excited about the school festival this Friday.
> Mike: Me, too. What can we do to advertise it, Andy?
> Andy: How about making posters?
> Mike: Great idea. We can post them in our neighborhood.
> Andy: Right. How long will it take to make them?
> Mike: Well, it will take about three hours.
> Andy: Okay, I hope many people come to the festival.

> Andy and Mike are excited about the school festival this Friday. To advertise it, they decide to _____(A)_____ and post them in _____(B)_____. It will take _____(C)_____ to make them. They want many people to come and enjoy _____(D)_____.

➡ (A) _____

(B) _____

(C) _____

(D) _____

[07~08] 다음 대화를 읽고 물음에 답하시오.

> Minsu: Hi, Emma. What's up?
> Emma: Hey, Minsu. Are you free this Saturday?
> Minsu: Yes. Why do you ask?
> Emma: Well, how about having lunch together?
> Minsu: (A) Sure.
> Emma: (B) Let's try the new Chinese restaurant, Ming's. It's near the school.
> Minsu: (C) Okay. How can I @<u>get</u> there from the school?
> Emma: (D) Make a left, and the restaurant will be on your left.
> Minsu: (E) All right. Let's meet at 12 o'clock.
> Emma: Wonderful. See you then.

07 위 대화의 (A)~(E) 중에서 다음 문장이 들어가기에 적절한 곳은?

> Come out from the school and go straight to Green Street.

① (A) ② (B) ③ (C) ④ (D) ⑤ (E)

08 위 대화의 밑줄 친 @<u>get</u>과 같은 의미로 쓰인 것은?

① <u>Get</u> me something to drink, please.

② We're going to be late. Let's <u>get</u> a taxi.

③ I didn't <u>get</u> your letter yesterday.

④ Jane will <u>get</u> the prize at the dancing contest.

⑤ You can <u>get</u> to the city hall by bus.

[09~10] 다음 대화를 읽고 물음에 답하시오.

> A: Excuse me. How can I get to the post office?
> B: Go straight to 1st Street and make a right. It will be on your right.
> A: (A)여기서 먼가요?
> B: No, it's not.
> A: Thank you very much.

출제율 90%

09 위 대화에 나타난 우체국의 위치를 우리말로 설명하시오.

➡ _____

출제율 95%

10 위 대화의 우리말 (A)를 영작하시오.

➡ _____

출제율 100%

11 다음 빈칸에 들어갈 말이 바르게 짝지어진 것은?

> • It is interesting _____ a book.
> • David saw me _____ a book in the library.

① reading – to read   ② read – reading
③ to read – reading   ④ read – to read
⑤ read – read

출제율 95%

12 다음 중 밑줄 친 부분의 쓰임이 다른 하나는?

① It was a bad idea to call you late at night.
② It was my mistake to give you my phone number.
③ It was the hat that I bought for him.
④ It is useful to discuss the issue.
⑤ It is strange for him to say so.

출제율 95%

13 주어진 단어를 활용하여 다음 우리말을 영어로 쓰시오.

> 나는 Kevin이 프랑스어를 말하는 것을 들었다.
> (hear / French)

➡ _____

출제율 90%

14 다음 우리말을 영어로 바르게 옮긴 것은?

> 목표를 정하고 최선을 다하는 것은 중요하다.

① It is important to set a goal and does your best.
② It is important to set a goal and do your best.
③ It is important setting a goal and to do your best.
④ It is important setting a goal and do your best.
⑤ It is important to set a goal and your best.

출제율 95%

15 다음 중 어법상 바르지 않은 것은?

① Jason heard two girls talking to each other loudly.
② It is not easy to take care of a pet.
③ Did you feel the house shaking?
④ I think it is important to listen to other people's opinion carefully.
⑤ Ms. Kim watched her students to solve the problems.

출제율 85%

16 주어진 단어를 활용하여 다음 우리말을 영어로 쓰시오.

> 그녀가 바이올린을 연주하는 것을 듣는 것은 좋은 기회야. (it / a good chance)

➡ _____

출제율 95%

17 다음 우리말을 영어로 쓰시오.

> 한 소년이 호수에서 수영하고 있는 것이 보이니?

➡ _____

[18~20] 다음 글을 읽고 물음에 답하시오.

White Nights Festival
Victor from St. Petersburg, Russia
Have you heard ___ⓐ___ the *White Nights*?
[A] During that time, we hold the White Nights Festival. It usually starts in May and lasts for about a month.
[B] A boat with red sails slowly appears on the river. Soon, fireworks begin and a water show follows. You can also hear musicians playing beautiful live music.
[C] Every summer, this amazing thing happens in my hometown. The night sky does not get completely dark.
[D] During the festival, there is a ballet or an opera almost every night. The most popular event is the Scarlet Sails celebration.

출제율 95%

18 다음 중 빈칸 ⓐ에 들어갈 말과 같은 말이 들어가는 것은?

① Emily gets tired _____ eating the same food.
② Jason came up _____ a brilliant idea.
③ My hobby is looking _____ plants in the garden.
④ I really look up _____ King Sejong.
⑤ They had to put _____ their event because of the bad weather.

출제율 90%

19 자연스러운 글이 되도록 [A]~[D]를 바르게 나열한 것은?

① [B] – [D] – [C] – [A]
② [B] – [C] – [A] – [D]
③ [C] – [B] – [D] – [A]
④ [C] – [A] – [D] – [B]
⑤ [D] – [B] – [A] – [C]

출제율 100%

20 다음 중 위 글을 읽고 답할 수 <u>없는</u> 것은?

① Where is St. Petersburg?
② What do people in Russia do during the White Nights?
③ What color of sails does the boat have?
④ What can people see after the firework?
⑤ How many musicians are there at the festival?

[21~22] 다음 글을 읽고 물음에 답하시오.

Holi, the Festival of Colors
Amala from Delhi, India
Holi is the most popular festival in my country. ① It is usually in March. During the festival, we say goodbye to cold winter and hello to warm spring. ② On the first day, people gather around a big fire at night and sing and dance. ③ The main event begins the next day. ④ Children and adults chase each other with *gulal*. ⑤ What is *gulal*? It is blue, yellow, green and pink powder. It's a lot of fun to run around and throw (A)colorful powder at everyone. We also join street parades!

출제율 90%

21 ①~⑤ 중 주어진 문장이 들어가기에 가장 적절한 곳은?

We celebrate the festival everywhere for two days.

①   ②   ③   ④   ⑤

출제율 95%

22 밑줄 친 (A)가 가리키는 것을 위 글에서 찾아 쓰시오.

➡ _____

[01~03] 다음 대화를 읽고 물음에 답하시오.

Minsu: Hi, Emma. What's up?

Emma: Hey, Minsu. Are you free this Saturday?

Minsu: Yes. Why do you ask?

Emma: Well, how about having lunch together?

Minsu: Sure.

Emma: Let's try the new Chinese restaurant, Ming's. It's near the school.

Minsu: Okay. How can I get there from the school?

Emma: Come out from the school and go straight to Green Street. Make a left, and the restaurant will be on your left.

Minsu: All right. Let's meet at 12 o'clock.

Emma: Wonderful. See you then.

01 What are Emma and Minsu going to do this Saturday?

➡ _____

_____

02 What time are Emma and Minsu going to meet?

➡ _____

03 중요 Minsu가 Ming's를 어떻게 찾아가야 하는지 우리말로 간략히 설명하시오.

➡ _____

_____

04 다음 빈칸에 call을 어법에 맞게 쓰시오.

• I heard someone _____ my name.
• I heard my name _____.

05 중요 주어진 단어를 활용하여 다음 우리말을 영어로 쓰시오.

나의 영어 실력을 향상시키는 것은 필수적이다.
(it / essential / skill / improve)

➡ _____

06 다음 대화의 빈칸에 알맞은 말을 다섯 단어로 쓰시오.

A: Do you think that having a balanced diet is important?
B: Sure. It is really important _____.

➡ _____

07 다음 두 문장을 하나의 문장으로 쓰시오.

• The cat jumped up onto the chair.
• Did you see that?

➡ _____

08 중요 주어진 단어를 바르게 배열하여 다음 우리말을 영어로 쓰시오.

나는 그 소년이 수영장에서 수영하고 있는 것을 보았다.
(in / the boy / I / the pool / saw / swimming)

➡ _____

Holi, the Festival of Colors

Amala from Delhi, India

Holi is the most popular festival in my country. It is usually in March. During the festival, we say goodbye to cold winter and hello to warm spring. We celebrate the festival everywhere for two days. On the first day, people gather around a big fire at night and sing and dance. The main event begins the next day. Children and adults chase each other with *gulal*. What is *gulal*? It is blue, yellow, green and pink powder. (A)주변을 뛰어다니며 형형색색의 가루를 모든 사람들에게 던지는 것은 정말 재미있어요. We also join street parades!

09 주어진 단어를 활용하여 밑줄 친 우리말 (A)를 영어로 쓰시오.

(a lot of / run around / colorful)

➡ _____

_____

10 위 글의 내용에 맞게 빈칸에 알맞은 말을 세 단어로 쓰시오.

A: Did you _____ _____ _____ at the Holi festival?

B: Yeah. People march in public to celebrate the festival. It was amazing.

11 When do people in India celebrate Holi? Answer in English with a full sentence.

➡ _____

I live in Gangneung. There are beautiful beaches in my neighborhood. It's a lot of fun to swim at the beach. Many people swim there. There is a famous hanok in Gangneung. It is called Ojukheon. Yulgok was born there. The most famous food in Gangneung is potato tteok. It is soft and sweet. Come and enjoy Gangneung!

12 다음 질문에 4 단어로 이루어진 한 문장으로 답하시오.

Q: Where is Ojukheon?

➡ _____

13 According to the passage, what can we see at the beach in Gangneung? Answer in English with a full sentence.

➡ _____

14 위 글의 내용에 맞게 빈칸에 알맞은 말을 쓰시오.

A: How is potato tteok?

B: _____

➡ _____

01 다음 지도에서 나타내는 Ming's의 위치와 일치하도록 빈칸에 알맞은 말을 넣어 가는 길을 설명하시오.

> Emma: Let's try the new Chinese restaurant, Ming's. It's near the school.
>
> Minsu: Okay. How can I get there from the school?
>
> Emma: _____
>
> Minsu: All right. Let's meet at 12 o'clock.
>
> Emma: Wonderful. See you then.

➡ _____

02 주어진 단어와 지각동사를 이용하여 축제에서 볼 수 있는 다양한 사람들을 묘사해 보시오.

> children   merchants   people

(1) _____
(2) _____
(3) _____

03 주어진 단어와 가주어 It과 진주어 to부정사를 활용하여 학교생활에서 유의해야 할 점에 대해 〈보기〉와 같이 써 보시오.

> important, necessary, essential, dangerous

> ═══ 보기 ═══
>
> It is important not to fall asleep during the class.

(1) _____
(2) _____
(3) _____
(4) _____

단원별 모의고사

01 다음 영영풀이가 가리키는 것을 고르시오.

> a small vehicle used for sliding over snow

① firework ② sled

③ boat ④ sail

⑤ shape

02 다음 주어진 문장의 밑줄 친 hold와 같은 의미로 쓰인 것은?

> We <u>hold</u> the White Nights Festival.

① Did Emily <u>hold</u> a large box?

② It is hard to <u>hold</u> a business meeting because of all this noise.

③ The girl was <u>holding</u> her mother's hand.

④ I'll <u>hold</u> the door for you.

⑤ Would you <u>hold</u> my place, please?

03 다음 대화의 빈칸에 들어갈 말로 어색한 것은?

> Sora: Excuse me. _____
>
> Tom: Oh, the library? Cross the street and go straight two blocks. Then make a left.
>
> Sora: Thank you very much.

① How can I get to the library?

② Where can I find the library?

③ Do you know where the library is?

④ Is there the library around here?

⑤ How long will it take to get to the library?

04 다음 우리말에 맞게 빈칸에 알맞은 말을 쓰시오.

(1) 그녀는 창문에 돌을 던졌다.

➡ She _____ stones at the window.

(2) Kate는 토론 대회에 참가했다.

➡ Kate took part in the debate _____.

(3) 마을이 거대한 시장으로 변하였다.

➡ The village was changed into the _____ market.

05 다음 문장의 빈칸에 들어갈 말을 〈보기〉에서 골라 쓰시오.

> ┤ 보기 ├
>
> go on / in front of / more and more / because of

(1) The festival will _____ for 5 days.

(2) _____ people are using the tablet PC.

(3) The boys couldn't go on a picnic _____ the bad weather.

(4) I felt so nervous _____ a large group of people.

06 다음 대화의 밑줄 친 우리말을 영작하시오.

> Amy: Jinho, hurry up. We're going to be late for the movie.
>
> Jinho: Okay. How long will it take to get to the theater?
>
> Amy: <u>버스로 약 15분 걸릴 거야.</u>
>
> Jinho: All right. I'm almost ready.

➡ _____

[07~08] 다음 대화를 읽고 물음에 답하시오.

> Man: Excuse me. How can I get to Suwon Hwaseong from here?
>
> Mina: ⓐ It's easy. Do you see the bus stop over there?
>
> Man: Yes, I do.
>
> Mina: Take the No. 11 bus and get ____ⓑ____ at the sixth stop.
>
> Man: How long will it take to get there?
>
> Mina: It will take about 20 minutes.
>
> Man: Thank you very much.
>
> Mina: No problem. Are you going there for the festival?
>
> Man: Yes. I heard it's a lot of fun.
>
> Mina: I hope you have a great time.

07 위 글의 밑줄 친 ⓐ가 가리키는 것을 우리말로 쓰시오.

➡ _____

08 위 글의 빈칸 ⓑ에 알맞은 말을 쓰시오.

➡ _____

09 다음 대화의 내용과 일치하지 <u>않는</u> 것은?

> Rachel: Chris, what will you do for the class party?
>
> Chris: I'll make sandwiches.
>
> Rachel: Great idea. How long will it take to make them?
>
> Chris: Maybe it'll take about an hour.
>
> Rachel: Then, I'll decorate the classroom.
>
> Chris: Sounds great.

① Rachel과 Chris는 학급 파티를 준비하고 있다.

② Chris는 학급 파티를 위해 샌드위치를 만들 것이다.

③ Chris는 샌드위치를 만드는 데 약 한 시간이 걸릴 것이다.

④ Rachel은 교실을 장식할 것이다.

⑤ Rachel은 교실을 장식하는 데 약 한 시간이 걸릴 것이다.

10 다음 주어진 우리말과 일치하도록 주어진 단어를 모두 배열하여 완성하시오.

(1) 너의 집에서 학교까지 가는 데 얼마나 걸리니?

(from / get / school / to / to / it / take / how / long / house / your / does)

➡ _____

(2) 은행까지 어떻게 가나요?

(the / to / I / get / can / bank / how)

➡ _____

(3) 길을 건너서 한 구역 곧장 가세요.

(street / and / the / cross / one / go / straight / block)

➡ _____

(4) 지하철로 대략 10분 정도 걸릴 거야.

(will / by / it / about / take / subway / 10 minutes)

➡ _____

11 다음 대화가 자연스럽게 이어지도록 순서대로 배열하시오.

> (A) Maybe it'll take about an hour.
>
> (B) I'll decorate the classroom.
>
> (C) What will you do for the class party?
>
> (D) Great idea. How long will it take to do it?

➡ _____

[12~13] 다음 대화를 읽고 물음에 답하시오.

A: How long does it take to get to school from your house?

B: It usually takes (a)about 10 minutes.

A: How do you go to school?

B: _____ (A)

12 위 대화의 빈칸 (A)에 들어갈 말로 적절한 것은?

① I walk to school.

② Go straight two blocks and you can find it on your right.

③ It will take about thirty minutes.

④ I'll decorate the classroom.

⑤ I'm almost ready.

13 위 대화의 밑줄 친 (a)와 같은 의미로 쓰인 것은?

① What is this book about?

② It is a story about wild animals.

③ My father is always worried about me.

④ We walked about five miles in the desert.

⑤ I can't understand why she's so angry about him.

14 다음 중 어법상 바르지 않은 것은?

① It is so great to be here with you.

② It is annoying to hear her to sing the same song.

③ Polly heard someone pounding on the door.

④ Christine saw her friend bounce a ball alone.

⑤ It is strange for him to be late today.

15 주어진 단어를 이용하여 다음 우리말을 영어로 쓰시오.

그녀는 비가 지붕 위로 떨어지는 소리를 들었다. (fall on)

➡ _____

16 다음 중 빈칸에 들어갈 말이 바르게 짝지어진 것은?

• Hamilton heard Simon _____ the blackboard.

• It was really irritating to hear someone _____ the blackboard.

① to scratch – to scratch

② scratching – to scratch

③ scratch – scratch

④ scratch – to scratch

⑤ scratch – scratched

17 다음 중 빈칸에 들어갈 수 있는 말을 모두 고르시오.

Jane _____ Thomas kick the wall.

① saw   ② made

③ wanted   ④ heard

⑤ would like

18 주어진 단어를 활용하여 다음 우리말을 영어로 쓰시오.

James는 무언가가 그의 팔을 무는 것을 느꼈다. (bite)

➡ _____

[19~20] 다음 글을 읽고 물음에 답하시오.

White Nights Festival

Victor from St. Petersburg, Russia

Have you heard of the *White Nights*? Every summer, this amazing thing happens in my hometown. The night sky does not get completely dark. (A)[While / During] that time, we hold the White Nights Festival. It usually starts in May and lasts for about a month. During the festival, there is a ballet or an opera almost every night. The most popular event is the Scarlet Sails celebration. A boat with red sails slowly (B)[appears / is appeared] on the river. Soon, fireworks begin and a water show follows. You can also hear musicians (C)[playing / to play] beautiful live music.

19 (A)~(C)에서 어법상 옳은 것끼리 바르게 짝지은 것은?

① While – appears – playing
② While – appears – to play
③ While – is appeared – to play
④ During – appears – playing
⑤ During – is appeared – playing

20 다음 중 위 글의 내용과 일치하지 <u>않는</u> 것은?

① You can experience the White Nights in Russia.
② It is hard to see something at night during the White Nights.
③ The White Nights Festival continues for about a month.
④ Musicians play live music at the festival.
⑤ You can see a ballet or an opera during the festival.

[21~23] 다음 글을 읽고 물음에 답하시오.

Kiruna Snow Festival

Ebba from Kiruna, Sweden

Winter is my favorite season (A)<u>because of</u> the Kiruna Snow Festival. The festival starts in the last week of January and goes on for five or six days. The largest event is the snow design competition. The artists shape huge piles of snow into animals, buildings, and other beautiful artworks. People watch the artists shaping their works from beginning to end. My favorite activity is the dog sled ride. (B)<u>개 썰매를 타고 눈 세상을 날아가는 것은 놀라워요.</u>

21 다음 중 밑줄 친 (A)를 대신하여 쓰일 수 있는 것은?

① because   ② due to   ③ since
④ as   ⑤ for

22 다음 중 위 글의 내용과 일치하는 것은?

① Ebba is not fond of the Kiruna Snow Festival.
② The festival lasts over a week.
③ The artists compete in the event by making something into a particular shape with snow.
④ There is only one mass of snow at the festival.
⑤ It is hard for people to watch the artists shape their works.

23 주어진 단어를 활용하여 밑줄 친 우리말 (B)를 영어로 쓰시오.

(it / through / on a dog sled)

➡ _____

Lesson 6

In Outer Space

의사소통 기능

- 알고 있는지 묻기
  A: Do you know who he is?
  B: Yes, I do. He is Albert Schweitzer.

- 용도 말하기
  A: What is it for?
  B: It's for making ink.

언어 형식

- 동등 비교
  A year on Mars is about twice **as long as** a year on Earth.

- 접속사 although
  Although there are many movies about Mars, no one has been there yet.

Words & Expressions

Key Words

- **adapt** [ədǽpt] 동 적응하다
- **although** [ɔːlðóu] 접 (비록) ~이긴 하지만
- **apply** [əplái] 동 지원하다
- **average** [ǽvəridʒ] 명 평균
- **blind** [blaind] 형 시각 장애가 있는, 눈이 먼
- **brave** [breiv] 형 용감한
- **communicate** [kəmjúːnəkèit] 동 의사소통하다
- **curious** [kjúəriəs] 형 호기심이 많은, 궁금한
- **deaf** [def] 형 청각 장애가 있는, 귀가 먹은
- **decorate** [dékərèit] 동 장식하다
- **difference** [dífərəns] 명 차이
- **electricity** [ilektrísəti] 명 전기
- **environment** [inváiərənmənt] 명 환경, 주위의 상황
- **exhibition** [èksəbíʃən] 명 전시회
- **farther** [fáːrðər] 형 더 먼 (far의 비교급) 부 더 멀리
- **following** [fálouiŋ] 형 다음에 나오는
- **friendly** [fréndli] 형 친절한, 상냥한
- **half** [hæf] 명 절반
- **include** [inklúːd] 동 포함하다
- **invention** [invénʃən] 명 발명
- **inventor** [invéntər] 명 발명가

- **lastly** [lǽstli] 부 마지막으로
- **lead** [liːd] 동 이끌다, 안내하다, 생활을 하다, 지내다
- **length** [leŋkθ] 명 기간, 길이
- **Mars** [maːrz] 명 화성
- **mission** [míʃən] 명 임무
- **necessary** [nésəsèri] 형 필요한, 없어서는 안 될
- **organization** [ɔ̀rgənizéiʃən] 명 조직, 단체
- **outgoing** [áutgouiŋ] 형 활발한
- **peel** [piːl] 동 껍질을 벗기다
- **planet** [plǽnit] 명 행성
- **produce** [prədjúːs] 동 생산하다
- **promise** [prámis] 동 약속하다
- **reason** [ríːzn] 명 이유
- **sense of humor** 유머 감각
- **several** [sévərəl] 형 몇몇의
- **similar** [símələr] 형 비슷한
- **slice** [slais] 동 (얇게) 썰다, 자르다
- **solar system** 태양계
- **space** [speis] 명 우주, 공간
- **spread** [spred] 동 바르다, 펼치다
- **stick** [stik] 명 나뭇가지, 막대

Key Expressions

- **be curious about** ~에 대해 궁금해 하다
- **be good at** ~을 잘하다
- **be made of** ~로 만들어지다, ~로 구성되다
- **cheer up** 기운을 내다, ~을 격려하다
- **from now on** 지금부터
- **get along with** ~와 잘 지내다

- **have a great time** 즐거운 시간을 보내다
- **in addition** 게다가
- **look for** ~을 찾다
- **make an invention** 발명하다
- **miss out** 놓치다
- **on average** 평균적으로

Word Power

※ 서로 반대되는 뜻을 가진 단어

☐ **wide** 넓은 → **narrow** 좁은

☐ **include** 포함하다 → **exclude** 제외하다

☐ **necessary** 필요한 → **unnecessary** 불필요한

☐ **produce** 생산하다 → **consume** 소비하다

※ 행성을 나타내는 단어

☐ **Mercury** 수성
☐ **Venus** 금성
☐ **Earth** 지구
☐ **Mars** 화성

☐ **Jupiter** 목성
☐ **Saturn** 토성
☐ **Uranus** 천왕성
☐ **Neptune** 해왕성

☐ **Pluto** 명왕성

※ 사람의 성격을 묘사하는 형용사

☐ **creative** 창의적인
☐ **curious** 호기심이 많은
☐ **friendly** 친절한
☐ **brave** 용감한

☐ **strong** 강한
☐ **outgoing** 활발한
☐ **shy** 수줍음이 많은
☐ **generous** 관대한

English Dictionary

☐ **adapt** 적응하다
→ to change your behavior in order to live in a new situation successfully
새로운 환경에서 성공적으로 살아가기 위해 당신의 행동을 바꾸다

☐ **apply** 지원하다
→ to ask formally for something such as a job, admission to a school, etc.
직장, 학교의 입학 허가 등과 같은 무언가를 공식적으로 요청하다

☐ **blind** 시각 장애가 있는, 눈이 먼
→ not able to see
볼 수 없는

☐ **deaf** 청각 장애가 있는, 귀가 먹은
→ not able to hear anything
어떤 것도 들을 수 없는

☐ **difference** 차이
→ the way in which two things are not like each other
두 가지 것들이 서로 같지 않은 방식

☐ **environment** 환경
→ the conditions that surround someone or something
누군가 또는 무언가를 둘러싸고 있는 주위의 상황

☐ **half** 절반
→ one of two equal parts into which something can be divided
무언가가 나누어질 수 있는 두 개의 똑같은 부분 중 하나

☐ **length** 기간
→ the amount of time that something lasts
무언가가 지속되는 시간의 양

☐ **mission** 임무
→ a task or job that someone is given to do
누군가에게 하도록 주어진 업무나 일

☐ **organization** 조직, 단체
→ a group such as a club or business that is formed for a particular purpose
특정한 목적을 위해 형성된 모임이나 사업과 같은 모임

☐ **peel** 껍질을 벗기다
→ to remove the skin from a fruit, vegetable, etc.
과일, 야채 등으로부터 껍질을 제거하다

☐ **similar** 비슷한
→ like somebody or something but not exactly the same
누군가 또는 무언가와 비슷하지만 완전히 같지는 않은

☐ **slice** (얇게) 썰다, 자르다
→ to cut something into thin pieces
무언가를 얇은 조각으로 자르다

☐ **stick** 나뭇가지, 막대
→ a thin piece of wood that has been broken from a tree
나무로부터 부러진 얇은 나무 조각

서답형

01 다음 짝지어진 단어의 관계가 같도록 빈칸에 알맞은 말을 쓰시오.

> increase : decrease = _____ : exclude

02 다음 주어진 단어 중 나머지 넷과 성격이 <u>다른</u> 것은?

① Mercury　　② Venus
③ Saturn　　④ Jupiter
⑤ Galaxy

중요

03 다음 영영풀이가 가리키는 것을 고르시오.

> a group such as a club or business that is formed for a particular purpose

① organization　　② mission
③ length　　④ average
⑤ invention

서답형

04 다음 괄호 안에서 알맞은 단어를 고르시오.

(1) Her (miss / mission) in life was to work for poor people.
(2) (Although / But) he was hungry, he could not eat.
(3) Could you (peel / feel) an orange for me?
(4) I need to (look after / look for) the book to do my homework.
(5) There are (several / severe) similar stores at the mall.

중요

05 다음 중 밑줄 친 부분의 뜻풀이가 바르지 <u>않은</u> 것은?

① <u>Although</u> he is short, he is very strong. 비록 ~일지라도
② I have to <u>adapt</u> quickly to the new system. 적응하다
③ Her grandfather is <u>blind</u>. 눈이 먼
④ Alice grew up in a good <u>environment</u>. 환경
⑤ He is a member of a large international <u>organization</u>. 유기체

서답형

06 다음 주어진 우리말과 일치하도록 빈칸에 알맞은 말을 쓰시오.

(1) 그는 일주일에 한 번씩 귀가 먼 아이들을 돕는다.
➡ He helps _____ children once a week.
(2) 10과 6의 평균값은 8이다.
➡ The _____ of 10 and 6 is 8.
(3) 나는 몇몇 다른 회사에 지원했다.
➡ I _____ to several different companies.

07 다음 밑줄 친 space의 의미가 나머지 넷과 <u>다른</u> 것은?

① In <u>space</u>, there is no gravity.
② The Earth looks beautiful from <u>space</u>.
③ Do you know who the first woman in <u>space</u> was?
④ I want to study <u>space</u> engineering in university.
⑤ There is not enough <u>space</u> between the two houses.

01 다음 주어진 우리말과 일치하도록 빈칸에 알맞은 말을 써 넣으시오.

(1) 그는 배드민턴을 잘 친다.
➡ He _____ playing badminton.

(2) 많은 팬들이 그의 새 앨범에 대해 궁금해 하고 있다.
➡ Many fans _____ his new album.

(3) 평균적으로 캥거루는 6년에서 8년 동안 산다.
➡ _____, kangaroos live for 6 to 8 years.

02 중요 다음 문장의 빈칸에 들어갈 말을 〈보기〉에서 골라 쓰시오.

┌─── 보기 ───────────────────┐
│ curious / blind / exhibition / similar / │
│ difference │
└──────────────────────────┘

(1) She is _____ in one eye.
(2) He is such a _____ boy, always asking questions.
(3) There's no _____ between the two bags.
(4) The brothers look very _____.
(5) There are several famous paintings at the _____.

03 다음 우리말에 맞게 주어진 단어를 사용하여 영작하시오.

(1) 우리는 매우 비슷한 관심사를 갖고 있다. (interests)
➡ _____
(2) 물은 생명을 위해 필요하다. (life)
➡ _____
(3) 여행 기간은 5일입니다. (trip)
➡ _____

04 다음 영영풀이가 가리키는 말을 한 단어로 쓰시오.

┌──────────────────────────┐
│ not able to see │
└──────────────────────────┘

➡ _____

05 중요 다음 주어진 우리말과 일치하도록 주어진 어구를 배열하여 완성하시오.

(1) 나는 자원봉사 프로그램에 지원할 것이다.
(apply / the / program / volunteer / I'll / for)
➡ _____

(2) 나는 평균적으로 한 달에 3권의 책을 읽는다.
(read / month / average / three books / I / a / on)
➡ _____

(3) 이 공은 저 공의 절반 크기이다.
(ball / that / of / one / the size / this / half / is)
➡ _____

06 대화의 내용과 일치하도록 다음 글의 빈칸을 완성하시오.

┌──────────────────────────┐
│ Sumi: Do you know what this is? │
│ Kevin: No, I don't. What is it? │
│ Sumi: It's a Socccket. │
│ Kevin: A Socccket? What is it for? │
│ Sumi: It produces electricity when you │
│   play with it. │
│ Kevin: Wow, that's great! │
└──────────────────────────┘
              ⬇
┌──────────────────────────┐
│ I think Sumi's Socccket is the best │
│ invention. When we play with it, it │
│ produces _____. It is very useful when │
│ we don't have any _____. │
└──────────────────────────┘

➡ _____

Conversation

① 알고 있는지 묻기

A Do you know who he is? 그가 누구인지 아니?

B Yes, I do. He is Albert Schweitzer. 응, 알아. 그는 Albert Schweitzer야.

■ 어떤 것에 관해 알고 있는지 물을 때는 'Do you know ~?'를 이용해 표현한다. 특정 인물에 관해 알고 있는지 물을 때는 'Do you know who ~ is?'로 표현하고, 사물에 관해 알고 있는지 물을 때는 'Do you know what ~ is?'로 표현한다.

알고 있는지 묻기

• Do you know who Jane Goodall is? Jane Goodall이 누구인지 알고 있니?

• Do you know about her? 그녀에 관해 알고 있니?

• Guess who she is. 그녀가 누군지 맞혀 봐.

• Can you guess what this is? 이게 무엇인지 추측할 수 있겠니?

핵심 Check

1. 다음 우리말과 일치하도록 빈칸에 알맞은 말을 쓰시오.

(1) **A:** He was an artist. He painted *the Mona Lisa*. Do you know ＿＿＿＿ ＿＿＿＿

＿＿＿＿? (그는 미술가야. 그는 모나리자를 그렸어. 그가 누구인지 아니?)

B: Yes, I do. He is Leonardo Da Vinci. (응, 알아. 그는 Leonardo Da Vinci야.)

(2) **A:** It looks like a man. It is made of snow. ＿＿＿＿ ＿＿＿＿ ＿＿＿＿ ＿＿＿＿

＿＿＿＿ ＿＿＿＿? (그것은 사람처럼 보여. 눈으로 만들어졌어. 무엇인지 알겠니?)

B: No, I don't. What is it? (아니, 모르겠어. 뭐니?)

A: It's a snowman. (눈사람이야.)

(3) **A:** It's for a rainy day. It has different colors. ＿＿＿＿ what it is.

(그것은 비 오는 날을 위한 것이야. 그것은 여러 가지 색들을 갖고 있어. 무엇인지 맞혀 봐.)

B: It's an umbrella. (우산이야.)

② 용도 말하기

A What is it for? 그것은 용도가 무엇이니?

B It's for making ink. 잉크를 만들기 위한 것이야.

■ 'What is it for?' 또는 'What are they for?'는 '용도가 무엇이니?'라는 뜻으로 특정 물건의 사용 목적이나 용도를 묻는 표현이다. 이에 대한 대답은 'It is[They are] for ~.'를 사용하여 물건의 사용 목적이나 용도를 말할 수 있다.

용도 말하기

• What is it for? 그것은 용도가 무엇이니?

• What are they used for? 그것들은 무엇을 위해 사용되니?

핵심 Check

2. 다음 우리말과 일치하도록 빈칸에 알맞은 말을 쓰시오.

(1) **A:** I've never seen it before. _____ _____ _____ _____?

(나는 전에 그것을 본 적이 없어. 그것은 용도가 무엇이니?)

B: It's for decorating your hair. (네 머리 장식을 위한 것이야.)

(2) **A:** Jane, _____ _____ this. It's a *Jige*. (Jane, 이것 좀 봐. 이것은 지게야.)

B: I have never seen it before. What is it _____?

(그것을 전에 본 적이 없어요. 용도가 무엇이에요?)

(3) **A:** _____ _____ _____ _____ _____? (그것들은 무엇을 위해 사용되나요?)

B: They are used for carrying many different things.

(그것들은 많은 다른 물건들을 옮기는 데 사용된다.)

 Listen and Speak 1-B

Ms. Lee: Hello, class! Jisu is today's ❶speaker for show and tell. Jisu?

Jisu: Hi, class! Do you know ❷who this man is? His name is Alexander Graham Bell. Bell was an ❸inventor. He ❹was interested in sound. What did he invent? Yes, the telephone! His mother and wife were ❺deaf. So he also made some inventions for deaf people and opened a school for ❻them.

Ms. Lee: 안녕하세요, 여러분! 지수가 오늘의 물건 가져와서 발표하기의 발표자예요. 지수야?

Jisu: 안녕, 얘들아! 이 사람이 누구인지 아니? 그의 이름은 Alexander Graham Bell이야. Bell은 발명가였어. 그는 소리에 관심이 있었어. 그가 무엇을 발명했지? 맞아, 전화기야! 그의 어머니와 아내는 청각 장애가 있었어. 그래서 그는 청각 장애인들을 위한 몇몇 발명품도 만들었고 그들을 위한 학교를 열었어.

❶ speaker: 발표자 show and tell 물건 가져와서 발표하기
❷ 간접의문문의 어순으로 '의문사+주어+동사'의 순서로 이어진다.
❸ inventor: 발명가
❹ be interested in: ~에 관심이 있다 = have an interest in
❺ deaf: 청각 장애가 있는
❻ them은 deaf people을 가리킨다.

Check(√) True or False

(1) Alexander Graham Bell invented the telephone.　　　　T ☐ F ☐

(2) Alexander Graham Bell was not able to hear.　　　　T ☐ F ☐

 Real Life Talk – Step 1

Judy: How was your weekend, Hojin?

Hojin: I ❶had a great time. I went to a science ❷exhibition with my brother.

Judy: Did you? I heard there were so many interesting things.

Hojin: Yes. Look at this. I bought it there. Do you know what it is?

Judy: Well, I'm not sure. What is it?

Hojin: It's a VR headset.

Judy: A VR headset? ❸What is it for?

Hojin: If you wear ❹it, you can experience another world.

Judy: Sounds cool. May I try it?

Hojin: Sure. Here you go.

Judy: 주말은 어땠니, 호진아?
Hojin: 즐거운 시간을 보냈어. 남동생과 과학 전시회에 갔었어.
Judy: 그랬니? 흥미로운 것들이 굉장히 많다고 들었어.
Hojin: 응. 이것 좀 봐. 거기에서 샀어. 이게 무엇인지 아니?
Judy: 음, 잘 모르겠어. 뭐니?
Hojin: VR 헤드셋이야.
Judy: VR 헤드셋? 용도가 뭐니?
Hojin: 그것을 쓰면 다른 세상을 경험할 수 있어.
Judy: 멋지다. 내가 써 봐도 될까?
Hojin: 물론이지. 여기 있어.

❶ have a great time: 즐거운 시간을 보내다
❷ exhibition: 전시회
❸ 용도를 묻는 표현이다.
❹ it은 a VR headset을 가리킨다.

Check(√) True or False

(3) Hojin went to a science exhibition and bought the VR headset.　　　　T ☐ F ☐

(4) The VR headset is for experiencing another world.　　　　T ☐ F ☐

Listen and Speak 1-A

Brian: Do you know what this is?

Amy: Um, it ❶looks like a ❷glue stick.

Brian: No, it's a butter stick.

Amy: Oh, is there butter in it?

Brian: Yes, you can ❸spread butter on the bread with ❹it.

❶ look like+명사(구): ～처럼 보이다
❷ glue: 풀
❸ spread: 바르다
❹ it은 a butter stick을 가리킨다.

Listen and Speak 2-A

Jane: ❶This looks interesting. ❷What is it for?

Mike: It's for ❸slicing eggs.

Jane: Really? May I try it?

Mike: Sure, here is an egg.

❶ look+형용사: ～처럼 보이다
❷ 용도를 묻는 표현으로 'What is it used for?'로 바꾸어 쓸 수 있다.
❸ slice: 썰다

Listen and Speak 2-B

Tom: Mom, ❶look at these slippers. I made ❷ them in science class.

Mom: Why did you make slippers in science class?

Tom: They are not ❸just for wearing.

Mom: Then, what are they for?

Tom: You can ❹put them on and clean the floor.

Mom: Oh, so you will clean your room ❺from now on?

Tom: Sure. Don't ❻worry about my room, Mom.

❶ look at: ～을 보다
❷ them은 slippers를 가리킨다.
❸ just: 단지, 오직
❹ put on: ～을 입다, 신다
❺ from now on: 지금부터
❻ worry about: ～에 대해 걱정하다

Listen and Speak 2-C

A: Jane, look at this. It's a meok.

B: I have never seen ❶it before. What is ❶it for?

A: ❶It's for making ink.

B: Oh, really? ❷That's interesting.

❶ it은 모두 meok(먹)을 가리킨다.
❷ That sounds interesting.으로 바꾸어 쓸 수 있다.

Real Life Talk – Step 2

A: Do you know what this is?

B: No, I don't. What is it?

A: It's a Clean Straw.

B: A Clean Straw? What is it for?

A: It cleans water ❶while you drink.

B: Wow, that's great!

❶ while은 '～하는 동안에'를 뜻하며 'while+주어+동사'가 이어지는 반면 during은 명사(구)가 이어진다.

• 다음 우리말과 일치하도록 빈칸에 알맞은 말을 쓰시오.

Listen & Speak 1-A

Brian: Do you know _____ this is?

Amy: Um, it _____ _____ a glue stick.

Brian: No, it's a _____ _____.

Amy: Oh, _____ _____ butter in it?

Brian: Yes, you can _____ butter on the bread with it.

Listen & Speak 1-B

Ms. Lee: Hello, class! Jisu is today's speaker for show and tell. Jisu?

Jisu: Hi, class! Do you know _____ _____ _____ _____?
His name is Alexander Graham Bell. Bell was an _____. He _____ _____ _____ sound. _____ did he _____?
Yes, the telephone! His mother and wife were _____. So he also made some _____ for deaf people and opened a school for them.

Listen & Speak 2-A

Jane: This looks _____. What is it for?

Mike: It's for _____ _____.

Jane: Really? May I _____ it?

Mike: Sure, _____ _____ an egg.

해석

Brian: 너는 이것이 무엇인지 아니?
Amy: 음, 막대 모양 풀 같아 보여.
Brian: 아니, 막대 모양 버터야.
Amy: 오, 그 안에 버터가 있니?
Brian: 응, 그걸로 빵 위에 버터를 바를 수 있어.

Ms. Lee: 안녕하세요, 여러분! 지수가 오늘의 물건 가져와서 발표하기의 발표자예요. 지수야?
Jisu: 안녕, 얘들아! 이 사람이 누구인지 아니? 그의 이름은 Alexander Graham Bell이야. Bell은 발명가였어. 그는 소리에 관심이 있었어. 그가 무엇을 발명했지? 맞아, 전화기야! 그의 어머니와 아내는 청각 장애가 있었어. 그래서 그는 청각 장애인들을 위한 몇몇 발명품도 만들었고 그들을 위한 학교를 열었어.

Jane: 이거 흥미롭게 생겼네. 용도가 뭐야?
Mike: 달걀을 얇게 썰기 위한 거야.
Jane: 정말? 내가 해 봐도 돼?
Mike: 물론이지, 여기 달걀이 있어.

Listen & Speak 2-B

Tom: Mom, _____ _____ these slippers. I made them in science class.

Mom: _____ did you _____ slippers in science class?

Tom: They are _____ _____ for wearing.

Mom: Then, _____ are they _____?

Tom: You can _____ _____ _____ and clean the floor.

Mom: Oh, so you will clean your room _____ _____ _____?

Tom: Sure. Don't _____ _____ my room, Mom.

Tom: 엄마, 이 슬리퍼를 보세요. 과학 시간에 만들었어요.
Mom: 왜 과학 시간에 슬리퍼를 만들었니?
Tom: 단지 신기 위한 게 아니에요.
Mom: 그럼 용도가 무엇이니?
Tom: 슬리퍼를 신고 바닥을 청소할 수 있어요.
Mom: 오, 그럼 앞으로는 네가 네 방을 청소하겠구나?
Tom: 물론이에요. 제 방은 걱정 마세요, 엄마.

Listen & Speak 2-C

A: Jane, _____ _____ this. It's a meok.

B: I _____ _____ _____ it before. _____ is it _____?

A: It's _____ _____ _____.

B: Oh, really? That's _____.

A: Jane, 이것 좀 봐. 먹이야.
B: 나는 그것을 전에 본 적이 없어. 용도가 무엇이니?
A: 잉크를 만들기 위한 거야.
B: 오, 정말? 그거 흥미롭다.

Real Life Talk – Step 1

Judy: _____ _____ your weekend, Hojin?

Hojin: I had a _____ _____. I went to a _____ _____ with my brother.

Judy: Did you? I heard _____ _____ so many interesting things.

Hojin: Yes. Look at this. I bought it there. Do you know _____ _____ _____?

Judy: Well, I'm _____ _____. What is it?

Hojin: It's a VR headset.

Judy: A VR headset? _____ _____ _____ _____?

Hojin: If you _____ it, you can experience _____ _____.

Judy: Sounds cool. May I _____ it?

Hojin: Sure. Here you go.

Judy: 주말은 어땠니, 호진아?
Hojin: 즐거운 시간을 보냈어. 남동생과 과학 전시회에 갔었어.
Judy: 그랬니? 흥미로운 것들이 굉장히 많다고 들었어.
Hojin: 응. 이것 좀 봐. 거기에서 샀어. 이게 무엇인지 아니?
Judy: 음, 잘 모르겠어. 뭐니?
Hojin: VR 헤드셋이야.
Judy: VR 헤드셋? 용도가 뭐니?
Hojin: 그것을 쓰면 다른 세상을 경험할 수 있어.
Judy: 멋지다. 내가 써 봐도 될까?
Hojin: 물론이지. 여기 있어.

[01~02] 다음 대화를 읽고 물음에 답하시오.

Jane: This looks interesting. (A)What is it for?
Mike: It's for slicing eggs.
Jane: Really? May I try it?
Mike: Sure, here is an egg.

01 위 대화의 밑줄 친 (A)의 의도로 적절한 것은?

① 용도 묻기　　　　② 직업 묻기
③ 사용 방법 묻기　　④ 취미 묻기
⑤ 선호도 묻기

02 What is Jane going to do with an egg?

➡ _____

[03~04] 다음 대화를 읽고 물음에 답하시오.

Sue: Do you know what this is?
Jack: No, I don't. What is it?
Sue: It's a Clean Straw.
Jack: A Clean Straw? What is it for?
Sue: _____
Jack: Wow, that's great!

03 위 대화의 주제로 적절한 것은?

① a new invention
② how to make a Clean Straw
③ how to use a Clean Straw
④ Sue's creativity
⑤ how to clean Jack's invention

04 위 대화의 빈칸에 들어갈 말을 주어진 단어를 모두 배열하여 완성하시오.

┌─ 보기 ─┐
water / you / it / cleans / drink / while

➡ _____

01 다음 짝지어진 대화가 어색한 것은?

① A: This looks interesting. What is it?
　 B: It's for slicing eggs.
② A: What are they for?
　 B: They are for cleaning the floor.
③ A: What is it used for?
　 B: You can use it for decorating your hair.
④ A: I've never seen this machine.
　 B: This is for peeling apples.
⑤ A: What are they for?
　 B: They are bineyos.

서답형

02 다음 대화가 자연스럽게 이어지도록 순서대로 배열하시오.

(A) It's for slicing eggs.
(B) Sure, here is an egg.
(C) Really? May I try it?
(D) This looks interesting. What is it for?

➡ _____

[03~04] 다음 대화를 읽고 물음에 답하시오.

Judy: How was your weekend, Hojin?
Hojin: I had a great time. I went to a science exhibition with my brother.
Judy: Did you? I heard there (A)[was / were] so many interesting things.
Hojin: Yes. Look at this. I bought it there. Do you know what it is?
Judy: Well, I'm not sure. What is it?
Hojin: It's a VR headset.
Judy: A VR headset? What is it for?
Hojin: If you wear it, you can experience (B)[another / other] world.
Judy: (C)[Sound / Sounds] cool. May I try it?
Hojin: Sure. Here you go.

중요

03 위 대화의 밑줄 친 (A)~(C)에 들어갈 말이 바르게 짝지어진 것은?

	(A)	(B)	(C)
①	was	another	Sound
②	was	other	Sounds
③	were	another	Sounds
④	were	other	Sound
⑤	were	another	Sound

서답형

04 위 대화의 내용과 일치하도록 다음 빈칸을 완성하시오.

Hojin visited a science exhibition with his brother last weekend. Hojin was so excited because there were _____(A)_____ to experience. He bought a VR headset, which made him _____(B)_____.

➡ (A) _____
　 (B) _____

[05~06] 다음 대화를 읽고 물음에 답하시오.

Tom: Mom, (A)look at these slippers. I made them in science class.
Mom: (B)Why did you make slippers in science class?
Tom: (C)They are not just for wearing.
Mom: Then, what are they for?
Tom: (D)You can put on them and clean the floor.
Mom: (E)Oh, so you will clean your room from now on?
Tom: Sure. Don't worry about my room, Mom.

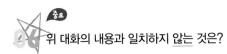

05 위 대화의 (A)~(E) 중 어법상 어색한 문장을 찾아 바르게 고쳐 쓰시오.

➡ _____

06 위 대화의 내용과 일치하지 않는 것은?

① Tom은 과학 시간에 슬리퍼를 만들었다.
② Tom은 슬리퍼를 단지 신기 위한 것이 아니라 청소할 수 있는 용도로 만들었다.
③ Tom은 앞으로 그의 방은 직접 청소할 것이다.
④ Tom은 엄마에게 그의 방은 걱정 말라고 말했다.
⑤ Tom은 엄마가 신을 수 있는 편안한 슬리퍼를 만들었다.

[07~08] 다음 대화를 읽고 물음에 답하시오.

Ms. Lee: Hello, class! Jisu is today's speaker for show and tell. Jisu?

Jisu: Hi, class! Do you know who this man is? His name is Alexander Graham Bell. Bell was an __(A)__ . He was interested in sound. What did he invent? Yes, the telephone! His mother and wife were deaf. So he also made some __(B)__ for deaf people and opened a school for them.

07 위 대화의 빈칸 (A)와 (B)에 invent를 알맞은 형태로 써 넣으시오.

➡ (A) _____ (B) _____

08 위 대화를 읽고 대답할 수 없는 질문은?

① Who was the speaker for show and tell?
② What did Alexander Graham Bell invent?
③ What was Alexander Graham Bell interested in?
④ What did Alexander Graham Bell do for deaf people?
⑤ What was the problem with Alexander Graham Bell's telephone?

[09~10] 다음 대화를 읽고 물음에 답하시오.

Brian: _____(A)_____
Amy: Um, it looks like a glue stick.
Brian: No, it's a butter stick.
Amy: Oh, is there butter in it?
Brian: Yes, you can spread butter on the bread with it.

09 위 대화의 빈칸 (A)에 들어갈 말을 다음 〈보기〉에 주어진 단어를 모두 배열하여 완성하시오.

┌─ 보기 ─┐
know / do / what / is / this / you
└────────┘

➡ _____

10 For what can the butter stick be used?

➡ _____

11 다음 주어진 문장 다음에 대화가 자연스럽게 이어지도록 순서대로 배열하시오.

┌─────────────────────────┐
Do you know what this is?
└─────────────────────────┘

┌─────────────────────────┐
(A) A Clean Straw? What is it for?
(B) It's a Clean Straw.
(C) It cleans water while you drink.
(D) Wow, that's great!
(E) No, I don't. What is it?
└─────────────────────────┘

➡ _____

[01~02] 다음 대화를 읽고 물음에 답하시오.

Jane: This looks interesting. (A)용도가 뭐예요? (for)
Mike: It's for slicing eggs.
Jane: Really? May I try it?
Mike: Sure, here is an egg.

01 위 대화의 밑줄 친 (A)의 우리말을 주어진 단어를 사용하여 4 단어로 영작하시오.

➡ _____

02 위 대화에서 설명하는 물건의 용도를 우리말로 간략히 설명하시오.

➡ _____

[03~05] 다음 대화를 읽고 물음에 답하시오.

Irene: Jane, look at this. It's a meok.
Jane: (A)나는 그것을 전에 본 적이 없어. (before, never) What is it for?
Irene: It's for making ink.
Jane: Oh, really? That's interesting.

03 위 대화의 밑줄 친 (A)의 우리말을 주어진 단어를 사용하여 6단어로 영작하시오.

➡ _____

04 What are Irene and Jane talking about?

➡ _____

05 What is a meok used for?

➡ _____

06 다음 대화의 내용과 일치하도록 주어진 표의 빈칸을 완성하시오.

Sue: Do you know what this is?
Jack: No, I don't. What is it?
Sue: It's a Clean Straw.
Jack: A Clean Straw? What is it for?
Sue: It cleans water while you drink.
Jack: Wow, that's great!

Sue's Invention	
Name	(A)
Use	It (B) while you drink.

➡ (A) _____ (B) _____

07 다음 대화의 내용과 일치하도록 표를 완성하시오.

Ms. Lee: Hello, class! Jisu is today's speaker for show and tell. Jisu?
Jisu: Hi, class! Do you know who this man is? His name is Alexander Graham Bell. Bell was an inventor. He was interested in sound. What did he invent? Yes, the telephone! His mother and wife were deaf. So he also made some inventions for deaf people and opened a school for them.

<Who is Alexander Graham Bell?>

Occupation	(A)
Interest	(B)
Achievement	(C)
Problems	(D)
Contribution	(E)

➡ (A) _____
(B) _____
(C) _____
(D) _____
(E) _____

교과서
Grammar

① 동등 비교

> • Jane is **as tall as** Mike. Jane은 Mike만큼 키가 크다.
> • My allowance is two times **as much as** my brother. 내 용돈은 내 남동생보다 두 배나 많다.

■ 'as+형용사/부사+as'는 두 대상을 비교하며 서로 동등할 때 쓰는 표현이다. '~만큼 …한'이라는 의미로 쓰인다. 서로가 같지 않음을 나타내는 동등비교의 부정형은 'not+as[so]+형용사/부사+as'의 형태로 쓰인다.

  • Your flower is **as beautiful as** mine. 너의 꽃은 내 꽃만큼 아름다워.
  • Karen's pumpkin pie is **not as[so] delicious as** her mother's.
    Karen의 호박파이는 그녀의 어머니 파이만큼 맛있지 않다.
  • The river is **not as[so] clean as** it used to be. 그 강은 예전만큼 깨끗하지 않다.

■ 동등 비교를 이용하여 배수 표현이 가능하다. '배수사(twice, three times 등)+as+형용사/부사+as'의 형태이며 '~의 몇 배 만큼 …한'이라는 의미로 쓰인다.

  • This ball is twice **as big as** that ball. 이 공은 저 공보다 두 배나 크다.
  • The demand is three times **as great as** the supply. 수요가 공급의 세 배이다.

■ 비교급은 일반적으로 형용사나 부사의 어미에 -er을 붙여서 만든다. 불규칙 변화하는 비교급 good-better, well-better, many-more, little-less 등이 있으며 의미에 따라 비교급 형태가 달라지는 것들에 유의한다.

  • The man looks **older than** his age. 그 남자는 자신의 나이보다 더 나이 들어 보인다.
  • He is **less clever than** his elder sister. 그는 누나보다 덜 영리하다.

핵심 Check

1. 다음 우리말과 일치하도록 빈칸에 알맞은 말을 쓰시오.
  (1) 개는 토끼만큼 빨리 달린다.
    ➡ Dogs run ＿＿＿＿ ＿＿＿＿ ＿＿＿＿ rabbits.
  (2) 이것은 저것보다 두 배나 좋다.
    ➡ This is ＿＿＿＿ ＿＿＿＿ ＿＿＿＿ ＿＿＿＿ that.
  (3) 나는 너만큼 용감하지 못해.
    ➡ I am ＿＿＿＿ ＿＿＿＿ ＿＿＿＿ ＿＿＿＿ you.

❷ 접속사 although

> • **Although** I was tired, I did my homework. 나는 피곤했지만, 숙제를 했다.
> • **Although** I like to swim in the river, I hate summer.
> 내가 강에서 수영하는 것을 좋아한다 해도, 나는 여름이 싫어.

■ '비록 ~이지만[~일지라도]'라는 의미로 쓰이는 although는 양보의 부사절을 이끄는 접속사이다. 이에 해당하는 접속사로는 though, even though, even if 등이 있다.

- **Though** he is old, he is quite strong. 그가 나이가 많다 할지라도, 꽤 힘이 세다.
- **Even though** she didn't invite me, I went to her party.
  그녀가 날 초대하지 않았지만, 나는 그녀의 파티에 갔다.
- **Even if** the cookies look great, they don't taste good. 그 쿠키들이 보기에는 좋지만, 맛이 있지는 않다.

■ 부사절을 이끄는 접속사는 주절의 앞뒤에 모두 위치할 수 있으며, 주절 앞에 올 경우 콤마를 쓴다.

- **Although** he wasn't hungry, he had dinner with her. 배가 고프지 않았지만, 그는 그녀와 함께 저녁을 먹었다.
- The waiters at the restaurant were polite **although** the service was slow.
  서비스가 느리긴 했지만, 그 식당의 웨이터들은 친절했다.
- **Although** I like the house, it's too far from my school. 나는 그 집을 좋아하지만, 학교에서 너무 멀다.

■ Despite(= In spite of)와 혼동하지 않도록 주의하자. Despite는 '~일지라도'라는 의미를 갖지만, 전치사로 명사구를 이끈다.

- **Despite** being late for the meeting, I had all the work done.

  = **Although** I was late for the meeting, I had all the work done.
  비록 회의에 늦었다 할지라도, 나는 모든 일을 처리하였다.

핵심 Check

2. 다음 우리말과 일치하도록 빈칸에 알맞은 말을 쓰시오.

(1) 물을 많이 마셨지만, 나는 목이 말랐다.

➡ _____ I drank a lot of water, I was thirsty.

(2) 졸렸지만 Julia는 공부했다.

➡ Julia studied _____ she was _____.

(3) 곤경에 처했다 해도, 너는 평정을 유지해야 한다.

➡ _____ _____ you are in trouble, you have to remain cool.

Grammar 시험대비 기본평가

01 다음 문장에서 어법상 <u>어색한</u> 부분을 바르게 고쳐 쓰시오.

(1) Because she was scared, she bravely went out.

_____ ➡ _____

(2) Kick the ball as hardly as you can.

_____ ➡ _____

(3) His speech is not as bored as it sounds.

_____ ➡ _____

02 다음 우리말에 맞게 주어진 말을 이용해 빈칸에 알맞은 말을 쓰시오.

(1) 진짜 과학은 공상 과학 소설만큼 재미있을 수 있다. (interesting)
= Real science can be _____ science fiction.

(2) 그는 대단히 침착했어요. (cool)
= He was _____ a cucumber.

(3) 내가 Sally만큼 예쁘지 않다고 생각하니? (pretty)
= Do you think I am _____ Sally?

(4) 그녀가 무례하다 할지라도, 그들은 그녀를 고용했다. (even)
= _____ she was rude, they hired her.

> (2) (as) cool as a cucumber: (곤란한 상황에서) 대단히 침착한

03 주어진 어구를 바르게 배열하여 다음 우리말을 영어로 쓰시오.

(1) 그녀는 부자였지만 계속해서 돈을 저축했다. (money / although / saving / she / rich / she / kept / was)

➡ _____

(2) 수영하는 법을 배우는 것은 보이는 것만큼 어렵지 않아요. (looks / as / it / as / learning / difficult / how / swim / is / to / not)

➡ _____

(3) 그들만큼 우리도 슬퍼요. (they / are / are / we / sad / as / as)

➡ _____

(4) 그녀는 예전만큼 매력적이지 않아. (used to / she / she / is / attractive / not / as / be / as)

➡ _____

> (1) keep Ving: 계속해서 V하다
> (2) how to V: V하는 방법
> (4) attractive: 매력적인

01 다음 중 빈칸에 들어갈 말로 알맞지 <u>않은</u> 것은?

> Julia is as _____ as Kelly.

① friendly   ② tall   ③ lovely
④ beautifully   ⑤ kind

02 다음 우리말을 영어로 바르게 옮긴 것은?

> 그것은 기차만큼 빠르게 달릴 수 없어요.

① It runs faster than a train.
② It runs as fast as a train.
③ A train doesn't run faster than it.
④ A train runs as fast as it.
⑤ It can't run as fast as a train.

03 다음 중 어법상 바르지 <u>않은</u> 것은?

> ①Even though ②what I said yesterday, I ③still love you ④as much as I ⑤can.

①   ②   ③   ④   ⑤

04 〔중요〕 다음 중 빈칸에 들어갈 말이 <u>다른</u> 하나는?

① _____ the news made him so sad, he started to cry.
② _____ it rained, we didn't go out.
③ _____ I was very tired, I couldn't sleep.
④ _____ Maria works out regularly, she is healthy.
⑤ _____ he was hungry, he wanted to eat something.

〔서답형〕

05 다음 문장을 지시대로 다시 쓰시오.

> David is 178cm tall. Richard is 182cm tall.

(1) tall, as ~ as를 사용할 것.
➡ _____

(2) short, as ~ as를 사용할 것.
➡ _____

06 다음 빈칸에 들어갈 말이 바르게 짝지어진 것은?

> • Sarah passed the exam _____ she didn't do her best.
> • Clark passed the exam _____ he studied hard.

① despite – because of
② although – when
③ in spite of – because
④ though – because
⑤ because – although

07 〔중요〕 다음 중 어법상 바르지 <u>않은</u> 것은?

① Your hair is twice as long as mine.
② Despite the bad weather, we were happy.
③ Call me as soon as you know something.
④ June is not as smart as Einstein.
⑤ Although he slept well last night, he is refreshed.

〔서답형〕

08 동등비교를 이용하여 주어진 문장과 같은 의미의 문장을 쓰시오.

> James is richer than Barry.

➡ _____

서답형

09 as ~ as를 이용하여 다음 문장과 같은 의미의 문장을 쓰시오.

> Brad is younger than he looks.

➡ _____

10 다음 대화의 밑줄 친 부분과 같은 의미의 문장은?

> A: How much did it cost? Seventy dollars?
> B: Not as much as that.

① I bought it with seventy dollars.
② It cost more than seventy dollars.
③ It didn't cost at all.
④ It cost seventy dollars.
⑤ It cost less than seventy dollars.

11 다음 중 주어진 문장의 빈칸에 들어갈 말과 같은 말이 들어가는 것은? (2개)

> _____ Kelly has a beautiful voice, she doesn't like to sing.

① _____ you called me, I was doing something.
② _____ I like June, I don't like the way she behaves.
③ _____ you are late again, you will be punished.
④ _____ they were poor, they were happy together.
⑤ _____ she is diligent, Emily works hard.

12 다음 중 어법상 바르지 않은 것은?

① Despite the pain, he kept walking.
② The first rope is three times as thick as the second rope.
③ His jacket is not as fancy as me.
④ I don't skip my meal although I am busy all the time.
⑤ You can have it as much as you want.

중요

13 다음 중 어법상 옳은 것끼리 바르게 짝지은 것은?

> • [Although / In spite of] what he heard, he couldn't accept it.
> • I came in as [quiet / quietly] as possible.
> • Sally's house is [bigger / as big as] than Toms' house.

① Although – quiet – bigger
② In spite of – quietly – bigger
③ Although – quitely – bigger
④ In spite of – quiet – as big as
⑤ Although – quitely – as big as

서답형

14 주어진 단어를 활용하여 다음 우리말을 영어로 쓰시오.

> 비록 그가 막 자신의 방을 청소했다 할지라도, 방은 여전히 더럽다.
> (just / still / though)

➡ _____

15 다음 우리말을 영어로 쓰시오.

> 너의 가방은 내 가방보다 두 배나 커.

➡ _____

16 주어진 문장과 같은 의미의 문장은?

> James still feels quite tired, but he felt a lot more tired yesterday.

① James feels more tired than he did yesterday.

② James feels as tired as he did yesterday.

③ James didn't feel as tired as he did the other day.

④ James doesn't feel as tired as he did yesterday.

⑤ James didn't feel more tired than he did yesterday.

17 다음 중 어법상 옳은 문장의 개수는?

> ⓐ Kevin is not as more creative as Jim.
> ⓑ Despite his success, Brad had trouble finding a publisher for his works.
> ⓒ Julian spends money as more as she wants.
> ⓓ Karl didn't hurry even though he was late for the meeting.
> ⓔ My time is as precious as your time.

① 1개   ② 2개   ③ 3개   ④ 4개   ⑤ 5개

18 다음 빈칸에 들어갈 말로 적절한 것을 <u>모두</u> 고르시오.

> _____ all my effort, my voice kept shaking.

① Though   ② Even if

③ Despite   ④ Because of

⑤ In spite of

19 다음 중 빈칸에 들어갈 수 <u>없는</u> 것은?

> Tom didn't give up _____ he kept failing.

① even though   ② although

③ though   ④ even if

⑤ unless

20 다음 빈칸에 들어갈 말로 적절한 것은?

> • Despite applying for tens of jobs, Mark is still out of job.
> = _____, Mark is still out of job.

① Because he applied for tens of jobs

② Even though he applied for tens of jobs

③ When he applied for tens of jobs

④ Although applied for tens of jobs

⑤ In spite applying for tens of jobs

21 다음 문장에서 어법상 <u>틀린</u> 것을 고쳐 문장을 다시 쓰시오.

> It is not as cheaper as I expected.

➡ _____

22 다음 우리말을 영어로 바르게 옮긴 것을 <u>모두</u> 고르시오.

> 그 영화는 내가 생각했던 것보다 짧았어.

① The movie was not as long as I thought.

② The movie was longer than I thought.

③ The movie was not as short as I thought.

④ The movie was shorter than I thought.

⑤ The movie was much longer than I thought.

01 동등 비교 표현을 이용하여 다음 문장과 같은 의미의 문장을 쓰시오.

> You spent more money than me.

➡ _____

02 주어진 형용사를 내용과 어법에 맞게 빈칸에 쓰시오.

> long   comfortable   fast   heavy

(1) I'm sorry I'm late, but I got here _____ I could.

(2) I'm going to sleep on the floor although it is _____ the bed.

(3) You can stay here _____ you like.

(4) Your box weighs 5 kilograms. My box weighs 10 kilograms. My box is _____ yours.

03 양보의 접속사를 이용하여 주어진 문장과 같은 의미의 문장을 쓰시오.

> In spite of being sick, Joe continues working.

➡ _____

04 다음 우리말을 영어로 쓰시오.

> BTS는 Justin Bieber만큼 유명하다.

➡ _____

05 주어진 단어를 이용하여 다음 우리말을 영어로 쓰시오. 콤마를 사용하지 마시오.

> 비록 네가 Bradley만큼 똑똑하다 할지라도, 너는 그만큼 현명하지는 못하다.
> (smart / wise)

➡ _____

_____

06 다음 두 문장을 하나의 문장으로 연결하시오.

> • It rained a lot.
> • The traffic was bad.
> • We have an important job.

> • We arrived on time.
> • We are not well paid.
> • We enjoyed our holiday.

➡ _____

➡ _____

➡ _____

07 지시에 맞게 다음 우리말을 영어로 쓰시오.

> 거북이는 토끼만큼 빠르지 않다.

(1) 동등 비교를 이용하여 문장을 쓰시오.

➡ _____

(2) slow를 이용하여 문장을 쓰시오.

➡ _____

08 주어진 단어를 이용하여 다음 문장과 같은 의미의 문장을 쓰시오.

> The new school was nearer than Tom expected.
> (not, as)

➡ _____

09 주어진 어휘를 어법에 맞게 빈칸에 쓰시오.

> despite   although   in spite of   though

(1) _____ our effort, we failed to win the first prize.

(2) Dana accepted the job _____ the salary was rather low.

(3) Dad can't quit smoking _____ the doctor's repeated warning.

(4) _____ he lied about everything, we decided to forgive him.

10 다음 문장을 동등 비교 문장을 이용하여 하나의 문장으로 쓰시오.

> Daivd has lived here for quite a long time. But I've lived here longer than he.

➡ _____

11 알맞은 접속사를 이용하여 주어진 문장과 같은 의미의 문장을 쓰시오.

> Despite being poor, Helen never lost her sense of humor.

➡ _____
_____

12 주어진 어구를 이용하여 다음 우리말을 영어로 쓰시오.

> 비록 이야기가 유치하긴 했지만, 나는 그 영화를 즐겼다. 그러나 그것은 내가 예상했던 것만큼 유치하지는 않았다.
> (although / silly / enjoy the film)

➡ _____
_____

13 주어진 어구를 바르게 배열하여 다음 우리말을 영어로 쓰시오.

> 그가 책을 출판했지만, 누구도 그 사실을 몰랐다.
> (the fact / though / knew / he / no one / a book / published)

➡ _____

14 다음 문장과 같은 의미의 문장을 완성하시오.

> The yellow car is not as expensive as the red car.

➡ The red car _____ .
➡ The yellow car _____ .

15 적절한 접속사를 이용하여 다음 우리말을 영어로 쓰시오.

> 어제 나는 배가 고팠지만, 아무것도 먹지 않았다.

➡ _____
_____

Fly Me to Mars

Live on MARS!
(어떤 장소에) 살다(자동사)
Do you want to live on another planet?
또 다른(another+단수명사)
The Korea Space Organization (KSO) is looking for people to go to
to부정사의 형용사적 용법(people 수식)
MARS! Our mission is to build a city on Mars.
to부정사의 명사적 용법(~하는 것)
We are looking for someone…

who is healthy.
주격 관계대명사(선행사: someone)
who is creative and curious.

who can get along with others.
= other people
who can adapt to a new environment quickly.
~에 적응하다
To apply, send us a short video. The video must include the answers
to부정사의 부사적 용법 중 목적(~하기 위해서)
to the following questions:

1. Why do you want to go to Mars?

2. Do you have a good sense of humor?

3. Why are you the perfect person for this mission?

This is a chance of a lifetime, so don't miss out!
부정명령문(~하지 마라)

Mars, the Second Earth?

Although there are many books and movies about Mars, no one has
many books에 수의 일치   누구도 ~하지 않다
been there yet. These days, scientists are looking at Mars as a new
아직   요즈음   (자격, 기능) ~로(서)
home. In fact, NASA and some companies are trying to send people
사실
there right now.

organization 조직. 단체	
mission 임무	
get along with ~와 잘 지내다	
adapt 적응하다	
environment 환경. 주위의 상황	
apply 지원하다	
include 포함하다	
following 다음에 나오는	
chance 기회	
lifetime 일생	
miss out 놓치다	
although (비록) ~이긴 하지만	

 확인문제

● 다음 문장이 본문의 내용과 일치하면 T, 일치하지 <u>않으면</u> F를 쓰시오.

1 To apply, you need to be healthy and creative. ☐

2 Getting along with others is not an important matter. ☐

3 Many people have been to Mars. ☐

4 NASA wants to send people to Mars. ☐

The big question is, "Can people live on Mars?" Many scientists believe so for several reasons. First, they think that there is water on Mars. This is great because water is necessary for all life. Second, Mars has hard land to build houses and buildings on. Third, the length of day and night on Mars is similar to that on Earth. In addition, Mars also has four seasons. So, people can lead similar lives. Lastly, Mars is not very far. It is the second closest planet to Earth.

Mars, however, has some differences from Earth. First, Mars is about half the size of Earth. It is the second smallest planet in the solar system. Second, a year on Mars is about twice as long as a year on Earth. Third, Mars is much colder than Earth. On average, it is about –60°C on Mars. This is because Mars is farther away from the Sun than Earth.

Although no one can answer the big question right now, it is exciting to imagine this new world. Who knows? You could be the first Korean on Mars!

단어
several 몇몇의
necessary 필요한, 없어서는 안 될
length 길이, 기간
similar 비슷한
in addition 게다가
lead 생활을 하다, 지내다
half 절반
solar system 태양계
twice 두 배
on average 평균적으로
exciting 신이 나는

 **확인문제**

● 다음 문장이 본문의 내용과 일치하면 T, 일치하지 <u>않으면</u> F를 쓰시오.

1 Many scientists think that it is possible for people to live on Mars. ☐

2 It is hard to say that there is water on Mars. ☐

3 Mars has fewer seasons as Earth has. ☐

4 Earth is about two times bigger than Mars. ☐

5 Being farther away from the Sun makes Mars colder than Earth. ☐

• 우리말을 참고하여 빈칸에 알맞은 말을 쓰시오.

1 Live _____ MARS!

2 Do you want _____ _____ _____ another planet?

3 The Korea Space Organization (KSO) is _____ _____ _____ _____ _____ to MARS!

4 Our mission is _____ _____ a city _____ Mars.

5 We are looking for someone…

_____ is _____.

_____ is _____ and _____.

_____ can _____ _____ _____ others.

_____ can _____ _____ a new environment quickly.

6 _____ _____, send us a short video.

7 The video _____ _____ the answers _____ the following questions:

8 1. Why do you _____ _____ _____ to Mars?

2. Do you have _____ _____ _____ _____ humor?

3. Why are you the perfect person _____ _____ _____?

9 This is _____ _____ _____ a lifetime, so don't _____ out!

10 Mars, _____ _____ _____?

11 _____ there are _____ _____ and _____ about Mars, no one has been there _____.

12 These days, scientists are _____ _____ Mars _____ a new home.

13 _____ _____, NASA and some companies _____ _____ _____ _____ people there right now.

1 화성에서 살아요!

2 다른 행성에서 살고 싶은가요?

3 한국 우주 기구(KSO)는 화성에 갈 사람들을 찾고 있습니다!

4 우리의 임무는 화성에 도시를 세우는 것입니다.

5 우리는 다음과 같은 사람을 찾고 있습니다.
건강한 사람.
창의적이고 호기심이 많은 사람.
다른 사람들과 잘 지낼 수 있는 사람.
새로운 환경에 빨리 적응할 수 있는 사람.

6 지원하려면 우리에게 짧은 동영상을 보내세요.

7 동영상은 다음의 질문에 관한 답을 포함해야 합니다.

8 1. 당신은 왜 화성에 가고 싶은가요?
2. 당신은 유머 감각이 있나요?
3. 왜 당신이 이 임무에 적합한 사람인가요?

9 이것은 일생에 단 한 번뿐인 기회이므로 놓치지 마세요!

10 화성, 제 2의 지구?

11 화성에 관한 많은 책과 영화가 있긴 하지만, 아직 화성에 가 본 사람은 아무도 없다.

12 요즘, 과학자들은 화성을 새로운 거주지로 보고 있다.

13 사실, NASA와 몇몇 회사들은 그곳에 사람들을 보내기 위해 바로 지금도 노력하고 있다.

14 The big question is, "_____ _____ _____ _____ Mars?"

15 Many scientists _____ _____ for several reasons.

16 First, they think _____ there is _____ on Mars.

17 This is great _____ water is _____ _____ all life.

18 Second, Mars has _____ _____ _____ _____ houses and buildings _____.

19 Third, the length of day and night on Mars _____ _____ _____ that on Earth.

20 _____ _____, Mars also _____ _____ _____.

21 So, people can _____ _____ _____.

22 Lastly, Mars is not _____ _____.

23 It is _____ _____ _____ planet to Earth.

24 Mars, _____, has _____ _____ _____ Earth.

25 First, Mars is _____ _____ the size of Earth.

26 It is _____ _____ _____ planet in the _____ system.

27 Second, a year on Mars is _____ _____ _____ _____ _____ a year on Earth.

28 Third, Mars is _____ _____ than Earth.

29 _____ _____, it is about –60℃ on Mars.

30 This is _____ Mars is _____ _____ from the Sun than Earth.

31 _____ no one can _____ the big question right now, it is _____ _____ _____ this new world.

32 Who knows? You could be _____ _____ Mars!

14 중요한 질문은 "화성에서 사람들이 살 수 있는가?"이다.

15 많은 과학자들은 몇몇 이유로 그렇게 믿고 있다.

16 첫째, 그들은 화성에 물이 있다고 생각한다.

17 물은 모든 생명체에 필수적이기 때문에 이것은 중요하다.

18 둘째, 화성은 집과 건물을 지을 수 있는 단단한 땅을 가지고 있다.

19 셋째, 화성의 낮과 밤의 길이는 지구의 낮과 밤의 길이와 비슷하다.

20 게다가, 화성은 사계절도 있다.

21 그래서 사람들이 비슷한 생활을 할 수 있다.

22 마지막으로, 화성은 그렇게 멀지 않다.

23 화성은 지구에서 두 번째로 가까운 행성이다.

24 그러나 화성은 지구와 다른 점이 몇 개 있다.

25 첫째, 화성은 지구의 약 절반 크기이다.

26 화성은 태양계에서 두 번째로 작은 행성이다.

27 둘째, 화성에서의 일 년은 지구에서의 일 년보다 약 두 배 길다.

28 셋째, 화성은 지구보다 훨씬 더 춥다.

29 평균적으로, 화성의 기온은 약 섭씨 영하 60도이다.

30 이것은 화성이 지구보다 태양에서 더 멀리 떨어져 있기 때문이다.

31 비록 누구도 그 중요한 질문에 지금 당장 답할 수는 없지만, 이 새로운 세상을 상상하는 것은 신이 난다.

32 누가 알겠는가? 당신이 화성에 발을 디디는 첫 번째 한국인이 될 수도 있다!

● 우리말을 참고하여 본문을 영작하시오.

1 화성에서 살아요!

➡ _____

2 다른 행성에서 살고 싶은가요?

➡ _____

3 한국 우주 기구(KSO)는 화성에 갈 사람들을 찾고 있습니다!

➡ _____

4 우리의 임무는 화성에 도시를 세우는 것입니다.

➡ _____

5 우리는 다음과 같은 사람을 찾고 있습니다.
건강한 사람. 창의적이고 호기심이 많은 사람. 다른 사람들과 잘 지낼 수 있는 사람.
새로운 환경에 빨리 적응할 수 있는 사람.

➡ _____

_____

6 지원하려면 우리에게 짧은 동영상을 보내세요.

➡ _____

7 동영상은 다음의 질문에 관한 답을 포함해야 합니다.

➡ _____

8 1. 당신은 왜 화성에 가고 싶은가요?

2. 당신은 유머 감각이 있나요?

3. 왜 당신이 이 임무에 적합한 사람인가요?

➡ 1. _____

2. _____

3. _____

9 이것은 일생에 단 한 번뿐인 기회이므로 놓치지 마세요!

➡ _____

10 화성, 제 2의 지구?

➡ _____

11 화성에 관한 많은 책과 영화가 있긴 하지만, 아직 화성에 가 본 사람은 아무도 없다.

➡ _____

12 요즘, 과학자들은 화성을 새로운 거주지로 보고 있다.

➡ _____

13 사실, NASA와 몇몇 회사들은 그곳에 사람들을 보내기 위해 바로 지금도 노력하고 있다.

➡ _____

14 중요한 질문은 "화성에서 사람들이 살 수 있는가?"이다.

➡ _____

15 많은 과학자들은 몇몇 이유로 그렇게 믿고 있다.

➡ _____

16 첫째, 그들은 화성에 물이 있다고 생각한다.

➡ _____

17 물은 모든 생명체에 필수적이기 때문에 이것은 중요하다.

➡ _____

18 둘째, 화성은 집과 건물을 지을 수 있는 단단한 땅을 가지고 있다.

➡ _____

19 셋째, 화성의 낮과 밤의 길이는 지구의 낮과 밤의 길이와 비슷하다.

➡ _____

20 게다가, 화성은 사계절도 있다.

➡ _____

21 그래서 사람들이 비슷한 생활을 할 수 있다.

➡ _____

22 마지막으로, 화성은 그렇게 멀지 않다.

➡ _____

23 화성은 지구에서 두 번째로 가까운 행성이다.

➡ _____

24 그러나 화성은 지구와 다른 점이 몇 개 있다.

➡ _____

25 첫째, 화성은 지구의 약 절반 크기이다.

➡ _____

26 화성은 태양계에서 두 번째로 작은 행성이다.

➡ _____

27 둘째, 화성에서의 일 년은 지구에서의 일 년보다 약 두 배 길다.

➡ _____

28 셋째, 화성은 지구보다 훨씬 더 춥다.

➡ _____

29 평균적으로, 화성의 기온은 약 섭씨 영하 60도이다.

➡ _____

30 이것은 화성이 지구보다 태양에서 더 멀리 떨어져 있기 때문이다.

➡ _____

31 비록 누구도 그 중요한 질문에 지금 당장 답할 수는 없지만, 이 새로운 세상을 상상하는 것은 신이 난다.

➡ _____

32 누가 알겠는가? 당신이 화성에 발을 디디는 첫 번째 한국인이 될 수도 있다!

➡ _____

[01~03] 다음 글을 읽고 물음에 답하시오.

Live on MARS!

Do you want to live ____(A)____ another planet?

The Korea Space Organization (KSO) is looking ____(B)____ people to go to MARS! Our mission is to build a city ____(C)____ Mars.

We are looking for someone...

who is healthy.

who is creative and curious.

who can get along with others.

who can adapt to a new environment quickly.

01 빈칸 (A)와 (C)에 공통으로 들어갈 말은?

① at ② by ③ of
④ to ⑤ on

02 다음 중 빈칸 (B)에 들어갈 말과 같은 말이 들어가는 것은?

① What brought _____ the change?
② James came back to care _____ the baby.
③ Can you please turn _____ the light?
④ I will pick you _____ at three.
⑤ Put _____ your coat. It's still cold.

03 다음 중 KSO에서 찾고 있는 사람과 가장 거리가 먼 사람은?

① Minsu is perfectly well.
② Jimmy is interested in many things.
③ Kelly makes friends easily wherever she goes.
④ Sheldon has hard time adjusting to a new environment.
⑤ Penny is inventive and exercises regularly.

[04~05] 다음 글을 읽고 물음에 답하시오.

To apply, send us a short video. The video must include the answers to the following questions:

1. Why do you want to go to Mars?
2. Do you have a good sense of humor?
3. Why are you the perfect person for this mission?

This is a chance of a lifetime, so (A)don't miss out!

04 다음 중 위 글을 읽고 답할 수 없는 질문은?

① What do we need to send to apply?
② How many questions do we need to answer?
③ What must be included in the video?
④ Where should we send the video?
⑤ How many videos should we send?

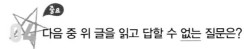

05 빈칸에 알맞은 말을 써서 글쓴이가 밑줄 친 (A)와 같이 말한 이유를 서술하시오.

➡ It's because _____.

[06~09] 다음 글을 읽고 물음에 답하시오.

Mars, the Second Earth?

Although there are many books and movies about Mars, no one has been there yet. ① These days, scientists are looking at Mars as a new home. ② In fact, NASA and some companies are trying to send people there right now. ③ Many scientists believe so for ____(A)____ reasons. ④ First, they think that there is water on Mars. ⑤ This is great because water is necessary for all life.

06 다음 중 빈칸 (A)에 들어갈 말로 적절하지 <u>않은</u> 것은?

① several   ② a few

③ a number of   ④ some

⑤ a great deal of

07 ①~⑤ 중 주어진 문장이 들어가기에 가장 적절한 곳은?

> The big question is, "Can people live on Mars?"

①   ②   ③   ④   ⑤

08 다음 중 위 글의 내용과 일치하지 <u>않는</u> 것은?

① There is no one who has been to Mars.

② We can easily find books and movies about Mars.

③ All living things need water to live.

④ Scientists believe that there is water on Mars.

⑤ NASA thinks that it is impossible to send people to Mars.

서답형

09 According to the passage, what is essential for all life? Answer the question in English with a full sentence.

➡ _____

[10~15] 다음 글을 읽고 물음에 답하시오.

Second, Mars has hard land to build houses and buildings _____(A)_____. Third, the length of day and night on Mars is similar to (B)<u>that</u> on Earth. In addition, Mars also has four seasons. So, people can lead similar lives. Lastly, Mars is not very far. It is the second closest planet to Earth. Mars, however, has some differences from Earth.

10 다음 중 빈칸 (A)에 들어갈 말로 가장 적절한 것은?

① at   ② on   ③ by

④ in   ⑤ to

서답형

11 밑줄 친 (B)가 가리키는 것을 위 글에서 찾아 쓰시오.

➡ _____

12 다음 중 위 글에 이어질 내용으로 가장 적절한 것은?

① the similarity between Earth and Mars

② how to build houses on Mars

③ merits of living on Mars

④ differences between Mars and Earth

⑤ difficulties of living on another planet

13 According to the passage, which is <u>NOT</u> true about Mars?

① It has hard land.

② It has four seasons.

③ It is not very far from Earth.

④ The length of day and night on Mars is similar to that on Earth.

⑤ It is the closest planet to Earth.

서답형

14 Write the reason why it is possible that people can lead similar lives on Mars. Use the phrase "It's because."

➡ _____

    _____

서답형

15 How close is Mars to Earth? Answer the question in English.

➡ _____

[16~20] 다음 글을 읽고 물음에 답하시오.

Mars, however, has some differences (A) [from / to] Earth. First, Mars is about half the size of Earth. It is the second smallest planet (B)[on / in] the solar system. Second, a year on Mars is about twice as long as a year on Earth. Third, Mars is much colder than Earth. On average, it is about –60℃ on Mars. ⓐ This is because Mars is farther away from the Sun than Earth.

(C)[Because / Although] no one can answer the big question right now, ⓑit is exciting to imagine ⓒthis new world. Who knows? You could be the first Korean on Mars!

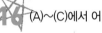

16 (A)~(C)에서 어법상 옳은 것끼리 바르게 짝지은 것은?

① from – on – Because
② to – in – Although
③ from – on – Although
④ to – on – Because
⑤ from – in – Although

서답형

17 밑줄 친 ⓐ가 의미하는 것을 우리말로 쓰시오.

➡ _____

18 다음 중 밑줄 친 ⓑ와 쓰임이 같은 것은?

① It is getting hotter and hotter.
② It is five kilometers from here to the station.
③ It looks like rain.
④ It is difficult to get there on time.
⑤ It will be soon Thanksgiving.

서답형

19 밑줄 친 ⓒ가 가리키는 것을 위 글에서 찾아 쓰시오.

➡ _____

중요

20 다음 중 위 글을 읽고 답할 수 없는 질문은?

① How many differences are there between Earth and Mars?
② How big is Mars?
③ How cold is Mars?
④ What is the average temperature of Earth?
⑤ Which is farther away from the Sun, Earth or Mars?

[21~23] 다음 글을 읽고 물음에 답하시오.

Do you want to live on another planet?
The Korea Space Organization (KSO) is looking for people to go to MARS! Our mission is ___(A)___ a city on Mars.
We are looking for someone...
who is healthy.
who is creative and curious.
who can get along with others.
who can adapt to a new environment quickly.

To apply, send us a short video. The video must include the answers to the following questions:
1. Why do you want to go to Mars?
2. Do you have a good sense of humor?
3. Why are you the perfect person for this mission?
This is a chance of a lifetime, so don't miss out!

서답형

21 동사 build를 어법에 맞게 빈칸 (A)에 쓰시오.

서답형 ➡ _____

22 다음과 같이 풀이되는 단어를 위 글에서 찾아 쓰시오.

a large, round object in space that moves around a star

➡ _____

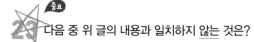
23 다음 중 위 글의 내용과 일치하지 <u>않는</u> 것은?

① KSO is looking for someone creative.

② KSO needs people who can get used to a new environment quickly.

③ Making a short video is necessary for you to apply.

④ You should answer some questions at the interview.

⑤ KSO needs someone who has curiosity.

[24~30] 다음 글을 읽고 물음에 답하시오.

Although there are many books and movies about Mars, no one has been there yet. These days, scientists are looking at Mars ①<u>as</u> a new home. In fact, NASA and some companies are trying ②<u>to send</u> people there right now.

The big question is, "Can people live on Mars?" Many scientists believe so ③<u>for</u> several reasons. First, they think (A)<u>that</u> there is water on Mars. This is great ④<u>because</u> water is necessary for all life. Second, Mars has hard land to build houses and buildings on. Third, the length of day and night on Mars is similar to ⑤<u>those</u> on Earth. (B), Mars also has four seasons.

24 다음 중 밑줄 친 (A)와 쓰임이 <u>다른</u> 하나는?

① The idea <u>that</u> Tom can swim that far is hard to accept.

② Danny suggests <u>that</u> we do exercise regularly.

③ He is the man <u>that</u> I have met at a party before.

④ It is not true <u>that</u> Kelly cheated on the exam.

⑤ Jason told me <u>that</u> he was not going to attend the class meeting.

25 다음 중 빈칸 (B)에 들어갈 말로 가장 적절한 것은?

① Therefore   ② Besides

③ However   ④ On the other hand

⑤ For example

26 What are NASA and some companies trying to do? Answer in English. Use the word 'to.'

➡ _____

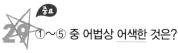
27 다음 중 위 글의 제목으로 가장 적절한 것은?

① Build a New House

② Mars, the Second Earth?

③ Where Do You Want to Live?

④ What Scientists Think about Earth

⑤ Mars, a New Resource for Water

서답형
28 위 글의 내용에 맞게 빈칸에 알맞은 말을 쓰시오.

There are several reasons why scientists believe that _____ .

➡ _____

중요
29 ①~⑤ 중 어법상 어색한 것은?

①   ②   ③   ④   ⑤

30 다음 중 위 글에서 반의어를 찾을 수 <u>없는</u> 것은?

① old   ② die   ③ vital

④ soft   ⑤ different

Reading **89**

[01~05] 다음 글을 읽고 물음에 답하시오.

Live on MARS!

Do you want to live on another planet?

The Korea Space Organization (KSO) is looking for people to go to MARS! Our mission is to build a city on Mars.

We are looking for someone...

who is healthy.

who is creative and curious.

who can get along with others.

who can adapt to a new environment quickly.

To apply, send us a short video. The video must include the answers to the following questions:

1. Why do you want to go to Mars?
2. Do you have a good sense of humor?
3. Why are you the perfect person for (A) this mission?

This is (B)일생에 단 한번뿐인 기회, so don't miss out!

01 밑줄 친 (A)가 의미하는 것을 우리말로 쓰시오.

➡ _____

02 밑줄 친 우리말 (B)를 영어로 쓰시오.

➡ _____

03 다음은 화성으로 가려는 사람의 지원서이다. 빈칸에 알맞은 말을 위 글에서 찾아 쓰시오.

> I am as _____ as an athlete. Also, I _____, so I always make people laugh.

➡ _____

04 위 글의 내용에 맞게 빈칸에 알맞은 말을 쓰시오.

> You should send _____ _____
> _____ _____ _____ in order to apply.

05 According to the passage, what must the video contain? Answer in English with a full sentence. Use the word 'some.'

➡ _____

[06~10] 다음 글을 읽고 물음에 답하시오.

Although there are many books and movies about Mars, no one has been there yet. These days, scientists are looking at Mars as a new home. In fact, NASA and some companies are trying to send people there right now.

The big question is, "Can people live on Mars?" Many scientists believe so for several reasons. First, they think that there is water on Mars. (A)This is great because water is necessary for all life. Second, Mars has hard land to build houses and buildings on. Third, the length of day and night on Mars is similar to that on Earth. In addition, Mars also has four seasons. So, people can lead similar lives. Lastly, Mars is not very far. It is the second closest planet to Earth.

06 밑줄 친 (A)가 가리키는 것을 위 글에서 찾아 쓰시오.

➡ _____

07 빈칸에 알맞은 말을 위 글에서 찾아 세 단어로 쓰시오.

> Life on Mars will _____ life on Earth.

08 위 글의 내용에 맞게 빈칸에 알맞은 말을 아홉 단어로 쓰시오.

> No one has been to Mars yet _____
> _____ .

➡ _____

09 위 글의 내용에 맞게 빈칸에 알맞은 말을 여섯 단어로 쓰시오.

> It is possible to _____
> because it has hard land.

➡ _____

10 How many seasons does Mars have? Answer in English with a full sentence.

➡ _____

[11~14] 다음 글을 읽고 물음에 답하시오.

Mars, however, has _____ (A) _____ from Earth. First, Mars is about half the size of Earth. It is the second smallest planet in the solar system. Second, a year on Mars is about twice as long as _____ (B) _____ . Third, Mars is much colder than Earth. On average, it is about −60℃ on Mars. This is because Mars is farther away from the Sun than Earth.

Although no one can answer the big question right now, it is exciting to imagine this new world. Who knows? You could be the first Korean on Mars!

11 빈칸 (A)에 알맞은 말을 두 단어로 쓰시오.

➡ _____

12 빈칸 (B)에 알맞은 말을 어법에 맞게 쓰시오.

➡ _____

13 Why is Mars much colder than Earth? Answer in English with a full sentence.

➡ _____

14 위 글의 내용에 맞게 빈칸에 알맞은 말을 쓰시오.

> Mars is _____ to the Sun as Earth.

[15~17] 다음 글을 읽고 물음에 답하시오.

My name is Suji Lee from Korea. I'm 15 years old. I want to go to Mars because I've been curious about space. I'm friendly and I enjoy _____ (A) _____ . I'm good at taking photos. I'm the perfect person for this mission because I can adapt to a new environment quickly. Although I'm young, I can communicate well with others. (B)저에게 화성에서 살 기회를 주세요!

15 make friends를 어법에 맞게 빈칸 (A)에 쓰시오.

➡ _____

16 밑줄 친 우리말 (B)를 영어로 쓰시오.

➡ _____

17 Write the reason why she is the perfect person for the mission she wants to participate in.

➡ _____

구석구석

Real Life Talk - Step 2

A: Do you know what this is?
간접의문문(의문사+주어+동사: 어순 주의)

B: No, I don't. What is it?

A: It's a Clean Straw.

B: A Clean Straw? What is it for?
용도를 묻는 표현

A: It cleans water while you drink.
(~ 동안에)+주어+동사. *cf.* during (~ 동안에)+명사(구)

B: Wow, that's great!

해석

A: 너는 이것이 무엇인지 아니?

B: 아니. 그건 뭐니?

A: Clean Straw야.

B: Clean Straw? 용도가 뭐니?

A: 네가 물을 마시는 동안 물을 깨끗이 해주는 거야.

B: 와, 멋지다!

Think and Write

My name is Suji Lee from Korea. I'm 15 years old. I want to go to Mars
to부정사를 목적어로 취하는 동사

because I've been curious about space. I'm friendly and I enjoy making
현재완료(계속 용법)   동명사를 목적어로 취하는 동사

friends. I'm good at taking photos. I'm the perfect person for this mission
동명사: 전치사 at의 목적어

because I can adapt to a new environment quickly. Although I'm young, I can
~에 적응하다   양보의 부사절을 이끄는 접속사

communicate well with others. Give me the chance to live on Mars!
other people   to부정사의 형용사적 용법

구문해설 • from: ~ 출신인 • Mars: 화성 • curious: 호기심 있는 • be good at: ~을 잘하다
• perfect: 완벽한 • mission: 임무 • communicate: 의사소통하다 • chance: 기회

제 이름은 수지이고 한국 출신입니다. 저는 15살입니다. 저는 쭉 우주에 호기심을 가져왔기 때문에 화성에 가고 싶습니다. 저는 상냥하고 친구들을 사귀는 것을 좋아합니다. 저는 사진을 잘 찍습니다. 저는 새로운 환경에 빨리 적응할 수 있기 때문에 이 임무에 적합한 사람입니다. 비록 저는 어리지만, 다른 사람들과 의사소통을 잘할 수 있습니다. 저에게 화성에서 살 기회를 주세요!

Project

Neptune

It has 14 moons. It's a very cold planet. It's named after the god of the sea. It's
Neptune   수동태   바다의 신

the farthest planet from the Sun in the solar system.
far의 최상급: 가장 먼

구문해설 • Neptune: 해왕성 • moon: 위성, 달 • be named after: ~의 이름을 따다
• the solar system: 태양계

해왕성

그것은 14개의 위성을 가지고 있다. 그곳은 아주 추운 행성이다. 그것은 바다의 신의 이름을 딴 것이다. 그것은 태양계에서 태양과 가장 멀리 떨어져 있다.

01 다음 주어진 단어 중 나머지 넷과 성격이 <u>다른</u> 것은?

① friendly　　　② brave
③ curious　　　④ outgoing
⑤ pretty

02 다음 영영풀이가 가리키는 것을 고르시오.

> to remove the skin from a fruit, vegetable, etc.

① peel　　　② slice
③ cut　　　④ boil
⑤ reduce

03 다음 빈칸에 들어갈 알맞은 말은?

> _____ we ran to the bus stop, we missed the bus.

① As　　　② If　　　③ Since
④ Because　　　⑤ Although

04 다음 중 밑줄 친 부분의 뜻풀이가 바르지 <u>않은</u> 것은?

① I will <u>peel</u> an apple for my little sister. 껍질을 벗기다
② <u>Several</u> people came to the meeting. 몇몇의
③ <u>Mars</u> is a planet in the solar system. 목성
④ We collected dry <u>sticks</u> for the campfire. 나뭇가지
⑤ She has an important <u>mission</u>. 임무

05 다음 우리말에 맞게 빈칸에 알맞은 말을 쓰시오.

(1) 나는 그녀에 대한 나의 생각을 말할 만큼 충분히 용감하지 않았다.
➡ I wasn't _____ enough to tell her what I thought of her.
(2) 우리는 오로지 이메일로 의사소통한다.
➡ We _____ only by email.
(3) 그는 빵 위에 버터를 발랐다.
➡ He _____ butter on bread.

06 다음 주어진 문장의 밑줄 친 lead[led]와 같은 의미로 쓰인 것은?

> I want to <u>lead</u> a happy life.

① This road will <u>lead</u> you to the library.
② I tried to <u>lead</u> the discussion.
③ If I could be born again, I would like to <u>lead</u> a luxury life.
④ Eating too much sugar can <u>lead</u> to health problems.
⑤ My teacher <u>led</u> us out into the grounds.

07 다음 문장에 공통으로 들어갈 말을 고르시오.

> • I visited the factory that _____s parts for the airplanes.
> • They will _____ a TV series about Korean history.
> • Creativity is needed to _____ artworks.

① promise　　　② produce
③ spread　　　④ build
⑤ apply

Conversation

[08~10] 다음 대화를 읽고 물음에 답하시오.

> **Ms. Lee:** Hello, class! (A)Jisu is today's speaker for show and tell. Jisu?
>
> **Jisu:** Hi, class! (B)Do you know who is this man? His name is Alexander Graham Bell. Bell was an inventor. (C)He was interested in sound. What did he invent? Yes, the telephone! (D)His mother and wife were deaf. (E)So he also made some inventions for deaf people and opened a school for them.

08 위 대화에서 다음 주어진 영영풀이가 가리키는 말을 찾아 쓰시오.

> not able to hear anything

➡ _____

09 위 대화의 (A)~(E) 중 어법상 어색한 문장을 고른 후 바르게 고쳐 쓰시오.

➡ _____

10 위 대화의 내용과 일치하지 <u>않는</u> 것은?

① 지수는 Alexander Graham Bell에 대해 발표하였다.

② Alexander Graham Bell은 소리에 관심이 있었다.

③ Alexander Graham Bell은 청각 장애인을 위해 전화기를 발명하였다.

④ Alexander Graham Bell의 어머니와 아내는 청각 장애가 있었다.

⑤ Alexander Graham Bell은 청각 장애인들을 위한 학교를 열었다.

[11~12] 다음 대화를 읽고 물음에 답하시오.

> **Brian:** (A)Do you know what this is?
>
> **Amy:** Um, (B)it looks a glue stick.
>
> **Brian:** No, it's a butter stick.
>
> **Amy:** Oh, is there butter in it?
>
> **Brian:** Yes, you can spread butter on the bread with it.

11 위 대화의 밑줄 친 (A)와 바꾸어 쓸 수 있는 것은?

① Have you ever heard about this?

② Guess what this is.

③ Do you want to know about this?

④ How can I get to know this?

⑤ Can you explain this?

12 위 대화의 밑줄 친 (B)를 어법에 맞게 고쳐 쓰시오.

➡ _____

[13~14] 다음 대화를 읽고 물음에 답하시오.

> **Judy:** How was your weekend, Hojin?
>
> **Hojin:** (A) I went to a science exhibition with my brother.
>
> **Judy:** (B) Did you? I heard there were so many interesting things.
>
> **Hojin:** (C) Yes. Look at this. I bought it there. Do you know what it is?
>
> **Judy:** (D) Well, I'm not sure. What is it?
>
> **Hojin:** (E) It's a VR headset.
>
> **Judy:** A VR headset? What is it for?
>
> **Hojin:** If you wear it, you can experience another world.
>
> **Judy:** Sounds cool. May I try it?
>
> **Hojin:** Sure. Here you go.

13 위 대화의 (A)~(E) 중 다음 주어진 문장이 들어가기에 적절한 곳은?

> I had a great time.

① (A)   ② (B)   ③ (C)   ④ (D)   ⑤ (E)

14 위 대화의 내용과 일치하지 <u>않는</u> 것은?

① Hojin은 주말에 남동생과 과학 전시회에 갔었다.
② Judy는 과학 전시회에는 흥미로운 것들이 굉장히 많다고 들었다.
③ Hojin은 VR 헤드셋을 과학 전시회에서 구매하였다.
④ VR 헤드셋을 쓰면 다른 세상을 경험할 수 있다.
⑤ Judy는 Hojin에게 VR 헤드셋의 용도를 설명하였다.

Grammar

15 주어진 단어를 활용하여 다음 우리말을 영어로 쓰시오.

> 비록 흐렸지만, 나는 선글라스를 썼다.
> (it / put on)

➡ _____

_____

16 다음 빈칸에 들어갈 말이 바르게 짝지어진 것은?

> • Christine couldn't get to sleep _____ there was a lot of noise.
> • Tom managed to get to sleep _____ the noise.

① when – although
② because – despite
③ as – even though
④ because of – even if
⑤ since – when

17 다음 우리말을 영어로 바르게 옮긴 것을 <u>모두</u> 고르시오.

> 그 시험은 내가 생각했던 것만큼 어렵지 않았어.

① The exam was not as difficult as I thought.
② The exam was as easy as I thought.
③ The exam was not as easy as I thought.
④ The exam was more difficult than I thought.
⑤ The exam was easier than I thought.

18 다음 중 밑줄 친 부분의 쓰임이 <u>잘못된</u> 것은?

① Kevin feels okay <u>although</u> he has a cold.
② Tony is in good shape <u>because</u> he gets a lot of exercise.
③ <u>Even though</u> he was busy, he answered all of my questions.
④ Angela doesn't speak French <u>because</u> she lived in Paris for years.
⑤ <u>Though</u> Jason is not rich, he always donates some money to the poor.

19 다음 중 주어진 문장과 같은 의미의 문장은?

> Susan used to have longer hair.

① Susan's hair is as long as it used to be.
② Susan's hair is not as short as it used to be.
③ Susan't hair is as short as it used to be.
④ Susan has longer hair than she used to have.
⑤ Susan's hair is not as long as it used to be.

20 다음 중 문맥상 어색한 문장은?

① Even though I told the truth, nobody believed me.

② Victoria is not as smart as you think.

③ I drive my car a lot because gas is so expensive.

④ Jackson has twice as many candies as I have.

⑤ We must be as kind to her as we can.

21 다음 빈칸에 들어갈 말로 가장 적절한 것은?

> • I eat less meat than you do.
> = I _____ you do.

① eat as much meat as

② don't eat meat like

③ eat as little meat as

④ don't eat as much meat as

⑤ eat as much meat like

22 다음 빈칸에 들어갈 말과 같은 말이 들어가는 것은?

> Larry didn't understand the joke _____ he laughed anyway.

① Tom wasn't tired _____ he took enough rest.

② I didn't wake up _____ the phone rang many times.

③ Stop talking _____ someone wants to talk to you.

④ He has been busy _____ he came here.

⑤ Give him this note _____ you see him.

23 두 문장의 의미가 통하도록 빈칸에 알맞은 말을 쓰시오.

> • You watch TV more than me.
> = I don't _____ you.

➡ _____

24 지시에 맞게 다음 우리말을 영어로 쓰시오.

> 테니스는 축구만큼 인기 있지 않지만, 나는 축구보다 테니스를 더 좋아한다.
> (동등 비교, 비교급을 한 번씩 사용할 것)

➡ _____

_____

Reading

[25~29] 다음 글을 읽고 물음에 답하시오.

Mars, the Second Earth?

____(A)____ there are many books and movies about Mars, no one (a)has been there yet. These days, scientists are looking at Mars as a new home. In fact, NASA and some companies are trying to send people there right now.

The big question is, "Can people live on Mars?" Many scientists believe so for several reasons. First, (b)they think that there is water on Mars. This is great because water is necessary for all life. Second, Mars has hard land to build houses and buildings on. Third, the length of day and night on Mars is similar to that on Earth. In addition, Mars also has four seasons. ____(B)____, people can lead similar lives. Lastly, Mars is not very far. It is the second closest planet to Earth.

25 빈칸 (A)에 들어갈 말로 적절한 것을 <u>모두</u> 고르시오.

① Even though   ② Because

③ Although   ④ Since

⑤ As

26 다음 중 (B)에 들어갈 말로 적절한 것은?

① However   ② Therefore

③ For example   ④ In addition

⑤ On the contrary

27 다음 중 밑줄 친 (a)와 쓰임이 같은 것은?

① Have you ever <u>visited</u> the museum?

② They <u>have</u> just <u>arrived</u> at the airport.

③ David <u>has gone</u> to the theater.

④ We <u>have known</u> each other for a year.

⑤ She <u>hasn't finished</u> her homework yet.

28 다음 중 위 글을 읽고 답할 수 <u>없는</u> 것은?

① Who considers Mars as a new home?

② Why do scientists believe people can live on Mars?

③ What is viewed as a new home by scientists?

④ How long does it take to get to Mars?

⑤ What makes it possible to build houses and buildings on Mars?

29 밑줄 친 (b)가 가리키는 것을 위 글에서 찾아 쓰시오.

➡ _____

[30~33] 다음 글을 읽고 물음에 답하시오.

  Mars, however, has some differences from Earth. First, ⓐ<u>Mars is about half the size of Earth</u>. It is the second smallest planet in the solar system. Second, a year on Mars is about twice as long as a year on Earth. Third, Mars is (A)[much / very] colder than Earth. On

average, it is about –60℃ on Mars. (B)[This is because / This is why] Mars is farther away from the Sun than Earth.

  Although no one can answer the big question right now, it is (C)[exciting / excited] ⓑ<u>to imagine</u> this new world. Who knows? You could be the first Korean on Mars!

30 위 글의 밑줄 친 ⓐ를 참고하여 다음 대화에 알맞은 말을 네 단어로 쓰시오.

> A: Do you know that Earth is _____ Mars?
>
> B: Really? I didn't know Mars is that small.

➡ _____

31 (A)~(C)에서 어법상 옳은 것끼리 바르게 묶은 것은?

① much – This is because – exciting

② much – This is why – excited

③ much – This is because – excited

④ very – This is why – exciting

⑤ very – This is because – exciting

32 다음 중 밑줄 친 ⓑ와 쓰임이 <u>다른</u> 하나는?

① <u>To sing</u> a song is my hobby.

② Is it possible <u>to change</u> her mind?

③ Is there anything <u>to ask</u>?

④ It is always fun <u>to talk</u> with her.

⑤ <u>To be</u> angry with them is not helpful.

33 위 글의 내용에 맞게 빈칸에 알맞은 말을 쓰시오.

> Mercury is the smallest planet in the solar system. So, Mars is _____ _____ _____ _____ Mercury.

01 다음 대화의 (A)~(C)에 들어갈 말로 적절한 것은?

Irene: Jane, (A)[look / to look] at this. It's a meok.

Jane: I (B)[was / have] never seen it before. What is it for?

Irene: It's for making ink.

Jane: Oh, really? That's (C)[interesting / interested].

	(A)	(B)	(C)
①	look	was	interesting
②	look	have	interesting
③	look	have	interested
④	to look	have	interested
⑤	to look	was	interested

02 다음 대화가 자연스럽게 이어지도록 순서대로 배열하시오.

(A) Yes, you can spread butter on the bread with it.

(B) Um, it looks like a glue stick.

(C) Do you know what this is?

(D) Oh, is there butter in it?

(E) No, it's a butter stick.

➡ _____

[03~05] 다음 대화를 읽고 물음에 답하시오.

Tom: Mom, look ⓐat these slippers. I made them in science class.

Mom: Why did you make slippers in science class?

Tom: They are not just for wearing.

Mom: Then, what are they ⓑfor?

Tom: You can put them ⓒoff and clean the floor.

Mom: Oh, so you will clean your room from now ⓓon?

Tom: Sure. Don't worry ⓔabout my room, Mom.

03 위 대화의 밑줄 친 ⓐ~ⓔ 중 문맥상 어색한 것을 찾아 바르게 고치시오.

➡ _____

04 What are the slippers Tom made for?

➡ _____
_____

05 위 대화를 읽고 대답할 수 없는 것은?

① What did Tom do in science class?

② What are the slippers Tom made for?

③ What did Tom promise his mom to do?

④ What can Tom do by wearing slippers?

⑤ What did Tom use to make the slippers in science class?

[06~08] 다음 대화를 읽고 물음에 답하시오.

Ms. Lee: Hello, class! Jisu is today's speaker for show and tell. Jisu?

Jisu: Hi, class! Do you know who this man is? His name is Alexander Graham Bell. Bell was an ___(A)___. He was interested in sound. What did he invent? Yes, the telephone! His mother and wife were deaf. So he also made some inventions for deaf people and opened a school for them.

06 위 대화의 빈칸 (A)에 다음 주어진 영영풀이가 가리키는 말을 쓰시오.

> a person who has invented something or whose job is inventing things

➡ _____

07 What did Alexander Graham Bell have an interest in?

➡ _____

08 What did Alexander Graham Bell do for deaf people?

➡ _____

_____

09 다음 짝지어진 대화가 <u>어색한</u> 것은?

① A: Do you know who she is?
   B: Um, it looks like a glue stick.
② A: Do you know what it is?
   B: No, I don't. What is it?
③ A: Do you know who he is?
   B: Yes, I do. He is Albert Schweitzer.
④ A: Guess what it is.
   B: I don't have any idea. Would you give me some hints?
⑤ A: Do you know about this man?
   B: Sure. I have seen him before.

[10~11] 다음 대화를 읽고 물음에 답하시오.

A: Do you know what this is?
B: No, I don't. What is ⓐit?
A: It's a Soccket.
B: A Soccket? What is ⓑit for?
A: ⓒIt produces electricity when you play with ⓓit.
B: Wow, ⓔIt sounds great!

10 위 대화에서 소개된 Soccket의 용도를 우리말로 간략히 설명하시오.

➡ _____

11 위 대화의 밑줄 친 ⓐ~ⓔ 중 나머지 넷과 가리키는 대상이 <u>다른</u> 것은?

① ⓐ   ② ⓑ   ③ ⓒ   ④ ⓓ   ⑤ ⓔ

12 다음 중 빈칸에 들어갈 말로 가장 적절한 것은?

> I didn't get hurt _____ I fell down the stairs.

① because   ② unless
③ though   ④ as soon as
⑤ but

13 다음 중 어법상 바르지 <u>않은</u> 것은?

① I don't know as many people as you.
② Even though I mailed the letter a week ago, it has not arrived yet.
③ The building is not as high as I expected.
④ I didn't return his call although he called me several times.
⑤ Your backpack is three times as big as me.

14 두 문장의 의미가 통하도록 빈칸에 알맞은 말을 여섯 단어로 쓰시오.

> • We played better than them.
> = They _____ .

➡ _____

15 다음 우리말을 영어로 바르게 옮긴 것을 <u>모두</u> 고르시오. 출제율 90%

> 사과는 배만큼 크지 않다.

① An apple is as big as a pear.
② A pear is not as big as an apple.
③ An apple is not bigger than a pear.
④ A pear is as small as an apple.
⑤ An apple is not as big as a pear.

16 다음 중 서로 의미가 같지 <u>않은</u> 것은? 출제율 95%

① Despite the rain, we went to the zoo last week.
  = We went to the zoo although it rained last week.
② The river is two times longer than the Han River.
  = The river is two times as long as the Han River.
③ Although my grandmother is ninety years old, she is still young at heart.
  = My grandmother is still young at heart even though she is ninety years old.
④ The festival was more exciting than we thought.
  = The festival was as exciting as we thought.
⑤ Today is not as cold as yesterday.
  = Yesterday was colder than today.

17 주어진 어구를 활용하여 다음 우리말을 영어로 쓰시오. 출제율 95%

> 그 빵은 어제만큼 촉촉하지 않더라도, 여전히 맛있다.
> (though / moist / it was / still)

➡ _____
_____

18 다음 빈칸에 알맞은 말을 쓰시오. 출제율 90%

> Halla Mountain is 1950 meters high. Fuji Mountain is 3776 meters high. Fuji Mountain is almost _____ _____ as _____ as Halla Mountain.

[19~22] 다음 글을 읽고 물음에 답하시오.

____(A)____ there are many books and movies about Mars, no one has been there ①ago. These days, scientists are looking at Mars as a new home. In fact, NASA and some companies ② are trying to send people there right now. The big question is, "Can people live on Mars?" Many scientists believe so for several reasons. First, they think that ③there is water on Mars. This is great ④because water is necessary for all life. Second, Mars has hard land to build houses and buildings on. Third, the length of day and night on Mars ⑤is similar to that on Earth. In addition, Mars also has four seasons. So, people can lead similar lives.

19 다음 중 빈칸 (A)에 들어갈 말과 같은 말이 들어가는 것은? 출제율 95%

① _____ you ask me a question, I will answer it.
② Stop bothering me _____ I am trying to study.
③ _____ I am broke, I don't need your help.
④ You will miss the bus _____ you wake up early.
⑤ It has been five years _____ you met me.

20 ①~⑤ 중 어법상 바르지 <u>않은</u> 것은? 출제율 100%

①   ②   ③   ④   ⑤

21 다음 중 위 글의 내용과 일치하는 것은?

① It is hard to find books and movies about Mars.

② Many people have already been to Mars.

③ People keep contacting NASA to go to Mars.

④ It is difficult to build houses on Mars.

⑤ Mars is not the planet which is the closest to Earth.

22 What is the fourth reason that scientists believe people can live on Mars? Answer in English with four words.

➡ _____

[23~26] 다음 글을 읽고 물음에 답하시오.

In addition, Mars also has four ①seasons. So, people can lead similar lives.

[A] It is the second smallest planet in ②the solar system. Second, a year on Mars is about twice as long as a year on Earth. Third, Mars is much colder than Earth.

[B] Lastly, Mars is not very far. It is the second closest planet to Earth. Mars, however, has some ③differences from Earth. First, Mars is about ④half the size of Earth.

[C] On ⑤average, it is about –60℃ on Mars. This is because Mars is farther away from the Sun than Earth.

Although no one can answer the big question right now, it is exciting to imagine this new world. Who knows? You could be the first Korean on Mars!

23 자연스러운 글이 되도록 [A]~[C]를 바르게 나열하시오.

➡ _____

24 밑줄 친 ①~⑤의 뜻풀이가 잘못된 것은?

① the main periods into which a year can be divided

② the sun and the planets that move around it

③ the way in which two things are not like each other

④ to cut something into pieces

⑤ the sum of the values in a set divided by their number

25 다음 우리말을 영어로 쓰시오.

> 화성은 내가 생각했던 것만큼 멀지 않다.

➡ _____

26 다음 중 위 글을 읽고 답할 수 없는 것은?

① Where can people lead similar lives?

② What is the smallest planet in the solar system?

③ How long is a year on Mars?

④ Why is Mars much colder than Earth?

⑤ How big is Earth compared with Mars?

[01~03] 다음 대화를 읽고 물음에 답하시오.

Judy: How was your weekend, Hojin?

Hojin: I had a great time. I went to a science exhibition with my brother.

Judy: Did you? I heard there were so many interesting things.

Hojin: Yes. Look at this. I bought it there. Do you know what it is?

Judy: Well, I'm not sure. What is it?

Hojin: It's a VR headset.

Judy: A VR headset? What is it for?

Hojin: If you wear it, you can experience another world.

Judy: Sounds cool. May I try it?

Hojin: Sure. Here you go.

01 With whom did Hojin go to the science exhibition?

➡ _____

02 What did Hojin buy at the science exhibition?

➡ _____

03 What is the VR headset for?

➡ _____

[04~05] 다음 대화를 읽고 물음에 답하시오.

Tom: Mom, look at these slippers. I made them in science class.

Mom: Why did you make slippers in science class?

Tom: They are not just for wearing.

Mom: Then, what are they for?

Tom: You can put them on and clean the floor.

Mom: Oh, so you will clean your room from now on?

Tom: Sure. Don't worry about my room, Mom.

04 In what class did Tom make slippers?

➡ _____

05 What promise did Tom make with his mother?

➡ _____

06 적절한 접속사를 사용하여 다음 대화의 빈칸에 알맞은 말을 쓰시오.

A: You turned on the air conditioner. Is the room still hot?

B: Yes. _____

➡ _____
_____

07 적절한 접속사를 이용하여 다음 두 문장을 하나의 문장으로 연결하시오.

• Hannah invited Tom to her party. But he didn't come without saying a word.

➡ _____
_____

08 주어진 문장과 같은 의미의 문장을 동등 비교 표현을 이용하여 쓰시오.

• Sally got up earlier than James.

➡ James _____ .
➡ Sally _____ .

09 다음 글을 읽고 지시에 맞게 빈칸에 알맞은 말을 쓰시오.

> Jason works very hard. He works 10 hours a day. Amelia works hard, but not that hard. She works 7 hours a day. Tom doesn't work very hard. He works only 5 hours a day.

(1) 동등 비교 표현을 이용하여
　➡ Amelia ＿＿＿＿＿＿＿＿＿ Jason.

(2) 비교급을 이용하여
　➡ But she ＿＿＿＿＿＿＿＿ Tom.

10 주어진 문장과 의미가 통하도록 빈칸에 알맞은 말을 8 단어로 쓰시오.

> • Health and happiness are more important than money.
> = Money ＿＿＿＿＿＿＿＿＿ .

➡ ＿＿＿＿＿＿＿＿＿＿＿＿＿＿＿

[11~12] 다음 글을 읽고 물음에 답하시오.

> Mars, the Second Earth?
>
> Although ①there are many books and movies about Mars, no one has been there yet. These days, scientists are looking at Mars as a new home. ②In fact, NASA and some companies are trying to send people there right now.
>
> The big question is, "Can people live on Mars?" ③Many scientists believe so for several reasons. First, they think that there is water on Mars. This is great because water is necessary for all life. Second, ④Mars has hard land to build houses and buildings. Third, the length of day and night on Mars is similar to that on Earth. ⑤In addition, Mars also has four seasons.

11 ①~⑤ 중 어법상 틀린 문장을 찾아 바르게 고쳐 쓰시오.

＿＿＿＿＿

➡ ＿＿＿＿＿＿＿＿＿＿＿＿＿＿＿

12 According to the passage, who thinks that there is water on Mars? Answer in English with a full sentence.

➡ ＿＿＿＿＿＿＿＿＿＿＿＿＿＿＿

[13~14] 다음 글을 읽고 물음에 답하시오.

> Mars, however, has some differences from Earth. First, (A)화성은 지구의 약 절반 크기이다. It is the second smallest planet in the solar system. Second, a year on Mars is about two times longer than a year on Earth. Third, Mars is much colder than Earth. On average, it is about −60℃ on Mars. This is because Mars is farther away from the Sun than Earth.

13 밑줄 친 우리말 (A)를 주어진 말을 써서 영어로 쓰시오. (about, size)

➡ ＿＿＿＿＿＿＿＿＿＿＿＿＿＿＿

14 위 글의 내용에 맞게 다음 글의 빈칸을 채우시오.

> I read about Mars today. Mars is not exactly the same as Earth. One of the most surprising differences is that a year on Mars is about ＿＿＿ ＿＿＿ ＿＿＿ ＿＿＿ ＿＿＿ a year on Earth.

01 다음 대화를 읽고 대화의 내용과 일치하도록 빈칸을 완성하시오.

> Tom: Mom, look at these slippers. I made them in science class.
>
> Mom: Why did you make slippers in science class?
>
> Tom: They are not just for wearing.
>
> Mom: Then, what are they for?
>
> Tom: You can put them on and clean the floor.
>
> Mom: Oh, so you will clean your room from now on?
>
> Tom: Sure. Don't worry about my room, Mom.

> Mon. Sep. 5th, 2019
>
> Today, I made special (A)_____ in science class. I came up with the idea to wipe the floor without any cloth. So, my slippers were designed not only for wearing but also for (B)_____. I promised my mother to (C)_____ myself.

02 다음 세 사람에 관한 이야기를 읽고 빈칸에 알맞은 말을 쓰시오. 괄호 안의 단어를 이용할 것.

> Jennifer: I am 25. I usually get up at 8. I don't have a car. I work at home.
>
> Michael: I am 27. I get up at 7:15. My car is gray. It takes 15 minutes to go to work.
>
> Christine: I am 27. I usually get up at 8. My car is black. It takes 45 minutes to go to work.

(1) Jennifer _____ Michael and Christine. (as)

(2) Jennifer and Christine _____ Michael. (as)

(3) Christine spends _____ Michael to go to work.

03 양보의 부사절 접속사를 활용하여 다음 문장을 하나의 문장으로 쓰시오.

> (1) The length of day and night on Mars is similar to that on Earth. A year on Mars is about twice as long as a year on Earth.
>
> (2) Mars has four seasons like Earth. Mars is much colder than Earth.
>
> (3) Mars has hard land to build houses and buildings on. It is really expensive to build them on Mars.

(1) _____

(2) _____

(3) _____

단원별 모의고사

01 다음 문장에 공통으로 들어갈 말을 고르시오.

- Would you tell me the _____ for your absence?
- Without any _____, Tom left for England.
- We tried to _____ out the answers to the questions.

① promise ② reason
③ difference ④ way
⑤ find

02 다음 문장의 빈칸에 들어갈 말을 〈보기〉에서 골라 쓰시오. 필요하면 어형 변화를 할 것.

┌─ 보기 ─┐
inventor / deaf / planet / organization / slice

(1) Wash and _____ the tomatoes.
(2) Thomas Edison was a great _____.
(3) Tony is a leader of an international _____.
(4) He's _____ in his right ear. So you should speak up.
(5) Mercury is the smallest of all the _____.

03 다음 우리말에 맞게 빈칸에 알맞은 말을 쓰시오.

(1) Alice와 잘 지내는 것은 불가능하다.
➡ It's impossible to _____ Alice.
(2) 그는 훌륭한 유머 감각이 있다.
➡ He has a good _____.
(3) 그는 영어를 매우 잘한다. 게다가, 그는 또한 스페인어와 독일어도 한다.
➡ He speaks English very well. _____, he speaks Spanish and German, too.

04 다음 대화가 자연스럽게 이어지도록 순서대로 배열하시오.

(A) Why did you make slippers in science class?
(B) Then, what are they for?
(C) They are not just for wearing.
(D) You can put them on and clean the floor.
(E) Mom, look at these slippers. I made them in science class.

➡ _____

05 다음 영어 뜻풀이에 해당하는 말은?

the sun and the planets that move around it

① earth ② sky
③ galaxy ④ universe
⑤ solar system

[06~07] 다음 대화를 읽고 물음에 답하시오.

Judy: How was your weekend, Hojin?
Hojin: I had a great time. I went to a science exhibition with my brother.
Judy: Did you? I heard there were so many interesting things.
Hojin: Yes. Look at this. I bought it there. Do you know what it is?
Judy: Well, I'm not sure. What is it?
Hojin: It's a VR headset.
Judy: A VR headset? _____(A)_____
Hojin: (B)그것을 쓰면 다른 세상을 경험할 수 있어.
Judy: Sounds cool. May I try it?
Hojin: Sure. Here you go.

06 위 대화의 빈칸 (A)에 들어갈 수 있는 말을 <u>모두</u> 고르시오.

① What should I do?
② What is it for?
③ What can I do for you?
④ What is it used for?
⑤ What do you do?

07 위 대화의 밑줄 친 우리말 (B)를 〈보기〉에 주어진 단어를 모두 배열하여 완성하시오.

---- 보기 ----
it / world / can / experience / you / another / if / wear / you

➡ _____

08 다음 대화의 빈칸에 들어갈 말로 적절한 것은?

A: I've never seen it. What is it for?
B: _____

① It looks like a stick.
② It is made of wood.
③ It is for decorating your hair.
④ How about wearing it?
⑤ I don't know how to use it.

[09~11] 다음 대화를 읽고 물음에 답하시오.

Ms. Lee: Hello, class! Jisu is today's speaker for show and tell. Jisu?

Jisu: Hi, class! Do you know (A)[who / which] this man is? ⓐ His name is Alexander Graham Bell. ⓑ Bell was an inventor. ⓒ He was (B)[interesting / interested] in sound. ⓓ Yes, the telephone! His mother and wife were deaf. ⓔ So he also made some inventions for deaf people and (C)[opened / opening] a school for them.

09 위 대화의 (A)~(C)에 들어갈 말로 바르게 짝지어진 것은?

	(A)	(B)	(C)
①	who	interesting	opened
②	who	interested	opening
③	who	interested	opened
④	which	interested	opening
⑤	which	interesting	opened

10 위 대화의 ⓐ~ⓔ 중 주어진 문장이 들어가기에 적절한 곳은?

What did he invent?

① ⓐ   ② ⓑ   ③ ⓒ   ④ ⓓ   ⑤ ⓔ

11 위 대화의 내용과 일치하지 <u>않는</u> 것은?

① Alexander Graham Bell invented the telephone.
② Alexander Graham Bell had an interest in sound.
③ Bell's mother and wife were not able to hear.
④ Alexander Graham Bell opened the school for his family.
⑤ Jisu introduced Alexander Graham Bell to her class.

12 다음 주어진 우리말과 일치하도록 주어진 단어를 모두 배열하여 완성하시오.

(1) Jimin은 반 친구들과 잘 지내는 것 같지 않다.
(classmates / get / to / along / with / his / seem / doesn't / Jimin)
➡ _____

(2) 태양계에서 가장 큰 행성은 무엇인가? (the / solar / what / planet / system / is / biggest / the / in)
➡ _____

13 다음 중 어법상 옳은 문장의 개수는?

ⓐ Although I felt sorry for her, I didn't apologize to her.
ⓑ Tom is richer than me. I am not as rich as Tom.
ⓒ Miranda went for a walk despite it was cold outside.
ⓓ I drink water two times as much as you are.
ⓔ The garden looks as tidy than it used to.

① 1개 ② 2개 ③ 3개 ④ 4개 ⑤ 5개

14 동등 비교 표현을 이용하여 다음 빈칸에 알맞은 말을 쓰시오.

Dad and I went for a run. Dad ran ten kilometers. I stopped after seven kilometers. I _____ Dad.

➡ _____

15 다음 우리말을 영어로 바르게 옮기지 <u>않은</u> 것은?

① 그녀의 병은 생각보다 심각하지 않았다.
→ Her illness was not as serious as we thought.

② 비록 네가 몸이 약하더라도, 항상 남을 도와라.
→ Always help others although you are weak.

③ 배가 부르진 않지만, 더 먹고 싶지 않아.
→ Though I am not full, I don't want to eat more.

④ 형편없는 성적에도 불구하고, 엄마는 나를 벌주지 않으셨다.
→ Despite the poor grade, Mom didn't punish me.

⑤ 그의 배낭은 나의 배낭보다 세 배 만큼 무겁다.
→ His backpack is three times as heavier as my backpack.

16 주어진 단어를 활용하여 다음 우리말을 영어로 쓰시오.

이 쿠키가 그 케이크만큼 맛있지 않더라도, 나는 이 쿠키를 먹을 거야.
(as ~ as / have)

➡ _____
_____

17 다음 빈칸에 알맞은 말을 쓰시오.

Bella couldn't finish her homework _____ there wasn't enough time. But Helen did everything she had to do _____ there wasn't enough time.

[18~21] 다음 글을 읽고 물음에 답하시오.

Do you want to live on another planet?
The Korea Space Organization (KSO) is looking ⓐ[at / for] people to go to MARS! Our mission is to build a city on Mars.
We are looking for someone...
who is healthy.
who is creative and curious.
who can get along with others.
who can ⓑ[adopt / adapt] to a new environment quickly.
Send us a short video (A)to apply. The video must ⓒ[include / exclude] the answers to the following questions:
1. Why do you want to go to Mars?
2. (B)당신은 훌륭한 유머 감각이 있나요?
3. Why are you the perfect person for this mission?

18 ⓐ~ⓒ에서 글의 흐름상 옳은 것끼리 바르게 짝지은 것은?

① for – adapt – exclude
② for – adapt – include
③ at – adopt – exclude
④ at – adopt – include
⑤ at – adapt – include

19 다음 중 밑줄 친 (A)와 쓰임이 같은 것은?

① I have many friends to play with.
② It is surprising for you to say so.
③ Anna went to the market to buy milk.
④ To jog in the morning makes me happy.
⑤ We decided to make a cake for Mom's birthday.

20 적절한 대명사를 이용하여 다음 물음에 완전한 문장의 영어로 답하시오.

> Q: What is the mission of KSO?

➡ _____

21 밑줄 친 우리말 (B)를 영어로 쓰시오.

➡ _____

[22~25] 다음 글을 읽고 물음에 답하시오.

The big question is, "Can people live on Mars?" Many scientists believe so for ① several reasons. First, they think that there is water on Mars. ②This is great because water is necessary for all life. Second, Mars has hard ③land to build houses and buildings on. Third, the length of day and night on Mars ④ is similar to that on Earth. In addition, Mars also has four seasons. So, people can lead similar lives. Lastly, Mars is not very far. It is the second closest planet to Earth.

___(A)___, Mars has some differences from Earth. First, Mars is about half the size of Earth. It is the second smallest planet in the solar system. Second, a year on Mars is about twice as long as a year on Earth. Third, Mars is much colder than Earth. On average, it is about −60℃ on Mars. This is because Mars is ⑤nearer to the Sun than Earth.

22 다음 중 빈칸 (A)에 들어갈 말로 가장 적절한 것은?

① For example   ② However
③ Therefore   ④ Thus
⑤ Moreover

23 다음 중 위 글의 내용과 일치하는 것은?

① Scientists don't think that it is possible for people to live on Mars.
② Mars doesn't have proper land to build houses on.
③ Mars is close to Earth and has four seasons.
④ Mars is the second smallest planet in the universe.
⑤ Mars is not as cold as Earth.

24 ①~⑤ 중 글의 흐름상 어색한 것을 골라 바르게 고치시오.

_____ ➡ _____

25 위 글의 표현을 이용하여 다음 우리말을 영어로 쓰시오.

> 화성은 지구와 다른 점이 몇 개 있지만, 과학자들은 사람들이 화성에서 살 수 있다고 믿는다.

➡ _____

Can I Trust It?

🎤 의사소통 기능

- 추천 요청하기

  A: Can you recommend a musical for me?

  B: How about *The Lion King*?

- 만족 여부 묻고 답하기

  A: How do you like your bicycle?

  B: I'm really happy with it.

🎤 언어 형식

- so ~ that

  The movie is **so** boring **that** I want to cry.

- 목적격 관계대명사

  In the ad, "Best Picture" is the award **which** the movie won.

Words & Expressions

Key Words

- **adventure** [ədvéntʃər] 명 모험
- **advertisement** [ədvərtáizmənt] 명 광고
- **author** [ɔ́:θər] 명 작가
- **award** [əwɔ́:rd] 명 상
- **backpack** [bǽkpæk] 명 배낭
- **belief** [bilí:f] 명 신념, 생각
- **boring** [bɔ́:riŋ] 형 지루한
- **connection** [kənékʃən] 명 관련성, 연관성
- **desert** [dézərt] 명 사막
- **difference** [dífərəns] 명 차이점
- **else** [els] 부 또 다른
- **especially** [ispéʃəli] 부 특히
- **explain** [ikspléin] 동 설명하다
- **express** [iksprés] 동 나타내다, 표현하다
- **fantasy** [fǽntəsi] 명 공상
- **friendship** [fréndʃip] 명 우정
- **genre** [ʒɑ́:nrə] 명 장르
- **lie** [lai] 동 거짓말하다
- **lift** [lift] 동 들어 올리다
- **meal** [mi:l] 명 식사
- **mix** [miks] 동 섞다

- **navy** [néivi] 명 남색
- **novel** [nɑ́vəl] 명 소설
- **opinion** [əpínjən] 명 의견
- **perfect** [pə́:rfikt] 형 완벽한
- **pocket** [pɑ́kit] 명 주머니
- **prove** [pru:v] 동 증명하다
- **purple** [pə́:rpl] 명 보라색, 자색
- **recommend** [rèkəménd] 동 추천하다
- **side** [said] 명 옆면, 측면
- **simple** [símpl] 형 간단한, 단순한
- **solve** [sɑlv] 동 해결하다, 풀다
- **strongly** [strɔ́:ŋli] 부 강력하게
- **touching** [tʌ́tʃiŋ] 형 감동적인
- **traditional** [trədíʃənl] 형 전통적인
- **trip** [trip] 명 여행
- **trust** [trʌst] 동 믿다, 신뢰하다
- **truth** [tru:θ] 명 진실, 사실
- **unlike** [ənláik] 전 ~와 달리
- **wisely** [wáizli] 부 현명하게
- **worth** [wə:rθ] 형 가치가 있는
- **yet** [jet] 부 아직

Key Expressions

- **based on** ~을 바탕으로
- **check out** ~을 확인하다
- **for example** 예를 들면
- **from now on** 지금부터
- **full of** ~로 가득한
- **hold on** 기다려, 멈춰

- **look for** ~을 찾다
- **main character** 주인공
- **make a choice** 선택하다
- **number one** (인기 순위) 1위
- **right now** 지금
- **worth it** 그만한 가치가 있는

Word Power

※ 서로 반대되는 뜻을 가진 어휘

- ☐ **simple** 간단한, 단순한 ↔ **complex** 복잡한
- ☐ **true** 사실의, 진실의 ↔ **false** 거짓의
- ☐ **boring** 지루한 ↔ **exciting** 신나는
- ☐ **perfect** 완벽한 ↔ **imperfect** 불완전한
- ☐ **ancient** 고대의 ↔ **modern** 현대의

- ☐ **worth** 가치가 있는 ↔ **worthless** 가치가 없는
- ☐ **wise** 지혜로운 ↔ **foolish** 미련한, 어리석은
- ☐ **fact** 사실 ↔ **opinion** 의견
- ☐ **like** ~처럼, ~같이 ↔ **unlike** ~와 달리
- ☐ **similarity** 유사점 ↔ **difference** 차이점

※ 색을 나타내는 단어

- ☐ **navy** 남색
- ☐ **orange** 주황색
- ☐ **burgundy** 진홍색

- ☐ **purple** 보라색
- ☐ **ivory** 상아색
- ☐ **violet** 보라색

- ☐ **gray** 회색
- ☐ **silver** 은색

- ☐ **brown** 갈색
- ☐ **khaki** 카키색

English Dictionary

- ☐ **advertisement** 광고
  → a notice, picture or short film telling people about something
  사람들에게 무언가에 대해 이야기하는 게시, 그림 또는 짧은 영화

- ☐ **award** 상
  → a prize such as money, etc. for something that somebody has done
  누군가가 한 무언가에 대한 돈 등과 같은 상

- ☐ **connection** 관련성
  → the way in which two things are related to each other
  두 개가 서로 관련되어 있는 방식

- ☐ **explain** 설명하다
  → to tell somebody about something in a way that is easy to understand
  이해하기 쉬운 방식으로 무언가에 대해 누군가에게 이야기하다

- ☐ **express** 나타내다, 표현하다
  → to show what you think or feel
  당신이 생각하거나 느끼는 것을 보여주다

- ☐ **lie** 거짓말하다
  → to say or write something that is not true
  사실이 아닌 무언가를 말하거나 쓰다

- ☐ **lift** 들어 올리다
  → to move something to a higher position
  무언가를 더 높은 위치로 옮기다

- ☐ **meal** 식사
  → the foods eaten or prepared at one time
  한 번에 먹거나 준비되는 음식

- ☐ **mix** 섞다
  → to add something to something else
  무언가를 다른 무언가에 더하다

- ☐ **opinion** 의견
  → ideas or feelings about something
  무언가에 대한 생각 또는 느낌

- ☐ **pocket** 주머니
  → a small bag that is attached to something
  무언가에 붙어 있는 작은 자루

- ☐ **prove** 증명하다
  → to use facts, evidence, etc. to show that something is true
  무언가가 진실이라는 것을 보여 주기 위해 사실, 증거 등을 사용하다

- ☐ **trust** 신뢰하다, 믿다
  → to believe that something is true
  무언가가 사실이라고 믿다

- ☐ **truth** 진실, 사실
  → the real facts about something
  무언가에 대한 실제의 사실

01 다음 짝지어진 단어의 관계가 같도록 빈칸에 알맞은 말을 쓰시오.

| tall : short = _____ : complex |

02 다음 영영풀이가 가리키는 것을 고르시오.

| a prize such as money, etc. for something that somebody has done |

① penalty   ② award
③ fare   ④ fee
⑤ price

03 다음 중 밑줄 친 부분의 뜻풀이가 바르지 <u>않은</u> 것은?

① I saw an <u>advertisement</u> for a ski camp in Toronto. 광고
② There is a <u>connection</u> between pollution and the death of plants. 관련성
③ The steak was <u>especially</u> good. 특히
④ Give me a chance. I'll <u>prove</u> it to you. 제공하다
⑤ My favorite color is <u>purple</u>. 보라색

서답형
04 다음 우리말에 맞게 빈칸에 알맞은 말을 써 넣으시오.

(1) 말로는 내 기분을 표현할 수 없다.
➡ Words cannot _____ my feelings.
(2) 같은 광고가 3개의 잡지에 등장했다.
➡ The same _____ appeared in three magazines.
(3) 그는 승리할 것이라는 자신의 능력에 강한 신념을 갖고 있다.
➡ He has a strong _____ in his ability to win.

05 다음 주어진 문장의 밑줄 친 touching과 같은 의미로 쓰인 것은?

| The movie was so <u>touching</u> that I cried a lot. |

① My daughter is <u>touching</u> a pet.
② Who is the boy <u>touching</u> an ant?
③ What a <u>touching</u> love story!
④ Avoid <u>touching</u> your eyes and nose with dirty hands.
⑤ <u>Touching</u> the keyboard, she told me about the plan.

06 다음 문장에 공통으로 들어갈 말을 고르시오.

| • My father served three years in the _____.
 • I dressed my son in the new _____ suit.
 • It's not bad, but I prefer the _____ skirt. |

① navy   ② pink   ③ yellow
④ purple   ⑤ brown

서답형
07 다음 문장의 빈칸에 들어갈 말을 〈보기〉에서 골라 쓰시오.

| 보기 |
| beliefs, purple, genre, friendship |

(1) Do you know the girl wearing the _____ jacket?
(2) You must respect other people's _____.
(3) Which _____ do you like most?
(4) A strong _____ grew between the two people.

01 다음 짝지어진 단어의 관계가 같도록 빈칸에 알맞은 말을 쓰시오.

> similar : different = similarity : _____

02 다음 우리말에 맞게 빈칸에 알맞은 말을 쓰시오.

(1) 나는 네게 거짓말하지 않았다. 모든 것은 진실이야.

➚ I didn't _____ to you. Everything is true.

(2) 주머니에 구멍이 났다.

➚ I have a hole in my _____.

(3) 그 만화 영화는 소설을 바탕으로 한다.

➚ The animation is _____ on a novel.

03 다음 문장의 빈칸에 들어갈 말을 〈보기〉에서 골라 쓰시오.

┌─ 보기 ─┐
fantasy, traditional, connection, author, desert, award
└─────┘

(1) I'm interested in _____ Korean culture.

(2) The land of Australia is primarily _____.

(3) This novel was written by a famous _____.

(4) There is a _____ between health and eating habits.

(5) Emma was really happy when she won the _____.

(6) I like to read _____ novel.

04 다음 우리말을 주어진 단어를 이용하여 영작하시오.

(1) 지금부터 축구 경기를 시작하겠습니다. (from, start, let's, playing)

➚ _____

(2) 나가기 전에, 전등을 다시 확인해 주세요. (light, you, check)

➚ _____

(3) 누가 이 영화의 주인공입니까? (main, this)

➚ _____

05 다음 우리말과 일치하도록 주어진 어구를 모두 배열하여 영작하시오.

(1) 게임 규칙을 설명해 줄 수 있나요?

(explain / the game / can / of / the rules / you)

➚ _____

(2) 당신이 빨간색과 파란색을 섞으면 보라색을 얻을 수 있어요.

(purple / get / you / blue / red / with / mix / you / can / if)

➚ _____

(3) 그가 유리창을 깨지 않았다는 것을 증명할 수 있어요.

(that / I / the window / didn't / can / break / prove / he)

➚ _____

(4) 신문에 난 그 광고 봤니?

(you / see/ did / the advertisement / the newspaper / on)

➚ _____

Conversation

1 추천 요청하기 및 추천하기

> **A** Can you recommend a musical for me? 제게 뮤지컬을 추천해 줄 수 있나요?
>
> **B** How about *The Lion King*? *The Lion King*은 어때?

■ 'Can you recommend ~?'는 '~을 추천해 줄 수 있나요?'라는 뜻으로 상대방에게 무엇인가를 추천해 달라고 부탁하는 표현이다. 대답으로 "How about ~?", "Why don't you ~?", "I recommend ~", "Try ~", "I think ~." 등의 표현을 사용해 추천해 줄 수 있다.

추천 요청하기

- What would you recommend? 무엇을 추천하나요?
- What do you think would be the best? 무엇이 가장 좋다고 생각하나요?
- Can you suggest a good movie? 좋은 영화를 추천해 줄 수 있나요?

추천하기

- How about *Frozen*? The music is so beautiful. *Frozen*은 어때? 음악이 매우 아름다워.
- Why don't you read *Frindle*? The story is really touching.
  *Frindle*을 읽어 보는 게 어때? 이야기가 정말 감동적이야.
- I recommend *Beauty and the Beast*. 나는 미녀와 야수를 추천해요.
- Try Antonio's. It's a good restaurant. Antonio's에 가 봐. 좋은 식당이야.
- I think this backpack is much better than that one. 제 생각에 이 배낭이 저것보다 훨씬 나을 거 같아요.

핵심 Check

1. 다음 주어진 우리말과 일치하도록 빈칸을 완성하시오.

(1) **A:** Can you _____ a movie for me? (영화를 추천해 줄 수 있나요?)

  B: _____ _____ *Spider Man*? It's interesting. (*Spiderman* 어때? 재밌어.)

(2) **A:** _____ _____ _____ a good novel for me? (제게 좋은 소설을 제안해 주시겠어요?)

  B: _____ don't you read *Harry Potter*? (*Harry Potter*를 읽어 보는 게 어때요?)

(3) **A:** _____ _____ _____ _____ _____ _____ the best musical?
  (최고의 뮤지컬이 무엇인 거 같아요?)

  B: I think *The Phantom of the Opera* is the best. (저는 오페라의 유령이 최고인 것 같아요.)

2 만족 여부 묻고 답하기

A How do you like your bicycle? 네 자전거는 마음에 드니?
B I'm really happy with it. 정말 마음에 들어.

■ 'How do you like ~?'는 '~이 마음에 드니?'라는 뜻으로 특정 물건이나 장소 등에 대해 만족하는지를 묻는 표현이다. 이에 대한 대답으로 만족을 표현할 때는 'I'm happy with ~.'로, 불만족을 표현할 때는 'I'm not happy with ~.'로, 표현할 수 있다.

만족 여부 묻기

• How do you like your new sneakers? 새 운동화가 마음에 드니?
• What do you like about the movie? 그 영화의 무엇이 마음에 드니?

만족 여부 답하기

• I'm satisfied with my job. 내 일에 만족해.
• I'm disappointed with the decision. 나는 그 결정에 실망했어.
• I'm pleased with the food. 음식이 마음에 들어.
• It's perfect. 완벽해.
• It's fantastic. 매우 좋아.

핵심 Check

2. 다음 주어진 우리말과 일치하도록 빈칸을 완성하시오.

(1) **A:** _____ _____ _____ _____ your new pants? (새 바지가 마음에 드니?)
   B: I'm really happy with them. (정말 마음에 들어.)

(2) **A:** How do you like your jacket? (재킷이 마음에 드니?)
   B: _____ _____ _____ _____ _____. (만족스럽지 않아.)

(3) **A:** _____ _____ _____ _____ about the bicycle?
   (그 자전거의 무엇이 마음에 드니?)
   B: It's light and fast. (가볍고 빨라요.)

Conversation 교과서 대화문 익히기

Listen and Speak 1 - B

W: ❶May I help you?

B: Yes. I'm ❷looking for a ❸backpack. Can you recommend ❹one?

W: ❺How about this red one? Red is the most popular color ❻these days.

B: My old backpack was red, so I want a different color.

W: How about this navy one? It has side pockets.

B: Oh, that looks good. I'll take ❼it.

W: 도와드릴까요?
B: 네. 배낭을 찾고 있어요. 하나 추천해 주시겠어요?
W: 이 빨간 배낭은 어떤가요? 빨간색은 요즘 가장 인기 있는 색이에요.
B: 제 옛 배낭이 빨간색이어서 다른 색을 원해요.
W: 이 남색 배낭은 어떤가요? 양옆에 주머니가 있어요.
B: 오, 좋아 보여요. 그걸로 살게요.

❶ 'May I help you?'는 '도와드릴까요?'라고 도움을 제안하는 표현으로 'How can I help you?' 또는 'Do you need any help?' 등으로 바꾸어 표현할 수 있다.

❷ look for: ~을 찾다　　❸ backpack: 배낭　　❹ one = a backpack

❺ 'How about ~?'은 '~하는 게 어때?'라고 추천하는 표현으로 'What about ~?'으로 바꾸어 쓸 수 있다.

❻ these days: 요즘 cf. those days: 그 당시에

❼ it은 the navy backpack with side pockets를 가리킨다.

Check(√) True or False

(1) The boy already had a red backpack.　　　　T ☐ F ☐

(2) The boy bought the backpack with side pockets.　　T ☐ F ☐

Listen and Speak 2 - B

Jack: Hi, Suji. ❶How did you like your trip to Gyeongju?

Suji: I was very happy with it.

Jack: Where did you visit?

Suji: I visited Cheomseongdae. It was great.

Jack: Where else did you go?

Suji: Bulguksa. It was a wonderful place.

Jack: Sounds like the perfect trip.

Suji: Yeah, but ❷walking up to Seokguram was difficult.

Jack: But I'm sure it was ❸worth it.

Jack: 안녕, 수지야. 경주 여행은 어땠니?
Suji: 매우 즐거웠어.
Jack: 어디를 방문했니?
Suji: 첨성대를 방문했어. 좋았어.
Jack: 또 어디를 방문했니?
Suji: 불국사. 멋진 곳이었어.
Jack: 완벽한 여행이었던 것 같네.
Suji: 응, 하지만 석굴암까지 걸어 올라가는 것은 힘들었어.
Jack: 하지만 그것이 그만한 가치가 있었을 것이라고 확신해.

❶ 경주 여행이 마음에 들었는지 묻는 표현이다.

❷ 동명사가 주어이므로 동사는 단수 형태로 쓰였다.

❸ worth it: 그만한 가치가 있는

Check(√) True or False

(3) Suji was happy with her trip to Gyeongju.　　　　T ☐ F ☐

(4) It was not hard for Suji to walk up to Seokguram.　　T ☐ F ☐

Listen and Speak 1-A

Brian: Can you ❶recommend a good movie?

Emily: Try *Star Wars*. I really liked ❷it.

Brian: Oh, I haven't seen ❷it yet.

Emily: ❷It's the ❸number one movie ❹right now.

❶ recommend: 추천하다
❷ it은 *Star Wars*를 가리킨다.
❸ number one: 1위의
❹ right now: 지금

Real Life Talk – Step 1

Brian: Mina, can you recommend a good pizza restaurant?

Mina: ❶Why don't you try Antonio's? ❷It's my favorite.

Brian: What do you like about ❷it?

Mina: The food is delicious. I recommend the bulgogi pizza.

Brian: How are the prices?

Mina: I think the prices are good, too.

Brian: Sounds like a good restaurant. How do you like the service?

Mina: It's ❸a little slow on the weekends.

Brian: Okay. I'll ❹check it out. Thanks.

Mina: No problem. Enjoy your meal!

❶ How about trying Antonio's?로 바꾸어 쓸 수 있다.
❷ It은 Antonio's를 가리킨다.
❸ a little: 조금
❹ check out: ~을 확인하다

Listen and Speak 1-C

A: Jiho, can you recommend a musical for me?

B: ❶How about *The Lion King*? The dancing is fantastic.

A: Okay. ❷Sounds good.

B: ❸I'm sure you'll like ❹it.

❶ How about ~?: ~는 어때?(=What about ~?)
❷ Sounds good.에는 앞 문장을 받는 주어 That이 생략되었다.
❸ I'm sure ~.: 나는 ~라고 확신해.
❹ it은 *The Lion King*을 가리킨다.

Real Life Talk – Step 2

Amy: Yujin, can you recommend a book for me?

Yujin: How about *The Little Prince*?

Amy: What do you like about ❶the book?

Yujin: I like the ❷main character. ❸He is very special.

Amy: Sounds good. I'll read it.

❶ the book은 *The Little Prince*를 가리킨다.
❷ main character: 주인공
❸ He = the main character

Listen and Speak 2-A

Sue: Tom, you got a new smartphone.

Tom: Yes, I did. I'm really happy with ❶it.

Sue: ❷What do you like most about ❶it?

Tom: I love the camera. It ❸takes great pictures.

❶ it은 a new smartphone을 가리킨다.
❷ 무엇이 마음에 드는지 묻는 표현이다.
❸ take a picture: 사진을 찍다

Conversation **117**

● 다음 우리말과 일치하도록 빈칸에 알맞은 말을 쓰시오.

Listen & Speak 1-A

Brian: Can you _____ a good movie?

Emily: Try *Star Wars*. I really liked it.

Brian: Oh, I haven't seen it _____.

Emily: It's the _____ _____ movie right now.

Brian: 좋은 영화를 추천해 줄래?
Emily: 'Star Wars'를 봐. 정말 좋았어.
Brian: 오, 나는 아직 그 영화를 본 적이 없어.
Emily: 지금 1위 영화야.

Listen & Speak 1-B

W: May I _____ you?

B: Yes. I'm looking for a _____. Can you _____ _____?

W: _____ _____ this red one? Red is the most popular color _____ _____.

B: My old backpack was red, so I want a _____ color.

W: How about this _____ one? It has side _____.

B: Oh, that looks good. I'll _____ it.

W: 도와드릴까요?
B: 네. 배낭을 찾고 있어요. 하나 추천해 주시겠어요?
W: 이 빨간 배낭은 어떤가요? 빨간색은 요즘 가장 인기 있는 색이에요.
B: 제 옛 배낭이 빨간색이어서 다른 색을 원해요.
W: 이 남색 배낭은 어떤가요? 양옆에 주머니가 있어요.
B: 오, 좋아 보여요. 그걸로 살게요.

Listen & Speak 2-A

Sue: Tom, you _____ a new smartphone.

Tom: Yes, I did. I'm really happy with it.

Sue: What do you _____ _____ _____ _____?

Tom: I love the camera. It _____ great pictures.

Sue: Tom, 새 스마트폰을 샀구나.
Tom: 응, 그래. 나는 정말 만족스러워.
Sue: 무엇이 가장 마음에 드니?
Tom: 카메라가 정말 좋아. 멋진 사진을 찍어.

Listen & Talk 2-B

Jack: Hi, Suji. How did you _____ your _____ to Gyeongju?

Suji: I was very _____ with it.

Jack: Where did you visit?

Suji: I visited Cheomseongdae. It was great.

Jack: _____ _____ did you go?

Suji: Bulguksa. It was a _____ _____.

Jack: Sounds like the _____ _____.

Suji: Yeah, but _____ _____ to Seokguram was difficult.

Jack: But I'm sure it was _____ _____.

Real Life Talk – Step 1

Brian: Mina, _____ _____ _____ a good pizza restaurant?

Mina: _____ _____ you try Antonio's? It's my favorite.

Brian: What do you like _____ it?

Mina: The food is _____. I _____ the bulgogi pizza.

Brian: How are _____ _____?

Mina: I _____ the prices are good, _____.

Brian: _____ _____ a good restaurant. _____ do you like _____ _____?

Mina: It's a little _____ on the weekends.

Brian: Okay. I'll _____ _____ _____. Thanks.

Mina: No _____. _____ your meal!

Real Life Talk – Step 2

Amy: Yujin, can you _____ _____ _____ _____ _____?

Yujin: How _____ *The Little Prince*?

Amy: _____ do you _____ about the book?

Yujin: I like the _____ _____. He is very _____.

Amy: _____ good. I'll read it.

해석

Jack: 안녕, 수지야. 경주 여행은 어땠니?
Suij: 매우 즐거웠어.
Jack: 어디를 방문했니?
Suij: 첨성대를 방문했어. 좋았어.
Jack: 또 어디를 방문했니?
Suij: 불국사. 멋진 곳이었어.
Jack: 완벽한 여행이었던 것 같네.
Suij: 응, 하지만 석굴암까지 걸어 올라가는 것은 힘들었어.
Jack: 하지만 그것이 그만한 가치가 있었을 것이라고 확신해.

Brian: 미나야, 괜찮은 피자 식당을 추천해 줄래?
Mina: Antonio's에 가 보는 게 어때? 내가 가장 좋아하는 곳이야.
Brian: 무엇이 좋은데?
Mina: 음식이 맛있어. 나는 불고기 피자를 추천해.
Brian: 가격은 어때?
Mina: 가격도 괜찮다고 생각해.
Brian: 괜찮은 식당 같네. 서비스는 어때?
Mina: 주말에는 좀 느려.
Brian: 알겠어. 내가 확인해 볼게. 고마워.
Mina: 천만에. 맛있게 먹어!

Amy: Yujin아, 내게 책을 추천해 줄래?
Yujin: '어린 왕자' 어때?
Amy: 책의 무엇이 마음에 드니?
Yujin: 나는 주인공이 마음에 들어. 그는 매우 특별해.
Amy: 좋은 책 같네. 내가 읽어 볼게.

[01~02] 다음 대화를 읽고 물음에 답하시오.

> Brian: _____?
> Emily: Try *Star Wars*. I really liked it.
> Brian: Oh, I haven't seen it yet.
> Emily: It's the number one movie right now.

01 위 대화의 빈칸에 들어갈 말을 〈보기〉에 주어진 단어를 모두 배열하여 영작하시오.

┌ 보기 ┐
> you / recommend / a / movie / can / good

➡ _____

02 위 대화의 내용과 일치하지 <u>않는</u> 것은?

① Brian은 Emily에게 좋은 영화를 추천해 줄 것을 요청하였다.
② Emily는 *Star Wars*를 볼 것을 추천하였다.
③ Emily는 *Star Wars*가 정말 좋았다.
④ Brain은 아직 *Star Wars*를 보지 않았다.
⑤ Brian은 지금 1위 영화를 보았다.

[03~04] 다음 대화를 읽고 물음에 답하시오.

> Sue: Tom, you got a new smartphone.
> Tom: Yes, I did. I'm really happy with (B)it.
> Sue: (A)무엇이 가장 마음에 드니?
> Tom: I love the camera. (C)It takes great pictures.

03 위 대화의 밑줄 친 (A)의 우리말을 주어진 단어를 모두 배열하여 영작하시오.

┌ 보기 ┐
> you / it / about / what / most / do / like

➡ _____

04 위 대화의 밑줄 친 (B)와 (C)의 <u>it</u>이 가리키는 것을 각각 찾아 쓰시오.

➡ (B) _____ (C) _____

[01~03] 다음 대화를 읽고 물음에 답하시오.

Jack: Hi, Suji. ①How did you like your trip to Gyeongju?

Suji: I was very happy ②with it.

Jack: Where did you visit?

Suji: I visited Cheomseongdae. It was great.

Jack: Where else did you go?

Suji: Bulguksa. It was a wonderful place.

Jack: ③Sounds like the perfect trip.

Suji: Yeah, ___(A)___ walking up to Seokguram ④were difficult.

Jack: ___(A)___ I'm sure it was ⑤worth it.

서답형

01 위 대화의 ①~⑤ 중 어법상 어색한 것을 찾아 바르게 고치시오.

➡ _____

02 위 대화의 빈칸 (A)에 들어갈 말로 적절한 것은?

① and / And
② but / But
③ so / So
④ for / For
⑤ because / Because

03 위 대화의 내용과 일치하지 <u>않는</u> 것은?

① Suji was satisfied with her trip to Gyeongju.

② Suji visited both Cheomseongdae and Bulguksa.

③ It was difficult for Suji to walk up to Seokguram.

④ Jack didn't think that it was worth while walking up to Cheomseongdae.

⑤ Suji thought that Bulguksa was a great place.

[04~05] 다음 대화를 읽고 물음에 답하시오.

Amy: Yujin, (A)내게 책을 추천해 줄래?(can)

Yujin: How about *The Little Prince*?

Amy: What do you like about the book?

Yujin: I like the main character. He is very special.

Amy: Sounds good. I'll read it.

서답형

04 위 대화의 밑줄 친 (A)의 우리말을 주어진 단어를 사용하여 영작하시오.

➡ _____

서답형

05 What does Yujin like about *The Little Prince*? Answer in English.

➡ _____

[06~08] 다음 대화를 읽고 물음에 답하시오.

Brian: Mina, can you recommend a good pizza restaurant?

Mina: (A) It's my favorite.

Brian: (B) What do you like about ⓐit?

Mina: (C) The food is delicious. I recommend the bulgogi pizza.

Brian: (D) How are the prices?

Mina: (E) I think the prices are good, too.

Brian: Sounds like a good restaurant. How do you like the service?

Mina: ⓑIt's a little slow on the weekends.

Brian: Okay. I'll check it out. Thanks.

Mina: No problem. Enjoy your meal!

06 위 대화의 (A)~(E) 중 주어진 문장이 들어가기에 적절한 곳은?

> Why don't you try Antonio's?

① (A) ② (B) ③ (C) ④ (D) ⑤ (E)

07 위 대화에서 밑줄 친 ⓐ와 ⓑ가 각각 가리키는 것을 찾아 쓰시오.

➡ ⓐ _____ ⓑ _____

08 위 대화의 내용과 일치하지 <u>않는</u> 것은?

① 미나는 괜찮은 피자 식당으로 Antonio's를 추천하였다.
② Antonio's는 미나가 가장 좋아하는 곳이다.
③ 미나는 Antonio's의 불고기 피자를 추천하였다.
④ 미나는 Antonio's의 가격이 괜찮다고 생각한다.
⑤ Antonio's의 서비스는 주중에는 좀 느리다.

[09~10] 다음 대화를 읽고 물음에 답하시오.

W: May I help you?
B: (A) Yes. I'm looking for a backpack. Can you recommend one?
W: (B) Red is the most popular color these days.
B: (C) My old backpack was red, so I want a different color.
W: (D) How about this navy one? It has side pockets.
B: (E) Oh, that looks good. I'll take it.

09 위 대화의 (A)~(E) 중 주어진 문장이 들어가기에 적절한 곳은?

> How about this red one?

① (A) ② (B) ③ (C) ④ (D) ⑤ (E)

10 위 대화를 읽고 대답할 수 <u>없는</u> 질문은?

① What was the boy looking for?
② What did the woman recommend at first?
③ Why didn't the boy want the red backpack?
④ What did the boy decide to buy?
⑤ How many pockets did the boy's old backpack have?

[11~12] 다음 대화를 읽고 물음에 답하시오.

Sue: Tom, you got a new smartphone.
Tom: Yes, I did. _____(A)_____
Sue: What do you like most about it?
Tom: I love the camera. It takes great pictures.

11 위 대화의 빈칸 (A)에 들어갈 말로 <u>어색한</u> 것은?

① I'm really happy with it.
② I'm satisfied with it.
③ I'm disappointed with it.
④ I'm pleased with it.
⑤ It's fantastic.

12 위 대화를 읽고 대답할 수 <u>없는</u> 질문은?

① What did Tom get?
② Does Tom like his new smartphone?
③ What does Tom like most about his smartphone?
④ Why does Tom love the camera in his smartphone?
⑤ When did Tom take great pictures?

[01~03] 다음 대화를 읽고 물음에 답하시오.

Brian: Can you recommend a good movie?
Emily: Try *Star Wars*. I really liked it.
Brian: Oh, (A)나는 아직 그것을 본 적이 없어. (yet)
Emily: It's the number one movie right now.

01 위 대화의 밑줄 친 (A)의 우리말을 주어진 단어를 사용하여 영작하시오.

➡ _____

02 What movie did Emily recommend to Brian?

➡ _____

03 What is the number one movie now?

➡ _____

[04~06] 다음 대화를 읽고 물음에 답하시오.

W: May I help you?
B: Yes. I'm looking for a backpack. Can you recommend one?
W: How about this red one? Red is the most popular color these days.
B: My old backpack was red, so I want a different color.
W: How about this navy one? It has side pockets.
B: Oh, that looks good. I'll take it.

04 What is the most popular color nowadays?

➡ _____

05 What is the feature of the navy backpack?

➡ _____

06 Why didn't the boy want to take the red backpack?

➡ _____

[07~08] 다음 대화를 읽고 물음에 답하시오.

Jack: Hi, Suji. ___(A)___ did you like your trip to Gyeongju?
Suji: I was very happy with it.
Jack: ___(B)___ did you visit?
Suji: I visited Cheomseongdae. It was great.
Jack: ___(C)___ else did you go?
Suji: Bulguksa. It was a wonderful place.
Jack: Sounds like the perfect trip.
Suji: Yeah, but walking up to Seokguram was difficult.
Jack: But I'm sure it was worth it.

07 위 대화의 빈칸 (A), (B), (C)에 들어갈 알맞은 의문사를 쓰시오.

➡ (A) _____ (B) _____ (C) _____

08 위 대화의 내용과 일치하도록 Suji의 일기를 완성하시오.

Sun, Nov 3rd, 2019
I took a trip to ___(A)___. It was a really nice and beautiful city. I visited ___(B)___ as well as Cheomseongdae. They are wonderful places. When I walked up to ___(C)___, I was tired but it was worth while to do it. I was so happy with the perfect trip to Gyeongju.

➡ (A) _____ (B) _____ (C) _____

Grammar

교과서

1 so ~ that

- **The hot chocolate was so hot that Jeremy couldn't drink it.**
  그 핫 초콜릿은 너무 뜨거워서 Jeremy는 그것을 마실 수 없었다.

- **I am so hungry that I could eat a horse.**
  나는 배가 너무 고파서 말 한 마리를 다 먹을 수 있을 정도야.

■ 'so+형용사/부사+that ~'은 '너무 …해서 ~하다'는 의미로 원인과 결과를 나타낼 때 사용한다.

- This book is **so** interesting **that** I can't put it down. 이 책은 너무 재미있어서 내려놓을 수가 없어.

- The sun is **so** hot **that** I have to drink lots of water. 태양이 너무 뜨거워서 나는 많은 물을 마셔야만 한다.

- The fox was **so** playful **that** he wanted to make play with the crane.
  그 여우는 장난기가 너무 많아서 학을 골탕 먹이고 싶었다.

■ 'so ~ that 주어 can't …'는 '너무 ~해서 …할 수 없다'는 의미로 'too ~ to V'로 표현할 수 있고, 'so ~ that 주어 can'은 '너무 ~해서 …할 수 있다'는 의미로 '~ enough to V'로 표현할 수 있다.

- I am **so** tired **that** I can't play with you.

  = I am **too** tired **to** play with you. 나는 너무 피곤해서 너와 함께 놀 수 없어.

- Julia was **so** tall **that** she played basketball very well.

  = Julia was tall **enough to** play basketball very well. Julia는 충분히 키가 커서 농구를 아주 잘했다.

핵심 Check

1. 다음 우리말과 같도록 빈칸에 알맞은 말을 쓰시오.

(1) 불빛이 너무 밝아서 나는 눈을 뜰 수 없어.

➡ The light is _____ _____ _____ I can't open my eyes.

(2) 그것은 너무 작아서 사람들은 그것을 보기 위해 현미경이 필요해요.

➡ It is _____ _____ _____ people need a microscope to see it.

(3) James는 너무 게을러서 모두가 그를 싫어한다.

➡ James is _____ _____ _____ everyone hates him.

2 목적격 관계대명사

- Mr. Han **whom** everyone respects teaches English.
  모두가 존경하는 한 선생님은 영어를 가르친다.

- The jacket **which** Sam got from his mother looks fancy.
  Sam이 엄마에게서 받은 재킷은 멋져 보인다.

■ 관계대명사는 두 개의 문장을 하나로 이어주는 접속사 역할을 하면서 동시에 (대)명사 역할을 한다. 전치사의 목적어 혹은 동사의 목적어였던 (대)명사를 목적격 관계대명사로 만들어 문장을 하나로 이어준다.

- There were many children at the zoo **which** Tom and Jane visited. 〈동사의 목적어〉
  Tom과 Jane이 방문했던 동물원에는 아이들이 많았다.

- Those boys **who[whom]** the woman is looking after look very cute. 〈전치사의 목적어〉
  그 여자가 돌보고 있는 저 소년들은 매우 귀여워 보인다.

■ 목적격 관계대명사 who(m), which는 that으로 대체할 수 있으며, 생략 가능하다. 관계대명사가 전치사의 목적어로 사용된 경우 전치사는 동사 뒤에 그대로 두거나, 전치사를 관계대명사 앞으로 보낼 수 있다. 단, 관계대명사 that은 전치사의 목적어로 쓰일 수 없음에 유의하자.

- The hotel (**which/that**) you stay in is famous for its breakfast.
  = The hotel **in which** you stay is famous for its breakfast.
  = The hotel in that you stay is famous for its breakfast. (×) 네가 머물고 있는 그 호텔은 아침식사로 유명하다.
- The missing girl (**who(m)/that**) people were looking for was found at the train station.
  = The missing girl for **whom** people were looking was found at the train station.
  = The missing girl for that people were looking was found at the train station. (×)
  사람들이 찾던 그 실종 소녀가 기차역에서 발견되었다.
- Tell me about the cats (**which/that**) you take care of on the streets.
  네가 길에서 돌보는 고양이들에 관해서 말해 줘.

핵심 Check

2. 다음 우리말과 같도록 빈칸에 알맞은 말을 쓰시오.

(1) 나는 Elizabeth가 만든 드레스를 입고 싶다.
➡ I want to wear the dress _____ _____ _____.

(2) Chris는 그가 어제 잃어버린 지갑을 찾고 있다.
➡ Chris is looking for the wallet _____ _____ _____ yesterday.

(3) 나는 Molly가 정말 좋아했던 책을 가지고 있다.
➡ I have the book _____ _____ _____ _____.

(4) 그녀는 꿈에서 본 남자를 찾고 있어.
➡ She is looking for a man _____ _____ _____ in her dream.

01 다음 문장에서 어법상 <u>어색한</u> 부분을 바르게 고쳐 쓰시오.

(1) The areas who you mentioned have some problems.

_____ ➡ _____

(2) Tell me about the patients which you cared for in the hospital.

_____ ➡ _____

(3) This necklace is very expensive that you will be shocked.

_____ ➡ _____

(4) Suji was so tired to do her homework.

_____ ➡ _____

02 다음 우리말과 같은 의미가 되도록 빈칸에 알맞은 말을 쓰시오.

(1) Tom이 많이 좋아하는 그 소녀는 내 친구이다.
= The girl _____ _____ _____ so much is my friend.

(2) 그 문제는 너무 쉬워서 모두가 그것을 풀 수 있다.
= The problem is _____ _____ _____ everyone can solve it.

(3) 그는 매우 부유해서 그가 원하는 어떤 것도 할 수 있다.
= He is _____ _____ _____ he can do anything _____ he wants.

(4) 내가 앉아 있는 이 의자는 편안하다.
= This chair _____ _____ _____ _____ is comfortable.

03 주어진 어구를 바르게 배열하여 다음 우리말을 영어로 쓰시오. 필요하다면 어형을 바꾸고 단어를 추가하시오.

(4) commute: 통근 (거리)

(1) 그녀는 좋아하지 않는 음식에 손도 대지 않았다. (she / she / didn't / didn't / like / touch / the food / that)

➡ _____

(2) 그 여자가 돌보고 있는 저 아기들은 매우 귀여워 보인다. (very cute / those babies / look after / look / whom / is / the woman)

➡ _____

(3) 구두가 너무 꼭 끼어서 내 발이 아파. (tight / hurt / the shoes / my feet / are / that)

➡ _____

(4) 그녀의 출퇴근 거리가 너무 멀어서 그녀는 차를 샀다. (a car / her commute / bought / so / she / far / was)

➡ _____

01 다음 우리말을 영어로 바르게 옮긴 것은?

> 그녀는 너무 피곤해서 일찍 잤어.

① She is very tired to go to bed early.
② She was too tired to go to bed early.
③ She was so tired that she couldn't go to sleep.
④ She was so tired that she went to bed early.
⑤ She went to bed so early that she was tired.

 02 다음 중 어법상 바르지 <u>않은</u> 것은?

> The woman ①whom I ②met yesterday ③was ④very friendly ⑤that I wanted to be friends with her.

①   ②   ③   ④   ⑤

03 다음 주어진 문장의 빈칸에 들어갈 말로 적절한 것을 <u>모두</u> 고르시오.

> The sofa _____ they bought last week looks expensive.

① whose   ② which   ③ who
④ that   ⑤ what

서답형

04 목적격 관계대명사를 이용하여 다음 두 문장을 하나의 문장으로 쓰시오.

> • The book was written by my mother.
> • You borrowed the book from the library.

➡ _____

_____

 05 주어진 문장과 같은 의미의 문장은?

> Tom was too scared to go out at night.

① Tom was scared enough to go out at night.
② Tom was very scared of going out at night.
③ Tom was so scared that he couldn't go out at night.
④ Tom was so scared that he could go out at night.
⑤ Tom was scared to go out at night.

06 다음 중 어법상 바르지 <u>않은</u> 것은?

① Minji is so smart that she can solve all the problems.
② The bike which Jason rides are fancy.
③ I know the house in which we used to live.
④ Some friends you invited are a little rude.
⑤ I was so upset that I didn't answer her phone.

 07 다음 빈칸에 들어갈 말이 바르게 짝지어진 것은?

> James kicked a ball so _____ that his foot hurt. The ball _____ James kicked was not found.

① hardly – whose   ② hardly – that
③ hard – who   ④ hard – whose
⑤ hard – that

서답형

08 주어진 단어를 활용하여 다음 우리말을 영어로 쓰시오.

> 그 컴퓨터는 너무 작아서 내가 가지고 다닐 수 있다. (so / carry around)

➡ _____

_____

09 다음 중 밑줄 친 부분을 생략할 수 없는 것은?

① The boy whom you ran across was one of my students.
② The banana which Jane ate was not hers.
③ Where are the coins that were under the sofa?
④ The car that Jimmy washed looked clean and shiny.
⑤ The children whom you play with are there.

10 다음 중 that의 쓰임이 나머지 넷과 다른 하나는?

① It is certain that Brady is alive.
② That he worried about you is true.
③ I lost the hat that you had bought me.
④ I told her that he was playing the piano.
⑤ Do you think that there will be lots of homework?

서답형

11 주어진 상황을 읽고 하나의 문장으로 표현하시오.

> There was an important examination. Julia studied hard to pass the exam. At last, she passed it.

➡ _____

_____

서답형

12 주어진 단어를 이용하여 알맞은 대답을 쓰시오.

> A: Why were you late?
> B: (that / traffic / heavy / here / be / on time)

➡ _____

_____

13 다음 빈칸에 공통으로 들어갈 말로 가장 적절한 것은?

> • The movie was so boring _____ most people fell asleep.
> • The plants _____ you cared for look very similar.

① who   ② which   ③ that
④ what   ⑤ whose

14 다음 중 서로 의미가 같지 않은 것은?

① Amelia was too talkative to listen to others.
  = Amelia was so talkative that she couldn't listen to others.
② I lent you some money. What will you do with it?
  = What will you do with the money that I lent you?
③ The boys are too noisy to be in the library.
  = The boys are so noisy that they can't be in the library.
④ Jacky wrote a popular song. People loved the song.
  = Jacky wrote a popular song which people loved.
⑤ Where is the dog? It follows you all the time.
  = Where is the dog you follow all the time?

15 같은 의미가 되도록 빈칸에 알맞은 말을 쓰시오.

> • The concert made me excited.
> • We watched the concert last week.
> = The concert _____ made me
>   excited.

➡ _____

16 다음 빈칸에 들어갈 말로 가장 적절한 것은?

> • My teeth were so painful that I went to
>   the dentist.
> = I went to the dentist _____ my teeth
>   were so painful.

① although　　② because
③ when　　　 ④ as soon as
⑤ unless

17 다음 우리말을 영어로 바르게 옮긴 것은?

> 그 노래가 나를 너무 슬프게 해서 나는 라디오를
> 껐다.

① The song was sad that I turned off the
   radio.
② The song made me so sad that I turned
   off the radio.
③ The song was too sad to turn off the
   radio.
④ I was so sad that I turned off the radio.
⑤ The song made me sadly so that I turned
   off the radio.

서답형

18 같은 의미의 문장이 되도록 빈칸에 알맞은 말을 쓰시오.

> • The song was beautiful.
> • They sang the song together.
> = The song _____ .

➡ _____

19 주어진 문장과 같은 의미의 문장은?

> I was so busy that I couldn't have lunch.

① I was busy although I couldn't have
   lunch.
② I was busy enough to have lunch.
③ I was busy because I couldn't have
   lunch.
④ I was busy having lunch.
⑤ I was too busy to have lunch.

20 다음 중 어법상 옳은 문장은?

① The necklace you wear look beautiful.
② The dress was so beautiful that I can't
   take my eyes off it.
③ The students whose you teach are noisy.
④ The apple you brought is tasty.
⑤ The man was so diligently that everyone
   liked him.

서답형

21 괄호 안의 말을 써서 주어진 문장과 같은 의미의 문장을 쓰시오.

> I can't talk in front of many people
> because I am too shy. (so ~ that)

➡ _____

서답형

22 다음 우리말을 영어로 쓸 때 빈칸에 알맞은 말을 쓰시오.

> 내가 흥미 있는 과목은 영어입니다.
> (subject / interested)

(1) The subject _____ _____
    _____ in is English.
(2) The subject in _____ _____
    _____ _____ is English.

01 주어진 단어를 바르게 배열하여 다음 우리말을 영어로 쓰시오.

> 네가 나에게 소개해 준 그 소녀는 매우 인기 있어.
> (very / is / me / popular / the girl / introduced / you / to / whom)

➡ _____

02 다음 대화를 읽고 빈칸에 알맞은 말을 쓰시오.

> A: Why didn't Sandra carry the box?
> B: It was too heavy.

➡ The box _____

_____ .

03 다음 두 문장을 하나의 문장으로 쓸 때 빈칸에 알맞은 말을 쓰시오.

> Ross wrote a poem. The poem was so amazing that I was moved to tears.

➡ The poem _____

_____ .

04 다음 빈칸에 알맞은 말을 쓰시오.

(1) The cats _____ you take care of look happy.

(2) The guests _____ are in the hall want something cold to drink.

(3) Some people _____ we can see over there are interested in our artworks.

05 주어진 문장과 같은 의미의 문장을 지시에 맞게 쓰시오. 주어 Penny로 문장을 시작할 것.

> Penny was too sick to eat anything.

(1) because를 써서

➡ _____

(2) so ~ that을 써서

➡ _____

06 자연스러운 문장이 되도록 두 문장을 연결하시오.

> • The car is not his.
> • Kevin picked some roses.
> • I know the person.

> • Catherine planted roses.
> • You took a trip with him.
> • Tom is driving a car.

(1) The car _____ .
(2) Kevin _____ .
(3) I _____ .

07 다음 대화를 읽고 빈칸에 알맞은 말을 쓰시오.

> A: Do you need to buy a coat, Avian?
> B: I don't need to buy another coat because I already have a coat which is really warm.

➡ Avian's coat is _____

_____ .

08 〈보기〉와 같이 두 문장을 하나의 문장으로 쓰시오.

> **보기**
>
> I was very grateful to her. I made a pie for her.
> → I was so grateful to her that I made a pie for her.

(1) Sally speaks English very well. You would think it is her native language.

➡ _____

_____

(2) The music was very loud. You could hear it from miles away.

➡ _____

_____

(3) Gabriel is very beautiful. Any man would love to be with her.

➡ _____

_____

09 원인과 결과를 나타내는 구문을 이용하여 다음 문장과 같은 의미의 문장을 쓰시오.

> The soup burned my tongue because it was too hot.

➡ _____

10 주어진 단어를 활용하여 다음 우리말을 영어로 쓰시오.

> Jody는 Ms. Galler가 찾고 있는 학생이다.
> (look for)

➡ _____

_____

11 다음 우리말을 영어로 쓰시오.

(1) 네가 어제 본 소년은 나의 남동생이야.

➡ _____

_____

(2) 그녀가 입고 있는 드레스는 유명한 사람에 의해 디자인된 거야.

➡ _____

_____

12 주어진 단어를 바르게 배열하여 다음 우리말을 영어로 쓰시오.

> 내가 가장 자주 전화하는 사람들은 나의 엄마와 내 여동생들이다.
> (my sisters / I / my mother / are / and / often / call / the people / most / whom)

➡ _____

_____

13 다음 대화를 읽고 빈칸에 알맞은 말을 쓰시오.

> A: Lisa must be really happy.
> B: Why do you say so, Jason?
> A: I can see her dancing in the room.

➡ According to Jason, Lisa is _____ she is dancing in the room.

14 주어진 문장을 'so'를 이용하여 하나의 문장으로 표현하시오.

> The party was very enjoyable. Therefore, no one wanted to leave.

➡ _____

_____

15 주어진 단어를 활용하여 다음 우리말을 영어로 쓰시오.

> 그녀는 너무 일찍 일어나서 피곤했어요.
> (so / early)

➡ _____

_____

Reading

교과서

Making Good Choices

Emma: What are you doing, Kyle?

Kyle: Oh, Emma. I'm watching the movie, *Y-Men 7* on my computer.
the movie = *Y-Men 7* 동격   ~로(수단)

Emma: How is it?

Kyle: Don't ask. It's so boring that I want to cry.
원인과 결과(너무 ~해서 …하다)

Emma: I'm sorry to hear that.
감정의 원인

Kyle: I'm so mad. The movie advertisement said it was "The Most Exciting Movie of the Year."
of+명사(비교의 범위를 나타냄)

Emma: Well, you can't believe everything that you read.
목적격 관계대명사

Kyle: They lied on the advertisement. I'm going to ask for my money back.

Emma: Hold on, Kyle! They didn't really lie because they used opinions, not facts.
(부정문에서) 꼭, 사실   이유를 나타내는 접속사
A. not B: B가 아니라 A

Kyle: Huh? I'm not following you.
I can't understand you. = I don't get it.

Emma: Opinions express people's feelings like, "The desert is beautiful." You can't say that it's true or not. But, facts can be proven. For example, "The Atacama Desert is in Chile," is a fact. You can check that on the map.
전치사(~와 같은)
say의 목적어를 이끄는 명사절 접속사
조동사가 있는 수동태
= The Atacama Desert is in Chile.

Kyle: Okay…. But what's the connection with movies?

boring 지루한
advertisement 광고
believe 믿다
lie 거짓말하다
ask for A back A를 돌려달라고 청하다
opinion 의견
express 나타내다, 표현하다
for example 예를 들어
check ~을 확인하다
connection 관련성

📎 **확인문제**

● 다음 문장이 본문의 내용과 일치하면 T, 일치하지 <u>않으면</u> F를 쓰시오.

1 Kyle feels like crying because of the movie. ☐

2 Emma tells Kyle to believe what he reads. ☐

3 It is hard to say that they told a lie on the advertisement. ☐

132 Lesson 7. Can I Trust It?

Emma: Let me explain. What's your favorite movie?
let+목적어+동사원형: 목적어가 ~하게 하다

Kyle: It's *Forrest Gump*.

Emma: Okay. Let's look for its advertisement. What does it say?
it = Forrest Gump   = its advertisement

Kyle: It says, "Winner of 6 Academy Awards including Best Picture."
~라고 되어[쓰여] 있다   수상작   전치사(~을 포함하여)

Emma: See? It uses facts unlike the *Y-Men 7* advertisement. Do you
전치사(~와는 달리)

see the difference?
알다, 이해하다

Kyle: Not exactly. The *Y-Men 7* ad says "Most Exciting Movie" and the
정확히는 아니다

Forrest Gump ad says "Best Picture." Aren't they both opinions?
= 'Most Exciting Movie' and 'Best Picture'

Emma: That's a great question, Kyle. When people use words like
전치사(~와 같은)

"best" or "most," they are usually expressing opinions. But in the

Forrest Gump ad, "Best Picture" is the award which the movie
목적격 관계대명사(선행사: award)

won. We can check that on the Internet. That's a fact.
"Best Picture" is the award which the movie won

Kyle: Aha! From now on I'm only going to trust ads with facts.
지금부터   ~을 가진, ~이 있는

Emma: It's not that simple. Most ads mix facts with opinions. So you
지시부사(그렇게, 그 정도로)

have to make a smart choice based on both of them.
facts and opinions

Kyle: Got it! Emma, do you want to watch the rest of *Y-Men 7* with me?
알았어!

Emma: Thanks, but no thanks. Enjoy the rest of the movie!
상대방이 권해 줘서 고맙지만 거절하고 싶을 때 쓸 수 있는 표현

---

explain 설명하다

favorite 가장 좋아하는

difference 차이

both 둘 다

trust 믿다

simple 간단한

mix A with B A와 B를 섞다

make a choice 선택하다

based on ~을 바탕으로

rest 나머지

확인문제

● 다음 문장이 본문의 내용과 일치하면 T, 일치하지 <u>않으면</u> F를 쓰시오.

1 Emma's favorite movie is *Forrest Gump*. ☐

2 *Forrest Gump* won seven Academy Awards. ☐

3 People use words like 'best' or 'most' when telling opinions. ☐

4 Kyle wants Emma to watch the movie with him. ☐

● 우리말을 참고하여 빈칸에 알맞은 말을 쓰시오.

1 Emma: What _____ you _____, Kyle?

2 Kyle: Oh, Emma. I'm _____ the movie, *Y-Men 7* _____ my computer.

3 Emma: _____ is it?

4 Kyle: Don't ask. It's _____ _____ _____ I want to cry.

5 Emma: I'm sorry _____ _____ _____ .

6 Kyle: I'm so mad. The movie _____ said _____ was "_____ _____ _____ _____ of the Year."

7 Emma: Well, you can't believe _____ _____ _____ _____ .

8 Kyle: They lied on the advertisement. I'm going to _____ _____ _____ _____ _____ .

9 Emma: _____ _____ , Kyle! They didn't really _____ _____ they used opinions, not facts.

10 Kyle: Huh? I'm _____ _____ _____ .

11 Emma: Opinions _____ _____ _____ like, "The desert is beautiful."

12 You can't say _____ it's true or not. But, facts _____ _____ _____ .

13 _____ _____ , "The Atacama Desert is in Chile," is a fact. You can _____ _____ _____ _____ _____ .

14 Kyle: Okay…. But what's _____ _____ _____ movies?

15 Emma: _____ _____ _____ . What's your favorite movie?

16 Kyle: _____ *Forrest Gump*.

17 Emma: Okay. Let's _____ _____ _____ _____. What does it say?

18 Kyle: _____ _____, "Winner of 6 Academy Awards including Best Picture."

19 Emma: See? It _____ _____ _____ the *Y-Men 7* advertisement.

20 Do you see _____ _____?

21 Kyle: Not _____. The *Y-Men 7* ad _____ "Most Exciting Movie" and the *Forrest Gump* ad _____ "Best Picture."

22 _____ they _____ _____?

23 Emma: That's a great question, Kyle. When people use _____ _____ "best" or "most," they are _____ _____ _____.

24 But in the *Forrest Gump* ad, "Best Picture" is the award _____ _____ _____ _____.

25 We can check _____ _____ _____ _____. That's a fact.

26 Kyle: Aha! _____ _____ _____ I'm only going to _____ ads _____ facts.

27 Emma: It's not _____ _____. Most ads _____ facts _____ opinions.

28 So you have to _____ _____ _____ _____ based on _____ of them.

29 Kyle: Got it! Emma, do you want _____ _____ the rest of *Y-Men 7* with me?

30 Emma: Thanks, but no thanks. Enjoy _____ _____ the movie!

16 Kyle: "Forest Gump"야.

17 Emma: 좋아. 그 영화의 광고를 찾아보자. 뭐라고 쓰여 있니?

18 Kyle: "Best Picture를 포함하여 아카데미 6개 부문 수상작"이라고 쓰여 있어.

19 Emma: 알겠니? "Y-Men 7" 광고와는 달리 사실을 사용하고 있어.

20 차이를 알겠니?

21 Kyle: 잘 모르겠어. "Y-Men 7" 광고는 "Most Exciting Movie"라고 쓰여 있고 "Forest Gump" 광고는 "Best Picture"라고 쓰여 있잖아.

22 둘 다 의견 아니니?

23 Emma: 좋은 질문이야, Kyle. 사람들이 'best'나 'most'와 같은 말을 사용할 때, 그들은 대개 의견을 표현하는 거야.

24 하지만 "Forest Gump" 광고에서 "Best Picture"는 영화가 받은 상이야.

25 우리는 인터넷에서 그것을 확인할 수 있어. 그건 사실이야.

26 Kyle: 아하! 지금부터 사실로 이루어진 광고만 믿겠어.

27 Emma: 그렇게 간단하지는 않아. 대부분의 광고는 사실과 의견이 섞여 있어.

28 그러니 그 둘을 바탕으로 현명한 선택을 해야 해.

29 Kyle: 알겠어! Emma, "Y-Men 7"의 남은 부분을 나와 함께 볼래?

30 Emma: 고맙지만 사양할게. 영화의 남은 부분 잘 봐!

● 우리말을 참고하여 본문을 영작하시오.

1 ▷ Emma: Kyle, 뭐 하고 있니?

➡ _____

2 ▷ Kyle: Emma. 나는 컴퓨터로 영화 "Y-Men 7"을 보고 있어.

➡ _____

3 ▷ Emma: 어때?

➡ _____

4 ▷ Kyle: 묻지 마. 너무 지루해서 울고 싶어.

➡ _____

5 ▷ Emma: 유감이야.

➡ _____

6 ▷ Klye: 난 정말 화가 나. 영화 광고에는 이것이 "올해의 가장 흥미진진한 영화"라고 쓰여 있었어.

➡ _____

7 ▷ Emma: 음, 넌 네가 읽는 것을 모두 믿을 수는 없어.

➡ _____

8 ▷ Kyle: 그들은 광고에 거짓말을 한 거야. 돈을 환불해 달라고 해야겠어.

➡ _____

9 ▷ Emma: 기다려, Kyle! 그들은 사실이 아닌 의견을 사용했기 때문에 꼭 거짓말을 한 것은 아니야.

➡ _____

10 ▷ Kyle: 뭐라고? 네 말을 이해하지 못하겠어.

➡ _____

11 ▷ Emma: 의견은 "사막은 아름다워."와 같이 사람들의 감정을 표현하는 것이야.

➡ _____

12 ▷ 그것이 사실인지 아닌지 말할 수는 없어. 하지만 사실은 증명할 수 있어.

➡ _____

13 ▷ 예를 들면, "아타카마 사막은 칠레에 있다."는 사실이야. 넌 그것을 지도에서 확인할 수 있어.

➡ _____

14 ▷ Kyle: 알겠어…. 하지만 그게 영화와 무슨 관련이 있니?

➡ _____

15 ▷ Emma: 설명해 줄게. 네가 가장 좋아하는 영화가 뭐니?

➡ _____

16 Kyle: "Forest Gump"야.

➡ _____

17 Emma: 좋아. 그 영화의 광고를 찾아보자. 뭐라고 쓰여 있니?

➡ _____

18 Kyle: "Best Picture를 포함하여 아카데미 6개 부문 수상작"이라고 쓰여 있어.

➡ _____

19 Emma: 알겠니? "Y-Men 7" 광고와는 달리 사실을 사용하고 있어.

➡ _____

20 차이를 알겠니?

➡ _____

21 Kyle: 잘 모르겠어. "Y-Men 7" 광고는 "Most Exciting Movie"라고 쓰여 있고 "Forest Gump" 광고는 "Best Picture"라고 쓰여 있잖아.

➡ _____

22 둘 다 의견 아니니?

➡ _____

23 Emma: 좋은 질문이야, Kyle. 사람들이 'best'나 'most'와 같은 말을 사용할 때, 그들은 대개 의견을 표현하는 거야.

➡ _____

24 하지만 "Forest Gump" 광고에서 "Best Picture"는 영화가 받은 상이야.

➡ _____

25 우리는 인터넷에서 그것을 확인할 수 있어. 그건 사실이야.

➡ _____

26 Kyle: 아하! 지금부터 사실로 이루어진 광고만 믿겠어.

➡ _____

27 Emma: 그렇게 간단하지는 않아. 대부분의 광고는 사실과 의견이 섞여 있어.

➡ _____

28 그러니 그 둘을 바탕으로 현명한 선택을 해야 해.

➡ _____

29 Kyle: 알겠어! Emma, "Y-Men 7"의 남은 부분을 나와 함께 볼래?

➡ _____

30 Emma: 고맙지만 사양할게. 영화의 남은 부분 잘 봐!

➡ _____

[01~05] 다음 글을 읽고 물음에 답하시오.

Emma: What are you doing, Kyle?

Kyle: Oh, Emma. I'm watching the movie, *Y-Men 7* on my computer.

Emma: How is it?

Kyle: Don't ask. It's so boring that I want to cry.

Emma: I'm sorry to hear that.

Kyle: I'm so mad. The movie advertisement said it was "The Most Exciting Movie of the Year."

Emma: Well, you can't believe everything ___(A)___ you read.

Kyle: They lied on the advertisement. I'm going to ask for my money back.

Emma: (B)Hold on, Kyle! They didn't really lie because they used opinions, not facts.

01 빈칸 (A)에 들어갈 말로 적절한 것을 <u>모두</u> 고르시오.

① which   ② that   ③ what
④ whose   ⑤ who

02 다음 중 위 글의 내용과 일치하지 <u>않는</u> 것은?

① Kyle is watching *Y-Men 7*.
② Emma is wondering what Kyle is doing.
③ Kyle is satisfied with the movie.
④ Kyle wants to get his money back.
⑤ Kyle thinks that he was fooled by the movie advertisement.

03 다음과 같이 풀이되는 단어를 위 글에서 찾아 쓰시오.

> ideas or feelings about something.

➡ _____

04 Write the reason why Kyle wants to cry. Answer in English with the phrase 'It's because.'

➡ _____

05 다음 중 밑줄 친 (B)를 대신하여 쓰일 수 있는 것은?

① Go ahead   ② Wait
③ Let me see   ④ Watch out
⑤ Way to go

[06~09] 다음 글을 읽고 물음에 답하시오.

Kyle: Huh? I'm not following you.

Emma: Opinions express people's feelings like, "The desert is beautiful." You can't say that it's true or not. But, facts can be proven. ___(A)___, "The Atacama Desert is in Chile," is a fact. You can check (B)<u>that</u> on the map.

Kyle: Okay.... But what's the connection with movies?

Emma: Let me explain. What's your favorite movie?

Kyle: It's *Forrest Gump*.

Emma: Okay. Let's look for its advertisement. What does it say?

Kyle: It says, "Winner of 6 Academy Awards including Best Picture."

Emma: See? It uses facts unlike the *Y-Men 7* advertisement. Do you see the difference?

06 다음 중 빈칸 (A)에 들어갈 말로 가장 적절한 것은?

① However   ② Therefore
③ Also   ④ For example
⑤ Nevertheless

서답형

07 밑줄 친 (B)가 가리키는 것을 15자 이내의 우리말로 쓰시오.

➡ _____

08 다음 중 위 글을 읽고 답할 수 없는 질문은?

① What is opinion?
② Where is Atacama Desert?
③ What is Emma's favorite movie?
④ How many academy awards did *Forrest Gump* win?
⑤ What does *Forrest Gump* advertisement say?

According to the passage, which one is a fact?

① Jimmy is the kindest person I have ever met.
② I think the river is dangerous to swim in.
③ It seems that the butterfly is saying hello to me.
④ Mrs. Simpson looked upset today.
⑤ Barack Obama is the 44th president of the United States of America.

[10~15] 다음 글을 읽고 물음에 답하시오.

Kyle: Not exactly. The *Y-Men 7* ad says "Most Exciting Movie" and the *Forrest Gump* ad says "Best Picture." Aren't they both ①opinion?
Emma: That's a great question, Kyle. When people use words like "best" or "most," they are usually expressing opinions. But ②in the *Forrest Gump* ad, "Best Picture" is the award ③which the movie won. We can check that ④on the Internet. That's ___(A)___.
Kyle: Aha! (B)지금부터 I'm only going to trust ⑤ads with facts.

Emma: It's not that simple. Most ads mix facts with opinions. So you have to make a smart choice based on (C)both of them.

서답형

10 빈칸 (A)에 알맞은 말을 위 글에서 찾아 어법에 맞게 쓰시오.

➡ _____

11 밑줄 친 우리말 (B)를 영어로 바르게 옮긴 것은?

① For a long time
② For the time being
③ From now on
④ From time to time
⑤ Now and then

서답형

12 밑줄 친 (C)가 가리키는 것을 영어로 쓰시오.

➡ _____

13 ①~⑤ 중 어법상 바르지 않은 것은?

① ② ③ ④ ⑤

서답형

14 What do people usually use when they express their opinions? Answer in English with a full sentence.

➡ _____

15 다음 중 위 글의 내용과 일치하지 않는 것은?

① There is a phrase "Most Exciting Movie" in the ad of *Y-Men 7*.
② *Forrest Gump* won the Best Picture award.
③ The ad of *Forrest Gump* used a fact.
④ There are many ads using only facts.
⑤ Kyle finally understands the difference between opinions and facts.

[16~20] 다음 글을 읽고 물음에 답하시오.

Emma: What are you doing, Kyle?

Kyle: Oh, Emma. I'm watching the movie, *Y-Men 7* on my computer.

Emma: (A)[What / How] is it?

Kyle: Don't ask. It's so (B)[boring / bored] that I want to cry.

Emma: I'm sorry ⓐto hear that.

Kyle: I'm so mad. The movie advertisement said it was "The Most Exciting Movie of the Year."

Emma: Well, you can't believe everything that you read.

Kyle: They lied on the advertisement. I'm going (C)[asking / to ask] for my money back.

Emma: Hold on, Kyle! They didn't really lie ____ⓑ____ they used opinions, not facts.

16 다음 중 밑줄 친 ⓐ와 쓰임이 같은 것은?

① David wants me to go with him to the theater.

② It is fun to spend time with you.

③ Julia made some cookies to give her friends.

④ There is a chance to win the race.

⑤ I am so happy to have such a nice teacher.

17 다음 중 빈칸 ⓑ에 들어갈 말로 가장 적절한 것은?

① so   ② while   ③ and

④ because   ⑤ though

서답형

18 What is Kyle doing? Answer in English with a full sentence.

➡ _____

19 (A)~(C)에서 어법상 옳은 것을 바르게 짝지은 것은?

① What – boring – asking

② What – boring – to ask

③ What – bored – to ask

④ How – boring – to ask

⑤ How – bored – asking

서답형

20 According to the passage, what did the movie advertisement say about the movie?

➡ _____

_____

[21~25] 다음 글을 읽고 물음에 답하시오.

Kyle: Huh? I'm not following you.

Emma: Opinions express people's feelings like, "The desert is beautiful." ① You can't say that it's true or not. ② But, facts can (A)[prove / be proven]. ③ For example, "The Atacama Desert is in Chile," is a fact. ④

Kyle: Okay.... But what's the connection with movies? ⑤

Emma: Let me (B)[explain / to explain]. What's your favorite movie?

Kyle: It's *Forrest Gump*.

Emma: Okay. Let's look for its advertisement. What does it say?

Kyle: It says, "Winner of 6 Academy Awards (C)[including / included] Best Picture."

Emma: See? It uses facts unlike the *Y-Men 7* advertisement. Do you see the difference?

21 ①~⑤ 중 주어진 문장이 들어가기에 가장 적절한 곳은?

You can check that on the map.

①   ②   ③   ④   ⑤

22 (A)~(C)에서 어법상 옳은 것을 바르게 짝지은 것은?

① be proven – explain – included
② be proven – explain – including
③ prove – to explain – included
④ prove – explain – including
⑤ prove – to explain – including

서답형

23 위 글의 내용을 참고하여 다음 빈칸에 알맞은 말을 쓰시오.

> According to the passage, "She is the most beautiful baby I've ever seen," is _____. On the other hand, "Mountain Everest is the highest mountain in the world." is _____.

24 According to the passage, who says an opinion?

① Jane: King Sejong invented Hanguel.
② Tim: Canada is rich in natural resources.
③ Brad: The longest river in the world is the Nile in Egypt.
④ Zoe: Going to the beach alone is not safe.
⑤ Kelly: Tom's house is located near the river.

25 다음 중 위 글의 내용과 일치하지 <u>않는</u> 것은?

① People's feelings are expressed in opinions.
② Emma wants to know what Kyle's favorite movie is.
③ Emma is explaining the difference between opinions and facts.
④ The *Forrest Gump* ad uses facts.
⑤ *Forrest Gump* won seven Academy Awards.

[26~29] 다음 글을 읽고 물음에 답하시오.

Emma: Do you see the difference?

(A) That's a great question. When people use words like "best" or "most," they are usually expressing opinions. But in the *Forrest Gump* ad, "Best Picture" is the award which the movie won. We can check (a)<u>that</u> on the Internet. That's a fact.

(B) It's not that simple. Most ads mix facts ___ⓐ___ opinions. So you have to make a smart choice based on both of them.

(C) Aha! From now on I'm only going to trust ads ___ⓑ___ facts.

(D) Not exactly. The *Y-Men 7* ad says "Most Exciting Movie" and the *Forrest Gump* ad says "Best Picture." Aren't they both opinions?

서답형

26 자연스러운 대화가 되도록 (A)~(D)를 바르게 나열하시오.

➡ _____

27 다음 중 빈칸 ⓐ와 ⓑ에 공통으로 들어갈 말은?

① in　② by　③ with　④ to　⑤ at

서답형

28 밑줄 친 (a)가 가리키는 것을 우리말로 쓰시오.

➡ _____

서답형

29 위 글의 내용에 맞게 빈칸에 알맞은 말을 쓰시오.

> We can find both _____ in most ads.

➡ _____

[01~05] 다음 글을 읽고 물음에 답하시오.

Emma: What are you doing, Kyle?

Kyle: Oh, Emma. I'm watching the movie, *Y-Men 7* on my computer.

Emma: How is it?

Kyle: Don't ask. (A)너무 지루해서 울고 싶어.

Emma: I'm sorry to hear that.

Kyle: I'm so mad. The movie advertisement said it was "The Most Exciting Movie of the Year."

Emma: Well, you can't believe everything that you read.

Kyle: They lied on the advertisement.
_____ (a) _____

Emma: Hold on, Kyle! (B)They didn't really lie because they used opinions, not facts.

⭐중요

01 주어진 단어를 바르게 배열하여 빈칸 (a)에 들어갈 말을 쓰시오.

(back / am / to / I / ask / money / for / my / going)

➡ _____

02 밑줄 친 우리말 (A)를 영어로 쓰시오.

➡ _____

고난이도

03 주어진 단어를 이용하여 밑줄 친 (B)와 같은 의미의 문장을 쓰시오.

(not A but B / so)

➡ _____

_____

04 What is the title of the movie that Kyle is watching?

➡ _____

05 글의 내용에 맞게 빈칸에 알맞은 말을 쓰시오.

Unlike the movie advertisement, Kyle did not feel _____ while he was watching the movie.

[06~10] 다음 글을 읽고 물음에 답하시오.

Kyle: Huh? I'm not following you.

Emma: Opinions express people's feelings like, "The desert is beautiful." You can't say that it's true or not. But, facts can _____(A)_____. For example, "(B)The Atacama Desert is in Chile," is a fact. You can check that on the map.

Kyle: Okay.... But what's the connection with movies?

Emma: Let me explain. What's your favorite movie?

Kyle: It's *Forrest Gump*.

Emma: Okay. Let's look for its advertisement. What does it say?

Kyle: It says, "Winner of 6 Academy Awards including Best Picture."

Emma: See? (C)It uses facts unlike the *Y-Men 7* advertisement. Do you see the difference?

06 주어진 단어를 빈칸 (A)에 어법에 맞게 쓰시오.

> prove

➡ _____

07 How can you know the underlined sentence (B) is a fact? Find the answer in the above passage.

➡ _____

08 다음 문장은 밑줄 친 문장 (C)를 읽고 알 수 있는 것이다. 빈칸에 알맞은 말을 쓰시오.

➡ The *Y-Men 7* ad _____.

09 위 글의 표현을 이용하여 다음 우리말을 영어로 쓰시오.

> 6개의 아카데미상을 수상한 그 영화를 보았니?

➡ _____

10 According to the passage, what is Kyle's favorite movie? Answer in English with a full sentence.

➡ _____

[11~14] 다음 글을 읽고 물음에 답하시오.

Kyle: Not exactly. The *Y-Men 7* ad says "Most Exciting Movie" and the *Forrest Gump* ad says "Best Picture." _____(A)_____

Emma: That's a great question, Kyle. When people use words like "best" or "most," they are usually expressing opinions. But in the *Forrest Gump* ad, (B)"Best Picture" is the award which the movie won. We can check that on the Internet. That's a fact.

Kyle: Aha! From now on I'm only going to trust ads with facts.

Emma: It's not that simple. Most ads mix facts with opinions. So you have to make a smart choice based on both of them.

11 주어진 단어를 바르게 나열하여 빈칸 (A)에 알맞은 말을 쓰시오.

> (opinions / they / aren't / both)?

➡ _____

12 밑줄 친 문장 (B)를 두 문장으로 나누어 쓰시오.

➡ _____

13 주어진 어구를 바르게 배열하여 다음 우리말을 영어로 쓰시오.

> 'best'나 'most'와 같은 말을 사용하는 사람들은 대개 의견을 표현하는 중이다.
> (opinions / people / use / are / expressing / usually / 'best' or 'most' / who / like / words)

➡ _____

_____

14 위 글의 내용에 맞게 빈칸에 알맞은 말을 쓰시오.

> When we make a decision, we should _____ our choice on _____ _____ _____.

Reading **143**

Listen and Speak 2-C

A: How do you like your bicycle?
'∼이 마음에 드니?' (만족하는지를 묻는 표현)

B: I'm not happy with it.
= the bicycle을 가리킨다.

A: Why not?
= Why are you not satisfied with it?

B: It's too heavy.

해석

A: 자전거가 마음에 드니?

B: 마음에 들지 않아.

A: 왜?

B: 너무 무거워.

Think and Write

Harry Potter is a fantasy novel. It was written by J. K. Rowling. Harry Potter
인칭대명사(Harry Potter 지칭)

is the main character of the book. When Harry goes to magic school, his
주인공

adventures begin. I especially like the friendship of Harry and his friends. The

book was so interesting that I couldn't put it down. I strongly recommend it to
흥미를 유발할 때 현재분사   so+형용사/부사+that ...: 너무 ∼해서 ...하다

everyone.

구문해설 • a fantasy novel: 공상 소설 • adventure: 모험 • especially: 특히
• friendship: 우정 • put A down: ∼를 내려놓다 • recommend: 추천하다

"해리포터"는 공상 소설이다. 이 책은 J. K. Rowling에 의해 쓰였다. Harry Potter 는 이 책의 주인공이다. Harry가 마법 학교에 가면서 그의 모험은 시작된다. 나는 특히 Harry와 그의 친구들의 우정을 좋아한다. 이 책은 너무 재미있어서 나는 책을 놓을 수가 없었다. 나는 모두에게 이 책을 강력히 추천한다.

Project

Korean folk village

Facts: It is located in Yongin. There are Korean traditional houses. Visitors
∼에 위치해 있다   ∼이 있다 (뒤에 나오는 명사에 수의 일치)

can watch nongak and jultagi.

Opinions: It's a fun place in Yongin. Korean traditional houses are beautiful.

Nongak and jultagi will be exciting.
감정을 유발할 때 현재분사

구문해설 • folk village: 민속촌 • traditional: 전통적인 • exciting: 신나는

한국 민속촌

사실: 그것은 용인에 있습니다. 한국 전통 가옥이 있습니다. 방문객들은 농악과 줄타기를 볼 수 있습니다.

의견: 그곳은 용인에 있는 재미있는 장소입니다. 한국 전통 가옥들은 아름답습니다. 농악과 줄타기는 신이 날 것입니다.

영역별 핵심문제

01 다음 짝지어진 단어의 관계가 같도록 빈칸에 알맞은 말을 쓰시오.

> increase : decrease = empty : _____

02 다음 영영풀이가 가리키는 것을 고르시오.

> to say or write something that is not true

① explain   ② tell
③ present   ④ lie
⑤ express

03 다음 중 밑줄 친 부분의 뜻풀이가 바르지 <u>않은</u> 것은?

① I like this <u>pocket</u> on the back of the suitcase. 주머니
② I can <u>trust</u> her word. 신뢰하다
③ She answered <u>wisely</u>. 현명하게
④ This book is <u>worth</u> reading. 세계
⑤ The bag comes in <u>navy</u> and green. 남색

04 다음 주어진 우리말과 일치하도록 주어진 단어를 모두 배열하여 영작하시오.

(1) 선물이 마음에 드니?
  (you / how / like / the / present / do)
  ➡ _____

(2) 그의 주장을 증명할 증거가 없다.
  (no / his / evidence / is / to / claim / there / prove)
  ➡ _____

05 주어진 단어를 이용해서 다음 우리말에 맞게 빈칸에 알맞은 말을 쓰시오.

(1) 가격을 비교해 보고 선택하는 게 어때?
  ➡ Why don't you _____ after comparing the prices? (make)

(2) 나는 네가 다시 한 번 서류를 확인해야 할 것 같아.
  ➡ I think you should _____ the documents again. (out)

(3) 야외 시장은 사람들로 가득 차 있었다.
  ➡ The outdoor market was _____ people. (of)

06 다음 주어진 문장의 밑줄 친 lie와 같은 의미로 쓰인 것은?

> Why did you <u>lie</u> to me? I'm so disappointed with you.

① I want to go home and <u>lie</u> on the bed.
② <u>Lie</u> down here and take a rest.
③ I'm innocent because I didn't <u>lie</u> for a second.
④ My children usually <u>lie</u> on the right side when they sleep.
⑤ You can't <u>lie</u> on the floor.

07 다음 문장에 공통으로 들어갈 말을 고르시오.

> • This gallery is _____ a visit.
> • This movie is _____ watching.
> • This souvenir is _____ $100.

① worth   ② cost
③ price   ④ value
⑤ expense

Conversation

[08~09] 다음 대화를 읽고 물음에 답하시오.

> Brian: (A)Can you recommend a good movie?
> Emily: _____ (B) _____ I really liked it.
> Brian: Oh, I haven't seen it yet.
> Emily: It's the number one movie right now.

08 위 대화의 밑줄 친 (A)와 바꾸어 쓸 수 있는 것은?

① What do you think about a good movie?
② Would you recommend a good movie?
③ What is a good movie?
④ Do you want to see a good movie?
⑤ What should I do to find a good movie?

09 위 대화의 빈칸 (B)에 들어갈 말로 어색한 것은?

① Try *Star Wars*.
② How about watching *Star Wars*?
③ Why did you watch *Star Wars*?
④ What about watching *Star Wars*?
⑤ I recommend *Star Wars*.

[10~12] 다음 대화를 읽고 물음에 답하시오.

> W: May I help you?
> B: Yes. I'm looking for a backpack. Can you recommend one?
> W: How about this red one? Red is the most popular color (A)these days.
> B: My old backpack was red, so I want a different color.
> W: How about this navy one? It has side pockets.
> B: Oh, that looks good. I'll take it.

10 위 대화의 여자와 소년의 관계로 적절한 것은?

① doctor – patient   ② clerk – customer
③ guide – tourist   ④ teacher – student
⑤ writer – reader

11 위 대화의 밑줄 친 (A)와 바꾸어 쓸 수 있는 것은?

① those days   ② nowadays
③ in the past   ④ the day before
⑤ in the future

12 위 대화의 내용과 일치하지 <u>않는</u> 것은?

① 소년은 배낭을 찾고 있다.
② 요즘 빨간색이 가장 인기 있는 색이다.
③ 소년의 옛 배낭이 빨간색이었다.
④ 남색 배낭은 양옆에 주머니가 있다.
⑤ 소년은 주머니가 있는 빨간색 가방을 샀다.

[13~15] 다음 대화를 읽고 물음에 답하시오.

> Jack: Hi, Suji. (A)경주 여행은 어땠니?
>   (Gyeongju, trip, how, like)
> Suji: I was very happy with it.
> Jack: Where did you visit?
> Suji: I visited Cheomseongdae. It was great.
> Jack: Where else did you go?
> Suji: Bulguksa. It was a wonderful place.
> Jack: Sounds like the perfect trip.
> Suji: Yeah, but walking up to Seokguram was difficult.
> Jack: But I'm sure it was worth it.

13 위 대화의 밑줄 친 (A)의 우리말을 주어진 단어를 사용하여 영작하시오.

➡ _____

14 위 대화에서 다음 주어진 영영풀이가 나타내는 말을 찾아 쓰시오.

> important, good or enjoyable enough for something

➡ _____

15 위 대화를 읽고 대답할 수 <u>없는</u> 질문은?

① Where did Suji travel?

② How did Suji like her trip to Gyeongju?

③ What did Suji think of Bulguksa?

④ What does Jack think about walking up to Seokguram?

⑤ How long did it take for Suji to walk up to Seokguram?

16 다음 짝지어진 대화가 <u>어색한</u> 것을 고르시오.

① A: Can you recommend a musical for me?

B: How about *The Lion King*?

② A: How do you like your bicycle?

B: I'm really happy with it.

③ A: Would you recommend a good movie?

B: Why don't you try *Star Wars*?

④ A: How do you like your jacket?

B: I'm not satisfied with it.

⑤ A: What do you like about your backpack?

B: I like it so much.

Grammar

17 다음 중 주어진 문장의 밑줄 친 부분과 쓰임이 같은 것은?

> The health-care worker <u>that</u> I spoke to was helpful.

① Hudson said <u>that</u> he refused the job offer.

② It is true <u>that</u> I don't like your attitude.

③ Patrick woke up so late <u>that</u> he couldn't attend the meeting again.

④ The fact <u>that</u> you lied to the police officer doesn't change.

⑤ This is the same kind of watch <u>that</u> I lost.

18 주어진 문장과 같은 의미의 문장은?

> We postponed our trip because the weather was bad.

① The weather was bad enough that we postponed our trip.

② The weather was so bad that we postponed our trip.

③ Although the weather was bad, we postponed our trip.

④ Because we postponed our trip, the weather was bad.

⑤ The weather was too bad to postpone our trip.

19 다음 빈칸에 들어갈 말로 적절한 것을 <u>모두</u> 고르시오.

> The children _____ Mr. Smith adopted are from three different countries.

① who ② that ③ whose

④ which ⑤ whom

20 주어진 문장과 같은 의미의 문장을 쓰시오.

> We went swimming because it was so hot yesterday. (so ~ that을 이용)

➡ _____

21 다음 중 빈칸에 들어갈 말로 적절한 것은?

> • She was so embarrassed that she wanted to run away and hide.
> = She wanted to run away and hide _____ she was embarrassed.

① although ② because ③ so

④ unless ⑤ therefore

22 다음 중 의미가 나머지 넷과 <u>다른</u> 하나는?

① Maya is so afraid of flying that she can't travel by plane.

② Maya can't travel by plane because she is afraid of flying.

③ Maya is afraid of flying, so she can't travel by plane.

④ Maya is too afraid of flying to travel by plane.

⑤ Although Maya is afraid of flying, she travels by plane.

23 주어진 단어를 이용하여 다음 우리말을 영어로 쓰시오.

> 그 남자가 훔친 약은 그의 아들을 위한 것이었다. (drug)

➡ _____

24 다음 중 밑줄 친 부분이 생략 가능하지 <u>않은</u> 것은?

① The painting <u>which</u> you drew looks amazing.

② The car <u>that</u> Brian borrowed from his brother was dirty.

③ A girl <u>who</u> was called Puddle fell in love with my brother.

④ I ordered an expensive meal at the restaurant <u>which</u> Clark runs.

⑤ Joy saw a man looking into the car <u>which</u> Tom bought.

25 다음 두 문장을 하나의 문장으로 쓰시오.

> We eat the carrots. My grandfather grew them on the farm.

➡ _____
_____

26 'so ~ that'을 이용하여 다음 두 문장을 한 문장으로 쓰시오.

> There are many leaves on a single tree. It is impossible to count them.

➡ _____
_____

27 주어진 단어를 이용하여 다음 우리말을 영어로 쓰시오.

> 네가 지난주에 방문한 박물관에 관해 말해 줘. (tell / visit)

➡ _____
_____

Reading

[28~30] 다음 글을 읽고 물음에 답하시오.

Emma: What are you doing, Kyle?

Kyle: Oh, Emma. I'm watching the movie, *Y-Men 7* on my computer.

Emma: How is it?

Kyle: Don't ask. (A)It's so boring that I want to cry.

Emma: I'm sorry to hear that.

Kyle: I'm so mad. The movie advertisement said it was "The Most Exciting Movie of the Year."

Emma: Well, you can't believe everything that you read.

Kyle: They lied on the advertisement. I'm going to ask for my money back.

Emma: Hold on, Kyle! They didn't really lie because they used opinions, not facts.

28 주어진 단어를 이용하여 다음 우리말을 영어로 쓰시오.

> Kyle이 선택한 영화는 광고에서 의견을 사용하였다. (chose / in the advertisement)

➡ _____

_____

29 다음 중 밑줄 친 (A)와 쓰임이 같은 것을 모두 고르시오.

① It is exciting to meet them this weekend.
② It is ten miles to Boston.
③ It will make our cake creamy.
④ It was windy and dark yesterday.
⑤ It means that they will quit as soon as possible.

30 다음 중 위 글을 읽고 답할 수 없는 질문은?

① What is Kyle doing?
② Why does Kyle want to cry?
③ How does Kyle feel about the movie?
④ Why does Kyle think they lied on the advertisement?
⑤ What does Emma think about Kyle?

[31~33] 다음 글을 읽고 물음에 답하시오.

Kyle: Not exactly. The *Y-Men 7* ad says "Most Exciting Movie" and the *Forrest Gump* ad says "Best Picture." Aren't they both opinions?

Emma: That's a great question, Kyle. When people use words like "best" or "most," they are usually expressing opinions. But in the *Forrest Gump* ad, "Best Picture" is the award ___(A)___ the movie won. We can check that on the Internet. That's a fact.

Kyle: Aha! From now on I'm only going to trust ads with facts.

Emma: (B)It's not that simple. Most ads mix facts with opinions. So you have to make a smart choice based on both of them.

31 다음 중 빈칸 (A)에 들어갈 말과 다른 하나는?

① I don't know _____ she is.
② The boys _____ you are looking at are my friends.
③ There are some flowers _____ Tom picked.
④ Many students _____ I teach are diligent.
⑤ A girl and a cat _____ are sitting together look happy.

32 다음은 좋은 영화를 고르기 위해 어떤 광고를 신뢰해야 하는지에 대한 조언이다. 올바른 조언을 한 사람은?

① Ben: Don't trust ads because they are full of lies.
② Amelia: Find ads which are full of facts.
③ Clark: Watch only movies that use opinions in their ads.
④ Molly: Choose a movie which only uses words like 'best' or 'most' in the ad.
⑤ Kevin: Check both facts and opinions and choose wisely.

33 Write the reason why Emma says like the underlined (B). Use the phrase "It's because."

➡ _____

01 다음 영영풀이가 가리키는 것을 고르시오.

> to add something to something else

① devide
② prove
③ lift
④ advertise
⑤ mix

02 다음 우리말에 맞게 빈칸에 알맞은 말을 쓰시오.

(1) 시간을 현명하게 써야 한다.
➡ You should spend your time _____.

(2) 좋은 식당을 추천해 줄래요?
➡ Can you _____ a good restaurant?

(3) 나는 강력하게 그의 의견에 동의한다.
➡ I _____ agree with his idea.

03 다음 문장의 빈칸에 들어갈 말을 〈보기〉에서 골라 쓰시오.

> ┤ 보기 ├
> hold on / right now / look for / number one / worth it

(1) Paris was the _____ destination for tourists.

(2) Would you help me _____ the information about Korean history?

(3) I'm working at the oil company _____.

(4) _____ for a moment. I'll bring my phone.

(5) I'm sure it'll _____.

04 다음 주어진 문장에 이어지는 대화가 자연스럽게 이어지도록 순서대로 배열하시오.

> May I help you?

(A) How about this red one? Red is the most popular color these days.
(B) Oh, that looks good. I'll take it.
(C) My old backpack was red, so I want a different color.
(D) How about this navy one? It has side pockets.
(E) Yes. I'm looking for a backpack. Can you recommend one?

➡ _____

05 다음 대화의 빈칸에 들어갈 말로 어색한 것은?

> A: How do you like your bicycle?
> B: I'm not satisfied with it.
> A: _____
> B: It's too heavy.

① What's wrong?
② Why not?
③ What's the problem?
④ What's the matter?
⑤ What do you like about it?

[06~08] 다음 대화를 읽고 물음에 답하시오.

Jack: Hi, Suji. (A)[What / How] did you like your trip to Gyeongju?

Suji: 여행은 매우 즐거웠어. (happy, it)

Jack: Where did you visit?

Suji: I visited Cheomseongdae. It was great.

Jack: Where else did you go?

Suji: Bulguksa. It was a wonderful place.

Jack: (B)[Sound / Sounds] like the perfect trip.

Suji: Yeah, but (C)[walk / walking] up to Seokguram was difficult.

Jack: But I'm sure it was worth it.

06 위 대화의 밑줄 친 우리말을 주어진 단어를 사용하여 영어로 쓰시오.

➡ _____

07 위 대화의 (A)~(C)에 들어갈 말로 적절한 것으로 짝지어진 것은?

	(A)	(B)	(C)
①	What	Sound	walk
②	What	Sounds	walking
③	How	Sounds	walk
④	How	Sounds	walking
⑤	How	Sound	walk

08 Check the places which Suji liked during the trip.

Cheomseongdae   Gyeongju National Museum

Seokguram   Bulguksa

➡ _____

09 다음 대화의 빈칸에 들어갈 말로 어색한 것은?

Bomi: Jiho, can you recommend a musical for me?
Jiho: How about *The Lion King*? _____
Bomi: Okay. Sounds good.
Jiho: I'm sure you'll like it.

① The story is exciting.
② The dancing is fantastic.
③ The music is so beautiful.
④ It is so popular these days.
⑤ I was so bored that I couldn't focus on it.

10 다음 대화의 내용과 일치하지 않는 것은?

Brian: Mina, can you recommend a good pizza restaurant?
Mina: Why don't you try Antonio's? It's my favorite.
Brian: What do you like about it?
Mina: The food is delicious. I recommend the bulgogi pizza.
Brian: How are the prices?
Mina: I think the prices are good, too.
Brian: Sounds like a good restaurant. How do you like the service?
Mina: It's a little slow on the weekends.
Brian: Okay. I'll check it out. Thanks.
Mina: No problem. Enjoy your meal!

① Brian is looking for a good pizza restaurant.
② Mina has eaten bulgogi pizza at Antonio's.
③ Mina thinks that the prices of Antonio's are resonable.
④ The service of Antonio's is a little slow on Saturdays and Sundays.
⑤ Brian is going to Antonio's to check whether the price is good or not.

11 다음 중 밑줄 친 부분의 쓰임이 다른 하나는?

① The girl who you invited didn't come.
② The man who gave me this ticket looks scary.
③ Can you tell me who they are?
④ The reporter who they hate wrote an article.
⑤ Tom is the boy who read lots of books.

12 다음 우리말을 영어로 바르게 옮긴 것은? 출제율 90%

> Jamie는 일을 너무 열심히 해서 병이 들었다.

① Jamie worked hardly to make himself sick.

② Jamie worked so that hard to become sick.

③ Jamie worked too hard to make himself sick.

④ Jamie worked so hard that he became sick.

⑤ Jamie worked so hardly that he became sick.

13 주어진 단어를 바르게 배열하여 다음 우리말을 영어로 쓰시오. 출제율 95%

> 네가 나에게서 빌려간 펜을 돌려줄래?
> (from / borrowed / the pen / me / can / you / back / give / you / me / that)

➡ _____

_____

14 다음 중 빈칸에 들어갈 말로 가장 적절한 것은? 출제율 100%

> That is the chair _____ your brother used to sit.

① which   ② on which   ③ who

④ on that   ⑤ that

15 다음 중 문장을 잘못 바꿔 쓴 것은? 출제율 90%

① Thomas is the man. You have to meet him.
   = Thomas is the man you have to meet.

② This is the copy machine. Polly bought it.
   = This is the copy machine that Polly bought.

③ Sally is too tired to do it.
   = Sally is so tired that she can't do it.

④ Joe is looking at the candle. Maya made it.
   = Joe is looking at the candle which Maya made.

⑤ Chris didn't know the man that his sister talked to.
   = Chris didn't know the man to that his sister talked.

16 주어진 단어를 활용하여 다음 우리말을 영어로 쓰시오. 출제율 95%

> 그 역기는 너무 가벼워서 내가 들어 올릴 수 있었어. (barbell / lift)

➡ _____

[17~21] 다음 글을 읽고 물음에 답하시오.

Kyle: Huh? (A)I'm not following you.

Emma: Opinions express people's feelings like, "The desert is beautiful." You can't say (B)that it's true or not. But, facts can be proven. For example, "The Atacama Desert is in Chile," is a fact. You can check that on the map.

Kyle: Okay.... But what's the connection with movies?

Emma: Let me explain. What's your favorite movie?

Kyle: It's *Forrest Gump*.

Emma: Okay. Let's look for its advertisement. What does it say?

Kyle: It says, "Winner of 6 Academy Awards including Best Picture."

Emma: See? It uses facts unlike the *Y-Men 7* advertisement. Do you see the difference?

Kyle: Not exactly. The *Y-Men 7* ad says "Most Exciting Movie" and the *Forrest Gump* ad says "Best Picture." Aren't they both opinions?

출제율 95%

17 다음 중 밑줄 친 (A) 대신에 쓸 수 있는 것은?

① I can't go after you.

② I can't understand you.

③ You are following me.

④ I need to follow up something.

⑤ It is hard to catch up with you.

출제율 100%

18 다음 중 밑줄 친 (B)와 쓰임이 다른 것은?

① He thinks that his friends are nice.

② Do you know the fact that the movie is bad?

③ It is true that she bought two tickets.

④ He is the boy that you want to see.

⑤ They said that I had to deal with the problem.

출제율 90%

19 글의 내용에 맞게 빈칸에 알맞은 말을 쓰시오.

Unlike _____, _____ cannot be proven.

출제율 85%

20 What are they mainly talking about? Answer in English with a full sentence.

➡ _____

_____

출제율 95%

21 다음 중 의견에 해당하는 것은?

① Bulguksa is located in Gyeongju.

② The Han River is not as long as the Nile River.

③ Watching movies is interesting.

④ Bill Gates founded Microsoft.

⑤ Mother Teresa was born in 1910.

[22~24] 다음 글을 읽고 물음에 답하시오.

Charlotte's Web is a children's novel. It was written by E. B. White. A little pig named Wilbur is the main character of the book. When Wilbur is in danger, his friend Charlotte helps him out. I especially like the friendship of Wilbur and Charlotte. _____(A)_____ I strongly recommend it to everyone.

출제율 90%

22 주어진 어구를 바르게 배열하여 빈칸 (A)에 들어갈 말을 쓰시오.

(touching / many times / the book / that / I / so / read / was / it)

➡ _____

출제율 95%

23 다음 중 위 글을 읽고 답할 수 없는 질문은?

① When did Charlotte help Wilbur?

② Who wrote the novel?

③ What is the name of the main character?

④ Who is Wilbur's friend?

⑤ How many friends does Wilbur have?

출제율 90%

24 다음 두 문장을 하나의 문장으로 쓰시오.

Charlotte's Web is a children's novel. E. B. White wrote the book.

➡ _____

서술형 실전문제

[01~03] 다음 대화를 읽고 물음에 답하시오.

> Brian: Mina, can you recommend a good pizza restaurant?
>
> Mina: Why don't you try Antonio's? It's my favorite.
>
> Brian: What do you like about it?
>
> Mina: The food is delicious. I recommend the bulgogi pizza.
>
> Brian: How are the prices?
>
> Mina: I think the prices are good, too.
>
> Brian: Sounds like a good restaurant. How do you like the service?
>
> Mina: It's a little slow on the weekends.
>
> Brian: Okay. I'll check it out. Thanks.
>
> Mina: No problem. Enjoy your meal!

01 What is Mina's favorite restaurant?

➡ _____

02  Which food does Mina recommend?

➡ _____

03 What does Mina think about the service?

➡ _____

04  다음 대화가 자연스럽게 이어지도록 순서대로 배열하시오.

> (A) What do you like most about it?
> (B) Yes, I did. I'm really happy with it.
> (C) Tom, you got a new smartphone.
> (D) I love the camera. It takes great pictures.

➡ _____

05 다음 두 문장을 하나의 문장으로 쓰시오.

> I can't find the cup. My husband likes to use it.

➡ _____

06 지시에 맞게 주어진 문장과 같은 의미의 문장을 쓰시오. 각각 The wind를 주어로 시작할 것.

> The wind was strong, so it blew my hat off my head.

(1) because를 이용하여

➡ _____
_____

(2) so ~ that을 이용하여

➡ _____
_____

07 두 문장이 같은 의미가 되도록 빈칸에 알맞은 말을 쓰시오.

> • Peter fell in love with a woman. She left him a few weeks ago.
> = The woman _____ a few weeks ago.

➡ _____
_____

08 다음 우리말에 맞게 빈칸에 알맞은 말을 쓰시오.

> The cookies _____ was _____ I ate all of them.
> 네가 구운 쿠키가 너무 맛있어서 내가 모두 먹어 버렸어.

09 주어진 단어를 활용하여 다음 우리말을 영어로 쓰시오.

> 그 보석은 너무 귀해서 값을 매길 수가 없다.
> (jewel / precious / that / priceless)

➡ _____

[10~13] 다음 글을 읽고 물음에 답하시오.

Kyle: Huh? I'm not following you.

Emma: Opinions express people's feelings like, "The desert is beautiful." You can't say that it's true or not. But, facts can be proven. For example, "The Atacama Desert is in Chile," is a fact. You can check that on the map.

Kyle: Okay.... But what's the connection with movies?

Emma: Let me explain. What's your favorite movie?

Kyle: It's *Forrest Gump*.

Emma: Okay. Let's look for its advertisement. What does it say?

Kyle: It says, "Winner of 6 Academy Awards including Best Picture."

Emma: See? It uses facts unlike the *Y-Men 7* advertisement. Do you see the difference?

10 What does the advertisement say about *Forrest Gump*?

➡ _____

_____

⭐ 중요
11 What is Emma using to explain the difference between facts and opinions? Answer in English.

➡ _____

12 According to the passage, what is the difference between facts and opinions? Answer in Korean.

➡ _____

⭐ 중요
13 글의 내용에 맞게 빈칸에 알맞은 말을 쓰시오.

> There are many _____ that we can't trust in the ads. We need an ad which has many _____ .

[14~15] 다음 글을 읽고 물음에 답하시오.

Harry Potter is a fantasy novel. It was written by J. K. Rowling. Harry Potter is the main character of the book. When Harry goes to magic school, his adventures begin. I especially like the friendship of Harry and his friends. (A)그 책은 아주 재미있어서 나는 책을 놓을 수가 없었다. I strongly recommend it to everyone.

14 밑줄 친 우리말 (A)를 영어로 쓰시오.

➡ _____

_____

15 What is the genre of the book, *Harry Potter*?

➡ _____

01 다음 대화의 내용과 일치하도록 Mina의 소개문을 완성하시오.

> Brian: Mina, can you recommend a good pizza restaurant?
>
> Mina: Why don't you try Antonio's? It's my favorite.
>
> Brian: What do you like about it?
>
> Mina: The food is delicious. I recommend the bulgogi pizza.
>
> Brian: How are the prices?
>
> Mina: I think the prices are good, too.
>
> Brian: Sounds like a good restaurant. How do you like the service?
>
> Mina: It's a little slow on the weekends.
>
> Brian: Okay. I'll check it out. Thanks.
>
> Mina: No problem. Enjoy your meal!

> I'll introduce my favorite restaurant, Antonio's. It is a good pizza restaurant. I recommend (A)_____, which is so delicious. The (B)_____ are reasonable. If you visit there on the weekends, the service can be (C)_____. How about trying Antonio's?

02 'so ~ that' 구문을 이용하여 다음 두 문장을 하나의 문장으로 써 보시오.

> Tom was busy. He couldn't answer the phone.
> The waves were high. We couldn't swim in the sea.

(1) _____

(2) _____

03 한국 민속촌에 관한 다음 글을 읽고 Facts와 Opinions를 구별하시오.

> I want to introduce Korean folk village. It is located in Yongin. It's a fun place in Yongin. There are Korean traditional houses. They are beautiful. Visitors can watch nongak and jultagi. Nongak and jultagi are very exciting to see.

Facts	Opinions

단원별 모의고사

[01~03] 다음 대화를 읽고 물음에 답하시오.

> Jack: Hi, Suji. How did you like your trip to Gyeongju?
> Suji: I was very happy with it.
> Jack: Where did you visit?
> Suji: I visited Cheomseongdae. It was great.
> Jack: Where else did you go?
> Suji: Bulguksa. It was a wonderful place.
> Jack: _____(A)_____
> Suji: Yeah, but walking up to Seokguram was difficult.
> Jack: But I'm sure it was worth it.

01 위 대화의 빈칸 (A)에 들어갈 말로 어색한 것은?

① That sounds great.
② Sounds like the perfect trip.
③ You seem to enjoy it a lot.
④ You seem to like it so much.
⑤ I'm sorry to hear that.

02 위 대화에서 알 수 있는 Suji의 심경으로 적절한 것은?

① disappointed
② satisfied
③ nervous
④ gloomy
⑤ upset

03 How was it to walk up to Seokguram for Suji?

➡ _____

[04~06] 다음 대화를 읽고 물음에 답하시오.

> W: May I help you?
> B: Yes. I'm looking for a backpack. Can you ____(A)____ one?
> W: How about this red one? Red is the most popular color these days.
> B: My old backpack was red, so I want a different color.
> W: _____(B)_____ It has side pockets.
> B: Oh, that looks good. I'll take it.

04 위 대화의 빈칸 (A)에 들어갈 수 있는 단어를 고르시오.

① watch
② guess
③ recommend
④ advise
⑤ introduce

05 위 대화의 빈칸 (B)에 들어갈 말로 어색한 것은?

① How about this navy one?
② I recommend this navy one.
③ What about this navy one?
④ Why don't you choose this navy one?
⑤ How was this navy one?

06 위 대화의 내용과 일치하도록 소년의 일기의 빈칸을 완성하시오.

> Mon, Nov 4th, 2019
> I was excited because I bought the new backpack. I used to wear the (A)_____ color backpack, so I wanted to buy (B)_____. The clerk recommended (C)_____, which had (D)_____. I liked it a lot and bought it. I'm looking forward to wearing the new backpack tomorrow.

[07~09] 다음 대화를 읽고 물음에 답하시오.

> Sue: Tom, you got a new smartphone.
> Tom: Yes, I did. I'm really happy with it.
> Sue: What do you like most about it?
> Tom: I love the camera. It takes great pictures.

07 What are Tom and Sue talking about?

➡ _____

08 How does Tom like his new smartphone?

➡ _____

09 What does Tom like most about his smartphone?

➡ _____

[10~11] 다음 대화를 읽고 물음에 답하시오.

> Brian: Mina, can you recommend a good pizza restaurant?
> Mina: Why don't you try Antonio's? It's my ⓐ <u>favorite</u>.
> Brian: What do you like about it?
> Mina: The food is delicious. I recommend the bulgogi pizza.
> Brian: How are the prices?
> Mina: I think the prices are good, too.
> Brian: ⓑ<u>Sounds</u> like a good restaurant. How do you like the service?
> Mina: It's ⓒ<u>a little</u> slow on the weekends.
> Brian: Okay. I'll ⓓ<u>check out it</u>. Thanks.
> Mina: No problem. ⓔ<u>Enjoy</u> your meal!

10 위 대화의 밑줄 친 ⓐ~ⓔ 중 어법상 어색한 것을 찾아 바르게 고치시오.

➡ _____

11 위 대화를 읽고 대답할 수 <u>없는</u> 질문은?

① What is Mina's favorite restaurant?
② What food did Mina recommend Brian to try at Antonio's?
③ How was the price of Antonio's?
④ When was the service of Antonio's slow?
⑤ How much was the bulgogi pizza at Antonio's?

12 다음 우리말에 맞게 주어진 단어를 사용하여 영작하시오.

(1) 버터를 설탕과 함께 섞으세요. (mix)

➡ _____

(2) Jack이 의자를 들어 올렸다. (lifted)

➡ _____

(3) 너는 진실을 말하고 있니? (telling)

➡ _____

13 다음 중 의미가 <u>다른</u> 하나는?

① It was so fine that we went out.
② We went out because of the fine weather.
③ It was fine, so we went out.
④ It was too fine for us to go out.
⑤ As it was fine, we went out.

14 다음 중 쓰임이 <u>다른</u> 하나는?

① The doll <u>that</u> Rose carries around all the time is made by her mother.
② I know the fact <u>that</u> she doesn't trust anyone.
③ The vase <u>that</u> the boy broke was not expensive.
④ The paper <u>that</u> Danny tore into pieces was an important document.
⑤ Who is the woman <u>that</u> Lisa is talking to?

15 주어진 단어를 활용하여 다음 우리말을 영어로 쓰시오.

> 그의 연설은 너무 유명해서 모두가 그것에 관해 알았다. (speech / that)

➡ _____

16 다음 중 어법상 바르지 <u>않은</u> 것은?

① Are these the keys you lost the other day?
② Is there anything that I can do for you?
③ The dog is so smart that everyone loves him.
④ What is the name of the movie that you are going to see?
⑤ The women whom I work with in the office is friendly.

17 주어진 문장과 같은 의미의 문장을 아홉 단어로 이루어진 한 문장으로 쓰시오.

> My mouth is frozen because it is so cold.

➡ _____

[18~23] 다음 글을 읽고 물음에 답하시오.

Emma: What are you doing, Kyle?
Kyle: ① _____
Emma: ② _____
Kyle: ③ _____
Emma: ④ _____
Kyle: I'm so mad. The movie advertisement said that it was "The Most Exciting Movie of the Year."
Emma: Well, you can't believe everything that you read.
Kyle: They lied on the advertisement. I'm going to ask for my money back.

Emma: Hold ___ⓐ___, Kyle! They didn't really ⓑlie because they used opinions, not facts.
Kyle: Huh? (A)I'm not following you.
Emma: Opinions express people's feelings like, "The desert is beautiful." You can't say (B)that it's true or not. But, facts can be ⓒproven. For example, "The Atacama Desert is in Chile," is a fact. You can check that on the map.
Kyle: Okay.... But what's the (C)connection with movies?
Emma: Let me explain. What's ⓓyour favorite movie?
Kyle: It's *Forrest Gump*.
Emma: Okay. Let's ⓔlook for its advertisement. What does (D)it say?
Kyle: It says, "Winner of 6 Academy Awards (E)including Best Picture."
Emma: See? It uses facts ⓕlike the *Y-Men 7* advertisement. Do you see the difference?

18 자연스러운 대화가 되도록 ①~④에 들어갈 말을 바르게 나열한 것은?

> ⓐ How is it?
> ⓑ I'm sorry to hear that.
> ⓒ Oh, Emma. I'm watching the movie, *Y-Men 7* on my computer.
> ⓓ Don't ask. It's so boring that I want to cry.

① ⓑ - ⓐ - ⓓ - ⓒ
② ⓑ - ⓓ - ⓒ - ⓐ
③ ⓒ - ⓐ - ⓓ - ⓑ
④ ⓒ - ⓑ - ⓐ - ⓓ
⑤ ⓓ - ⓑ - ⓐ - ⓒ

19 빈칸 ⓐ에 들어갈 말로 가장 적절한 것은?

① in ② at ③ by ④ on ⑤ out

20 다음 중 위 글의 내용과 일치하는 것은?

① It is hard to prove facts.

② Ads always tell lies about their products.

③ We had better believe everything that we read.

④ It is not allowed to use opinions in ads.

⑤ People who advertise products use not only facts but also opinions.

21 다음 중 (A)~(E)에 관한 설명으로 바르지 않은 것은?

① (A): 'I can't understand you.'로 바꾸어 쓸 수 있다.

② (B): 접속사로 동사 say의 목적어가 되는 명사절을 이끌고 있다.

③ (C): the way in which two things are related to each other로 풀이되는 말이다.

④ (D): "Forest Gump"를 가리키는 대명사이다.

⑤ (E): '~을 포함하여'라는 의미의 전치사이다.

22 밑줄 친 ⓑ~ⓕ 중 내용상 어색한 것을 골라 바르게 고치시오.

➡ _____

23 글의 내용에 맞게 빈칸에 알맞은 말을 쓰시오.

According to the passage, if something can be proven, it is a _____. However, if it is hard to say something is true or not, you can say it is _____ _____.

[24~25] 다음 글을 읽고 물음에 답하시오.

Charlotte's Web is a children's novel. It was written by E. B. White. A little pig named Wilbur is the main character of the book. When Wilbur is in danger, his friend Charlotte helps him out. I especially like the friendship of Wilbur and Charlotte. The book was so touching that I read it many times. I strongly recommend it to everyone.

24 Which is NOT true about the passage?

① The writer of the book is E. B. White.

② Wilbur is the name of the main character.

③ Wilbur and Charlotte are friends.

④ Charlotte ignores Wilbur when he is in danger.

⑤ The writer read the book many times.

25 위 글의 표현을 이용하여 다음 우리말을 영어로 쓰시오.

내가 읽은 책은 너무 감동적이어서 나는 그것을 너에게 추천하고 싶어.

➡ The book _____
   I want to _____.

INSIGHT
on the textbook
교과서 파헤치기

※ 다음 영어를 우리말로 쓰시오.

01 arrow _____

02 neighborhood _____

03 appear _____

04 dark _____

05 solve _____

06 decorate _____

07 far _____

08 firework _____

09 follow _____

10 gather _____

11 shape _____

12 amazing _____

13 huge _____

14 last _____

15 advertise _____

16 competition _____

17 festival _____

18 sled _____

19 almost _____

20 completely _____

21 post _____

22 musician _____

23 celebrate _____

24 outdoor _____

25 chase _____

26 pile _____

27 artwork _____

28 powder _____

29 adult _____

30 colorful _____

31 hold _____

32 throw _____

33 hometown _____

34 bakery _____

35 each other _____

36 out of hand _____

37 from beginning to end _____

38 between A and B _____

39 go on _____

40 because of _____

41 more and more _____

42 on one's right _____

43 in front of _____

※ 다음 우리말을 영어로 쓰시오.

01 빵집, 제과점

02 축하하다, 기념하다

03 형형색색의

04 페레이드, 행진

05 (시간이) 걸리다

06 ～ 동안

07 돛

08 예술 작품

09 뒤쫓다

10 개최하다

11 고향

12 배, 선박

13 가로지르다

14 라이브의, 실황인

15 가까운, 가까이에 있는

16 가루

17 야외의

18 블록, 구획

19 더미

20 성인, 어른

21 던지다

22 장식하다

23 모이다, 모으다

24 광고하다

25 해결하다

26 지속하다

27 나타나다

28 근처, 이웃, 인근

29 대회, 시합, 경쟁

30 불꽃놀이

31 거대한

32 화살

33 완전히

34 따르다

35 더욱 더

36 내리다

37 서로

38 ～ 앞에

39 ～ 때문에

40 ～ 옆에

41 지속되다, 계속되다

42 A와 B 사이에

43 처음부터 끝까지

Step3

※ 다음 영영풀이에 알맞은 단어를 <보기>에서 골라 쓴 후, 우리말 뜻을 쓰시오.

1 _____ : to move something or someone to a higher position: _____

2 _____ : a fully grown person: _____

3 _____ : to follow and try to catch: _____

4 _____ : objects produced by artists: _____

5 _____ : an event or contest in which people compete: _____

6 _____ : a day or period of celebration: _____

7 _____ : a small vehicle used for sliding over snow: _____

8 _____ : to continue in time: _____

9 _____ : the city or town where you were born or grew up: _____

10 _____ : to come together to form a group: _____

11 _____ : to have a meeting, competition, conversation, etc.: _____

12 _____ : a mass of something that has been placed somewhere: _____

13 _____ : to tell the public about goods to make people buy them: _____

14 _____ : to make something into a particular shape: _____

15 _____ : to do something special for an important event, holiday, etc.: _____

16 _____ : to make something look more beautiful by putting things on it: _____

보기			
sled	chase	artwork	lift
decorate	pile	hometown	competition
adult	celebrate	advertise	last
shape	hold	gather	festival

※ 다음 우리말과 일치하도록 빈칸에 알맞은 말을 쓰시오.

Listen and Speak 1-A

Sora: Excuse me. _____ _____ _____ _____ _____ _____ _____?

Tom: Oh, the library? _____ the street and _____ _____ two blocks. Then _____ _____ _____.

Sora: _____ _____ very much.

Sora: 실례합니다. 도서관까지 어떻게 가나요?
Tom: 아, 도서관이요? 길을 건너서 두 구역을 곧장 가세요. 그런 다음 왼쪽으로 도세요.
Sora: 정말 고마워요.

Listen and Speak 1-B

(*A phone rings.*)

Minsu: Hi, Emma. _____ _____?

Emma: Hey, Minsu. _____ you _____ _____ _____?

Minsu: Yes. _____ _____ you _____?

Emma: Well, how _____ _____ _____ together?

Minsu: Sure.

Emma: _____ _____ the new _____ _____, Ming's. It's _____ the school.

Minsu: Okay. _____ _____ _____ _____ _____ _____ _____ _____ _____?

Emma: _____ _____ from the school and _____ _____ to Green Street. _____ _____ _____, and the restaurant will _____ _____ _____ _____ _____.

Minsu: _____ _____. _____ _____ _____ 12 o'clock.

Emma: Wonderful. _____ _____ _____.

(전화벨이 울린다.)
Minsu: 안녕, Emma. 잘 지내니?
Emma: 안녕, 민수야. 이번 토요일에 한가하니?
Minsu: 응. 왜 묻는 거니?
Emma: 음, 함께 점심 먹는 게 어떠니?
Minsu: 좋아.
Emma: Ming's라는 새로 생긴 중국 음식점에 가 보자. 학교 근처에 있어.
Minsu: 좋아. 학교에서 거기까지 어떻게 가니?
Emma: 학교에서 나와서 Green Street 까지 곧장 가. 왼쪽으로 돌면 음식점이 네 왼쪽에 있을 거야.
Minsu: 알겠어. 12시에 만나자.
Emma: 좋아. 그때 보자.

Listen and Speak 1-C

A: _____ _____. How _____ I _____ _____ _____ the post office?

B: _____ _____ to 1st Street and _____ _____ _____. It _____ _____ _____ _____ _____.

A: _____ it _____ _____ here?

B: _____, it's _____.

A: _____ _____ very much.

A: 실례합니다. 우체국에 어떻게 갈 수 있나요?
B: 1st Street까지 곧장 가서 오른쪽으로 도세요. 그것은 오른쪽에 있을 거예요.
A: 여기서 먼가요?
B: 아니요, 멀지 않아요.
A: 정말 고마워요.

Listen and Speak 2-A

Amy: Jinho, _____ _____. We're _____ _____ _____ _____ the movie.

Jinho: Okay. _____ _____ _____ _____ _____ _____ _____ _____ _____ _____ _____ _____?

Amy: It will _____ _____ 15 minutes _____ _____.

Jinho: All right. I'm _____ _____.

Amy: 진호야, 서둘러. 우리 영화 시간에 늦겠어.

Jinho: 응. 영화관까지 가는 데 시간이 얼마나 걸릴까?

Amy: 버스로 대략 15분 정도 걸릴 거야.

Jinho: 알겠어. 나 거의 준비됐어.

Listen and Speak 2-B

Andy: I'm so _____ _____ the school festival _____ _____.

Mike: _____, _____. What _____ we _____ _____ _____ it, Andy?

Andy: How _____ _____ posters?

Mike: Great idea. We _____ _____ _____ _____ in our _____.

Andy: Right. _____ _____ _____ _____ _____ _____ _____ make them?

Mike: Well, it will _____ _____ _____ _____ _____.

Andy: Okay, _____ _____ many people _____ _____.

Andy: 나는 이번 금요일 학교 축제가 정말 기대돼.

Mike: 나도. 축제를 광고하기 위해 무엇을 할 수 있을까, Andy?

Andy: 포스터를 만들면 어떨까?

Mike: 좋은 생각이야. 이 근방에 포스터를 붙일 수 있겠다.

Andy: 맞아. 포스터를 만드는 데 시간이 얼마나 걸릴까?

Mike: 음, 대략 세 시간 정도 걸릴 거야.

Andy: 좋아. 많은 사람들이 축제에 왔으면 좋겠다.

Real Life Talk

Man: _____ me. _____ — _____ I _____ _____ Suwon Hwaseong from here?

Mina: It's _____. Do you see the bus stop _____ _____?

Man: Yes, _____ _____.

Mina: _____ the No. 11 bus and _____ _____ at the sixth stop.

Man: _____ _____ _____ _____ _____ _____ _____ _____ _____?

Mina: It will _____ _____ _____ _____.

Man: Thank you _____ _____.

Mina: No _____. _____ you _____ there for _____ _____?

Man: Yes. I heard _____ _____ _____ _____ _____.

Mina: _____ _____ you _____ _____ _____.

Man: 실례합니다. 여기에서 수원 화성까지 어떻게 가나요?

Mina: 쉬워요. 저쪽에 버스 정류장 보이세요?

Man: 네, 보여요.

Mina: 11번 버스를 타서 여섯 번째 정류장에서 내리세요.

Man: 그곳까지 가는 데 시간이 얼마나 걸릴까요?

Mina: 대략 20분 정도 걸릴 거예요.

Man: 정말 고마워요.

Mina: 별말씀을요. 그곳에 축제 때문에 가시는 건가요?

Man: 네. 그 축제가 무척 재미있다고 들었어요.

Mina: 즐거운 시간 보내길 바라요.

※ 다음 우리말에 맞도록 대화를 영어로 쓰시오.

Listen and Speak 1-A

Sora: _____

Tom: _____

Sora: _____

Sora: 실례합니다. 도서관까지 어떻게 가나요?

Tom: 아, 도서관이요? 길을 건너서 두 구역을 곧장 가세요. 그런 다음 왼쪽으로 도세요.

Sora: 정말 고마워요.

Listen and Speak 1-B

(*A phone rings.*)

Minsu: _____

Emma: _____

Minsu: _____

Emma: _____

Minsu: _____

Emma: _____

Minsu: _____

Emma: _____
_____

Minsu: _____

Emma: _____

(전화벨이 울린다.)

Minsu: 안녕, Emma. 잘 지내니?

Emma: 안녕, 민수야. 이번 토요일에 한가하니?

Minsu: 응. 왜 묻는 거니?

Emma: 음, 함께 점심 먹는 게 어떠니?

Minsu: 좋아.

Emma: Ming's라는 새로 생긴 중국 음식점에 가 보자. 학교 근처에 있어.

Minsu: 좋아. 학교에서 거기까지 어떻게 가니?

Emma: 학교에서 나와서 Green Street까지 곧장 가. 왼쪽으로 돌면 음식점이 네 왼쪽에 있을 거야.

Minsu: 알겠어. 12시에 만나자.

Emma: 좋아. 그때 보자.

Listen and Speak 1-C

A: _____

B: _____

A: _____

B: _____

A: _____

A: 실례합니다. 우체국에 어떻게 갈 수 있나요?

B: 1st Street까지 곧장 가서 오른쪽으로 도세요. 그것은 오른쪽에 있을 거예요.

A: 여기서 먼가요?

B: 아니요, 멀지 않아요.

A: 정말 고마워요.

Listen and Speak 2-A

Amy: _____

Jinho: _____

Amy: _____

Jinho: _____

Amy: 진호야, 서둘러. 우리 영화 시간에 늦겠어.
Jinho: 응. 영화관까지 가는 데 시간이 얼마나 걸릴까?
Amy: 버스로 대략 15분 정도 걸릴 거야.
Jinho: 알겠어. 나 거의 준비됐어.

Listen and Speak 2-B

Andy: _____

Mike: _____

Andy: _____

Mike: _____

Andy: _____

Mike: _____

Andy: _____

Andy: 나는 이번 금요일 학교 축제가 정말 기대돼.
Mike: 나도. 축제를 광고하기 위해 무엇을 할 수 있을까, Andy?
Andy: 포스터를 만들면 어떨까?
Mike: 좋은 생각이야. 이 근방에 포스터를 붙일 수 있겠다.
Andy: 맞아. 포스터를 만드는 데 시간이 얼마나 걸릴까?
Mike: 음, 대략 세 시간 정도 걸릴 거야.
Andy: 좋아, 많은 사람들이 축제에 왔으면 좋겠다.

Real Life Talk

Man: _____

Mina: _____

Man: _____

Mina: _____

Man: _____

Mina: _____

Man: _____

Mina: _____

Man: _____

Mina: _____

Man: 실례합니다. 여기에서 수원 화성까지 어떻게 가나요?
Mina: 쉬워요. 저쪽에 버스 정류장 보이세요?
Man: 네, 보여요.
Mina: 11번 버스를 타서 여섯 번째 정류장에서 내리세요.
Man: 그곳까지 가는 데 시간이 얼마나 걸릴까요?
Mina: 대략 20분 정도 걸릴 거예요.
Man: 정말 고마워요.
Mina: 별말씀을요. 그곳에 축제 때문에 가시는 건가요?
Man: 네. 그 축제가 무척 재미있다고 들었어요.
Mina: 즐거운 시간 보내길 바라요.

※ 다음 우리말과 일치하도록 빈칸에 알맞은 것을 골라 쓰시오.

1 Holi, the _____ of _____

A. Colors   B. Festival

2 Amala _____ _____, India

A. from   B. Delhi

3 Holi is the _____ _____ festival in _____ country.

A. popular   B. my   C. most

4 It _____ _____ _____ March.

A. usually   B. is   C. in

5 _____ the festival, we _____ goodbye to cold winter and _____ to warm spring.

A. say   B. during   C. hello

6 We _____ the festival _____ _____ two days.

A. everywhere   B. for   C. celebrate

7 _____ the first day, people _____ _____ a big fire _____ night and sing and dance.

A. around   B. at   C. on   D. gather

8 The _____ event _____ the _____ day.

A. next   B. main   C. begins

9 Children and adults _____ _____ _____ with *gulal*.

A. each   B. chase   C. other

10 _____ is *gulal*? It is blue, yellow, _____ and pink _____.

A. powder   B. what   C. green

11 It's a lot of fun to _____ _____ and _____ colorful powder _____ everyone.

A. throw   B. run   C. at   D. around

12 We _____ _____ street _____!

A. join   B. parades   C. also

13 _____ _____ Festival

A. Nights   B. White

14 Victor _____ St. _____, _____

A. Russia   B. Petersburg   C. from

15 _____ you _____ _____ the *White Nights*?

A. heard   B. have   C. of

16 _____ summer, this _____ thing _____ in my hometown.

A. amazing   B. every   C. happens

1 홀리, 색의 축제

2 인도, 델리의 Amala

3 '홀리'는 우리나라에서 가장 인기 있는 축제예요.

4 그것은 보통 3월에 있어요.

5 축제 기간 동안에, 우리는 추운 겨울에게 작별 인사를 하고 따뜻한 봄을 맞는 인사를 해요.

6 우리는 이틀 동안 어디서든 축제를 기념해요.

7 첫째 날, 사람들은 밤에 큰 모닥불 주변에 모여 노래하고 춤을 춰요.

8 주요 행사는 다음 날에 시작돼요.

9 어린이들과 어른들이 'gulal'을 지니고 서로를 쫓아다녀요.

10 'gulal'이 무엇이냐고요? 그것은 파랑, 노랑, 초록, 분홍의 가루예요.

11 주변을 뛰어다니며 형형색색의 가루를 모든 사람들에게 던지는 것은 정말 재미있어요.

12 우리는 거리 행진에도 참가해요!

13 백야 축제

14 러시아, 상트페테르부르크의 Victor

15 '백야'에 대해 들어 봤나요?

16 매년 여름, 이 놀라운 일이 나의 고향에서 벌어져요.

17 The night sky does not _____ _____ _____ .
A. completely   B. get   C. dark

18 _____ that time, we _____ the White Nights Festival.
A. hold   B. during

19 It usually starts _____ May and _____ for _____ a month.
A. lasts   B. about   C. in

20 During the festival, _____ is a ballet or an opera _____ _____ night.
A. every   B. there   C. almost

21 The _____ _____ event is the Scarlet Sails _____ .
A. celebration   B. popular   C. most

22 A boat _____ red sails slowly _____ _____ the river.
A. appears   B. with   C. on

23 Soon, fireworks _____ and a water show _____ .
A. follows   B. begin

24 You can _____ _____ musicians _____ beautiful live music.
A. playing   B. hear   C. also

25 _____ Snow _____
A. Festival   B. Kiruna

26 Ebba _____ _____ , Sweden
A. Kiruna   B. from

27 Winter is my _____ season _____ the Kiruna Snow Festival.
A. because   B. favorite   C. of

28 The festival _____ in the _____ week of January and _____ _____ for five or six days.
A. on   B. last   C. goes   D. starts

29 The _____ _____ is the snow design _____ .
A. competition   B. event   C. largest

30 The artists _____ huge piles of snow _____ animals, buildings, and _____ beautiful artworks.
A. shape   B. other   C. into

31 People _____ the artists _____ their works beginning _____ end.
A. shaping   B. to   C. from   D. watch

32 My favorite _____ is the dog _____ .
A. sled   B. activity   C. ride

33 It is amazing _____ fly _____ a world of snow _____ a dog sled.
A. on   B. through   C. to

---

17 밤하늘이 완전히 어두워지지 않아요.

18 그 시기 동안, 우리는 백야 축제를 열어요.

19 축제는 보통 5월에 시작되고 약 한 달 동안 지속돼요.

20 축제 기간 동안 거의 매일 밤 발레나 오페라 공연이 있어요.

21 가장 인기 있는 행사는 '붉은 돛 축하 행사'예요.

22 빨간 돛을 단 배가 강 위에 서서히 나타나요.

23 곧 불꽃놀이가 시작되고 물 쇼가 이어져요.

24 또한 여러분은 음악가들이 아름다운 라이브 음악을 연주하는 것을 들을 수 있어요.

25 키루나 눈 축제

26 스웨덴, 키루나의 Ebba

27 겨울은 키루나 눈 축제 때문에 내가 가장 좋아하는 계절이에요.

28 축제는 1월 마지막 주에 시작해서 5일이나 6일 동안 계속돼요.

29 가장 큰 행사는 '눈 디자인 대회'예요.

30 미술가들이 거대한 눈 덩어리를 동물, 건물, 다른 아름다운 작품의 모양으로 만들어요.

31 사람들은 미술가들이 그들의 작품을 만드는 것을 처음부터 끝까지 지켜봐요.

32 내가 가장 좋아하는 활동은 개썰매 타기예요.

33 개썰매를 타고 눈 세상을 날아가는 것은 정말 놀라워요.

※ 다음 우리말과 일치하도록 빈칸에 알맞은 말을 쓰시오.

1 Holi, the _____ _____ _____

2 Amala _____ _____, _____

3 Holi is _____ _____ _____ _____ in my country.

4 It _____ _____ _____ _____.

5 _____ the festival, we _____ _____ to cold winter and

_____ to _____ _____.

6 We _____ the festival everywhere _____ _____ _____.

7 _____ the first day, people _____ _____ a big fire

_____ _____ and _____ _____ _____.

8 The _____ event _____ _____ _____ _____.

9 Children and adults _____ _____ _____ _____ _____ _____ *gulal*.

10 _____ is *gulal*? It is blue, yellow, green and pink _____.

11 It's a lot of fun _____ _____ _____ and _____ colorful

powder _____ _____.

12 We _____ _____ _____ _____ _____!

13 _____ _____ Festival

14 Victor _____ St. Petersburg, _____

15 _____ _____ _____ _____ _____ the *White Nights*?

16 Every summer, this _____ thing _____ in my hometown.

1 홀리, 색의 축제

2 인도, 델리의 Amala

3 '홀리'는 우리나라에서 가장 인기 있는 축제예요.

4 그것은 보통 3월에 있어요.

5 축제 기간 동안에, 우리는 추운 겨울에게 작별 인사를 하고 따뜻한 봄을 맞는 인사를 해요.

6 우리는 이틀 동안 어디서든 축제를 기념해요.

7 첫째 날, 사람들은 밤에 큰 모닥불 주변에 모여 노래하고 춤을 춰요.

8 주요 행사는 다음 날에 시작돼요.

9 어린이들과 어른들이 'gulal'을 지니고 서로를 쫓아다녀요.

10 'gulal'이 무엇이냐고요? 그것은 파랑, 노랑, 초록, 분홍의 가루예요.

11 주변을 뛰어다니며 형형색색의 가루를 모든 사람들에게 던지는 것은 정말 재미있어요.

12 우리는 거리 행진에도 참가해요!

13 백야 축제

14 러시아, 상트페테르부르크의 Victor

15 '백야'에 대해 들어 봤나요?

16 매년 여름, 이 놀라운 일이 나의 고향에서 벌어져요.

17 The night sky _____ _____ _____ _____ _____.

18 _____ that time, we _____ the White Nights Festival.

19 It _____ _____ _____ May and _____ _____ _____ a month.

20 _____ the festival, _____ _____ a ballet or an opera _____ _____ _____.

21 The _____ _____ event is the Scarlet Sails _____.

22 A boat with red sails slowly _____ _____ _____ _____.

23 Soon, _____ _____ and a water show _____.

24 You can _____ _____ musicians _____ beautiful live music.

25 Kiruna _____ _____

26 Ebba _____ _____, _____

27 Winter is _____ _____ _____ _____ _____ _____ the Kiruna Snow Festival.

28 The festival _____ _____ _____ _____ _____ of January and _____ _____ _____ five or six days.

29 _____ _____ _____ is the snow design _____.

30 The artists _____ _____ _____ of snow _____ animals, buildings, and _____ beautiful artworks.

31 People _____ the artists _____ their works _____ _____ _____ _____.

32 My _____ _____ is the _____ _____ _____.

33 _____ is _____ _____ _____ _____ a world of snow _____ a dog sled.

17 밤하늘이 완전히 어두워지지 않아요.

18 그 시기 동안, 우리는 백야 축제를 열어요.

19 축제는 보통 5월에 시작되고 약 한 달 동안 지속돼요.

20 축제 기간 동안 거의 매일 밤 발레나 오페라 공연이 있어요.

21 가장 인기 있는 행사는 '붉은 돛 축하 행사'예요.

22 빨간 돛을 단 배가 강 위에 서서히 나타나요.

23 곧 불꽃놀이가 시작되고 물 쇼가 이어져요.

24 또한 여러분은 음악가들이 아름다운 라이브 음악을 연주하는 것을 들을 수 있어요.

25 키루나 눈 축제

26 스웨덴, 키루나의 Ebba

27 겨울은 키루나 눈 축제 때문에 내가 가장 좋아하는 계절이에요.

28 축제는 1월 마지막 주에 시작해서 5일이나 6일 동안 계속돼요.

29 가장 큰 행사는 '눈 디자인 대회'예요.

30 미술가들이 거대한 눈 덩어리를 동물, 건물, 다른 아름다운 작품의 모양으로 만들어요.

31 사람들은 미술가들이 그들의 작품을 만드는 것을 처음부터 끝까지 지켜봐요.

32 내가 가장 좋아하는 활동은 개썰매 타기예요.

33 개썰매를 타고 눈 세상을 날아가는 것은 정말 놀라워요.

※ 다음 문장을 우리말로 쓰시오.

1 ▷ Holi, the Festival of Colors

➡ _____

2 ▷ Amala from Delhi, India

➡ _____

3 ▷ Holi is the most popular festival in my country.

➡ _____

4 ▷ It is usually in March.

➡ _____

5 ▷ During the festival, we say goodbye to cold winter and hello to warm spring.

➡ _____

6 ▷ We celebrate the festival everywhere for two days.

➡ _____

7 ▷ On the first day, people gather around a big fire at night and sing and dance.

➡ _____

8 ▷ The main event begins the next day.

➡ _____

9 ▷ Children and adults chase each other with *gulal*.

➡ _____

10 ▷ What is *gulal*? It is blue, yellow, green and pink powder.

➡ _____

11 ▷ It's a lot of fun to run around and throw colorful powder at everyone.

➡ _____

12 ▷ We also join street parades!

➡ _____

13 ▷ White Nights Festival

➡ _____

14 ▷ Victor from St. Petersburg, Russia

➡ _____

15 ▷ Have you heard of the *White Nights*?

➡ _____

16 ▷ Every summer, this amazing thing happens in my hometown.

➡ _____

17 The night sky does not get completely dark.

➡ _____

18 During that time, we hold the White Nights Festival.

➡ _____

19 It usually starts in May and lasts for about a month.

➡ _____

20 During the festival, there is a ballet or an opera almost every night.

➡ _____

21 The most popular event is the Scarlet Sails celebration.

➡ _____

22 A boat with red sails slowly appears on the river.

➡ _____

23 Soon, fireworks begin and a water show follows.

➡ _____

24 You can also hear musicians playing beautiful live music.

➡ _____

25 Kiruna Snow Festival

➡ _____

26 Ebba from Kiruna, Sweden

➡ _____

27 Winter is my favorite season because of the Kiruna Snow Festival.

➡ _____

28 The festival starts in the last week of January and goes on for five or six days.

➡ _____

29 The largest event is the snow design competition.

➡ _____

30 The artists shape huge piles of snow into animals, buildings, and other beautiful artworks.

➡ _____

31 People watch the artists shaping their works from beginning to end.

➡ _____

32 My favorite activity is the dog sled ride.

➡ _____

33 It is amazing to fly through a world of snow on a dog sled.

➡ _____

※ 다음 괄호 안의 단어들을 우리말에 맞도록 바르게 배열하시오.

1 (the / Colors / Holi, / of / Festival)
➡ _____

2 (from / Amala / India / Delhi,)
➡ _____

3 (is / Holi / most / the / festival / popular / country. / my / in)
➡ _____

4 (is / it / usually / March. / in)
➡ _____

5 (the / during / festival, / say / we / to / goodbye / cold / and / winter / spring. / warm / to / hello)
➡ _____

6 (celebrate / we / festival / the / for / everywhere / days. / two)
➡ _____

7 (the / day, / on / first / people / around / gather / fire / big / a / night / at / and / dance. / and / sing)
➡ _____

8 (main / the / begins / event / day. / next / the)
➡ _____

9 (and / children / chase / adults / other / each / *gulal*. / with)
➡ _____

10 (*gulal*? / is / what // is / it / blue, / green / yellow, / and / powder. / pink)
➡ _____

11 (a / it's / of / lot / fun / run / to / around / and / colorful / throw / everyone. / at / powder)
➡ _____

12 (join / also / we / parades! / street)
➡ _____

13 (Nights / White / Festival)
➡ _____

14 (from / Victor / Russia / St. Petersburg)
➡ _____

15 (you / have / of / heard / *Nights*? / *White* / the)
➡ _____

16 (summer, / every / amazing / this / happens / thing / hometown. / my / in)
➡ _____

1 홀리, 색의 축제

2 인도, 델리의 Amala

3 '홀리'는 우리나라에서 가장 인기 있는 축제예요.

4 그것은 보통 3월에 있어요.

5 축제 기간 동안에, 우리는 추운 겨울에게 작별 인사를 하고 따뜻한 봄을 맞는 인사를 해요.

6 우리는 이틀 동안 어디서든 축제를 기념해요.

7 첫째 날, 사람들은 밤에 큰 모닥불 주변에 모여 노래하고 춤을 춰요.

8 주요 행사는 다음 날에 시작돼요.

9 어린이들과 어른들이 'gulal'을 지니고 서로를 쫓아다녀요.

10 'gulal'이 무엇이냐고요? 그것은 파랑, 노랑, 초록, 분홍의 가루예요.

11 주변을 뛰어다니며 형형색색의 가루를 모든 사람들에게 던지는 것은 정말 재미있어요.

12 우리는 거리 행진에도 참가해요!

13 백야 축제

14 러시아, 상트페테르부르크의 Victor

15 '백야'에 대해 들어 봤나요?

16 매년 여름, 이 놀라운 일이 나의 고향에서 벌어져요.

17 (night / sky / the / not / does / completely / dark. / get)
➡ _____

18 (that / during / time, / hold / we / the / White / Festival. / Nights)
➡ _____

19 (usually / it / in / starts / May / and / for / lasts / about / month. / a)
➡ _____

20 (the / festival, / during / is / there / ballet / a / or / opera / an / night. / every / almost)
➡ _____

21 (most / the / is / event / popular / Scarlet / the / celebration. / Sails)
➡ _____

22 (boat / a / red / with / sails / appears / slowly / river. / the / on)
➡ _____

23 (fireworks / soon, / begin / and / water / a / follows. / show)
➡ _____

24 (can / you / hear / also / playing / musicians / music. / live / beautiful)
➡ _____

25 (Festival / Snow / Kiruna)
➡ _____

26 (from / Sweden / Ebba / Kiruna,)
➡ _____

27 (is / winter / favorite / season / my / of / because / the / Festival. / Snow / Kiruna)
➡ _____

28 (festival / starts / the / in / last / the / week / January / of / and / on / goes / for / days. / six / or / five)
➡ _____
_____

29 (largest / the / event / is / snow / the / competition. / design)
➡ _____

30 (artists / shape / the / piles / huge / snow / of / animals, / into / buildings, / and / artworks. / beautiful / other)
➡ _____
_____

31 (watch / people / artists / the / shaping / works / their / from / end. / to / beginning)
➡ _____
_____

32 (favorite / my / activity / is / dog / the / ride. / sled)
➡ _____

33 (is / it / amazing / fly / to / a / through / world / snow / of / on / sled. / dog / a)
➡ _____

17 밤하늘이 완전히 어두워지지 않아요.

18 그 시기 동안, 우리는 백야 축제를 열어요.

19 축제는 보통 5월에 시작되고 약 한 달 동안 지속돼요.

20 축제 기간 동안 거의 매일 밤 발레나 오페라 공연이 있어요.

21 가장 인기 있는 행사는 '붉은 돛 축하 행사'예요.

22 빨간 돛을 단 배가 강 위에 서서히 나타나요.

23 곧 불꽃놀이가 시작되고 물 쇼가 이어져요.

24 또한 여러분은 음악가들이 아름다운 라이브 음악을 연주하는 것을 들을 수 있어요.

25 키루나 눈 축제

26 스웨덴, 키루나의 Ebba

27 겨울은 키루나 눈 축제 때문에 내가 가장 좋아하는 계절이에요.

28 축제는 1월 마지막 주에 시작해서 5일이나 6일 동안 계속돼요.

29 가장 큰 행사는 '눈 디자인 대회'예요.

30 미술가들이 거대한 눈 덩어리를 동물, 건물, 다른 아름다운 작품의 모양으로 만들어요.

31 사람들은 미술가들이 그들의 작품을 만드는 것을 처음부터 끝까지 지켜봐요.

32 내가 가장 좋아하는 활동은 개썰매 타기예요.

33 개썰매를 타고 눈 세상을 날아가는 것은 정말 놀라워요.

※ 다음 우리말을 영어로 쓰시오.

1 홀리, 색의 축제

➡ _____

2 인도, 델리의 Amala

➡ _____

3 '홀리'는 우리나라에서 가장 인기 있는 축제예요.

➡ _____

4 그것은 보통 3월에 있어요.

➡ _____

5 축제 기간 동안에, 우리는 추운 겨울에게 작별 인사를 하고 따뜻한 봄을 맞는 인사를 해요.

➡ _____

6 우리는 이틀 동안 어디서든 축제를 기념해요.

➡ _____

7 첫째 날, 사람들은 밤에 큰 모닥불 주변에 모여 노래하고 춤을 춰요.

➡ _____

8 주요 행사는 다음 날에 시작돼요.

➡ _____

9 어린이들과 어른들이 'gulal'을 지니고 서로를 쫓아다녀요.

➡ _____

10 'gulal'이 무엇이냐고요? 그것은 파랑, 노랑, 초록, 분홍의 가루예요.

➡ _____

11 주변을 뛰어다니며 형형색색의 가루를 모든 사람들에게 던지는 것은 정말 재미있어요.

➡ _____

12 우리는 거리 행진에도 참가해요!

➡ _____

13 백야 축제

➡ _____

14 러시아, 상트페테르부르크의 Victor

➡ _____

15 '백야'에 대해 들어 봤나요?

➡ _____

16 매년 여름, 이 놀라운 일이 나의 고향에서 벌어져요.

➡ _____

17 밤하늘이 완전히 어두워지지 않아요.

➡ _____

18 그 시기 동안, 우리는 백야 축제를 열어요.

➡ _____

19 축제는 보통 5월에 시작되고 약 한 달 동안 지속돼요.

➡ _____

20 축제 기간 동안 거의 매일 밤 발레나 오페라 공연이 있어요.

➡ _____

21 가장 인기 있는 행사는 '붉은 돛 축하 행사'예요.

➡ _____

22 빨간 돛을 단 배가 강 위에 서서히 나타나요.

➡ _____

23 곧 불꽃놀이가 시작되고 물 쇼가 이어져요.

➡ _____

24 또한 여러분은 음악가들이 아름다운 라이브 음악을 연주하는 것을 들을 수 있어요.

➡ _____

25 키루나 눈 축제

➡ _____

26 스웨덴, 키루나의 Ebba

➡ _____

27 겨울은 키루나 눈 축제 때문에 내가 가장 좋아하는 계절이에요.

➡ _____

28 축제는 1월 마지막 주에 시작해서 5일이나 6일 동안 계속돼요.

➡ _____

29 가장 큰 행사는 '눈 디자인 대회'예요.

➡ _____

30 미술가들이 거대한 눈 덩어리를 동물, 건물, 다른 아름다운 작품의 모양으로 만들어요.

➡ _____

31 사람들은 미술가들이 그들의 작품을 만드는 것을 처음부터 끝까지 지켜봐요.

➡ _____

32 내가 가장 좋아하는 활동은 개썰매 타기예요.

➡ _____

33 개썰매를 타고 눈 세상을 날아가는 것은 정말 놀라워요.

➡ _____

※ 다음 우리말과 일치하도록 빈칸에 알맞은 말을 쓰시오.

Listen and Speak 2 - C

1. A: Chris, what _____ you _____ for the _____ _____?

2. B: I'll _____ _____.

3. A: Great idea. _____ _____ will it _____ _____ make them?

4. B: _____ it'll _____ _____ _____ _____.

1. A: Chris, 학급 파티를 위해 무엇을 할 거니?
2. B: 나는 샌드위치를 만들 거야.
3. A: 좋은 생각이야. 그것들을 만드는 데 얼마가 걸릴까?
4. B: 아마도 약 한 시간 정도 걸릴 거야.

Think and Write

1. I _____ Gangneung

2. I _____ _____ Gangneung.

3. _____ _____ beautiful beaches in my _____.

4. It's _____ _____ _____ fun _____ _____ at the beach.

5. There is a _____ _____ _____ Gangneung.

6. It _____ _____ Ojukheon. Yulgok _____ _____ there.

7. _____ _____ _____ _____ in Gangneung is potato tteok.

8. It is soft and sweet. _____ _____ _____ Gangneung!

1. 강릉이 정말 좋아요
2. 저는 강릉에 살아요.
3. 나의 이웃에는 아름다운 해변들이 있어요.
4. 해변에서 수영하는 것은 정말 재미있어요.
5. 강릉에는 유명한 한옥이 있어요.
6. 그것은 오죽헌이라고 불려요. 율곡이 거기에서 태어났어요.
7. 강릉에서 가장 유명한 음식은 감자떡이에요.
8. 그것은 부드럽고 달콤해요. 와서 강릉을 즐기세요!

Project Culture

1. I want _____ _____ Boryeong Mud Festival.

2. It _____ _____ _____ Daecheon Beach _____ _____.

3. There are _____ _____ _____ _____ in the festival.

4. First, you can _____ _____ _____ Ssireum in mud.

5. Also _____ is fun _____ _____ colorful mud body _____ on your body.

6. _____, there is an _____ _____.

7. You can _____ _____ _____ beautiful musics.

1. 나는 보령 진흙 축제를 소개하고 싶어요.
2. 그것은 7월에 대천 해수욕장에서 열립니다.
3. 축제에는 많은 흥미로운 행사가 있습니다.
4. 우선, 당신은 사람들이 진흙 속에서 씨름하는 것을 볼 수 있어요.
5. 또한 당신의 몸에 형형색색의 진흙을 바르는 것은 재미있어요.
6. 마지막으로, 실외 콘서트가 있습니다.
7. 당신은 음악가들이 아름다운 음악을 연주하는 것을 들을 수 있습니다.

※ 다음 우리말을 영어로 쓰시오.

Listen and Speak 2 - C

1. A: Chris, 학급 파티를 위해 무엇을 할 거니?
➡ _____

2. B: 나는 샌드위치를 만들 거야.
➡ _____

3. A: 좋은 생각이야. 그것들을 만드는 데 얼마가 걸릴까?
➡ _____

4. B: 아마도 약 한 시간 정도 걸릴 거야.
➡ _____

Think and Write

1. 강릉이 정말 좋아요
➡ _____

2. 저는 강릉에 살아요.
➡ _____

3. 나의 이웃에는 아름다운 해변들이 있어요.
➡ _____

4. 해변에서 수영하는 것은 정말 재미있어요.
➡ _____

5. 강릉에는 유명한 한옥이 있어요.
➡ _____

6. 그것은 오죽헌이라고 불려요. 율곡이 거기에서 태어났어요.
➡ _____

7. 강릉에서 가장 유명한 음식은 감자떡이에요.
➡ _____

8. 그것은 부드럽고 달콤해요. 와서 강릉을 즐기세요!
➡ _____

Project Culture

1. 니는 보령 진흙 축제를 소개하고 싶어요.
➡ _____

2. 그것은 7월에 대천 해수욕장에서 열립니다.
➡ _____

3. 그 축제에는 많은 흥미로운 행사가 있습니다.
➡ _____

4. 우선, 당신은 사람들이 진흙 속에서 씨름하는 것을 볼 수 있어요.
➡ _____

5. 또한 당신의 몸에 형형색색의 진흙을 바르는 것은 재미있어요.
➡ _____

6. 마지막으로, 실외 콘서트가 있습니다.
➡ _____

7. 당신은 음악가들이 아름다운 음악을 연주하는 것을 들을 수 있습니다.
➡ _____

※ 다음 영어를 우리말로 쓰시오.

01	inventor		22	following
02	lastly		23	several
03	apply		24	length
04	environment		25	adapt
05	blind		26	necessary
06	promise		27	organization
07	communicate		28	curious
08	similar		29	peel
09	deaf		30	mission
10	average		31	difference
11	decorate		32	slice
12	space		33	electricity
13	outgoing		34	in addition
14	brave		35	miss out
15	exhibition		36	on average
16	although		37	from now on
17	farther		38	be made of
18	friendly		39	get along with
19	include		40	cheer up
20	spread		41	make an invention
21	invention		42	be curious about
			43	be good at

※ 다음 우리말을 영어로 쓰시오.

01	발명	
02	눈이 먼	
03	비슷한	
04	전기	
05	청각 장애가 있는	
06	평균	
07	장식하다	
08	약속하다	
09	발명가	
10	마지막으로	
11	필요한	
12	조직, 단체	
13	(얇게) 썰다, 자르다	
14	환경, 주위의 상황	
15	호기심이 많은, 궁금한	
16	의사소통하다	
17	친절한, 상냥한	
18	이유	
19	태양계	
20	껍질을 벗기다	
21	활발한	

22	나뭇가지, 막대	
23	전시회	
24	용감한	
25	생산하다	
26	임무	
27	(비록) ~이긴 하지만	
28	포함하다	
29	지원하다	
30	다음에 나오는	
31	몇몇의	
32	기간, 길이	
33	적응하다	
34	차이	
35	놓치다	
36	지금부터	
37	~와 잘 지내다	
38	평균적으로	
39	게다가	
40	~로 구성되다	
41	~에 대해 궁금해 하다	
42	기운을 내다, ~을 격려하다	
43	즐거운 시간을 보내다	

※ 다음 영영풀이에 알맞은 단어를 <보기>에서 골라 쓴 후, 우리말 뜻을 쓰시오.

1 _____ : not able to see: _____

2 _____ : the amount of time that something lasts: _____

3 _____ : a task or job that someone is given to do: _____

4 _____ : to cut something into thin pieces: _____

5 _____ : not able to hear anything: _____

6 _____ : to put a layer of something on top of something else: _____

7 _____ : like somebody or something but not exactly the same: _____

8 _____ : to remove the skin from a fruit, vegetable, etc.: _____

9 _____ : the way in which two things are not like each other: _____

10 _____ : the conditions that surround someone or something: _____

11 _____ : one of two equal parts into which something can be divided: _____

12 _____ : a person who has invented something or whose job is inventing things: _____

13 _____ : to change your behavior in order to live in a new situation successfully: _____

14 _____ : a thin piece of wood that has been broken from a tree: _____

15 _____ : to ask formally for something such as a job, admission to a school, etc.: _____

16 _____ : a group such as a club or business that is formed for a particular purpose: _____

보기			
mission	difference	slice	environment
peel	blind	length	apply
half	inventor	organization	adapt
stick	similar	deaf	spread

※ 다음 우리말과 일치하도록 빈칸에 알맞은 말을 쓰시오.

Listen & Speak 1-A

Brian: Do you know _____ _____ _____?

Amy: Um, it _____ _____ a glue stick.

Brian: No, it's a _____ _____.

Amy: Oh, _____ _____ _____ _____ _____?

Brian: Yes, you _____ _____ _____ on the bread _____ it.

Listen & Speak 1-B

Ms. Lee: Hello, class! Jisu is today's speaker for _____ _____ _____. Jisu?

Jisu: Hi, class! Do you know _____ _____ _____ _____? His name is Alexander Graham Bell. Bell was an _____. He _____ _____ _____ sound. _____ did he _____? Yes, the telephone! His mother and wife were _____. So he also _____ _____ _____ for _____ and _____ a school for them.

Listen & Speak 2-A

Jane: This _____ _____. _____ is it _____?

Mike: It's _____ _____ _____.

Jane: Really? May I _____ it?

Mike: Sure, _____ _____ _____ _____.

Listen & Speak 2-B

Tom: Mom, _____ _____ these slippers. I made them _____

_____ _____.

Mom: _____ did you _____ slippers in science class?

Tom: They are _____ _____ _____ _____.

Mom: Then, _____ are they _____?

Tom: You can _____ _____ _____ and _____ _____ _____.

Mom: Oh, so you _____ _____ your room _____ _____

_____?

Tom: Sure. _____ _____ _____ my room, Mom.

Tom: 엄마, 이 슬리퍼를 보세요. 과학 시간에 만들었어요.
Mom: 왜 과학 시간에 슬리퍼를 만들었니?
Tom: 단지 신기 위한 게 아니에요.
Mom: 그럼 용도가 무엇이니?
Tom: 슬리퍼를 신고 바닥을 청소할 수 있어요.
Mom: 오, 그럼 앞으로는 네가 네 방을 청소하겠구나?
Tom: 물론이에요. 제 방은 걱정 마세요, 엄마.

Listen & Speak 2-C

A: Jane, _____ _____ this. It's a meok.

B: I _____ _____ it _____. _____ is it _____?

A: It's _____ _____ _____.

B: Oh, really? That's _____.

A: Jane, 이것 좀 봐. 먹이야.
B: 나는 그것을 전에 본 적이 없어. 용도가 무엇이니?
A: 잉크를 만들기 위한 거야.
B: 오, 정말? 그거 흥미롭다.

Real Life Talk – Step 1

Judy: _____ _____ your weekend, Hojin?

Hojin: I _____ _____ _____ _____. I went to a _____

_____ _____ my brother.

Judy: Did you? I _____ _____ _____ so many interesting things.

Hojin: Yes. _____ _____ this. I bought it there. Do you know

_____ _____ _____?

Judy: Well, I'm _____ _____. What is it?

Hojin: It's a VR headset.

Judy: A VR headset? _____ _____ _____ _____?

Hojin: If you _____ it, you _____ _____ _____ _____.

Judy: _____ cool. May I _____ it?

Hojin: Sure. _____ you _____.

Judy: 주말은 어땠니, 호진아?
Hojin: 즐거운 시간을 보냈어. 남동생과 과학 전시회에 갔었어.
Judy: 그랬니? 흥미로운 것들이 굉장히 많다고 들었어.
Hojin: 응. 이것 좀 봐. 거기에서 샀어. 이게 무엇인지 아니?
Judy: 음, 잘 모르겠어. 뭐니?
Hojin: VR 헤드셋이야.
Judy: VR 헤드셋? 용도가 뭐니?
Hojin: 그것을 쓰면 다른 세상을 경험할 수 있어.
Judy: 멋지다. 내가 써 봐도 될까?
Hojin: 물론이지. 여기 있어.

※ 다음 우리말에 맞도록 대화를 영어로 쓰시오.

Listen & Speak 1-A

Brian: _____

Amy: _____

Brian: _____

Amy: _____

Brian: _____

Brian: 너는 이것이 무엇인지 아니?
Amy: 음, 막대 모양 풀 같아 보여.
Brian: 아니, 막대 모양 버터야.
Amy: 오, 그 안에 버터가 있니?
Brian: 응, 그걸로 빵 위에 버터를 바를 수 있어.

Listen & Speak 1-B

Ms. Lee: _____

Jisu: _____

_____

_____

_____

Ms. Lee: 안녕하세요, 여러분! 지수가 오늘의 물건 가져와서 발표하기의 발표자예요. 지수야?
Jisu: 안녕, 얘들아! 이 사람이 누구인지 아니? 그의 이름은 Alexander Graham Bell이야. Bell은 발명가였어. 그는 소리에 관심이 있었어. 그가 무엇을 발명했지? 맞아, 전화기야! 그의 어머니와 아내는 청각 장애가 있었어. 그래서 그는 청각 장애인들을 위한 몇몇 발명품도 만들었고 그들을 위한 학교를 열었어.

Listen & Speak 2-A

Jane: _____

Mike: _____

Jane: _____

Mike: _____

Jane: 이거 흥미롭게 생겼네. 용도가 뭐야?
Mike: 달걀을 얇게 썰기 위한 거야.
Jane: 정말? 내가 해 봐도 돼?
Mike: 물론이지, 여기 달걀이 있어.

Listen & Speak 2-B

Tom: _____

Mom: _____

Tom: _____

Mom: _____

Tom: _____

Mom: _____

Tom: _____

Tom: 엄마, 이 슬리퍼를 보세요. 과학 시간에 만들었어요.
Mom: 왜 과학 시간에 슬리퍼를 만들었니?
Tom: 단지 신기 위한 게 아니에요.
Mom: 그럼 용도가 무엇이니?
Tom: 슬리퍼를 신고 바닥을 청소할 수 있어요.
Mom: 오, 그럼 앞으로는 네가 네 방을 청소하겠구나?
Tom: 물론이에요. 제 방은 걱정 마세요, 엄마.

Listen & Speak 2-C

A: _____

B: _____

A: _____

B: _____

A: Jane, 이것 좀 봐. 먹이야.
B: 나는 그것을 전에 본 적이 없어. 용도가 무엇이니?
A: 잉크를 만들기 위한 거야.
B: 오, 정말? 그거 흥미롭다.

Real Life Talk – Step 1

Judy: _____

Hojin: _____

Judy: _____

Hojin: _____

Judy: _____

Hojin: _____

Judy: _____

Hojin: _____

Judy: _____

Hojin: _____

Judy: 주말은 어땠니, 호진아?
Hojin: 즐거운 시간을 보냈어. 남동생과 과학 전시회에 갔었어.
Judy: 그랬니? 흥미로운 것들이 굉장히 많다고 들었어.
Hojin: 응. 이것 좀 봐. 거기에서 샀어. 이게 무엇인지 아니?
Judy: 음, 잘 모르겠어. 뭐니?
Hojin: VR 헤드셋이야.
Judy: VR 헤드셋? 용도가 뭐니?
Hojin: 그것을 쓰면 다른 세상을 경험할 수 있어.
Judy: 멋지다. 내가 써 봐도 될까?
Hojin: 물론이지. 여기 있어.

※ 다음 우리말과 일치하도록 빈칸에 알맞은 것을 골라 쓰시오.

1 _____ _____ MARS!

A. on   B. Live

2 Do you want to _____ _____ _____ planet?

A. another   B. on   C. live

3 The Korea Space Organization (KSO) is _____ _____ people _____ go to MARS!

A. for   B. to   C. looking

4 Our mission is _____ _____ a city _____ Mars.

A. build   B. on   C. to

5 We are looking for someone…

who is _____.

who is creative and _____.

who can get _____ with others.

who can _____ to a new environment quickly.

A. adapt   B. curious   C. healthy   D. along

6 _____ _____, _____ us a short video.

A. apply   B. to   C. send

7 The video _____ the answers _____ the _____ questions:

A. following   B. include   C. to   D. must

8 1. _____ do you _____ to _____ to Mars?

A. want   B. go   C. why

2. Do you have a _____ _____ of _____?

A. humor   B. sense   C. good

3. Why are you the _____ person _____ this _____?

A. perfect   B. mission   C. for

9 This is a _____ of a lifetime, _____ don't _____ _____!

A. chance   B. out   C. miss   D. so

10 Mars, _____ _____ _____?

A. Earth   B. Second   C. the

11 _____ there are many books and movies about Mars, no _____ has _____ there _____.

A. one   B. yet   C. although   D. been

12 _____ days, scientists are _____ _____ Mars _____ a new home.

A. as   B. these   C. at   D. looking

13 _____ _____, NASA and some companies are _____ to send people there _____ now.

A. right   B. fact   C. trying   D. in

---

1 화성에서 살아요!

2 다른 행성에서 살고 싶은가요?

3 한국 우주 기구(KSO)는 화성에 갈 사람들을 찾고 있습니다!

4 우리의 임무는 화성에 도시를 세우는 것입니다.

5 우리는 다음과 같은 사람을 찾고 있습니다.

건강한 사람.

창의적이고 호기심이 많은 사람.

다른 사람들과 잘 지낼 수 있는 사람.

새로운 환경에 빨리 적응할 수 있는 사람.

6 지원하려면 우리에게 짧은 동영상을 보내세요.

7 동영상은 다음의 질문에 관한 답을 포함해야 합니다.

8 1. 당신은 왜 화성에 가고 싶은가요?

2. 당신은 유머 감각이 있나요?

3. 왜 당신이 이 임무에 적합한 사람인가요?

9 이것은 일생에 단 한 번뿐인 기회이므로 놓치지 마세요!

10 화성, 제 2의 지구?

11 화성에 관한 많은 책과 영화가 있긴 하지만, 아직 화성에 가 본 사람은 아무도 없다.

12 요즘, 과학자들은 화성을 새로운 거주지로 보고 있다.

13 사실, NASA와 몇몇 회사들은 그곳에 사람들을 보내기 위해 바로 지금도 노력하고 있다.

14 The _____ question is, "Can people _____ _____ Mars?"
A. on   B. live   C. big

15 Many scientists _____ _____ for _____ _____.
A. reasons   B. believe   C. several   D. so

16 First, they _____ _____ there is _____ on Mars.
A. that   B. water   C. think

17 This is great _____ water is _____ _____ all life.
A. for   B. because   C. necessary

18 Second, Mars has _____ _____ to _____ houses and buildings _____.
A. on   B. land   C. build   D. hard

19 Third, the _____ of day and night on Mars is _____ _____ _____ on Earth.
A. similar   B. length   C. to   D. that

20 _____ _____, Mars also _____ four _____.
A. seasons   B. addition   C. has   D. in

21 _____, people can _____ similar _____.
A. lives   B. so   C. lead

22 _____, Mars is not _____ _____.
A. far   B. lastly   C. very

23 It is _____ _____ _____ planet to Earth.
A. second   B. the   C. closest

24 Mars, _____, has some _____ _____ Earth.
A. differences B. from   C. however

25 First, Mars is _____ _____ the _____ of Earth.
A. half   B. size   C. about

26 It is the _____ _____ planet in the _____ _____.
A. solar   B. second   C. smallest   D. system

27 Second, a _____ on Mars is _____ _____ as long _____ a year on Earth.
A. twice   B. as   C. about   D. year

28 Third, Mars is _____ _____ _____ Earth.
A. colder   B. than   C. much

29 _____ _____, it is _____ −60℃ on Mars.
A. about   B. average   C. on

30 This is _____ Mars is _____ _____ from the Sun _____ Earth.
A. farther   B. because   C. than   D. away

31 _____ no one can _____ the big question right now, it is _____ to _____ this new world.
A. answer   B. imagine   C. exciting   D. although

32 Who knows? You could _____ _____ first _____ Mars!
A. Korean   B. on   C. be   D. the

14 중요한 질문은 "화성에서 사람들이 살 수 있는가?"이다.

15 많은 과학자들은 몇몇 이유로 그렇게 믿고 있다.

16 첫째, 그들은 화성에 물이 있다고 생각한다.

17 물은 모든 생명체에 필수적이기 때문에 이것은 중요하다.

18 둘째, 화성은 집과 건물을 지을 수 있는 단단한 땅을 가지고 있다.

19 셋째, 화성의 낮과 밤의 길이는 지구의 낮과 밤의 길이와 비슷하다.

20 게다가, 화성은 사계절도 있다.

21 그래서 사람들이 비슷한 생활을 할 수 있다.

22 마지막으로, 화성은 그렇게 멀지 않다.

23 화성은 지구에서 두 번째로 가까운 행성이다.

24 그러나 화성은 지구와 다른 점이 몇 개 있다.

25 첫째, 화성은 지구의 약 절반 크기이다.

26 화성은 태양계에서 두 번째로 작은 행성이다.

27 둘째, 화성에서의 일 년은 지구에서의 일 년보다 약 두 배 길다.

28 셋째, 화성은 지구보다 훨씬 더 춥다.

29 평균적으로, 화성의 기온은 약 섭씨 영하 60도이다.

30 이것은 화성이 지구보다 태양에서 더 멀리 떨어져 있기 때문이다.

31 비록 누구도 그 중요한 질문에 지금 당장 답할 수는 없지만, 이 새로운 세상을 상상하는 것은 신이 난다.

32 누가 알겠는가? 당신이 화성에 발을 디디는 첫 번째 한국인이 될 수도 있다!

※ 다음 우리말과 일치하도록 빈칸에 알맞은 말을 쓰시오.

1 _____ _____ MARS!

2 Do you want _____ _____ _____ _____ planet?

3 The _____ _____ _____ (KSO) is _____ _____ _____ _____ _____ to MARS!

4 _____ _____ is _____ _____ a city _____ Mars.

5 We _____ _____ _____ someone...
_____ is _____.
_____ is _____ and _____.
_____ can _____ _____ _____ others.
_____ can _____ a _____ _____ quickly.

6 _____ _____, _____ _____ a short video.

7 The video _____ _____ the answers _____ the _____ _____:

8 1. Why do you _____ _____ _____ to Mars?
2. Do you have _____ _____ _____ _____ _____ _____?
3. Why are you the _____ _____ _____ _____?

9 This is _____ _____ _____ a lifetime, so _____ _____ out!

10 Mars, _____ _____ _____?

11 _____ there are _____ _____ and _____ about Mars, no one _____ _____ there _____.

12 _____ _____, scientists are _____ _____ Mars _____ a new home.

13 _____ _____, NASA and some companies _____ _____ _____ _____ people there _____ _____.

---

1 화성에서 살아요!

2 다른 행성에서 살고 싶은가요?

3 한국 우주 기구(KSO)는 화성에 갈 사람들을 찾고 있습니다!

4 우리의 임무는 화성에 도시를 세우는 것입니다.

5 우리는 다음과 같은 사람을 찾고 있습니다.
건강한 사람.
창의적이고 호기심이 많은 사람.
다른 사람들과 잘 지낼 수 있는 사람.
새로운 환경에 빨리 적응할 수 있는 사람.

6 지원하려면 우리에게 짧은 동영상을 보내세요.

7 동영상은 다음의 질문에 관한 답을 포함해야 합니다.

8 1. 당신은 왜 화성에 가고 싶은가요?
2. 당신은 유머 감각이 있나요?
3. 왜 당신이 이 임무에 적합한 사람인가요?

9 이것은 일생에 단 한 번뿐인 기회이므로 놓치지 마세요!

10 화성, 제 2의 지구?

11 화성에 관한 많은 책과 영화가 있긴 하지만, 아직 화성에 가 본 사람은 아무도 없다.

12 요즘, 과학자들은 화성을 새로운 거주지로 보고 있다.

13 사실, NASA와 몇몇 회사들은 그곳에 사람들을 보내기 위해 바로 지금도 노력하고 있다.

14 The big question is, "_____ _____ _____ _____ Mars?"

15 Many scientists _____ _____ for _____.

16 First, they think _____ there is _____ _____ Mars.

17 This is great _____ water is _____ _____ all life.

18 Second, Mars has _____ _____ _____ _____ houses and buildings _____.

19 Third, the _____ of day and night on Mars _____ _____ _____ _____ on Earth.

20 _____ _____, Mars also _____ _____ _____.

21 So, people _____ _____ _____ _____ _____.

22 Lastly, Mars is _____ _____.

23 It is _____ _____ _____ _____ to Earth.

24 Mars, _____, has _____ _____ _____ Earth.

25 First, Mars is _____ _____ the size of Earth.

26 It is _____ _____ planet in the _____ system.

27 Second, a year on Mars is _____ _____ _____ _____ _____ a year on Earth.

28 Third, Mars is _____ _____ _____ Earth.

29 _____ _____, it is _____ −60℃ on Mars.

30 This is _____ Mars is _____ _____ _____ the Sun than Earth.

31 _____ no one can _____ the big question _____ _____, it is _____ _____ this new world.

32 Who knows? You could be _____ _____ Mars!

14 중요한 질문은 "화성에서 사람들이 살 수 있는가?"이다.

15 많은 과학자들은 몇몇 이유로 그렇게 믿고 있다.

16 첫째, 그들은 화성에 물이 있다고 생각한다.

17 물은 모든 생명체에 필수적이기 때문에 이것은 중요하다.

18 둘째, 화성은 집과 건물을 지을 수 있는 단단한 땅을 가지고 있다.

19 셋째, 화성의 낮과 밤의 길이는 지구의 낮과 밤의 길이와 비슷하다.

20 게다가, 화성은 사계절도 있다.

21 그래서 사람들이 비슷한 생활을 할 수 있다.

22 마지막으로, 화성은 그렇게 멀지 않다.

23 화성은 지구에서 두 번째로 가까운 행성이다.

24 그러나 화성은 지구와 다른 점이 몇 개 있다.

25 첫째, 화성은 지구의 약 절반 크기이다.

26 화성은 태양계에서 두 번째로 작은 행성이다.

27 둘째, 화성에서의 일 년은 지구에서의 일 년보다 약 두 배 길다.

28 셋째, 화성은 지구보다 훨씬 더 춥다.

29 평균적으로, 화성의 기온은 약 섭씨 영하 60도이다.

30 이것은 화성이 지구보다 태양에서 더 멀리 떨어져 있기 때문이다.

31 비록 누구도 그 중요한 질문에 지금 당장 답할 수는 없지만, 이 새로운 세상을 상상하는 것은 신이 난다.

32 누가 알겠는가? 당신이 화성에 발을 디디는 첫 번째 한국인이 될 수도 있다!

※ 다음 문장을 우리말로 쓰시오.

1 Live on MARS!

➡ _____

2 Do you want to live on another planet?

➡ _____

3 The Korea Space Organization (KSO) is looking for people to go to MARS!

➡ _____

4 Our mission is to build a city on Mars.

➡ _____

5 We are looking for someone... who is healthy. who is creative and curious.

who can get along with others. who can adapt to a new environment quickly.

➡ _____

_____

6 To apply, send us a short video.

➡ _____

7 The video must include the answers to the following questions:

➡ _____

8 1. Why do you want to go to Mars?

2. Do you have a good sense of humor?

3. Why are you the perfect person for this mission?

➡ 1. _____

2. _____

3. _____

9 This is a chance of a lifetime, so don't miss out!

➡ _____

10 Mars, the Second Earth?

➡ _____

11 Although there are many books and movies about Mars, no one has been there yet.

➡ _____

12 These days, scientists are looking at Mars as a new home.

➡ _____

13 In fact, NASA and some companies are trying to send people there right now.

➡ _____

14 The big question is, "Can people live on Mars?"
➡ _____

15 Many scientists believe so for several reasons.
➡ _____

16 First, they think that there is water on Mars.
➡ _____

17 This is great because water is necessary for all life.
➡ _____

18 Second, Mars has hard land to build houses and buildings on.
➡ _____

19 Third, the length of day and night on Mars is similar to that on Earth.
➡ _____

20 In addition, Mars also has four seasons.
➡ _____

21 So, people can lead similar lives.
➡ _____

22 Lastly, Mars is not very far.
➡ _____

23 It is the second closest planet to Earth.
➡ _____

24 Mars, however, has some differences from Earth.
➡ _____

25 First, Mars is about half the size of Earth.
➡ _____

26 It is the second smallest planet in the solar system.
➡ _____

27 Second, a year on Mars is about twice as long as a year on Earth.
➡ _____

28 Third, Mars is much colder than Earth.
➡ _____

29 On average, it is about –60°C on Mars.
➡ _____

30 This is because Mars is farther away from the Sun than Earth.
➡ _____

31 Although no one can answer the big question right now, it is exciting to imagine this new world.
➡ _____

32 Who knows? You could be the first Korean on Mars!
➡ _____

※ 다음 괄호 안의 단어들을 우리말에 맞도록 바르게 배열하시오.

1 (MARS / on / Live)
➡ _____

2 (want / you / do / live / to / planet? / another / on)
➡ _____

3 (Korea / The / Oraganization / Space / (KSO) / looking / is / for / MARS! / to / go / people / to)
➡ _____

4 (mission / our / to / is / a / build / Mars. / on / city)
➡ _____

5 (are / we / for / looking / someonc... / is / who / healthy. // who / curious. / and / creative / is // can / who / with / get / others. / along // can / who / to / adapt / a / environment / new / quickly.)
➡ _____
_____

6 (apply, / to / us / send / video. / short / a)
➡ _____

7 (video / the / include / must / answers / the / to / following / the / questions:)
➡ _____

8 1. (do / why / want / you / go / to / Mars? / to)
2. (you / do / have / good / a / sense / humor? / of)
3. (are / why / the / you / person / perfect / mission? / this / for)
➡ 1. _____
2. _____
3. _____

9 (is / this / chance / a / of / lifetime, / a / don't / so / out! / miss)
➡ _____

10 (the / Mars, / Earth? / Second)
➡ _____

11 (there / although / many / are / books / and / about / movies / Mars, / one / no / been / has / yet. / there)
➡ _____
_____

12 (days / these / are / scientists / looking / at / as / Mars / home. / new / a)
➡ _____

13 (fact, / in / NASA / and / companies / some / trying / are / send / to / there / people / now. / right)
➡ _____
_____

1 화성에서 살아요!

2 다른 행성에서 살고 싶은가요?

3 한국 우주 기구(KSO)는 화성에 갈 사람들을 찾고 있습니다!

4 우리의 임무는 화성에 도시를 세우는 것입니다.

5 우리는 다음과 같은 사람을 찾고 있습니다.
건강한 사람.
창의적이고 호기심이 많은 사람.
다른 사람들과 잘 지낼 수 있는 사람.
새로운 환경에 빨리 적응할 수 있는 사람.

6 지원하려면 우리에게 짧은 동영상을 보내세요.

7 동영상은 다음의 질문에 관한 답을 포함해야 합니다.

8 1. 당신은 왜 화성에 가고 싶은가요?
2. 당신은 유머 감각이 있나요?
3. 왜 당신이 이 임무에 적합한 사람인가요?

9 이것은 일생에 단 한 번뿐인 기회이므로 놓치지 마세요!

10 화성, 제 2의 지구?

11 화성에 관한 많은 책과 영화가 있긴 하지만, 아직 화성에 가 본 사람은 아무도 없다.

12 요즘, 과학자들은 화성을 새로운 거주지로 보고 있다.

13 사실, NASA와 몇몇 회사들은 그곳에 사람들을 보내기 위해 바로 지금도 노력하고 있다.

14 (big / the / is, / question / people / "can / live / Mars?" / on)
➡ _____

15 (scientists / many / so / believe / for / reasons. / several)
➡ _____

16 (first, / think / they / there / that / water / is / Mars. / on)
➡ _____

17 (is / this / because / great / is / water / for / necessary / life. / all)
➡ _____

18 (second, / has / Mars / land / hard / build / to / houses / and / on. / buildings)
➡ _____

19 (the / third, / length / day / of / night / and / Mars / on / similar / is / that / to / Earth. / on)
➡ _____

20 (addition, / in / also / Mars / four / seasons. / has)
➡ _____

21 (people / so, / lead / can / lives. / similar)
➡ _____

22 (Mars / lastly, / not / is / far. / very)
➡ _____

23 (is / it second / the / planet / closest / Earth. / to)
➡ _____

24 (however, / Mars, / some / has / differences / Earth. / from)
➡ _____

25 (Mars / first, / about / is / the / half / Earth. / of / size)
➡ _____

26 (is / it second / the / planet / smallest / the / in / system. / solar)
➡ _____

27 (a / second, / year / Mars / on / about / is / as / twice / long / as / year / a / Earth. / on)
➡ _____

28 (Mars / third, / is / colder / much / Earth. / than)
➡ _____

29 (average, / on / is / it / about / on / –60°C / Mars.)
➡ _____

30 (is / this / Mars / because / farther / is / from / away / the / Earth. / than / Sun)
➡ _____
_____

31 (no / although / one / answer / can / big / the / right / question / now, / is / it / to / exciting / this / imagine / world. / new)
➡ _____
_____

32 (knows? / who // could / you / the / be / Korean / first / Mars! / on)
➡ _____

---

14 중요한 질문은 "화성에서 사람들이 살 수 있는가?"이다.

15 많은 과학자들은 몇몇 이유로 그렇게 믿고 있다.

16 첫째, 그들은 화성에 물이 있다고 생각한다.

17 물은 모든 생명체에 필수적이기 때문에 이것은 중요하다.

18 둘째, 화성은 집과 건물을 지을 수 있는 단단한 땅을 가지고 있다.

19 셋째, 화성의 낮과 밤의 길이는 지구의 낮과 밤의 길이와 비슷하다.

20 게다가, 화성은 사계절도 있다.

21 그래서 사람들이 비슷한 생활을 할 수 있다.

22 마지막으로, 화성은 그렇게 멀지 않다.

23 화성은 지구에서 두 번째로 가까운 행성이다.

24 그러나 화성은 지구와 다른 점이 몇 개 있다.

25 첫째, 화성은 지구의 약 절반 크기이다.

26 화성은 태양계에서 두 번째로 작은 행성이다.

27 둘째, 화성에서의 일 년은 지구에서의 일 년보다 약 두 배 길다.

28 셋째, 화성은 지구보다 훨씬 더 춥다.

29 평균적으로, 화성의 기온은 약 섭씨 영하 60도이다.

30 이것은 화성이 지구보다 태양에서 더 멀리 떨어져 있기 때문이다.

31 비록 누구도 그 중요한 질문에 지금 당장 답할 수는 없지만, 이 새로운 세상을 상상하는 것은 신이 난다.

32 누가 알겠는가? 당신이 화성에 발을 디디는 첫 번째 한국인이 될 수도 있다!

※ **다음 우리말을 영어로 쓰시오.**

1 화성에서 살아요!

➡ _____

2 다른 행성에서 살고 싶은가요?

➡ _____

3 한국 우주 기구(KSO)는 화성에 갈 사람들을 찾고 있습니다!

➡ _____

4 우리의 임무는 화성에 도시를 세우는 것입니다.

➡ _____

5 우리는 다음과 같은 사람을 찾고 있습니다.
건강한 사람. 창의적이고 호기심이 많은 사람. 다른 사람들과 잘 지낼 수 있는 사람.
새로운 환경에 빨리 적응할 수 있는 사람.

➡ _____

_____

6 지원하려면 우리에게 짧은 동영상을 보내세요.

➡ _____

7 동영상은 다음의 질문에 관한 답을 포함해야 합니다.

➡ _____

8 1. 당신은 왜 화성에 가고 싶은가요?

2. 당신은 유머 감각이 있나요?

3. 왜 당신이 이 임무에 적합한 사람인가요?

➡ 1. _____

2. _____

3. _____

9 이것은 일생에 단 한 번뿐인 기회이므로 놓치지 마세요!

➡ _____

10 화성, 제 2의 지구?

➡ _____

11 화성에 관한 많은 책과 영화가 있긴 하지만, 아직 화성에 가 본 사람은 아무도 없다.

➡ _____

12 요즘, 과학자들은 화성을 새로운 거주지로 보고 있다.

➡ _____

13 사실, NASA와 몇몇 회사들은 그곳에 사람들을 보내기 위해 바로 지금도 노력하고 있다.

➡ _____

14 중요한 질문은 "화성에서 사람들이 살 수 있는가?"이다.
➡ _____

15 많은 과학자들은 몇몇 이유로 그렇게 믿고 있다.
➡ _____

16 첫째, 그들은 화성에 물이 있다고 생각한다.
➡ _____

17 물은 모든 생명체에 필수적이기 때문에 이것은 중요하다.
➡ _____

18 둘째, 화성은 집과 건물을 지을 수 있는 단단한 땅을 가지고 있다.
➡ _____

19 셋째, 화성의 낮과 밤의 길이는 지구의 낮과 밤의 길이와 비슷하다.
➡ _____

20 게다가, 화성은 사계절도 있다.
➡ _____

21 그래서 사람들이 비슷한 생활을 할 수 있다.
➡ _____

22 마지막으로, 화성은 그렇게 멀지 않다.
➡ _____

23 화성은 지구에서 두 번째로 가까운 행성이다.
➡ _____

24 그러나 화성은 지구와 다른 점이 몇 개 있다.
➡ _____

25 첫째, 화성은 지구의 약 절반 크기이다.
➡ _____

26 화성은 태양계에서 두 번째로 작은 행성이다.
➡ _____

27 둘째, 화성에서의 일 년은 지구에서의 일 년보다 약 두 배 길다.
➡ _____

28 셋째, 화성은 지구보다 훨씬 더 춥다.
➡ _____

29 평균적으로, 화성의 기온은 약 섭씨 영하 60도이다.
➡ _____

30 이것은 화성이 지구보다 태양에서 더 멀리 떨어져 있기 때문이다.
➡ _____

31 비록 누구도 그 중요한 질문에 지금 당장 답할 수는 없지만, 이 새로운 세상을 상상하는 것은 신이 난다.
➡ _____

32 누가 알겠는가? 당신이 화성에 발을 디디는 첫 번째 한국인이 될 수도 있다!
➡ _____

※ 다음 우리말과 일치하도록 빈칸에 알맞은 말을 쓰시오.

Real Life Talk - Step 2

1. A: Do you know _____ _____ _____?

2. B: _____, I _____. _____ is _____?

3. A: It's a _____ _____.

4. B: A Clean Straw? _____ _____ _____ _____?

5. A: It cleans water _____ _____ _____.

6. B: Wow, _____ _____!

1. A: 너는 이것이 무엇인지 아니?
2. B: 아니. 그게 뭐니?
3. A: Clean Straw야.
4. B: Clean Straw? 용도가 뭐니?
5. A: 네가 물을 마시는 동안 물을 깨끗이 해주는 거야.
6. B: 와, 멋지다!

Think and Write

1. My name is Suji Lee _____ _____. I'm 15 _____ _____.

2. I _____ _____ go to Mars _____ I've _____ _____ _____ space.

3. I'm _____ and I _____ _____ _____.

4. I'm _____ _____ _____ photos.

5. I'm the _____ _____ for this mission because I can _____ to a _____ _____ quickly.

6. _____ I'm young, I can _____ _____ _____ _____.

7. Give me _____ _____ _____ _____ on Mars!

1. 제 이름은 수지이고 한국 출신입니다. 저는 15살입니다.
2. 저는 쭉 우주에 호기심을 가져왔기 때문에 화성에 가고 싶습니다.
3. 저는 상냥하고 친구들을 사귀는 것을 좋아합니다.
4. 저는 사진을 잘 찍습니다.
5. 저는 새로운 환경에 빨리 적응할 수 있기 때문에 이 임무에 적합한 사람입니다.
6. 비록 저는 어리지만, 다른 사람들과 의사소통을 잘할 수 있습니다.
7. 저에게 화성에서 살 기회를 주세요!

Project

1. _____

2. It has 14 _____. It's a very _____ _____.

3. It's _____ _____ the _____ _____ _____ _____.

4. It's _____ _____ _____ from the Sun in _____ _____ _____.

1. 해왕성
2 그것은 14개의 위성을 가지고 있다. 그곳은 아주 추운 행성이다.
3 그것은 바다의 신의 이름을 딴 것이다.
4 그것은 태양계에서 태양과 가장 멀리 떨어져 있다.

※ 다음 우리말을 영어로 쓰시오.

Real Life Talk - Step 2

1. A: 너는 이것이 무엇인지 아니?
   ➡ _____

2. B: 아니. 뭐니?
   ➡ _____

3. A: Clean Straw야.
   ➡ _____

4. B: Clean Straw? 용도가 뭐니?
   ➡ _____

5. A: 네가 물을 마시는 동안 물을 깨끗이 해주는 거야.
   ➡ _____

6. B: 와, 멋지다!
   ➡ _____

Think and Write

1. 제 이름은 수지이고 한국 출신입니다. 저는 15살입니다.
   ➡ _____

2. 저는 쭉 우주에 호기심을 가져왔기 때문에 화성에 가고 싶습니다.
   ➡ _____

3. 저는 상냥하고 친구들을 사귀는 것을 좋아합니다.
   ➡ _____

4. 저는 사진을 잘 찍습니다.
   ➡ _____

5. 저는 새로운 환경에 빨리 적응할 수 있기 때문에 이 임무에 적합한 사람입니다.
   ➡ _____

6. 비록 저는 어리지만, 다른 사람들과 의사소통을 잘할 수 있습니다.
   ➡ _____

7. 저에게 화성에서 살 기회를 주세요!
   ➡ _____

Project

1. 해왕성
   ➡ _____

2. 그것은 14개의 위성을 가지고 있다. 그곳은 아주 추운 행성이다.
   ➡ _____

3. 그것은 바다의 신의 이름을 딴 것이다.
   ➡ _____

4. 그것은 태양계에서 태양과 가장 멀리 떨어져 있다.
   ➡ _____

※ 다음 영어를 우리말로 쓰시오.

01 author _____

02 backpack _____

03 perfect _____

04 connection _____

05 trip _____

06 award _____

07 difference _____

08 mix _____

09 trust _____

10 adventure _____

11 traditional _____

12 explain _____

13 simple _____

14 friendship _____

15 especially _____

16 unlike _____

17 truth _____

18 lie _____

19 advertisement _____

20 worth _____

21 fantasy _____

22 belief _____

23 strongly _____

24 lift _____

25 wisely _____

26 meal _____

27 prove _____

28 express _____

29 solve _____

30 navy _____

31 recommend _____

32 boring _____

33 touching _____

34 opinion _____

35 for example _____

36 full of _____

37 based on _____

38 from now on _____

39 hold on _____

40 make a choice _____

41 right now _____

42 check out _____

43 worth it _____

※ 다음 우리말을 영어로 쓰시오.

01 믿다, 신뢰하다 _____

02 작가 _____

03 완벽한 _____

04 감동적인 _____

05 나타내다, 표현하다 _____

06 지루한 _____

07 여행 _____

08 남색 _____

09 모험 _____

10 보라색, 자색 _____

11 소설 _____

12 의견 _____

13 광고 _____

14 주머니 _____

15 간단한, 단순한 _____

16 상 _____

17 가치가 있는 _____

18 특히 _____

19 식사 _____

20 우정 _____

21 강력하게 _____

22 들어 올리다 _____

23 해결하다, 풀다 _____

24 증명하다 _____

25 설명하다 _____

26 전통적인 _____

27 차이점 _____

28 섞다 _____

29 공상 _____

30 추천하다 _____

31 신념, 생각 _____

32 ～와 달리 _____

33 현명하게 _____

34 진실, 사실 _____

35 ～을 확인하다 _____

36 ～을 찾다 _____

37 지금부터 _____

38 선택하다 _____

39 예를 들면 _____

40 ～로 가득한 _____

41 ～을 바탕으로 _____

42 지금 _____

43 기다려, 멈춰 _____

※ 다음 영영풀이에 알맞은 단어를 <보기>에서 골라 쓴 후, 우리말 뜻을 쓰시오.

1 _____ : to believe that something is true: _____

2 _____ : ideas or feelings about something: _____

3 _____ : to add something to something else: _____

4 _____ : to move something to a higher position: _____

5 _____ : the real facts about something: _____

6 _____ : the foods eaten or prepared at one time: _____

7 _____ : to show what you think or feel: _____

8 _____ : to say or write something that is not true: _____

9 _____ : a small bag that is attached to something: _____

10 _____ : to tell someone that something is good or useful: _____

11 _____ : a notice, picture or short film telling people about something:

_____

12 _____ : the way in which two things are related to each other: _____

13 _____ : to tell somebody about something in a way that is easy to understand:

_____

14 _____ : to use facts, evidence, etc. to show that something is true: _____

15 _____ : a prize such as money, etc. for something that somebody has done:

_____

16 _____ : a large area of land that has very little water and very few plants growing

on it: _____

보기			
award	explain	advertisement	lie
mix	opinion	desert	express
prove	connection	pocket	recommend
trust	lift	meal	truth

Step1

※ 다음 우리말과 일치하도록 빈칸에 알맞은 말을 쓰시오.

Listen & Speak 1-A

Brian: Can you _____ _____ _____ _____?

Emily: Try *Star Wars*. I _____ _____ it.

Brian: Oh, I _____ _____ it _____.

Emily: It's the _____ _____ movie _____ _____.

Listen & Speak 1-B

W: May I _____ you?

B: Yes. I'm _____ _____ a _____. Can you _____ _____?

W: _____ _____ this red one? Red is _____ _____ _____ _____ _____ _____.

B: _____ _____ _____ was red, so I want a _____ _____.

W: _____ _____ this _____ one? It _____ _____ _____ _____.

B: Oh, that _____ _____. I'll _____ it.

Listen & Speak 2-A

Sue: Tom, you _____ a _____ _____.

Tom: Yes, I did. I'm _____ _____ _____ it.

Sue: _____ do you _____ _____ _____ _____?

Tom: I love the camera. It _____ _____ _____.

Listen & Speak 2-B

Jack: Hi, Suji. _____ _____ you _____ your _____ to Gyeongju?

Suji: I was very _____ _____ it.

Jack: _____ did you _____?

Suji: I _____ Cheomseongdae. It was great.

Jack: _____ _____ _____ you _____?

Suji: Bulguksa. It was a _____ _____.

Jack: _____ _____ the _____ _____.

Suji: Yeah, but _____ _____ to Seokguram _____ _____.

Jack: But _____ _____ it was _____ _____.

Jack: 안녕, 수지야. 경주 여행은 어땠니?
Suji: 매우 즐거웠어.
Jack: 어디를 방문했니?
Suji: 첨성대를 방문했어. 좋았어.
Jack: 또 어디를 방문했니?
Suji: 불국사. 멋진 곳이었어.
Jack: 완벽한 여행이었던 것 같네.
Suji: 응, 하지만 석굴암까지 걸어 올라가는 것은 힘들었어.
Jack: 하지만 그것이 그만한 가치가 있었을 것이라고 확신해.

Real Life Talk – Step 1

Brian: Mina, _____ _____ _____ a good pizza restaurant?

Mina: _____ _____ you try Antonio's? It's _____ _____.

Brian: _____ do you _____ _____ it?

Mina: The food is _____. I _____ the bulgogi pizza.

Brian: _____ are _____ _____?

Mina: I _____ the prices are good, _____.

Brian: _____ _____ a good restaurant. _____ do you _____ _____ _____?

Mina: It's a _____ _____ on the weekends.

Brian: Okay. I'll _____ _____ _____. Thanks.

Mina: No _____. _____ your meal!

Brian: 미나야. 괜찮은 피자 식당을 추천해 줄래?
Mina: Antonio's에 가 보는 게 어때? 내가 가장 좋아하는 곳이야.
Brian: 무엇이 좋은데?
Mina: 음식이 맛있어. 나는 불고기 피자를 추천해.
Brian: 가격은 어때?
Mina: 가격도 괜찮다고 생각해.
Brian: 괜찮은 식당 같네. 서비스는 어때?
Mina: 주말에는 좀 느려.
Brian: 알겠어. 내가 확인해 볼게. 고마워.
Mina: 천만에. 맛있게 먹어!

Real Life Talk – Step 2

Amy: Yujin, can you _____ _____ _____ _____ _____?

Yujin: _____ _____ The Little Prince?

Amy: _____ _____ _____ _____ about the book?

Yujin: I like the _____ _____. He is very _____.

Amy: _____ good. I'll _____ it.

Amy: Yujin아, 내게 책을 추천해 줄래?
Yujin: '어린 왕자' 어때?
Amy: 책의 무엇이 마음에 드니?
Yujin: 나는 주인공이 마음에 들어. 그는 매우 특별해.
Amy: 좋은 책 같네. 내가 읽어 볼게.

Step2

※ 다음 우리말에 맞도록 대화를 영어로 쓰시오.

Listen & Speak 1-A

Brian: _____

Emily: _____

Brian: _____

Emily: _____

Brian: 좋은 영화를 추천해 줄래?
Emily: 'Star Wars'를 봐. 정말 좋았어.
Brian: 오, 나는 아직 그 영화를 본 적이 없어.
Emily: 지금 1위 영화야.

Listen & Speak 1-B

W: _____

B: _____

W: _____

B: _____

W: _____

B: _____

W: 도와드릴까요?
B: 네. 배낭을 찾고 있어요. 하나 추천해 주시겠어요?
W: 이 빨간 배낭은 어떤가요? 빨간색은 요즘 가장 인기 있는 색이에요.
B: 제 옛 배낭이 빨간색이어서 다른 색을 원해요.
W: 이 남색 배낭은 어떤가요? 양옆에 주머니가 있어요.
B: 오, 좋아 보여요. 그걸로 살게요.

Listen & Speak 2-A

Sue: _____

Tom: _____

Sue: _____

Tom: _____

Sue: Tom, 새 스마트폰을 샀구나.
Tom: 응, 그래. 나는 정말 만족스러워.
Sue: 무엇이 가장 마음에 드니?
Tom: 카메라가 정말 좋아. 멋진 사진을 찍어.

Listen & Speak 2-B

Jack: _____

Suji: _____

Jack: _____

Suji: _____

Jack: _____

Suji: _____

Jack: _____

Suji: _____

Jack: _____

Jack: 안녕, 수지야. 경주 여행은 어땠니?
Suij: 매우 즐거웠어.
Jack: 어디를 방문했니?
Suij: 첨성대를 방문했어. 좋았어.
Jack: 또 어디를 방문했니?
Suij: 불국사. 멋진 곳이었어.
Jack: 완벽한 여행이었던 것 같네.
Suij: 응, 하지만 석굴암까지 걸어 올라가는 것은 힘들었어.
Jack: 하지만 그것이 그만한 가치가 있었을 것이라고 확신해.

Real Life Talk – Step 1

Brian: _____

Mina: _____

Brian: _____

Mina: _____

Brian: _____

Mina: _____

Brian: _____

Mina: _____

Brian: _____

Mina: _____

Brian: 미나야, 괜찮은 피자 식당을 추천해 줄래?
Mina: Antonio's에 가 보는 게 어때? 내가 가장 좋아하는 곳이야.
Brian: 무엇이 좋은데?
Mina: 음식이 맛있어. 나는 불고기 피자를 추천해.
Brian: 가격은 어때?
Mina: 가격도 괜찮다고 생각해.
Brian: 괜찮은 식당 같네. 서비스는 어때?
Mina: 주말에는 좀 느려.
Brian: 알겠어. 내가 확인해 볼게. 고마워.
Mina: 천만에. 맛있게 먹어!

Real Life Talk – Step 2

Amy: _____

Yujin: _____

Amy: _____

Yujin: _____

Amy: _____

Amy: Yujin아, 내게 책을 추천해 줄래?
Yujin: '어린 왕자' 어때?
Amy: 책의 무엇이 마음에 드니?
Yujin: 나는 주인공이 마음에 들어. 그는 매우 특별해.
Amy: 좋은 책 같네. 내가 읽어 볼게.

※ 다음 우리말과 일치하도록 빈칸에 알맞은 것을 골라 쓰시오.

1 Emma: What _____ you _____, Kyle?
A. doing　　　　B. are

2 Kyle: Oh, Emma. I'm _____ the movie, *Y-Men 7* _____ my _____.
A. on　　　　B. watching　　　　C. computer

3 Emma: _____ is _____?
A. it　　　　B. how

4 Kyle: _____ ask. It's _____ _____ _____ I want to cry.
A. so　　　　B. don't　　　　C. that　　　　D. boring

5 Emma: I'm _____ _____ _____ that.
A. to　　　　B. sorry　　　　C. hear

6 Kyle: I'm so _____. The movie _____ _____ it was "The Most Exciting Movie of the Year."
A. advertisement　　B. mad　　　　C. said

7 Emma: Well, you can't_____ _____ _____ you _____.
A. that　　　　B. believe　　　　C. everything　　　　D. read

8 Kyle: They _____ _____ the advertisement. I'm going to ask _____ my money _____.
A. for　　　　B. on　　　　C. back　　　　D. lied

9 Emma: _____ on, Kyle! They didn't really _____ _____ they used _____, not facts.
A. hold　　　　B. because　　　　C. lie　　　　D. opinions

10 Kyle: Huh? I'm _____ _____ _____.
A. you　　　　B. following　　　　C. not

11 Emma: Opinions _____ people's _____ _____, "The desert is beautiful."
A. like　　　　B. express　　　　C. feelings

12 You can't say _____ it's true or _____. But, _____ can be _____.
A. not　　　　B. that　　　　C. proven　　　　D. facts

13 _____ _____, "The Atacama Desert is in Chile," is a fact. You can _____ that _____ the map.
A. on　　　　B. check　　　　C. example　　　　D. for

14 Kyle: Okay…. But what's _____ _____ _____ movies?
A. with　　　　B. connection　　　　C. the

15 Emma: _____ me _____. What's your _____ movie?
A. explain　　　　B. favorite　　　　C. let

1 Emma: Kyle, 뭐 하고 있니?

2 Kyle: Emma. 나는 컴퓨터로 영화 "Y-Men 7"을 보고 있어.

3 Emma: 어때?

4 Kyle: 묻지 마. 너무 지루해서 울고 싶어.

5 Emma: 유감이야.

6 Klye: 난 정말 화가 나. 영화 광고에는 이것이 "올해의 가장 흥미진진한 영화"라고 쓰여 있었어.

7 Emma: 음, 넌 네가 읽는 것을 모두 믿을 수는 없어.

8 Kyle: 그들은 광고에 거짓말을 한 거야. 돈을 환불해 달라고 해야겠어.

9 Emma: 기다려, Kyle! 그들은 사실이 아닌 의견을 사용했기 때문에 꼭 거짓말을 한 것은 아니야.

10 Kyle: 뭐라고? 네 말을 이해하지 못하겠어.

11 Emma: 의견은 "사막은 아름다워."와 같이 사람들의 감정을 표현하는 것이야.

12 그것이 사실인지 아닌지 말할 수는 없어. 하지만 사실은 증명할 수 있어.

13 예를 들면, "아타카마 사막은 칠레에 있다."는 사실이야. 넌 그것을 지도에서 확인할 수 있어.

14 Kyle: 알겠어… 하지만 그게 영화와 무슨 관련이 있니?

15 Emma: 설명해 줄게. 네가 가장 좋아하는 영화가 뭐니?

16 Kyle: _____ _Forrest_ _____.

    A. _Gump_   B. it's

17 Emma: Okay. _____ look for _____ _____. What does it _____?

    A. say   B. its   C. let's   D. advertisement

18 Kyle: It _____, "Winner of 6 Academy _____ _____ Best Picture."

    A. says   B. including   C. Awards

19 Emma: See? It _____ _____ _____ the _Y-Men 7_ advertisement.

    A. unlike   B. uses   C. facts

20 _____ you _____ the _____?

    A. see   B. difference   C. do

21 Kyle: Not _____. The _Y-Men 7_ ad _____ "Most Exciting Movie" and the _Forrest Gump_ _____ says "Best Picture."

    A. says   B. ad   C. exactly

22 _____ they _____ _____?

    A. opinions   B. aren't   C. both

23 Emma: That's a great _____, Kyle. When people use words _____ "best" or "most," they are usually _____ _____.

    A. like   B. expressing   C. question   D. opinions

24 But in the _Forrest Gump_ _____, "Best Picture" is the _____ which the _____ _____.

    A. award   B. movie   C. ad   D. won

25 We can _____ that _____ the Internet. That's a _____.

    A. fact   B. on   C. check

26 Kyle: Aha! _____ now _____ I'm only going to _____ ads _____ facts.

    A. with   B. from   C. trust   D. on

27 Emma: It's not _____ _____. Most ads _____ facts _____ opinions.

    A. with   B. mix   C. simple   D. that

28 So you _____ to _____ a smart _____ based on _____ of them.

    A. both   B. choice   C. make   D. have

29 Kyle: _____ it! Emma, do you want to _____ the _____ of _Y-Men 7_ _____ me?

    A. rest   B. watch   C. with   D. got

30 Emma: Thanks, but _____ _____. Enjoy the _____ of the movie!

    A. rest   B. thanks   C. no

---

16 Kyle: "Forest Gump"야.

17 Emma: 좋아. 그 영화의 광고를 찾아보자. 뭐라고 쓰여 있니?

18 Kyle: "Best Picture를 포함하여 아카데미 6개 부문 수상작"이라고 쓰여 있어.

19 Emma: 알겠니? "Y-Men 7" 광고와는 달리 사실을 사용하고 있어.

20 차이를 알겠니?

21 Kyle: 잘 모르겠어. "Y-Men 7" 광고는 "Most Exciting Movie"라고 쓰여 있고 "Forest Gump" 광고는 "Best Picture"라고 쓰여 있잖아.

22 둘 다 의견 아니니?

23 Emma: 좋은 질문이야, Kyle. 사람들이 'best'나 'most'와 같은 말을 사용할 때, 그들은 대개 의견을 표현하는 거야.

24 하지만 "Forest Gump" 광고에서 "Best Picture"는 영화가 받은 상이야.

25 우리는 인터넷에서 그것을 확인할 수 있어. 그건 사실이야.

26 Kyle: 아하! 지금부터 사실로 이루어진 광고만 믿겠어.

27 Emma: 그렇게 간단하지는 않아. 대부분의 광고는 사실과 의견이 섞여 있어.

28 그러니 그 둘을 바탕으로 현명한 선택을 해야 해.

29 Kyle: 알겠어! Emma, "Y-Men 7"의 남은 부분을 나와 함께 볼래?

30 Emma: 고맙지만 사양할게. 영화의 남은 부분 잘 봐!

※ 다음 우리말과 일치하도록 빈칸에 알맞은 말을 쓰시오.

1 Emma: _____ _____ you _____, Kyle?

2 Kyle: Oh, Emma. I'm _____ _____ _____, *Y-Men 7* _____ my computer.

3 Emma: _____ is _____?

4 Kyle: _____ ask. It's _____ _____ _____ I want _____ _____.

5 Emma: I'm _____ _____ _____ _____.

6 Kyle: I'm so _____. The movie _____ said _____ was "_____ _____ _____ _____ of the Year."

7 Emma: Well, you _____ _____ _____ _____ _____ _____.

8 Kyle: They _____ _____ the advertisement. I'm going to _____ _____ _____ _____.

9 Emma: _____ _____, Kyle! They didn't really _____ they _____ _____, not _____.

10 Kyle: Huh? I'm _____ _____ _____.

11 Emma: Opinions _____ _____ _____ like, "The desert is beautiful."

12 You can't say _____ it's _____ _____ _____. But, facts _____ _____ _____.

13 _____ _____, "The Atacama Desert is in Chile," is a fact. You can _____ _____ _____ _____ _____.

14 Kyle: Okay…. But what's _____ _____ _____ movies?

15 Emma: _____ _____ _____. What's your favorite movie?

---

1 Emma: Kyle, 뭐 하고 있니?

2 Kyle: Emma. 나는 컴퓨터로 영화 "Y-Men 7"을 보고 있어.

3 Emma: 어때?

4 Kyle: 묻지 마. 너무 지루해서 울고 싶어.

5 Emma: 유감이야.

6 Klye: 난 정말 화가 나. 영화 광고에는 이것이 "올해의 가장 흥미진진한 영화"라고 쓰여 있었어.

7 Emma: 음, 넌 네가 읽는 것을 모두 믿을 수는 없어.

8 Kyle: 그들은 광고에 거짓말을 한 거야. 돈을 환불해 달라고 해야겠어.

9 Emma: 기다려, Kyle! 그들은 사실이 아닌 의견을 사용했기 때문에 꼭 거짓말을 한 것은 아니야.

10 Kyle: 뭐라고? 네 말을 이해하지 못하겠어.

11 Emma: 의견은 "사막은 아름다워."와 같이 사람들의 감정을 표현하는 것이야.

12 그것이 사실인지 아닌지 말할 수는 없어. 하지만 사실은 증명할 수 있어.

13 예를 들면, "아타카마 사막은 칠레에 있다."는 사실이야. 넌 그것을 지도에서 확인할 수 있어.

14 Kyle: 알겠어… 하지만 그게 영화와 무슨 관련이 있니?

15 Emma: 설명해 줄게. 네가 가장 좋아하는 영화가 뭐니?

16 Kyle: _____ *Forrest Gump.*

17 Emma: Okay. _____ _____ _____ _____ _____.
What does it say?

18 Kyle: _____ _____, "Winner of 6 Academy Awards _____
Best Picture."

19 Emma: See? It _____ _____ _____ the *Y-Men 7*
advertisement.

20 Do you see _____ _____?

21 Kyle: Not _____. The *Y-Men 7* ad _____ "Most Exciting
Movie" and the *Forrest Gump* ad _____ "Best Picture."

22 _____ they _____ _____?

23 Emma: That's a great question, Kyle. When people use _____
_____ "best" or "most," they are _____ _____ _____.

24 But in the *Forrest Gump* ad, "Best Picture" is the _____
_____ _____ _____ _____.

25 We can _____ _____ _____ _____ _____. That's a
fact.

26 Kyle: Aha! _____ _____ _____ I'm only going to _____
ads _____ facts.

27 Emma: It's not _____ _____. Most ads _____ _____
_____ _____.

28 So you have to _____ _____ _____ _____
_____ _____ of them.

29 Kyle: Got it! Emma, do you want _____ _____
_____ of *Y-Men 7* with me?

30 Emma: Thanks, but _____ _____. Enjoy _____ _____
_____ the movie!

16 Kyle: "Forest Gump"야.

17 Emma: 좋아. 그 영화의 광고를 찾아보자. 뭐라고 쓰여 있니?

18 Kyle: "Best Picture를 포함하여 아카데미 6개 부문 수상작"이라고 쓰여 있어.

19 Emma: 알겠니? "Y-Men 7" 광고와는 달리 사실을 사용하고 있어.

20 차이를 알겠니?

21 Kyle: 잘 모르겠어. "Y-Men 7" 광고는 "Most Exciting Movie"라고 쓰여 있고 "Forest Gump" 광고는 "Best Picture"라고 쓰여 있잖아.

22 둘 다 의견 아니니?

23 Emma: 좋은 질문이야. Kyle. 사람들이 'best'나 'most'와 같은 말을 사용할 때, 그들은 대개 의견을 표현하는 거야.

24 하지만 "Forest Gump" 광고에서 "Best Picture"는 영화가 받은 상이야.

25 우리는 인터넷에서 그것을 확인할 수 있어. 그건 사실이야.

26 Kyle: 아하! 지금부터 사실로 이루어진 광고만 믿겠어.

27 Emma: 그렇게 간단하지는 않아. 대부분의 광고는 사실과 의견이 섞여 있어.

28 그러니 그 둘을 바탕으로 현명한 선택을 해야 해.

29 Kyle: 알겠어! Emma, "Y-Men 7"의 남은 부분을 나와 함께 볼래?

30 Emma: 고맙지만 사양할게. 영화의 남은 부분 잘 봐!

※ 다음 문장을 우리말로 쓰시오.

1 Emma: What are you doing, Kyle?

➡ _____

2 Kyle: Oh, Emma. I'm watching the movie, *Y-Men 7* on my computer.

➡ _____

3 Emma: How is it?

➡ _____

4 Kyle: Don't ask. It's so boring that I want to cry.

➡ _____

5 Emma: I'm sorry to hear that.

➡ _____

6 Kyle: I'm so mad. The movie advertisement said it was "The Most Exciting Movie of the Year."

➡ _____

7 Emma: Well, you can't believe everything that you read.

➡ _____

8 Kyle: They lied on the advertisement. I'm going to ask for my money back.

➡ _____

9 Emma: Hold on, Kyle! They didn't really lie because they used opinions, not facts.

➡ _____

10 Kyle: Huh? I'm not following you.

➡ _____

11 Emma: Opinions express people's feelings like, "The desert is beautiful."

➡ _____

12 You can't say that it's true or not. But, facts can be proven.

➡ _____

13 For example, "The Atacama Desert is in Chile," is a fact. You can check that on the map.

➡ _____

14 Kyle: Okay.... But what's the connection with movies?

➡ _____

15 Emma: Let me explain. What's your favorite movie?

➡ _____

16 Kyle: It's *Forrest Gump*.

➡ _____

17 Emma: Okay. Let's look for its advertisement. What does it say?

➡ _____

18 Kyle: It says, "Winner of 6 Academy Awards including Best Picture."

➡ _____

19 Emma: See? It uses facts unlike the *Y-Men 7* advertisement.

➡ _____

20 Do you see the difference?

➡ _____

21 Kyle: Not exactly. The *Y-Men 7* ad says "Most Exciting Movie" and the *Forrest Gump* ad says "Best Picture."

➡ _____

_____

22 Aren't they both opinions?

➡ _____

23 Emma: That's a great question, Kyle. When people use words like "best" or "most," they are usually expressing opinions.

➡ _____

24 But in the *Forrest Gump* ad, "Best Picture" is the award which the movie won.

➡ _____

25 We can check that on the Internet. That's a fact.

➡ _____

26 Kyle: Aha! From now on I'm only going to trust ads with facts.

➡ _____

27 Emma: It's not that simple. Most ads mix facts with opinions.

➡ _____

28 So you have to make a smart choice based on both of them.

➡ _____

29 Kyle: Got it! Emma, do you want to watch the rest of *Y-Men 7* with me?

➡ _____

30 Emma: Thanks, but no thanks. Enjoy the rest of the movie!

➡ _____

※ 다음 괄호 안의 단어들을 우리말에 맞도록 바르게 배열하시오.

1 (Emma: / are / what / doing, / you / Kyle?)
➡ _____

2 (Kyle: / Emma. / oh, // watching / I'm / movie, / the / on / 7 / *Y-Men* / computer. / my)
➡ _____

3 (Emma: / is / it? / how)
➡ _____

4 (Kyle: / ask. / don't // so / it's / that / boring / cry. / to / want / I)
➡ _____

5 (Emma: / sorry / I'm / that. / hear / to)
➡ _____

6 (Klye: / so / mad. / I'm // movie / the / advertisement / it / said / was / Most / "The / Movie / Exciting / of / Year." / the)
➡ _____

7 (Emma: / well, / can't / you / everything / believe / that / read. / you)
➡ _____

8 (Kyle: / lied / they / the / on / advertisement. // going / I'm / ask / to / my / for / back. / money)
➡ _____

9 (Emma: / on, / hold / Kyle! // didn't / they / lie / really / they / because / used / opinions, / facts. / not)
➡ _____

10 (Kyle: / huh? // not / I'm / you. / following)
➡ _____

11 (Emma: / express / opinions / feelings / people's / like, / desert / "the / beautiful." / is)
➡ _____

12 (can't / you / say / it's / that / or / true / not. // but, / can / proven. / be / facts)
➡ _____

13 (example, / for / "The / Desert / Atacama / in / is / Chile," / fact. / a / is // can / you / that / check / map. / the / on)
➡ _____

14 (Kyle: / okay / ..... / what's / but / connection / the / movies? / with)
➡ _____

15 (Emma: / me / let / explain. // your / what's / movie? / favorite)
➡ _____

1 Emma: Kyle, 뭐 하고 있니?

2 Kyle: Emma. 나는 컴퓨터로 영화 "Y-Men 7"을 보고 있어.

3 Emma: 어때?

4 Kyle: 묻지 마. 너무 지루해서 울고 싶어.

5 Emma: 유감이야.

6 Klye: 난 정말 화가 나. 영화 광고에는 이것이 "올해의 가장 흥미진진한 영화"라고 쓰여 있었어.

7 Emma: 음, 넌 네가 읽는 것을 모두 믿을 수는 없어.

8 Kyle: 그들은 광고에 거짓말을 한 거야. 돈을 환불해 달라고 해야겠어.

9 Emma: 기다려, Kyle! 그들은 사실이 아닌 의견을 사용했기 때문에 꼭 거짓말을 한 것은 아니야.

10 Kyle: 뭐라고? 네 말을 이해하지 못하겠어.

11 Emma: 의견은 "사막은 아름다워."와 같이 사람들의 감정을 표현하는 것이야.

12 그것이 사실인지 아닌지 말할 수는 없어. 하지만 사실은 증명할 수 있어.

13 예를 들면, "아타카마 사막은 칠레에 있다."는 사실이야. 넌 그것을 지도에서 확인할 수 있어.

14 Kyle: 알겠어… 하지만 그게 영화와 무슨 관련이 있니?

15 Emma: 설명해 줄게. 네가 가장 좋아하는 영화가 뭐니?

16 (Kyle: / *Forrest* / it's / *Gump*.)
➡ _____

17 (Emma: / okay. / look / let's / for / advertisement. / its // say? / what / it / does)
➡ _____

18 (Kyle: / says, / it / "winner / 6 / of / Awards / Academy / Best / Picture." / including)
➡ _____

19 (Emma: / see? // uses / it / unlike / facts / the / advertisement. / 7 / *Y-Men*)
➡ _____

20 (you / do / see / difference? / the)
➡ _____

21 (Kyle: / exactly. / not // *Y-Men 7* / the / says / ad / "Most Exciting Movie" / and / says / the / "Best Picture." / *Forrest Gump* / ad)
➡ _____

22 (they / aren't / opinions? / both)
➡ _____

23 (Emma: / a / questions, / that's / Kyle. // people / when / words / use / "most," / or / "best" / like / are / they / usually / opinions. / expressing)
➡ _____

24 (in / but / *Forrest Gump* / the / ad, / "Best Picture" / the / is / which / award / won. / movie / the)
➡ _____

25 (can / we / that / check / the / on / Internet. // fact. / a / that's)
➡ _____

26 (Kyle: / aha! // now / from / on / only / I'm / to / going / trust / facts. / with / ads)
➡ _____

27 (Emma: / not / it's / simple. / that // ads / most / facts / mix / opinions. / with)
➡ _____

28 (you / so / to / have / make / smart / a / based / choice / both / on / them. / of)
➡ _____

29 (Kyle: / it! / got / Emma, / you / do / want / watch / to / rest / the / *Y-Men 7* / of / me? / with)
➡ _____

30 (Emma: / but / thanks, / thanks. / no // the / enjoy / rest / movie! / of / the)
➡ _____

16 Kyle: "Forest Gump"야.

17 Emma: 좋아. 그 영화의 광고를 찾아보자. 뭐라고 쓰여 있니?

18 Kyle: "Best Picture를 포함하여 아카데미 6개 부문 수상작"이라고 쓰여 있어.

19 Emma: 알겠니? "Y-Men 7" 광고와는 달리 사실을 사용하고 있어.

20 차이를 알겠니?

21 Kyle: 잘 모르겠어. "Y-Men 7" 광고는 "Most Exciting Movie"라고 쓰여 있고 "Forest Gump" 광고는 "Best Picture"라고 쓰여 있잖아.

22 둘 다 의견 아니니?

23 Emma: 좋은 질문이야. Kyle. 사람들이 'best'나 'most'와 같은 말을 사용할 때. 그들은 대개 의견을 표현하는 거야.

24 하지만 "Forest Gump" 광고에서 "Best Picture"는 영화가 받은 상이야.

25 우리는 인터넷에서 그것을 확인할 수 있어. 그건 사실이야.

26 Kyle: 아하! 지금부터 사실로 이루어진 광고만 믿겠어.

27 Emma: 그렇게 간단하지는 않아. 대부분의 광고는 사실과 의견이 섞여 있어.

28 그러니 그 둘을 바탕으로 현명한 선택을 해야 해.

29 Kyle: 알겠어! Emma, "Y-Men 7"의 남은 부분을 나와 함께 볼래?

30 Emma: 고맙지만 사양할게. 영화의 남은 부분 잘 봐!

※ 다음 우리말을 영어로 쓰시오.

1 ▶ Emma: Kyle, 뭐 하고 있니?

➡ _____

2 ▶ Kyle: Emma. 나는 컴퓨터로 영화 "Y-Men 7"을 보고 있어.

➡ _____

3 ▶ Emma: 어때?

➡ _____

4 ▶ Kyle: 묻지 마. 너무 지루해서 울고 싶어.

➡ _____

5 ▶ Emma: 유감이야.

➡ _____

6 ▶ Klye: 난 정말 화가 나. 영화 광고에는 이것이 "올해의 가장 흥미진진한 영화"라고 쓰여 있었어.

➡ _____

7 ▶ Emma: 음, 넌 네가 읽는 것을 모두 믿을 수는 없어.

➡ _____

8 ▶ Kyle: 그들은 광고에 거짓말을 한 거야. 돈을 환불해 달라고 해야겠어.

➡ _____

9 ▶ Emma: 기다려, Kyle! 그들은 사실이 아닌 의견을 사용했기 때문에 꼭 거짓말을 한 것은 아니야.

➡ _____

10 ▶ Kyle: 뭐라고? 네 말을 이해하지 못하겠어.

➡ _____

11 ▶ Emma: 의견은 "사막은 아름다워."와 같이 사람들의 감정을 표현하는 것이야.

➡ _____

12 ▶ 그것이 사실인지 아닌지 말할 수는 없어. 하지만 사실은 증명할 수 있어.

➡ _____

13 ▶ 예를 들면, "아타카마 사막은 칠레에 있다."는 사실이야. 넌 그것을 지도에서 확인할 수 있어.

➡ _____

14 ▶ Kyle: 알겠어…. 하지만 그게 영화와 무슨 관련이 있니?

➡ _____

15 ▶ Emma: 설명해 줄게. 네가 가장 좋아하는 영화가 뭐니?

➡ _____

16 Kyle: "Forest Gump"야.

➡ _____

17 Emma: 좋아. 그 영화의 광고를 찾아보자. 뭐라고 쓰여 있니?

➡ _____

18 Kyle: "Best Picture를 포함하여 아카데미 6개 부문 수상작"이라고 쓰여 있어.

➡ _____

19 Emma: 알겠니? "Y-Men 7" 광고와는 달리 사실을 사용하고 있어.

➡ _____

20 차이를 알겠니?

➡ _____

21 Kyle: 잘 모르겠어. "Y-Men 7" 광고는 "Most Exciting Movie"라고 쓰여 있고 "Forest Gump" 광고는 "Best Picture"라고 쓰여 있잖아.

➡ _____

22 둘 다 의견 아니니?

➡ _____

23 Emma: 좋은 질문이야, Kyle. 사람들이 'best'나 'most'와 같은 말을 사용할 때, 그들은 대개 의견을 표현하는 거야.

➡ _____

24 하지만 "Forest Gump" 광고에서 "Best Picture"는 영화가 받은 상이야.

➡ _____

25 우리는 인터넷에서 그것을 확인할 수 있어. 그건 사실이야.

➡ _____

26 Kyle: 아하! 지금부터 사실로 이루어진 광고만 믿겠어.

➡ _____

27 Emma: 그렇게 간단하지는 않아. 대부분의 광고는 사실과 의견이 섞여 있어.

➡ _____

28 그러니 그 둘을 바탕으로 현명한 선택을 해야 해.

➡ _____

29 Kyle: 알겠어! Emma, "Y-Men 7"의 남은 부분을 나와 함께 볼래?

➡ _____

30 Emma: 고맙지만 사양할게. 영화의 남은 부분 잘 봐!

➡ _____

※ 다음 우리말과 일치하도록 빈칸에 알맞은 말을 쓰시오.

Listen and Speak 2 - C

1. A: _____ _____ _____ _____ your bicycle?

2. B: I'm _____ _____ _____ it.

3. A: Why _____?

4. B: It's _____ _____.

1. A: 자전거가 마음에 드니?
2. B: 마음에 들지 않아.
3. A: 왜?
4. B: 너무 무거워.

Think and Write

1. *Harry Potter* is a _____ _____.

2. It _____ _____ _____ J. K. Rowling.

3. Harry Potter is _____ _____ _____ of the book.

4. When Harry goes to _____ _____, his _____ begin.

5. I _____ _____ the _____ of Harry and his friends.

6. The book was _____ _____ _____ I couldn't _____ it

   _____.

7. I _____ _____ it to everyone.

1. "해리포터"는 공상 소설이다.
2. 이 책은 J. K. Rowling에 의해 쓰였다.
3. Harry Potter는 이 책의 주인공이다.
4. Harry가 마법 학교에 가면서 그의 모험은 시작된다.
5. 나는 특히 Harry와 그의 친구들의 우정을 좋아한다.
6. 이 책은 너무 재미있어서 나는 책을 놓을 수가 없었다.
7. 나는 모두에게 이 책을 강력히 추천한다.

Project

1. Korean _____ _____

2. Facts: It _____ _____ _____ Yongin.

3. There are _____ _____ _____.

4. Visitors _____ _____ nongak and jultagi.

5. Opinions: It's _____ _____ _____ in Yongin.

6. Korean _____ are beautiful.

7. Nongak and jultagi _____ _____ _____.

1. 한국 민속촌
2. 사실: 그것은 용인에 있습니다.
3. 한국 전통 가옥이 있습니다.
4. 방문객들은 농악과 줄타기를 볼 수 있습니다.
5. 의견: 그곳은 용인에 있는 재미있는 장소입니다.
6. 한국 전통 가옥들은 아름답습니다.
7. 농악과 줄타기는 신이 날 겁니다.

※ 다음 우리말을 영어로 쓰시오.

Listen and Speak 2 - C

1. A: 자전거가 마음에 드니?
   ➡ _____

2. B: 마음에 들지 않아.
   ➡ _____

3. A: 왜?
   ➡ _____

4. B: 너무 무거워.
   ➡ _____

Think and Write

1. "해리포터"는 공상 소설이다.
   ➡ _____

2. 이 책은 J. K. Rowling에 의해 쓰였다.
   ➡ _____

3. Harry Potter는 이 책의 주인공이다.
   ➡ _____

4. Harry가 마법 학교에 가면서 그의 모험은 시작된다.
   ➡ _____

5. 나는 특히 Harry와 그의 친구들의 우정을 좋아한다.
   ➡ _____

6. 이 책은 너무 재미있어서 나는 책을 놓을 수가 없었다.
   ➡ _____

7. 나는 모두에게 이 책을 강력히 추천한다.
   ➡ _____

Project

1. 한국 민속촌
   ➡ _____

2. 사실: 그것은 용인에 있습니다.
   ➡ _____

3. 한국 전통 가옥이 있습니다.
   ➡ _____

4. 방문객들은 농악과 줄타기를 볼 수 있습니다.
   ➡ _____

5. 의견: 그곳은 용인에 있는 재미있는 장소입니다.
   ➡ _____

6. 한국 전통 가옥들은 아름답습니다.
   ➡ _____

7. 농악과 줄타기는 신이 날 겁니다.
   ➡ _____

MEMO

영어 기출 문제집

적중100

2학기

정답 및 해설

동아 | 이병민

중 2

적중100

영어 기출 문제집

적중100

2학기

정답 및 해설

동아 | 이병민

중 2

Come One, Come All

시험대비 실력평가　　　　　　　　　p.08

01 far　　　02 hometown　　　　　03 ①
04 (1) neighborhood　(2) parade　(3) advertise
(4) pile　(5) regularly　　　05 ①　　　06 ⑤
07 (1) sled　(2) colorful　(3) arrow

01 주어진 단어는 반의어 관계를 나타낸다. far: 먼, near: 가까운
02 '당신이 태어나거나 자란 도시나 마을'을 가리키는 것은 hometown(고향)이다.
03 ①번 문장에서 sail은 '돛'을 의미한다. rake: 갈퀴로 긁다, 긁어 모으다
04 neighborhood: 근처, 이웃, parade: 퍼레이드, 행진, advertise: 광고하다, pile: 더미, regularly: 규칙적으로
05 주어진 문장에서 live는 형용사로 '실황인, 라이브의'를 의미하며 이와 같은 의미로 쓰인 것은 ①번이다. 나머지는 모두 '살다'나 '살아 있다'를 의미한다.
06 주어진 문장에서 cross는 '건너다'와 '십자, X표'를 의미한다.
07 sled: 썰매, colorful: 형형색색의, arrow: 화살

서술형 시험대비　　　　　　　　　　p.09

01 disappear　02 (1) live　(2) fireworks　(3) almost
(4) artwork　03 (1) to end　(2) more and more
(3) come out　(4) out of hand
04 (1) When will the music festival be held?
(2) I enjoyed decorating the Christmas tree.
(3) People gathered together to see the singer.
05 (1) People celebrate the festival everywhere for two days.
(2) It was amazing to see my favorite singer in person.
(3) People watch the artists shaping their works from beginning to end.

01 주어진 단어는 반의어 관계를 나타낸다. appear: 나타나다, disappear: 사라지다
02 live: 라이브의, 실황인, almost: 거의, fireworks: 불꽃놀이, artwork: 예술 작품
03 from beginning to end: 처음부터 끝까지, more and more: 더욱 더, come out: 나오다, out of hand: 손을 쓸 수 없는

04 hold: 개최하다, decorate: 장식하다, gather: 모이다, 모으다
05 (2) in person: 직접 (3) from beginning to end: 처음부터 끝까지

교과서 Conversation

핵심 Check　　　　　　　　　　　p.10~11

1 (1) How can I get to
(2) Cross the street, go straight
(3) Is there a hospital / just around
2 (1) take about half an hour
(2) How long will it take to / by bus
(3) How long will it take to decorate the classroom / take about two hours

교과서 대화문 익히기

 Check(√) True or False　　　　p.12

1 T　2 F　3 T　4 F

교과서 확인학습　　　　　　　　p.14~15

Listen and Speak 1-A
How can I get to the library / Cross, go straight, make

Listen and Speak 1-B
What's up / free / Why, ask / having / Let's, near / How can I get there from the school / Come out, go straight, Make a left, on your left / Let's meet / See, then

Listen and Speak 1-C
How can, get to / Go straight, make, be on your right / far from / not

Listen and Speak 2-A
be late for / How long will it take to get to the theater / take about, by bus / almost

Listen and Speak 2-B
excited / Me, too, advertise / about making / post them, neighborhood / How long will it take to / take about / come to

Real Life Talk
get to / over there / Take, get off / How long will it take to get there / take about / the festival / it's a lot of fun / have a great time

01 It will take about 5 minutes by car.
02 (B) → (E) → (C) → (D) → (A)
03 ⓒ → and　　　　　　　04 ⑤

02 (B) 길 묻기 → (E) 길 안내하기 → (C) 거리가 먼지 질문 → (D) 대답 → (A) 감사 표현
03 between A and B: A와 B 사이에

 시험대비 실력평가　　　　　p.17~18

01 How long will it take to get to the theater?
02 ①　　　　　03 why don't we have lunch together?
04 ⑤　　　　　05 advertise　　06 ⓐ the school festival
ⓑ the posters　　　　　07 ⑤
08 He will go there by bus.
09 Because he heard (that) it's a lot of fun.
10 He should take the number 11 bus.
11 (A) get　(B) Go straight　(C) a right　(D) one block　(E) fron

02 by bus: 버스로
03 how about ~?=why don't we ~?= ~하는 게 어때?
04 위 대화를 읽고 Emma가 Ming's까지 가는 데 걸리는 시간은 알 수 없다.
05 '사람들이 물건을 사게 만들도록 물건에 대해 대중에게 이야기하다'를 가리키는 말은 advertise(광고하다)이다.
07 Andy와 Mike가 그들의 이웃들과 포스터를 게시할 것이라는 설명은 대화의 내용과 일치하지 않는다.
11 Green Street까지 직진하세요. 우회전하세요. 한 구역 곧장 간 후 길을 건너면 마켓이 당신 앞에 있을 것입니다.

 서술형 시험대비　　　　　p.19

01 How can I get to the library?
02 make a left 또는 turn left　03 ⓐ → excited
04 They are going to advertise the school festival.
05 They are going to make posters.
06 (A) Go straight to 1st Street and make a right
(B) left

01 이어지는 대답으로 보아 길을 묻는 질문이 적절하다.
02 make a left: 왼쪽으로 돌다
03 exciting: 흥분시키는, excited: 신나는, 흥분한
04 Andy와 Mike는 학교 축제를 홍보할 것이다.
05 Andy와 Mike는 포스터를 만들 것이다.
06 극장에 가기 위해 1st Street까지 곧장 간 후 오른쪽으로 돌면 왼쪽에 있다.

핵심 Check　　　　　　　　　　p.20~21

1 (1) It, to exercise　(2) It, to drive　(3) to lie
2 (1) felt, follow(ing)　(2) saw, enter(ing)
(3) made[had], clean

01 (1) get → to get　(2) to changing → to change
(3) said → say(또는 saying)
(4) to dance → dance(또는 dancing)
02 (1) fall 또는 falling　(2) to go
(3) break 또는 breaking　(4) to play
03 (1) I heard the baby cry(ing).
(2) It is a good idea for you to wake up early.
(3) Emma saw them swim(ming) around the island.
(4) People watch the artists create their works from beginning to end.

01 (1) 가주어 it에 의미상의 주어 'for+목적격'이 쓰였으므로 진주어로 to부정사를 쓰는 것이 옳다. (2) to부정사의 형태는 'to+동사원형'이다. (3), (4) 지각동사의 목적어가 목적격보어의 행위의 주체가 될 경우 목적격보어로 원형부정사나 현재분사를 쓰는 것이 옳다.
02 (1), (3) 지각동사의 목적격보어는 목적어와의 관계가 능동일 경우 원형부정사나 현재분사가 쓰인다. (2), (4) 진주어로 to부정사를 쓸 수 있다.
03 (1), (3) '아기가 우는 소리', '그들이 수영하는 것'은 모두 목적어가 목적격보어의 주체가 되므로 목적격보어로 원형부정사나 현재분사를 쓰는 것이 옳다. (2) 일찍 일어나는 것의 주체가 '너'이므로 의미상의 주어로 '너'를 명시하여 for you를 써야 한다. (4) 미술가들이 작품을 만드는 것을 지켜보는 것이므로 목적어로 the artists, 목적격 보어로 create their works를 쓴다.

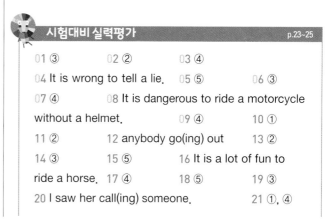

01 ③　　　　　02 ②　　　　　03 ④
04 It is wrong to tell a lie.　05 ⑤　　　　06 ③
07 ④　　　　　08 It is dangerous to ride a motorcycle without a helmet.　　　　09 ④　　　　10 ①
11 ②　　　　12 anybody go(ing) out　　13 ②
14 ③　　　　15 ⑤　　　　16 It is a lot of fun to ride a horse.　17 ④　　　　18 ⑤　　　　19 ③
20 I saw her call(ing) someone.　　21 ①, ④

22 ⑤   23 I saw the boy fall(ing) off the tree yesterday.   24 using his phone   25 It is not safe to stay here.

01 ③ 모두 가주어 It이지만 ③번은 인칭대명사 It이다. 전자는 해석되지 않지만 후자는 '그것'이라고 해석된다.

02 see는 지각동사로 목적격보어로 원형부정사 혹은 현재분사, 과거분사를 받을 수 있다. 친구들이 축구를 하는 주체가 되므로 play(ing)가 빈칸에 들어가는 것이 적절하다.

03 '이 책을 읽는 것'이 주어이므로 to read this book이라고 쓰고 어려웠다는 것은 과거이므로 was difficult를 쓴다.

04 '거짓말을 하는 것'을 진주어로 하여 문장을 만든다.

05 make가 사역동사로 쓰였으므로 목적격보어로 원형부정사 형태를 쓰는 것이 옳다.

06 '부부가 싸우는 소리', '집이 흔들리는 것'이므로 ③번이 옳다.

07 listen to는 지각동사이다. 따라서 목적격보어로 원형부정사나 현재분사를 쓰는 것이 옳다.

08 to가 필요하다.

09 '최선을 다하는 것'이 주어이므로 to do your best를 써서 진주어를 만들고 가주어 It을 쓴 것이 답이다.

10 남자가 차에 타는 것이므로 get 혹은 getting을 쓰는 것이 옳다. dormitory: 기숙사

11 모두 주어로 쓰인 to부정사이지만 ②번은 부사로 쓰인 to부정사로 감정의 원인을 나타낸다.

12 누가 나가는 것을 보지 못했다는 의미이다. anybody는 go out의 주체가 되므로 go out 혹은 going out을 쓸 수 있다.

13 hear는 지각동사이며 you가 들어오는 것이므로 원형부정사 혹은 현재분사를 목적격보어로 써야 한다.

14 (A), (C) 목적어와의 관계로 보아 지각동사의 목적격보어로 원형부정사나 현재분사를 쓰는 것이 옳으며, (B) 진주어이므로 to부정사를 쓰는 것이 옳다.

15 주어진 문장의 It은 가주어이다. ①, ② 시간, 명암을 나타내는 비인칭 주어, ③, ④ 인칭대명사, ⑤ 가주어

16 '말을 타는 것'이 주어이므로 가주어 it을 활용하여 문장을 만든다.

17 '나는 Brad가 길을 걷고 있는 것을 보았다'가 옳다.

18 make는 목적격보어로 원형부정사를 취하여 사역동사의 의미를 갖는다.

19 네가 창문을 닫는 것을 내가 보았다는 의미가 된다. 따라서 ③번이 가장 적절하다.

20 '그녀가 누군가에게 전화하는 것'이므로 목적어로 her, 목적격보어로 call 또는 calling을 쓸 수 있다.

21 It is fun 다음에는 진주어로 동명사를 쓸 수도 있으며, see는 지각동사에 해당하므로 목적격보어로 원형부정사나 현재분사를 쓴다.

22 to부정사의 형태는 'to+동사원형'이다.

23 '나는 그 소년이 어제 나무에서 떨어지는 것을 보았다'라고 쓸 수 있다.

24 using을 대신하여 use를 써도 무방하다.

25 가주어 it과 진주어로 to부정사를 이용하여 문장을 만든다.

서술형 시험대비
p.26~27

01 you ride(또는 riding) a bike yesterday
02 It is bad to run on the stairs.
03 Did you see the accident happen?
04 It was good
05 It is not a good idea to allow students to use cell phones in school.
06 saw her cross(ing) the street
07 It is rude of you not to bow politely.
08 (1) To save water is important.
　 (2) It is important to save water.
09 open(ing) the window
10 It is difficult to shoot an arrow.
11 to reduce food waste in school cafeteria
12 musicians play(ing) beautiful live music, play(ing) catch, sing(ing) a song
13 It is easy to look up a word in a dictionary.
14 I heard someone play(ing) the piano.
15 It is important to be honest and fair.
16 잘못된 곳: to do → do(ing) 고친 이유: 지각동사의 목적격 보어로 원형부정사나 현재분사를 쓰는 것이 옳다.
17 It is not easy to be a doctor.
18 to watch them move the table
19 I felt someone follow(ing) me yesterday.

01 어제 네가 자전거를 타는 것을 보았기 때문이라고 답할 수 있다.

02 stairs: 계단

03 '사고가 발생하는 것을 보았니?'라는 문장으로 쓸 수 있다. happen: 발생하다

04 to부정사를 맨 뒤로 보낸 것으로 보아 가주어 it을 써야 함을 알 수 있다.

05 allow+목적어+to부정사: 목적어가 V하도록 허락하다

06 Susan이 길을 건너는 것을 보았다고 답하는 것이 적절하다. 'Susan이 길을 건너는 것'이므로 지각동사의 목적격보어로 원형부정사나 현재분사를 사용하여 답한다.

07 '예의 바르게 인사하지 않는 것'이 주어이다. to부정사의 부정은 to V 앞에 부정어를 써서 나타내므로 진주어를 not to bow politely라고 쓰는 것이 옳다.

08 '물을 절약하는 것'이 주어이므로 to save water라고 쓴다.

09 어떤 남자가 창문을 여는 것을 보았지만 그가 누구인지는 모른다고 답할 수 있다. 지각동사 see의 목적어로 창문을 여는 주체

인 a man이 쓰이고 있으므로 원형부정사나 현재분사를 목적격
보어로 쓰는 것이 옳다.

10 'To shoot an arrow is difficult.'라고 써도 무방하다.

11 학교에서 음식물 쓰레기를 줄이려는 것이 힘들었다는 대답이 들
어가는 것이 자연스럽다.

12 공원에서 너는 음악가들이 아름다운 즉석 연주를 하는 것을 들
을 수 있다. 또한 너는 아이들이 캐치볼 놀이를 하고, 커플들이
노래를 부르는 것을 볼 수 있다.

13 difficult의 반의어는 easy이므로 사전에서 단어를 찾는 것은
쉽다고 답할 수 있다. 'To look up a word in a dictionary
is easy.'라고 써도 좋다.

14 '누군가가 피아노를 연주하는' 소리이므로 목적어와 목적격보어
로 someone play(ing) the piano를 쓰는 것이 옳다

15 fair: 공정한

16 해석: Brady는 Clara가 무언가를 하는 것을 보았고 그녀가 무
엇을 하는지 궁금했다.

17 to become a doctor로 써도 무방하다.

18 move를 대신하여 moving을 써도 무방하다.

19 feel은 지각동사로 목적어와 목적격보어를 취하는 동사이
다. '누군가가 나를 따라오는 것'이라고 하였으므로 목적어로
someone을 쓰고 목적격보어로
follow 혹은 following을 쓰는 것이 옳다.

교과서 Reading

확인문제　　　　　　p.28

1 T　2 F　3 F　4 T

확인문제　　　　　　p.29

1 T　2 F　3 T　4 F　5 T

교과서 확인학습 A　　　　　p.30~31

01 Festival
02 from
03 the most popular
04 is usually
05 say goodbye, hello
06 celebrate, for
07 On, gather around, at night
08 begins the next day
09 chase each other
10 What, powder
11 to run around, throw, at
12 join street parades
13 White Nights
14 from
15 Have, heard of
16 amazing, happens

17 does not get completely
18 During, hold
19 starts in, lasts, about
20 there is, almost every night
21 popular, celebration
22 appears on the river
23 begin, follows
24 hear, playing
25 Snow Festival
26 from
27 my favorite season because of
28 starts in the last week, goes on
29 The largest event
30 shape, into, other
31 watch, shaping, from, to
32 favorite activity
33 to fly through, on

교과서 확인학습 B　　　　　p.32~33

1 Holi, the Festival of Colors
2 Amala from Delhi, India
3 Holi is the most popular festival in my country.
4 It is usually in March.
5 During the festival, we say goodbye to cold winter and hello to warm spring.
6 We celebrate the festival everywhere for two days.
7 On the first day, people gather around a big fire at night and sing and dance.
8 The main event begins the next day.
9 Children and adults chase each other with *gulal*.
10 What is *gulal*? It is blue, yellow, green and pink powder.
11 It's a lot of fun to run around and throw colorful powder at everyone.
12 We also join street parades!
13 White Nights Festival
14 Victor from St. Petersburg, Russia
15 Have you heard of the *White Nights*?
16 Every summer, this amazing thing happens in my hometown.
17 The night sky does not get completely dark.
18 During that time, we hold the White Nights Festival.
19 It usually starts in May and lasts for about a month.
20 During the festival, there is a ballet or an opera almost every night.
21 The most popular event is the Scarlet Sails celebration.
22 A boat with red sails slowly appears on the river.
23 Soon, fireworks begin and a water show follows.
24 You can also hear musicians playing beautiful live music.

25 Kiruna Snow Festival

26 Ebba from Kiruna, Sweden

27 Winter is my favorite season because of the Kiruna Snow Festival.

28 The festival starts in the last week of January and goes on for five or six days.

29 The largest event is the snow design competition.

30 The artists shape huge piles of snow into animals, buildings, and other beautiful artworks.

31 People watch the artists shaping their works from beginning to end.

32 My favorite activity is the dog sled ride.

33 It is amazing to fly through a world of snow on a dog sled.

시험대비 실력평가 p.34~37

01 ④　　　　02 to run　　　03 ③

04 Holi is the most popular festival in India.

05 gather　　　06 ⑤　　　　07 ②

08 the White Nights　　　09 ⑤

10 We can see a ballet or an opera almost every night.　　　11 shape (또는 shaping)　　　12 ②

13 ⑤　　　14 It lasts five or six days.　　　15 ②

16 ④　　　　17 ⑤

18 chase[chasing] each other with gulal

19 We should go to the festival on the second day.

20 play(ing)　　　21 every summer　　　22 ⑤

23 ④　　　24 ②　　　25 ⑤

26 shaping their works　　　27 ④　　　28 ③, ⑤

01 at night: 밤에, throw something at someone: ~에게 ~을 던지다

02 가주어 it이 쓰이고 있으므로 진주어를 써야 한다. 병렬로 연결된 동사 throw의 형태로 미루어 보아 to run을 쓰는 것이 옳다.

03 주요 행사는 다음 날에 시작된다고 하였다. 따라서 ③번은 일치하지 않는다.

04 인도에서 가장 인기 있는 축제는 '홀리'라고 하였다.

05 사람들이 한 무리로 모이는 것은 gather이다.

06 colorful powder를 던진다고 하였다.

07 (A)에서 쓰인 현재완료는 '경험'이다. 따라서 '~에 가본 적이 있다'는 경험을 나타내는 has been to가 옳다.

08 '이 놀라운 것'이라는 것은 '백야'를 의미한다.

09 (C)는 '개최하다'는 의미로 쓰였다. ①, ③ ~을 쥐다, 잡다, ② 지탱하다, ④ (수화기를 들고) 기다리다, ⑤ 개최하다

10 축제 동안 거의 매일 밤 발레나 오페라가 있다고 하였다.

11 지각동사 watch의 목적격보어 자리이다. 목적어와 능동 관계에

있으므로 원형부정사 혹은 현재분사를 쓴다.

12 (A) 명사구가 이어지고 있으므로 because of (B) 복수명사가 이어지고 있으므로 other (C) 놀라움을 유발하는 것이므로 현재분사 amazing을 쓰는 것이 옳다.

13 ⑤ 몇 명의 미술가가 눈 디자인 대회에 참가하는지는 알 수 없다.

14 축제는 5~6일 동안 지속된다고 하였다.

15 (A) 출신을 나타내는 전치사 from, (B) 월, 연도 앞에는 전치사 in, (C) 특정 기간을 나타내어 '~ 동안'이라는 의미는 during

16 ④ 축제 첫 날 밤에 사람들이 큰 모닥불 주변에 모여 노래하고 춤을 춘다고 하였다.

17 join은 타동사이므로 전치사 없이 목적어를 취한다. 따라서 join이라고 쓰는 것이 어법상 옳다.

18 축제 마지막 날인 둘째 날에는 어린이들과 어른들이 gulal을 지니고 서로를 쫓아다니는 모습을 볼 수 있다.

19 둘째 날에 주요 행사가 있다고 하였다. 따라서 주요 행사만 보고 싶다면 둘째 날 축제에 가야 한다.

20 목적어와 능동 관계에 있으므로 지각동사 hear의 목적보어로 원형부정사나 현재분사를 쓸 수 있다.

21 백야 축제는 매년 여름마다 거행된다고 하였다.

22 배가 어디에서 오는지는 알 수 없다.

23 배가 서서히 나타난다고 하였으므로 ④번은 옳지 않다.

24 go on: 계속되다

25 ⑤ 눈 덩어리를 동물 모양으로 만드는 사람들은 미술가들이라고 하였다.

26 지각동사 see의 목적격보어 자리이므로 shape their works라고 써도 좋다.

27 ④ 미술가들은 눈덩이로 동물, 건물, 다른 아름다운 작품의 모양을 만든다고 하였다.

28 밑줄 친 (A)는 가주어 it이다. ①, ④ 인칭대명사 ② 비인칭 주어

서술형 시험대비 p.38~39

01 They celebrate the festival for two days.

02 gather around, sing and dance

03 is a lot of fun to run around and throw, colorful powder at everyone.

04 India in March

05 It is blue, yellow, green and pink powder.

06 St. Petersburg, Russia

07 It usually starts in May and lasts for about a month.

08 The night sky does not get completely dark.

09 There are a ballet or an opera almost every night and the Scarlet Sails celebration.

10 slowly appear(ing) on the river

11 to fly

12 Winter is Ebba's favorite season because of the Kiruna Snow Festival.

13 Kiruna, the snow design competition

14 It lasts for five or six days.

15 I am watching the artist shaping a huge pile of snow into an elephant.

01 축제는 이틀 동안 지속된다고 하였다.

02 gathering around, singing and dancing이라고 써도 좋다.

03 가주어를 이용하여 문장을 다시 쓸 수 있다.

04 홀리 축제를 보려면 3월에 인도로 가야 한다.

05 gulal은 파랑, 노랑, 초록, 분홍의 가루라고 하였다.

06 러시아 상트페테르부르크가 글쓴이의 고향이다.

07 빈도부사의 위치는 보통 일반동사 앞, be동사나 조동사 뒤이다.

08 밤하늘이 완전히 어두워지지 않는 것이 백야이다.

09 축제 행사로는 발레, 오페라, 붉은 돛 축하 행사가 있다고 하였다.

10 배가 강 위에 서서히 나타나는 것을 보았다고 쓸 수 있다. '배가 나타나는 것'이므로 지각동사의 목적어로 원형부정사나 현재분사를 쓰는 것이 옳다.

11 진주어이므로 to fly를 쓴다.

12 키루나 눈 축제 때문에 Ebba는 겨울을 가장 좋아한다고 하였다.

13 키루나 눈 축제를 보기 위해서 키루나를 방문할 것이라면 축제에서 가장 큰 행사인 눈 디자인 대회를 보아야 한다고 말하는 것이 옳다.

14 축제는 5일이나 6일 동안 계속된다고 하였다.

15 '미술가가 ~을 바꾸는 것'이므로 목적어로 the artist, 목적격보어로 shaping ~을 쓰는 것이 옳다.

영역별 핵심문제   p.41~45

01 dark   02 ①   03 ④

04 (1) Go straight, make   (2) each other   (3) get off

05 ②   06 (1) Where is your hometown?

(2) It is across from the museum.

(3) My friends gathered to celebrate my birthday.

07 How can I get there from the school?

08 ④   09 I hope many people come to the festival.   10 ⑤   11 ⑤   12 ④

13 ⑤   14 ⑤   15 ②   16 ④

17 to see him shouting at someone   18 ③

19 ⑤   20 to hearing → to hear

21 It is exciting to learn English.   22 ②

23 ③   24 I felt someone touch(ing) my shoulder.   25 celebrate   26 ④

27 ③   28 ⑤   29 ③

30 We can see the artists shape huge piles of snow into animals, buildings, and other beautiful artworks.   31 ④

32 It is interesting to watch the artists shaping their works from beginning to end.   33 sled

01 주어진 단어는 반의어 관계를 나타낸다. dark: 어두운, bright: 밝은

02 '따라가서 잡으려고 노력하다'를 가리키는 말은 chase(뒤쫓다)이다.

03 ④번 문장에서 chase는 '뒤쫓다'를 의미한다.

04 make a left: 왼쪽으로 돌다, each other: 서로, get off: 내리다

05 주어진 문장에서 sail은 '돛'을 의미하며 이와 같은 의미로 쓰인 문장은 ②번이다. 나머지는 모두 '항해하다'를 의미한다. retirement: 은퇴, navigator: 항해사, extend: 펼치다

06 hometown: 고향, across from: ~ 건너편에, celebrate: 축하하다

08 민수는 학교에서 나와서 Green Street까지 곧장 간 후 왼쪽으로 돌아야 음식점을 찾을 수 있다

10 Andy와 Mike가 포스터를 어디에서 만들지는 알 수 없다.

11 ⑤번을 제외한 나머지는 모두 감사에 대한 대답 표현이다.

12 (A)는 수원 화성에 어떻게 가는지 질문하는 문장이므로 get(도착하다)이 적절하다. (B) get on the bus: 버스를 타다, get off the bus: 버스에서 내리다 (C) 그곳까지 가는 데 소요 시간을 질문하고 있으므로 'How long will it take to ~?'가 적절하다.

13 Mina가 수원 화성 축제에 방문해 본 적이 있는지는 알 수 없다.

14 빈칸에는 목적격보어로 원형부정사를 쓰는 동사가 들어가야 한다. encourage는 목적격보어로 to부정사를 사용하는 동사이다.

15 모두 날씨, 날짜, 거리, 명암, 시간 등을 표현할 때 쓰이는 비인칭 주어 it이지만 ②번은 가주어 it이다.

16 누군가가 문을 열고 나가는 것이므로 open the door와 go out의 주체는 someone이 된다. 따라서 ④번이 옳다.

17 그가 누군가에게 소리 지르는 것을 보는 것은 놀라움을 주었다고 답하는 것이 자연스럽다.

18 ③ 소년들이 공을 차는 주체가 되므로 kick 혹은 kicking을 쓰는 것이 옳다.

19 밑줄 친 부분은 진주어로 쓰인 to부정사이다. 각각의 to부정사는 ① 목적격보어로 쓰인 명사적 용법 ② 부사적 용법 중 목적 ③ 명사를 꾸미는 형용사 ④ 동사의 목적어로 쓰인 명사적 용법 ⑤ 진주어로 쓰인 to부정사이다.

20 진주어는 to부정사이다. 따라서 to hear로 쓰는 것이 옳다.

21 '영어를 배우는 것'이 주어이므로 to learn English를 진주어로 하여 문장을 만든다.

22 ⓒ listen to는 지각동사이므로 tell 혹은 telling을 쓰는 것이 옳다. ⓓ 지각동사 see가 쓰였으므로 목적격보어로 원형부정사나 현재분사를 쓰는 것이 옳다.

23 첫 번째 빈칸은 진주어 자리이므로 to부정사를 쓰는 것이 옳으며, 두 번째 빈칸에는 지각동사의 목적격보어가 들어가야 하므로 ③번이 옳다.

24 '누군가가 내 어깨를 만지는 것'이므로 목적어로 someone, 목적격보어로 touch(ing)을 쓰는 것이 옳다.

25 중요한 행사나 명절을 위해 특별한 무언가를 하는 것은 '축하하다, 기념하다(celebrate)'이다.

26 아이들과 어른들이 gulal을 지니고 서로를 쫓아다닌다는 말이 먼저 나온 후 gulal이 무엇인지 설명해 주는 것이 자연스럽다.

27 ⓑ는 진주어로 쓰인 to부정사로 명사적 용법이다. 따라서 ③번이 옳다. ① 부사적 용법 중 목적 ② 감정의 원인 ④ 형용사적 용법 ⑤ 부사적 용법 중 형용사 수식

28 축제에 있는 사람들이 얼마나 많은 양의 gulal을 가지고 있는지는 알 수 없다.

29 go on은 '계속되다'는 의미이다. 따라서 continue가 옳다.

30 눈 디자인 대회에서는 미술가들이 거대한 눈 덩어리를 동물, 건물, 다른 아름다운 작품의 모양으로 만드는 모습을 볼 수 있다. shaping을 써도 무방하다.

31 가장 큰 행사는 개썰매 타기가 아니라 눈 디자인 대회라고 하였다.

32 지각동사 watch의 목적어와 목적격보어가 능동 관계에 있으므로 shape를 써도 무방하다.

33 '눈 위로 미끄러지는 데 사용되는 작은 탈 것'은 '썰매'이다.

단원별 예상문제 p.46~49

01 bank(오른쪽 맨 위 건물)   02 Go straight two blocks and make a left. The bakery is between the hospital and the bus stop.   03 ⑤   04 How long will it take to get there?   05 ①
06 (A) make posters   (B) their neighborhood
(C) about three hours   (D) the (school) festival
07 ④   08 ⑤   09 1st Street까지 곧장 간 후 우회전하면 오른쪽에 우체국이 있다.
10 Is it far from here?   11 ③   12 ③
13 I heard Kevin speak(ing) French.
14 ②   15 ⑤
16 It is a good chance to hear her play(ing) the violin.
17 Do you see a boy swim(ming) in the lake?
18 ①   19 ④   20 ⑤   21 ②
22 gulal

03 길을 묻는 질문에 소요 시간을 답하고 있으므로 ⑤번은 어색하다.

06 Andy와 Mike는 이번 주 금요일의 학교 축제로 매우 신이 났다. 이를 홍보하기 위해 그들은 포스터를 만들고 근방에 포스터를 붙이기로 결정한다. 포스터를 만드는 데 약 세 시간이 걸릴 것이다. 그들은 많은 사람들이 축제에 와서 즐기기를 원한다.

07 주어진 문장은 길을 안내해 주는 표현이므로 길을 묻는 표현 다음에 이어지는 (D)가 적절하다

08 ⓐ의 get은 '도착하다'라는 의미로 이와 같이 쓰인 것은 ⑤번이다. ①번은 '가져오다', ②번은 '타다', ③, ④번은 '받다'는 의미로 쓰였다.

11 진주어로 to부정사를 쓸 수 있으며 지각동사의 목적격보어로 원형부정사나 현재분사를 쓰는 것이 옳다.

12 모두 가주어 it이지만 ③번은 It was ~ that 강조 용법이다.

13 'Kevin이 프랑스어를 말하는 것'이므로 목적어로 Kevin, 목적격보어로 speak(ing) French를 써야 한다.

14 '목표를 설정하고 최선을 다하는 것'은 to set a goal and (to) do your best이다. 따라서 ②번이 옳다.

15 watch는 지각동사이며 목적어와 목적격보어의 관계가 능동이므로 원형부정사나 현재분사를 쓰는 것이 옳다.

16 '그녀가 바이올린을 연주하는 것'이므로 목적어로 her, 목적격보어로 play(ing) the violin을 써서 문장을 만든다.

17 '한 소년이 수영하고 있는 것'이므로 목적어로 a boy, 목적격보어로 swim(ming)을 쓰는 것이 옳다.

18 빈칸 ⓐ에는 전치사 of가 들어간다. ① get tired of: ~에 싫증이 나다 ② come up with: ~을 떠올리다 ③ look after: ~을 돌보다 ④ look up to: ~을 존경하다 ⑤ put off: ~을 미루다

19 백야에 대해 들어봤느냐는 질문에 - [C] 백야 설명 (this amazing thing이 'the White Nights' 지칭) - [A] 백야 기간 동안 축제를 엶 - [D] 축제 기간에 행사를 하고, 가장 인기 있는 축제는 '붉은 돛 축하 행사'임 - [B] 붉은 돛 축하 행사 설명

20 축제에 몇 명의 음악가들이 있는지는 알 수 없다.

21 홀리 축제를 이틀 동안 기념한다고 말한 후 첫째 날과 둘째 날에 어떤 행사가 있는지에 대한 설명이 이어지는 것이 자연스럽다.

22 형형색색의 가루는 gulal이다.

서술형 실전문제 p.50~51

01 They are going to have lunch together at the new Chinese restaurant, Ming's.
02 They are going to meet at 12 o'clock.
03 학교에서 나와서 Green Street까지 곧장 간 후 왼쪽으로 돌면 왼쪽에 있다.
04 call(ing) / called
05 It is essential to improve my English skill.
06 to have a balanced diet
07 Did you see the cat jump(ing) up onto the chair?
08 I saw the boy swimming in the pool.
09 It's a lot of fun to run around and throw colorful powder at everyone.
10 join street parades
11 People in India celebrate Holi in March.
12 It is in Gangneung.
13 We can see people swim(ming) at the beach.
14 It is soft and sweet.

04 someone은 나의 이름을 부르는 주체가 될 수 있으므로 현재분사나 원형부정사를 쓰고, 나의 이름은 '불리는 것'이므로 called를 쓰는 것이 옳다.

05 improve: 향상시키다

06 균형 잡힌 식사를 하는 것은 정말로 중요하다고 답할 수 있다. 다섯 단어이므로 to부정사로 만들어 답한다.

07 고양이가 의자로 뛰어오른 것을 보았는지 묻는 말로 쓸 수 있다.

09 'To run around and throw colorful powder at everyone is a lot of fun.' 혹은 'Running around and throwing colorful powder at everyone is a lot of fun.'으로 써도 무방하다.

10 이어지는 대답이 행진을 설명하는 말이므로 '거리 행진에 참가했니?'라고 묻는 것이 옳다.

11 홀리 축제는 3월에 있다고 하였다.

12 오죽헌은 강릉에 있다.

13 사람들이 해변에서 수영하는 것을 볼 수 있다.

14 감자떡이 어떤지를 묻는 말이다. 글쓴이는 감자떡이 부드럽고 달콤하다고 하였다.

창의사고력 서술형 문제   p.52

|모범답안|

01 Come out from the school and go straight to Green Street. Make a left, and the restaurant will be on your left.

02 (1) You can see many children chasing each other.
  (2) I can see many merchants selling their things.
  (3) I can hear people laughing happily at a festival.

03 (1) It is important to do your homework.
  (2) It is necessary to obey the school rules.
  (3) It is essential to pay attention to what a teacher says.
  (4) It is dangerous to run in the hall.

단원별 모의고사   p.53~56

01 ②   02 ②   03 ⑤
04 (1) threw (2) competition (3) huge
05 (1) go on (2) More and more (3) because of
(4) in front of 06 It will take about 15 minutes by bus.   07 이곳에서 수원 화성에 가는 것
08 off   09 ⑤
10 (1) How long does it take to get to school from your house?
  (2) How can I get to the bank?
  (3) Cross the street and go straight one block.
  (4) It will take about 10 minutes by subway.
11 (C) → (B) → (D) → (A)   12 ①   13 ④

14 ②   15 She heard the rain fall(ing) on the roof.   16 ③   17 ①, ②, ④
18 James felt something biting his arm.
19 ④   20 ②   21 ②   22 ③
23 It is amazing to fly through a world of snow on a dog sled.

01 '눈 위에서 미끄러지기 위해 사용되는 작은 탈 것'을 가리키는 말은 sled(썰매)이다.

02 주어진 문장에서 hold는 '개최하다, 열다'를 의미하며 이와 같은 의미로 쓰인 것은 ②번이다. ①, ③, ④번은 '잡다, 쥐다'를 의미하며 ⑤는 '맡다, 보유하다'를 의미한다. ⑤ 내 자리 좀 맡아 주실래요?

03 이어지는 대화로 보아 길을 묻는 표현이 적절하다. ⑤번은 소요 시간을 묻는 표현이다.

04 throw: 던지다, competition: 경쟁, 대회, huge: 거대한

05 go on: 지속되다, 계속되다, more and more: 더욱 더, because of: ~ 때문에, in front of: ~ 앞에

08 get off: 내리다

09 교실 장식의 소요 시간은 언급되지 않았다.

11 (C) 계획 질문 → (B) 계획 설명 → (D) 소요 시간 질문 → (A) 소요 시간 대답

12 학교에 어떻게 가는지 묻고 있으므로 ①번이 적절하다.

13 (a)는 부사로 쓰여 '거의, 대략'을 의미하며 이와 같은 의미로 쓰인 것은 ④번이다. 나머지는 모두 전치사로 '~에 관하여, ~에 대해'를 의미한다.

14 ② 지각동사의 목적격보어는 목적어와 능동의 관계에 있을 경우 원형부정사나 현재분사를 쓴다. 따라서 sing 혹은 singing을 쓰는 것이 옳다. pound on: ~을 마구 두드리다

15 '비가 지붕 위로 떨어지는 소리'이므로 목적어로 the rain, 목적격보어로 fall(ing)을 쓰는 것이 옳다.

16 두 문장 모두 지각동사의 목적격보어로 원형부정사나 현재분사를 쓸 수 있다. irritate: 짜증나게 하다

17 빈칸에는 목적격보어로 원형부정사를 취할 수 있는 동사가 와야 한다. 따라서 사역동사와 지각동사가 옳다.

18 '무언가가 그의 팔을 무는 것'이므로 목적어로 something, 목적격보어로 biting 혹은 bite을 써서 문장을 만든다.

19 (A) 명사가 따라오고 있으므로 전치사 During, (B) appear는 자동사이므로 수동태로 쓸 수 없다. (C) 연주자들이 연주를 하는 주체가 되므로 지각동사의 목적격보어로 원형부정사나 현재분사를 쓴다.

20 ② 밤하늘이 완전히 어두워지지 않는다고 하였으므로 무언가를 보는 것이 어렵다는 것은 글의 내용과 일치하지 않는다.

21 due to: ~ 때문에

22 눈 디자인 대회에서는 예술가들이 눈으로 특정한 모양을 만들며 겨룬다고 하였다.

23 fly through: ~을 날다

Lesson 6

In Outer Space

시험대비 실력평가 p.60

01 include   02 ⑤   03 ①
04 (1) mission (2) Although (3) peel (4) look for
(5) several   05 ⑤   06 (1) deaf (2) average
(3) applied   07 ⑤

01 주어진 관계는 반의어 관계를 나타낸다. include: 포함하다,
exclude: 제외하다
02 나머지는 모두 행성을 가리키지만 ⑤번은 은하를 뜻한다.
03 특정한 목적을 위해 형성된 모임이나 사업과 같은 단체를 가리
키는 말은 organization(조직, 단체)이다.
04 mission: 임무, although: ~이긴 하지만, peel: 껍질을 벗기
다, look for: ~을 찾다, several: 몇몇의
05 organization: 조직, 단체
07 나머지는 모두 '우주'를 뜻하지만 ⑤번은 '공간'을 뜻한다.

서술형 시험대비 p.61

01 (1) is good at   (2) are curious about
(3) On average   02 (1) blind (2) curious
(3) difference (4) similar (5) exhibition
03 (1) We have very similar interests.
  (2) Water is necessary for life.
  (3) The length of the trip is five days.
04 blind
05 (1) I'll apply for the volunteer program.
  (2) I read three books a month on average.
  (3) This ball is half the size of that one.
06 electricity

01 be good at: ~을 잘하다, be curious about: ~을 궁금해 하
다, on average:평균적으로
02 curious: 호기심 많은, blind: 눈이 먼, exhibition: 전시회,
similar: 비슷한, difference: 차이
04 '볼 수 없는'을 가리키는 말은 blind(시각 장애가 있는)이다.
06 나는 수미의 Soccket이 최고의 발명품이라고 생각한다. 우리가
이것을 갖고 놀 때, 이것은 전기를 만들어 낸다. 우리가 전기가
없을 때 이것은 매우 유용하다.

Conversation

핵심 Check p.62~63

1 (1) who he is (2) Do you know what it is
(3) Guess   **2** (1) What is it for (2) look at / for
(3) What are they used for

교과서 대화문 익히기

Check(√) True or False p.64

1 T 2 F 3 T 4 T

교과서 확인학습 p.66~67

Listen & Speak 1-A
what / looks like / butter stick / is there / spread

Listen & Speak 1-B
who this man is, inventor, was interested in, What,
invent, deaf, inventions

Listen & Speak 2-A
interesting / slicing eggs / try / here is

Listen & Speak 2-B
look at / Why, make / not just / what, for / put them on /
from now on / worry about

Listen & Speak 2-C
look at / have never seen, What, for / for making ink /
interesting

Real Life Talk – Step 1
How was / great time, science exhibition / there were
/ what it is / not sure / What is it for / wear, another
world / try

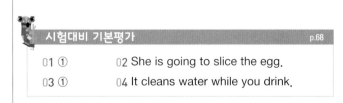

시험대비 기본평가 p.68

01 ①   02 She is going to slice the egg.
03 ①   04 It cleans water while you drink.

02 Jane은 달걀을 얇게 썰 것이다.

시험대비 실력평가

p.69~70

01 ⑤   02 (D) → (A) → (C) → (B)   03 ③
04 (A) so many interesting things
   (B) experience another world
05 (D) → You can put them on and clean the floor.
06 ⑤   07 (A) inventor   (B) inventions
08 ⑤   09 Do you know what this is?
10 It can be used to spread butter on the bread.
11 (E) → (B) → (A) → (C) → (D)

01 용도를 묻고 있는 질문에 '그것들은 비녀이다.'라고 대답하는 것은 어색하다.

02 (D) 용도 묻기 → (A) 용도 설명 → (C) 허락 요청 → (B) 대답

03 (A) 이어지는 주어가 복수이므로 were가 알맞다. (B) other 뒤에는 셀 수 있는 복수 명사가 이어진다. (C) 주어 That이 생략되어 있으므로 Sounds가 적절하다.

04 호진은 그의 남동생과 과학 전시회를 방문했다. 그는 경험할 흥미로운 것들이 매우 많았기 때문에 매우 신났었다. 그는 VR 헤드셋을 샀는데, 이것은 그를 다른 세계를 경험할 수 있게 만들어 주었다.

05 구동사(put on)의 목적어가 인칭대명사일 때 그 대명사는 동사와 부사(on) 사이에 위치한다.

06 Tom은 신고 청소할 수 있는 슬리퍼를 만들었으므로 엄마가 신을 수 있는 편리한 슬리퍼를 만들었다는 설명은 대화의 내용과 일치하지 않는다.

07 (A) inventor: 발명가, (B) make an invention: 발명하다

08 ⑤ 위 대화를 통해 Alexander Graham Bell의 전화기에 무슨 문제가 있었는지는 알 수 없다.

10 버터 스틱은 빵에 버터를 바를 때 사용될 수 있다.

11 (E) 모른다고 대답 및 설명 요청 → (B) 설명 → (A) 용도 질문 → (C) 용도 설명 → (D) 반응

서술형 시험대비

p.71

01 What is it for?   02 달걀을 얇게 써는 것
03 I have never seen it before.
04 They are talking about a meok.
05 It is used for making ink.
06 (A) Clean Straw   (B) cleans water
07 (A) inventor   (B) sound   (C) He invented the
   telephone.   (D) His mother and wife were deaf.
   (E) He made some inventions and opened a
   school for deaf people.

04 Irene과 Jane은 먹에 대해 이야기하고 있다.

05 먹은 잉크를 만드는 데 사용된다.

07 occupation: 직업, interest: 흥미, achievement: 업적, contribution: 기여

교과서

Grammar

핵심 Check

p.72~73

1 (1) as fast as   (2) twice as good as
  (3) not as[so] brave as
2 (1) Although[Though]   (2) although[though], sleepy
  (3) Even though[if]

시험대비 기본평가

p.74

01 (1) Because → Although[Though]
  (2) hardly → hard   (3) bored → boring
02 (1) as interesting as   (2) as cool as
  (3) not as[so] pretty as   (4) Even though
03 (1) Although she was rich, she kept saving
   money.
  (2) Learning how to swim is not as difficult as it
   looks.
  (3) We are as sad as they are.
  (4) She is not as attractive as she used to be.

01 (1) 문맥상 양보의 접속사를 써야 한다. (2), (3) as ~ as 사이에는 형용사나 부사의 원급이 온다. hard는 '세게'라는 의미의 부사이며 hardly는 '거의 ~하지 않는'이라는 의미의 부사로 쓰인다. 연설은 지루함을 유발하는 것이므로 boring을 쓴다.

02 (1) 흥미를 유발하는 주체이므로 interesting을 쓰는 것에 유의한다. (4) Even if, Although, Though를 써도 무방하다.

03 (1) although를 주절 뒤에 배치할 경우 콤마 없이 쓴다. (2), (4) 동등비교의 부정을 써서 표현한다.

시험대비 실력평가

p.75~77

01 ④   02 ⑤   03 ①   04 ③
05 (1) David is not as[so] tall as Richard.
  (2) Richard is not as[so] short as David.
06 ④   07 ⑤
08 Barry is not as[so] rich as James.
09 Brad is not as[so] old as he looks.   10 ⑤
11 ②, ④   12 ③   13 ②
14 Though he has just cleaned his room, it is still
   dirty.

01 be동사의 보어가 빠져 있으므로 빈칸에는 보어 역할을 할 수 있는 형용사가 들어가는 것이 옳다. 따라서 부사는 답이 될 수 없다. ① 명사+ly: 형용사

02 '그것'이 기차만큼 빠르게 달릴 수 없다고 하였으므로 주어는 It으로 하고 can't run을 쓰는 것이 옳다.

03 ① what I said라는 명사절을 이끌고 있으므로 In spite of 혹은 Despite를 쓰는 것이 옳다.

04 모두 원인과 결과의 절을 이어주는 because나 as가 들어가지만, ③번에는 앞뒤로 상반되는 내용을 이어주는 although가 적절하다.

05 'David는 Richard만큼 크지 않다, Richard는 David만큼 작지 않다'라고 쓸 수 있다.

06 위 문장은 앞뒤 내용이 상반되는 내용을 이어주는 말이, 아래 문장은 원인과 결과를 이어주는 말이 들어가는 것이 적절하다.

07 ⑤ Although가 아닌 Because[As]가 들어가는 것이 적절하다.

08 James가 Barry보다 부자라고 하였으므로 Barry는 James만큼 부자가 아니라는 문장을 쓸 수 있다.

09 Brad는 보이는 것보다 젊다는 의미이므로 보이는 것만큼 늙지 않았다는 말로 쓸 수 있다.

10 비용이 70달러만큼 들지 않았다는 말은 70달러보다 적게 들었다는 의미이다.

11 주어진 문장에는 양보의 접속사가 들어가는 것이 옳다. 따라서 앞뒤가 상반된 내용인 ②, ④번이 답이다.

12 ③ 그의 외투와 나의 외투를 비교하는 것이므로 me가 아닌 mine으로 쓰는 것이 옳다.

13 전치사의 목적어 역할을 하는 what절이 이어지고 있으므로 In spite of, '조용히'라는 부사가 들어가는 것이 내용상 옳으며 I came in이 완선한 설이므로 부사 quietly, than이 있으므로 비교급

14 방 청소를 방금 완료했음에도 방이 여전히 더럽다고 하였으므로 양보의 접속사를 이용하여 문장을 만든다.

15 two times bigger than이라고 써도 무방하다.

16 James는 여전히 꽤 피곤하지만 어제 더 피곤함을 느꼈다고 하였으므로, James는 어제만큼 피곤하지 않다는 말로 쓸 수 있다.

17 ⓑ, ⓓ, ⓔ가 옳은 문장이다. ⓐ as creative as, ⓒ as much as

18 노력에도 불구하고 목소리가 계속 떨렸다는 의미가 옳다. 명사구를 이끌고 있으므로 전치사(구)를 써야 한다.

19 내용상 양보의 접속사가 들어가는 것이 적절하다.

20 even though, although는 양보의 접속사로 완전한 절을 이끈다.

21 as와 as 사이에는 형용사나 부사의 원급이 온다.

22 생각했던 것보다 짧았다는 것을 동등 비교의 부정을 이용하여 '생각했던 것만큼 길지 않았다'라고도 쓸 수 있다.

🦉 서술형 시험대비   p.78~79

01 네가 나보다 돈을 더 많이 썼다고 하였으므로 '나는 너만큼 돈을 쓰지 않았다'는 문장으로 쓸 수 있다.

02 (1) 늦어서 죄송해요, 하지만 할 수 있는 한 빨리 이곳에 왔어요. (2) 침대만큼 편하진 않지만 나는 바닥에서 잘 서야. (3) 너는 네가 원하는 만큼 오래 이곳에 머물러도 좋다. (4) 나의 상자는 너의 상자보다 두 배나 무겁다. two times heavier than으로 써도 좋다.

03 Although 대신 Though, Even though, Even if 등을 써도 좋다.

04 동등 비교 표현을 이용하여 문장을 만들 수 있다. famous: 유명한

05 콤마를 사용하지 않으려면 양보의 부사절을 주절 뒤에 배치해야 하며, 양보의 부사절에서 Bradley 만큼 똑똑하지 않다는 내용을 이끌어야 한다. although를 대신하여 though나 even

though를 써도 무방하다.

06 Although를 대신하여 다른 양보의 접속사를 사용해도 좋다. 단, 부사절을 주절 뒤로 배치할 경우 콤마를 쓰지 않는 것에 유의한다.

07 동등 비교의 부정을 이용하여 문장을 만들 수 있으며, slow를 이용할 경우 비교급을 써서 나타낼 수 있다.

08 동등 비교의 부정문을 이용하여 같은 의미의 문장을 쓸 수 있다. 학교가 생각보다 가깝다고 하였으므로 생각만큼 멀지 않다고 말할 수 있다.

09 (1), (3)번 답과 (2), (4)번 답을 바꾸어 써도 무방하다. in spite of, despite는 전치사(구)로 명사구나 명사절을 이끌고, although와 though는 접속사로 부사절을 이끄는 것에 유의하여 답을 쓴다.

10 David는 이곳에서 꽤 오랫동안 살았지만 내가 그보다 더 오래 살았다고 하였으므로 'David는 나만큼 이곳에서 오래 살지 않았다'는 문장을 쓸 수 있다.

11 Despite와 같은 의미의 접속사는 although[though]이다.

12 양보의 부사절을 주절 뒤에 쓸 경우 콤마 없이 주절에 이어주는 것에 유의한다. 예상했던 것만큼 유치하지 않다는 것은 동등 비교의 부정문으로 표현할 수 있다.

13 publish: 출판하다

14 노란색 차는 빨간색 차만큼 비싸지 않다는 것은, 빨간색 차가 노란색 차보다 더 비싸다는 의미이다. 주어에 따라 more, less를 써서 같은 의미의 문장을 만들 수 있다.

15 I didn't eat anything 대신에 I ate nothing을 써도 무방하다. 부사절을 주절 앞에 배치할 경우 콤마를 쓰는 것에 유의한다.

[교과서]
Reading

확인문제 p.80

1 T 2 F 3 F 4 T

확인문제 p.81

1 T 2 F 3 F 4 T 5 T

교과서 확인학습 A p.82~83

01 on
02 to live on
03 looking for people to go
04 to build, on
05 who, healthy / who, creative, curious / who, get along with / who, adapt to
06 To apply
07 must include, to

08 want to go / a good sense of / for this mission
09 a chance of, miss
10 the Second Earth
11 Although, many books, movies, yet
12 looking at, as
13 In fact, are trying to send
14 Can people live on
15 believe so
16 that, water
17 because, necessary for
18 hard land to build, on
19 is similar to
20 In addition, has four seasons
21 lead similar lives
22 very far
23 the second closest
24 however, some differences from
25 about half
26 the second smallest, solar
27 about twice as long as
28 much colder
29 On average
30 because, farther away
31 Although, answer, exciting to imagine
32 the first Korean on

교과서 확인학습 B p.84~85

1 Live on MARS!

2 Do you want to live on another planet?

3 The Korea Space Organization (KSO) is looking for people to go to MARS!.

4 Our mission is to build a city on Mars.

5 We are looking for someone... who is healthy. who is creative and curious. who can get along with others. who can adapt to a new environment quickly.

6 To apply, send us a short video.

7 The video must include the answers to the following questions:

8 Why do you want to go to Mars? / Do you have a good sense of humor? / Why are you the perfect person for this mission?

9 This is a chance of a lifetime, so don't miss out!

10 Mars, the Second Earth?

11 Although there are many books and movies about Mars, no one has been there yet.

12 These days, scientists are looking at Mars as a new home.

13 In fact, NASA and some companies are trying to send people there right now.

14 The big question is, "Can people live on Mars?"

15 Many scientists believe so for several reasons.

16 First, they think that there is water on Mars.

17 This is great because water is necessary for all life.

18 Second, Mars has hard land to build houses and buildings on.

19 Third, the length of day and night on Mars is similar to that on Earth.

20 In addition, Mars also has four seasons.

21 So, people can lead similar lives.

22 Lastly, Mars is not very far.

23 It is the second closest planet to Earth.

24 Mars, however, has some differences from Earth.

25 First, Mars is about half the size of Earth.

26 It is the second smallest planet in the solar system.

27 Second, a year on Mars is about twice as long as a year on Earth.

28 Third, Mars is much colder than Earth.

29 On average, it is about −60℃ on Mars.

30 This is because Mars is farther away from the Sun than Earth.

31 Although no one can answer the big question right now, it is exciting to imagine this new world.

32 Who knows? You could be the first Korean on Mars!

시험대비 실력평가   p.86~89

01 ⑤   02 ②   03 ④   04 ④

05 this is a chance of a lifetime   06 ⑤

07 ③   08 ⑤   09 Water is essential for all life.   10 ②   11 the length of day and night   12 ④   13 ⑤

14 It's because Mars has four seasons and the length of day and night on Mars is similar to that on Earth.

15 Mars is the second closest planet to Earth.

16 ⑤   17 화성의 기온이 약 섭씨 영하 60도인 것

18 ④   19 Mars   20 ④

21 to build (또는 building)   22 planet   23 ④

24 ③   25 ②

26 NASA and some companies are trying to send people to Mars right now.

27 ②   28 people can live on Mars

29 ⑤   30 ③

01 '~에 살다'는 의미로 live on이 가장 적절하다.

02 (B) look for: ~을 찾다 bring about: ~을 초래하다, care

for: ~을 돌보다, turn off: ~을 끄다, pick somebody up: ~을 태우러 가다, put on: ~을 입다

03 ④ 새로운 환경에 빨리 적응할 수 있는 사람을 찾는다고 하였으므로 Sheldon이 가장 거리가 멀다. have hard time Ving: ~하느라 힘든 시간을 보내다, be well: 건강하다

04 ④ 동영상을 어디로 보내야 하는지는 위 글을 읽고 알 수 없다.

05 일생에 단 한번뿐인 기회이기 때문에 놓치지 말라고 하였다.

06 a great deal of는 셀 수 없는 명사를 수식한다.

07 believe so에서 so가 의미하는 것은 '화성에서 사람들이 살 수 있다.'이다.

08 ⑤ NASA에서 사람들을 화성으로 보내려고 노력하고 있다 하였다.

09 essential을 대신하여 necessary를 써도 좋다.

10 땅 '위에' 건물을 짓는 것이므로 전치사 on을 쓰는 것이 옳다.

11 낮과 밤의 길이를 가리킨다.

12 마지막 문장에서 화성과 지구는 다른 점이 몇 가지 있다고 하였으므로 이어질 내용으로는 ④번이 적절하다.

13 지구에서 두 번째로 가까운 행성이라고 하였다.

14 사람들이 화성에서 비슷한 생활을 할 수 있는 이유는 화성에 사계절이 있기 때문이다.

15 화성은 지구에서 두 번째로 가까운 행성이다.

16 (A) differences from: ~와의 차이점 (B) 태양계 '내에서'를 의미하므로 전치사 in (C) 주절과 부사절의 내용이 상반되므로 양보의 접속사 although

17 앞 문장의 내용을 가리키는 말이다.

18 가주어 it으로 쓰인 것은 ④번이다. 나머지는 모두 비인칭 주어이다.

19 화성을 의미하는 말이다.

20 지구의 평균 온도는 글을 읽고 알 수 없다.

21 be동사의 보어 자리이므로 to부정사나 동명사를 쓰는 것이 옳다.

22 우주에서 별 주변을 도는 크고 둥근 물체는 '행성(planet)'이다.

23 인터뷰가 아닌 영상에서 몇 가지 질문에 답해야 한다.

24 밑줄 친 (A)는 명사절을 이끄는 접속사로 완전한 절을 이끈다. ③번은 관계대명사로 쓰였으며 불완전한 절을 이끈다.

25 also라는 말로 화성과 지구의 유사점을 이어 말하고 있으므로 '게다가'가 들어가는 것이 옳다.

26 NASA와 몇몇 회사들은 화성에 사람들을 보내기 위해 바로 지금도 노력하고 있다고 하였다.

27 화성이 두 번째 지구가 될 수 있는지에 관한 글이다. 따라서 ②번이 적절하다.

28 몇 가지 이유로 과학자들은 화성에서 사람이 살 수 있다고 믿는다고 하였다.

29 단수명사 the length of day and night을 가리키는 지시대명사이므로 that이 옳다.

30 vital은 necessary와 동의어로 볼 수 있다.

01 화성으로 가서 도시를 세우는 것

02 a chance of a lifetime

03 healthy, have a good sense of humor

04 a short video to them

05 It must contain the answers to some questions.

06 There is water on Mars.   07 be similar to

08 although there are many books and movies about it

09 build houses and buildings on Mars

10 It has four seasons.   11 some differences

12 a year on Earth (또는 that on Earth)

13 Because it is farther away from the Sun than Earth.

14 not as[so] close   15 making friends

16 Give me the chance to live on Mars!

17 Because she can adapt to a new environment quickly.

---

01 화성으로 가서 도시를 세울 사람을 찾고 있다고 하였다.

02 chance: 기회, lifetime: 일생

03 동등 비교의 대상이 운동선수이므로 healthy가 적합하고, 사람들을 웃게 한다고 했으므로 유머 감각이 있다는 말이 들어가는 것이 적절하다.

04 지원하려면 짧은 동영상을 보내야 한다.

05 영상은 몇 가지 질문에 관한 답을 포함해야 한다고 하였다. contain: 포함하다

06 화성에 물이 있는 것이 좋다는 의미이다.

07 화성에서의 삶은 지구에서의 삶과 비슷할 것이다.

08 많은 책과 영화가 있긴 하지만 아직 화성에 가 본 사람은 없다고 하였다. although를 주절 뒤에 쓸 경우 콤마를 사용하지 않는 것에 유의한다.

09 화성은 단단한 땅을 가지고 있기 때문에 집과 건물을 지을 수 있다고 하였다.

10 화성은 사계절을 가지고 있다고 하였다.

11 some 대신에 several을 써도 무방하다.

12 비교 대상이 화성에서의 일 년과 지구에서의 일 년이다. 따라서 a year on Earth를 쓰는 것이 옳다.

13 화성이 지구보다 훨씬 더 추운 이유는 화성이 지구보다 태양에서 더 멀리 떨어져 있기 때문이다.

14 화성은 지구만큼 태양에 가깝지 않다는 의미이다.

15 enjoy는 동명사를 목적어로 취하는 동사이다.

16 '살 기회'이므로 to부정사가 the chance를 수식하도록 문장을 만든다.

17 새로운 환경에 빨리 적응할 수 있기 때문에 자신이 임무에 적합하다고 하였다.

01 ⑤   02 ①   03 ⑤   04 ③

05 (1) brave   (2) communicate   (3) spread

06 ③   07 ②   08 deaf

09 (B) → Do you know who this man is?

10 ③   11 ②

12 it looks like a glue stick.   13 ①   14 ⑤

15 Though[Even though, Although] it was cloudy, I put on my sunglasses.

16 ②   17 ①, ⑤   18 ④   19 ⑤

20 ③   21 ④   22 ②

23 watch TV as much as

24 Although tennis is not as popular as football, I like tennis more than football.

25 ①, ③   26 ②   27 ①   28 ④

29 Many scientists   30 twice as big[large] as

31 ①   32 ③   33 not as[so] small as

---

01 ⑤번을 제외한 나머지는 모두 사람의 성격을 묘사하는 형용사이다.

02 '과일, 야채 등으로부터 껍질을 제거하다'를 나타내는 말은 peel(껍질을 벗기다)이다.

03 Although: ~이긴 하지만

04 Mars: 화성

06 주어진 문장에서 lead는 '생활을 하다, 지내다'를 뜻하며 이와 같은 의미로 쓰인 것은 ③번이다. 나머지는 '이끌다'를 의미한다.

07 produce: 생산하다, 제작하다

08 어떤 것도 들을 수 없음을 나타내는 말은 deaf(귀가 먼)이다

09 간접의문의 어순은 '의문사+주어+동사'이다.

12 look+형용사, look like+명사

13 주어진 문장은 주말이 어땠는지에 대한 질문에 대한 대답으로 적절하므로 (A)가 알맞다.

15 양보의 부사절을 주절 뒤에 쓸 경우 콤마를 사용하지 않는 것에 유의한다. put on: ~을 쓰다

16 절을 이끌며 원인과 결과를 나타내는 문장이므로 because, the noise는 명사로 전치사를 써야 하므로 despite가 옳다.

17 생각했던 것만큼 어렵지 않았다는 것은 생각했던 것보다 더 쉬웠다는 의미가 된다.

18 ④ 내용상 앞뒤가 상반되는 내용이므로 양보의 접속사로 이어주는 것이 좋다.

19 '머리가 전에는 더 길었다.'는 것은 지금은 전만큼 길지 않다는 의미이다. used to V: (과거에) ~이었다

20 ③ because → although[though]

21 '나는 너보다 고기를 덜 먹는다'는 말은 '나는 너 만큼 고기를 먹지 않는다.'는 의미이다.

22 앞뒤 절의 내용이 상반되는 ②번이 옳다. ①, ③ because [as] ④ since ⑤ if[when]

15

23 나는 너만큼 TV를 많이 보지 않는다는 말로 쓸 수 있다.

24 'Although football is more popular than tennis, I don't like football as much as tennis.'라고 써도 좋다.

25 앞뒤의 절이 상반된 내용이므로 양보의 부사절 접속사 although, even though가 들어가는 것이 옳다.

26 사람들이 비슷한 생활을 할 수 있다는 '결과를 이끄는 연결사'가 들어가는 것이 옳다.

27 (a)는 경험을 나타내는 현재완료이다. ① 경험 ② 완료 ③ 결과 ④ 계속 ⑤ 완료

28 화성으로 가는 데 얼마만큼의 시간이 걸리는지는 위 글을 읽고 알 수 없다.

29 앞 문장에 언급된 많은 과학자들을 가리키는 말이다.

30 '배수사+as+원급+as'를 이용하여 같은 의미의 문장을 쓸 수 있다.

31 (A) 비교급 강조부사 much (2) 원인을 이끌고 있으므로 This is because (3) 새로운 세상을 상상하는 것은 신나는 감정을 유발하는 것이므로 exciting을 쓰는 것이 옳다.

32 ⓑ는 진주어로 쓰인 to부정사이다. ③은 anything을 수식하는 형용사로 쓰인 to부정사이다.

33 화성은 태양계에서 두 번째로 작은 행성이라고 하였고, 수성이 가장 작은 행성이므로 화성은 수성만큼 작은 행성이 아니다.

단원별 예상문제   p.98~101

01 ②   02 (C) → (B) → (E) → (D) → (A)

03 ⓒ → on

04 They are not just for wearing but also for cleaning the floor.   05 ⑤

06 inventor   07 He had an interest in sound.

08 He made some inventions for deaf people and opened a school for them.

09 ①   10 이것을 갖고 놀 때 전기를 만들어 낸다.

11 ⑤   12 ③   13 ⑤

14 didn't play as[so] well as us[we did]

15 ③, ⑤   16 ④

17 Though the bread is not as[so] moist as it was yesterday, it is still delicious.

18 two times, high   19 ③   20 ①

21 ⑤   22 Mars has four seasons.

23 [B]–[A]–[C]   24 ④

25 Mars is not as far as I thought.   26 ②

01 (A) 명령문이므로 look, (B) 경험을 나타내는 현재완료 (have+p.p) 형태가 적절하다. (C) interesting: 흥미로운, interested: 흥미를 갖고 있는

02 (C) 알고 있는지 묻기 → (B) 추측 → (E) 정확한 설명 → (D) 버터가 있는지 구체적인 질문 → (A) 대답

---

03 put off는 '미루다'는 뜻으로 문맥의 흐름상 '(신발을) 신다'를 나타내기 위해 'put on'이 적절하다.

04 Tom이 만든 슬리퍼는 신는 것뿐만 아니라 바닥을 청소하기 위한 것이다.

05 Tom이 과학 시간에 슬리퍼를 만들기 위해 무엇을 사용했는지 알 수 없다.

06 '무언가를 발명한 사람 또는 그의 직업이 무언가를 발명하는 사람'을 가리키는 말은 inventor(발명가)이다.

07 Alexander Graham Bell은 소리에 관심을 갖고 있었다.

08 Alexander Graham Bell은 청각 장애인들을 위한 몇몇 발명품도 만들고 그들을 위한 학교도 열었다.

11 ⓔ를 제외한 나머지는 모두 a Soccket을 가리킨다.

12 계단에서 넘어졌지만 다치지 않았다고 말하는 것이 가장 자연스럽다. 따라서 양보의 부사절 접속사를 쓰는 것이 옳다.

13 비교 대상이 배낭이므로 my backpack 혹은 mine이라고 쓰는 것이 옳다.

14 우리가 그들보다 더 잘했다는 것은 그들이 우리만큼 하지 못했다는 의미이다.

15 사과가 배만큼 크지 않다고 하였으므로 사과가 배보다 크지 않다고도 말할 수 있다.

17 moist: 촉촉한, 수분이 있는

18 후지산은 한라산보다 두 배만큼 높다는 의미이다.

19 (A)에는 양보의 부사절 접속사 although가 쓰인다. ① When ② while ③ Although ④ unless ⑤ since

20 과거를 나타내는 어구인 ago는 현재완료 시제와 함께 사용될 수 없다. ago → yet

21 화성이 지구에서 두 번째로 가까운 행성이라고 하였다.

22 사람이 화성에서 살 수 있다고 과학자들이 믿는 네 번째 이유로 화성에 사계절이 있기 때문이라고 하였다.

23 [B] 사람들이 비슷한 생활을 할 수 있는 마지막 이유로 지구에서 두 번째로 가까운 행성이라고 언급한 후 '그러나'로 차이점을 언급하며 첫 번째는 크기임 → [A] 화성은 태양계에서 두 번째로 작은 행성임을 언급하고 두 번째와 세 번째 차이(화성이 지구보다 훨씬 더 추움) 언급 → [C] 평균 온도가 섭씨 영하 60도임을 언급

24 ④번은 slice를 설명하는 말이다.

25 as+형용사/부사의 원급+as: ~만큼 …한

26 태양계에서 가장 작은 행성이 무엇인지는 글에 나와 있지 않다.

서술형 실전문제   p.102~103

01 He went there with his brother.

02 He bought a VR headset.

03 It is for experiencing another world.

04 He made them in science class.

05 He made a promise to clean his room from now on.

06 Although[Though] I turned on the air conditioner, the room is still hot.

07 Although[Though] Hannah invited Tom to her party, he didn't come without saying a word.

08 didn't get up as[so] early as Sally /
didn't get up as[so] late as James

09 (1) doesn't work as[so] hard as
(2) works harder than

10 is not as[so] important as health and happiness

11 ④번 → Mars has hard land to build houses and buildings on.

12 Many scientists think that there is water on Mars.

13 Mars is about half the size of Earth.

14 two times as long as

01 호진은 과학 전시회에 남동생과 같이 갔다.

02 호진은 과학 전시회에서 VR 헤드셋을 샀다.

03 VR 헤드셋은 다른 세상을 경험하기 위한 것이다.

04 Tom은 과학시간에 슬리퍼를 만들었다.

05 Tom은 엄마에게 이제부터 그의 방을 청소할 것을 약속하였다.

06 '에어컨을 틀었지만 방은 여전히 덥다'는 문장을 쓸 수 있다. although를 주절 뒤에 배치할 경우 콤마를 쓰지 않는 것에 유의한다.

07 해석: Hannah가 Tom을 파티에 초대했지만, 그는 말 한마디도 없이 오지 않았다.

08 Sally는 James보다 일찍 일어났다는 것은 Sally가 James만큼 늦게 일어나지 않았고, James는 Sally만큼 일찍 일어나지 않았다는 의미이다.

09 Amelia는 Jason만큼 일하지 않지만 Tom보다는 더 열심히 일한다. 일하는 시간을 비교해 보면 Jason은 Tom보다 두 배 만큼 많이 일한다.

10 건강과 행복은 돈보다 더 중요하다는 것은 '돈은 건강과 행복만큼 중요하지 않다'는 것이다.

11 build houses and building on hard land이므로 전치사 on을 쓰는 것이 옳다.

12 많은 과학자들이 화성에 물이 있다고 생각한다.

13 about: 대략 half: 절반

14 화성에서의 일 년은 지구에서의 일 년보다 약 두 배 길다고 하였으므로 two times as long as를 써서 나타낼 수 있다.

|모범답안|

01 (A) slippers (B) cleaning the floor
(C) clean my room

02 (1) is not as[so] old as
(2) don't get up as[so] early as
(3) three times as much time as

03 (1) Although the length of day and night on Mars is similar to that on Earth, a year on Mars is about twice as long as a year on Earth.
(2) Although Mars has four seasons like Earth, Mars is much colder than Earth.
(3) Although Mars has hard land to build houses and buildings on, it is really expensive to build them on Mars.

01 오늘 나는 과학시간에 특별한 슬리퍼를 만들었다. 나는 어떤 천도 없이 바닥을 청소할 수 있는 아이디어를 생각해 냈다. 그래서 내 슬리퍼는 단지 신기 위한 것뿐만 아니라 바닥을 청소하기 위해 디자인되었다. 나는 엄마에게 스스로 내 방을 청소할 것을 약속했다.

02 (1) Jennifer는 Michael과 Christine만큼 나이 들지 않았다.
(2) Jennifer와 Christine은 Michael만큼 일찍 일어나지 않는다. (3) Christine은 직장에 가기 위해서 Michael보다 세 배나 더 많은 시간을 소비한다.

01 ②   02 (1) slice (2) inventor
(3) organization (4) deaf (5) planets

03 (1) get along with (2) sense of humor
(3) In addition

04 (E) → (A) → (C) → (B) → (D)   05 ⑤

06 ②, ④

07 If you wear it, you can experience another world.

08 ③   09 ③   10 ④   11 ④

12 (1) Jimin doesn't seem to get along with his classmates.
(2) What is the biggest planet in the solar system?

13 ②   14 didn't run as[so] much(또는 far) as

15 ⑤

16 Although[Though] this cookie is not as[so] delicious as the cake, I will have this cookie.

17 because, although   18 ②   19 ③

20 Their mission is to build a city on Mars.

21 Do you have a good sense of humor?

22 ②   23 ③

24 ⑤번 → farther away from

25 Although Mars has some differences from Earth, scientists believe that people can live on Mars.

01 reason: 이유; 추론하다

02 inventor: 발명가, deaf: 청각 장애가 있는, planet: 행성, organization: 조직, 단체, slice: 얇게 썰다

04 (E) 과학 시간에 슬리퍼를 만든 것을 설명 → (A) 과학 시간에 만든 이유 질문 → (C) 용도 설명 → (B) 구체적인 용도 질문 → (D) 구체적인 용도 설명

05 태양 주위에서 움직이는 행성이나 태양을 일컫는 말은 solar system(태양계)이다.

06 용도를 묻는 표현이 들어가야 한다.

08 용도를 묻고 있으므로 이에 대한 대답인 ③번이 적절하다.

09 (A)는 의문사로 누구를 가리키는 'who' (B) be interested in: ~에 관심이 있다 (C) 동사 opened가 적절하다.

10 그가 무엇을 발명했는지 묻는 질문에 전화기를 발명했다는 대답이 이어지므로 ⓓ가 적절하다.

11 ④ Alexander Graham Bell이 가족을 위해 학교를 열었다는 설명은 대화의 내용과 일치하지 않는다.

13 ⓐ, ⓑ가 옳은 문장이다. ⓒ despite → although ⓓ you are → you do ⓔ as tidy than → as tidy as

14 나는 아빠만큼 많이 달리지 않았다는 말을 쓰는 것이 옳다.

15 as heavy as라고 쓰는 것이 옳다.

16 쿠키가 케이크만큼 맛있지 않다고 하였으므로 동등 비교의 부정문을 이용하여 문장을 만들 수 있다.

17 앞 문장은 원인과 결과를 이어주는 말이 들어가는 것이 옳으며, 뒷문장의 내용은 서로 상반되므로 양보의 부사절 접속사를 쓰는 것이 옳다. because 대신에 as, although 대신에 though나 even though를 써도 무방하다.

18 ⓐ 화성으로 갈 사람을 찾는 것이므로 look for ⓑ 새로운 환경에 빠르게 적응한다는 의미이므로 adapt ⓒ 질문에 대한 대답을 포함해야 한다는 의미이므로 include가 적절하다.

19 (A)는 부사적 용법 중 '목적'으로 쓰인 to부정사이다. 따라서 '~하기 위해서'라고 해석되는 ③번이 옳다.

20 그들의 임무는 화성에 도시를 세우는 것이라고 하였다.

21 a sense of humor: 유머 감각

22 앞 문단과 상반되는 내용이 이어지고 있으므로 역접의 접속부사 '그러나'가 옳다.

23 ③ 화성은 지구와 가깝고 사계절이 있다고 하였다.

24 화성이 지구보다 태양에서 더 멀기 때문에 더 추운 것이다.

25 Although절을 주절 뒤에 쓸 경우 콤마를 쓰지 않는 것에 유의한다.

18 정답 및 해설

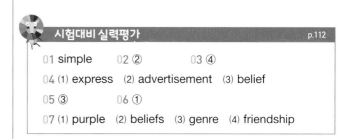

Lesson
7

Can I Trust It?

시험대비 실력평가   p.112

01 simple   02 ②   03 ④
04 (1) express   (2) advertisement   (3) belief
05 ③   06 ①
07 (1) purple   (2) beliefs   (3) genre   (4) friendship

01 주어진 단어의 관계는 반의어 관계를 나타낸다. simple: 간단한, complex: 복잡한

02 누군가가 한 무언가에 대한 돈 등과 같은 상을 가리키는 말은 award(상)이다. penalty: 벌금 fare: 운임 fee: 요금

03 prove: 증명하다

05 주어진 문장에서 touching은 '감동적인'을 뜻하며 이와 같은 의미로 쓰인 것은 ③번이다. 나머지는 모두 '만지다'를 의미한다.

06 navy: 해군, 남색

07 belief: 신념, purple: 보라색, genre: 장르, friendship: 우정

서술형 시험대비   p.113

01 difference   02 (1) lie   (2) pocket   (3) based
03 (1) traditional   (2) desert   (3) author
     (4) connection   (5) award   (6) fantasy
04 (1) From now on, let's start playing the soccer game.
     (2) Before you go out, check out the light again.
     (3) Who is the main character in this movie?
05 (1) Can you explain the rules of the game?
     (2) If you mix red with blue, you can get purple.
     (3) I can prove that he didn't break the window.
     (4) Did you see the advertisement on the newspaper?

01 주어진 빈칸에 different의 명사형 difference가 와야 한다.

02 lie: 거짓말하다, pocket: 주머니, be based on: ~을 바탕으로 하다

03 fantasy: 공상, traditional: 전통적인, connection: 연관성, author: 작가, desert: 사막, award: 상 primarily: 주로

Conversation 교과서

핵심 Check
p.114~115

1 (1) recommend / How about (2) Can you suggest / Why (3) What do you think would be
2 (1) How do you like (2) I'm not satisfied with it
  (3) What do you like

교과서 대화문 익히기

Check(√) True or False
p.116

1 T 2 T 3 T 4 F

교과서 확인학습
p.118~119

Listen & Speak 1-A

recommend / yet / number one

Listen & Speak 1-B

help / backpack, recommend one / How about, these days / different / navy, pockets / take

Listen & Speak 2-A

got / like most about it / takes

Listen & Talk 2-B

like, trip / happy / Where else / wonderful place / perfect trip / walking up / worth it

Real Life Talk – Step 1

can you recommend / Why don't / about / delicious, recommend / the prices / think, too / Sounds like, How, the service / slow / check it out / problem, Enjoy

Real Life Talk – Step 2

recommend a book for me / about / What, like / main character, special / Sounds

시험대비 기본평가
p.120

01 Can you recommend a good movie?
02 ⑤   03 What do you like most about it?
04 (B) the new smartphone (C) the camera

시험대비 실력평가
p.121~122

01 ④ → was 02 ②   03 ④
04 can you recommend a book for me?
05 She likes the main character.
06 ①   07 ⓐ Antonio's ⓑ the service
08 ⑤   09 ②   10 ⑤   11 ③
12 ⑤

01 동명사가 주어로 쓰였으므로 동사는 단수 형태인 was가 적절하다.
02 문맥상 상반의 접속사 but이 알맞다.
03 ④ Jack은 석굴암까지 걸어 올라가는 것이 가치가 있었을 것이라고 믿었다.
06 주어진 문장은 식당을 추천하고 있는 표현이므로 (A)가 적절하다.
09 이어지는 대화에서 빨간색을 추천한 이유를 설명하고 있으므로 (B)가 적절하다.
10 소년의 오래된 배낭이 얼마나 많은 주머니를 갖고 있었는지는 알 수 없다.
11 (A)의 빈칸에 들어갈 말로 만족을 나타내는 표현이 알맞다. ③은 실망을 나타내고 있다.
12 ⑤ 위 대화를 통해 Tom이 언제 멋진 사진을 찍었는지 알 수 없다.

서술형 시험대비
p.123

01 I haven't seen it yet.
02 She recommended *Star Wars*.
03 It's *Star Wars*.   04 It is red.
05 It has side pockets.
06 Because his old backpack was red.
07 (A) How (B) Where (C) Where
08 (A) Gyeongju (B) Bulguksa (C) Seokguram

02 Emily는 Brian에게 *Star Wars*를 추천하였다.
03 지금 1위 영화는 *Star Wars*이다.
04 요즘 가장 인기 있는 색은 빨간색이다.
05 남색 가방은 양옆에 주머니가 있다.
06 소년이 빨간색 배낭을 원하지 않은 이유는 그의 옛 배낭이 빨간색이기 때문이다.
08 나는 경주 여행을 갔다. 이곳은 정말로 멋지고 아름다운 도시였다. 나는 첨성대뿐만 아니라 불국사도 방문했다. 그들은 모두 훌륭한 곳이었다. 나는 석굴암까지 올라갔을 때 피곤했다. 그러나 그것은 가치있는 일이었다. 나는 경주로 간 완벽한 여행이 정말 마음에 들었다.

Grammar

핵심 Check
p.124~125

1 (1) so bright that (2) so small that (3) so lazy that

2 (1) that(또는 which) Elizabeth made

(2) that(또는 which) he lost

(3) that(또는 which) Molly really liked

(4) who(m)(또는 that) she saw

시험대비 기본평가
p.126

01 (1) who → which(또는 that)

(2) which → who(m)(또는 that) (3) very → so

(4) so → too

02 (1) who(m) Tom likes (2) so easy that

(3) so rich that, that (4) that I sit on[in]

03 (1) She didn't touch the food that she didn't like.

(2) Those babies whom the woman is looking after look very cute.

(3) The shoes are so tight that my feet hurt.

(4) Her commute was so far that she bought a car.

01 (1), (2) 목적격 관계대명사가 쓰이고 있으므로 생략해도 무방하다. (3) 'so ~ that'은 원인과 결과를 나타내는 어구이며 that은 완전한 절을 이끈다. 'too ~ to V'는 '너무 ~해서 …할 수 없는'의 의미이다.

02 (1), (4) 'Tom이 많이 좋아하는 그 소녀', '내가 앉아 있는 이 의자'이므로 관계사절로 명사를 수식할 수 있다. (2), (3) 'so ~ that'은 원인과 결과를 나타내는 어구이다.

03 (1), (2) '좋아하지 않는 음식', '그 여자가 돌보고 있는 저 아기들'이므로 the food that she didn't like, the babies whom she is looking after로 쓰는 것이 옳다.

시험대비 실력평가

p.127~129

01 ④ **02** ④ **03** ②, ④

04 The book which[that] you borrowed from the library was written by my mother.

05 ③ **06** ② **07** ⑤

08 The computer is so small that I can carry it around.

09 ③ **10** ③

11 Julia studied so hard that she could pass the important exam.

12 The traffic was so heavy that I couldn't be here on time.

13 ③ **14** ⑤ **15** which[that] we watched last week **16** ② **17** ②

18 that they sang together was beautiful **19** ⑤

20 ④ **21** I am so shy that I can't talk in front of many people.

22 (1) which[that] I am interested

(2) which I am interested

01 피곤한 것이 원인이고 일찍 잔 것은 결과이므로 ④번이 옳다.

02 어제 만난 여자가 너무 상냥해서 친구가 되고 싶었다는 의미이다. 원인과 결과를 나타내는 어구인 'so ~ that' 구문을 쓰는 것이 옳다.

03 목적격 관계대명사가 적절하다. 사물이 선행사이므로 which나 that이 옳다.

04 목적격 관계대명사를 이용하면 '네가 도서관에서 빌린 그 책은 우리 엄마에 의해 쓰였다.'는 의미의 문장을 만들 수 있다.

05 'too ~ to V'는 '너무 ~해서 V할 수 없는'이라는 의미이다. 'so ~ that ... can't'와 같다.

06 ② 핵심 주어인 자전거는 단수이므로 is라고 쓰는 것이 옳다.

07 hard는 부사로 '세게'라는 의미를 갖는다. hardly 역시 부사이지만 '거의 ~하지 않는'이라는 의미이다. 두 번째 빈칸에는 목적격 관계대명사가 쓰이므로 that 혹은 which가 온다.

08 컴퓨터가 너무 작은 것이 원인이 되어 내가 가지고 다닐 수 있게 되었다. 따라서 'so ~ that' 구문을 이용하여 문장을 만들 수 있다. carry around: 휴대하다, 가지고 다니다

09 ③번은 주격 관계대명사이다. 목적격 관계대명사 혹은 '주격 관계대명사+be동사'는 생략 가능하다. run across: 우연히 마주치다

10 모두 완전한 명사절을 이끄는 접속사 that이지만, ③번은 불완전한 절을 이끄는 관계대명사 that이다.

11 Julia가 공부를 열심히 해서 그 결과 시험에 합격할 수 있었다는 하나의 문장을 쓸 수 있다.

12 원인과 결과를 나타내는 어구를 이용하여 늦은 이유를 설명하면 된다. 주어진 단어를 이용한다면 '교통 체증이 너무 심해서 제때에 올 수 없었다.'라고 쓸 수 있다.

13 결과를 나타내는 절을 이끌거나 목적격 관계대명사 역할을 할 수 있는 것은 that이다.

14 ⑤ 'Where is the dog which follows you all the time?'이라고 쓰는 것이 옳다.

15 목적격 관계대명사이므로 that을 써도 무방하다.

16 'so ~ that'은 원인과 결과를 나타내는 어구이다. 같은 의미가 되기 위해서는 빈칸에 because를 쓰는 것이 옳다.

17 나를 슬프게 하는 것이 원인이고 라디오를 끈 것이 결과이므로 ②번이 가장 적절하다.

18 목적격 관계대명사 that을 대신하여 which를 쓰거나 생략해도 무방하다.

19 'too ~ to V'는 '너무 ~해서 V할 수 없는'이란 의미이다. 따라서 ⑤번이 옳다.

20 ① looks ② couldn't ③ whom(또는 that) ⑤ diligent

21 너무 수줍어서 많은 사람들 앞에서 말할 수 없다는 문장을 쓸 수 있다.

22 관계대명사 that은 전치사의 목적어로 쓰일 수 없는 것에 유의하여 답을 쓴다.

서술형 시험대비
p.130~131

01 The girl whom you introduced to me is very popular.

02 was so heavy that Sandra couldn't carry it. 또는 was too heavy for Sandra to carry

03 which Ross wrote was so amazing that I was moved to tears

04 (1) which(또는 that) (2) who(또는 that)
   (3) whom(또는 that)

05 (1) Penny couldn't eat anything because she was very sick.
   (2) Penny was so sick that she couldn't eat anything.

06 (1) which Tom is driving is not his
   (2) picked some roses which Catherine planted
   (3) know the person who(m) you took a trip with

07 so warm that he doesn't need to buy another coat

08 (1) Sally speaks English so well that you would think it is her native language.
   (2) The music was so loud that you could hear it from miles away.
   (3) Gabriel is so beautiful that any man would love to be with her.

09 The soup was so hot that it burned my tongue.

10 Jody is the student who(m) Ms. Galler is looking for.

11 (1) The boy who(m) you saw yesterday is my brother.
   (2) The dress which she is wearing was designed by a famous person.

12 The people whom I call most often are my mother and my sisters.

13 so happy that

14 The party was so enjoyable that no one wanted to leave.

15 She woke up so early that she was tired.

01 '네가 나에게 소개해 준 그 소녀'이므로 관계사절이 the girl을 수식하도록 문장을 만든다.

02 상자가 너무 무거워서 Sandra는 그것을 나르지 않았다고 쓸 수 있다.

03 which 대신 that을 쓰거나 또는 생략할 수 있다.

04 (1), (3)번에 쓰인 관계대명사는 목적격이므로 생략해도 무방하다.

05 Penny는 너무 아파서 아무것도 먹을 수 없었다는 의미이다.

06 목적격 관계대명사를 이용하여 하나의 문장으로 이어주었으므로 모두 that으로 쓰거나 생략해도 무방하다.

07 Avian의 외투가 너무 따뜻해서 다른 것을 살 필요가 없다는 문장을 쓸 수 있다.

08 원인과 결과를 나타내는 'so ~ that' 구문을 이용하여 문장을 하나로 만든다.

09 수프가 너무 뜨거워서 혀를 데였다는 문장으로 쓸 수 있다.

10 목적격 관계대명사이므로 that을 쓰거나 생략해도 무방하다.

11 모두 목적격 관계대명사이므로 that으로 쓰거나 생략해도 무방하다.

12 '내가 가장 자주 전화하는'이 '사람들'을 수식하고 있으므로 관계사절 The people whom I call most often이라고 쓰는 것이 옳다.

13 Jason에 따르면 Lisa는 너무 행복해서 방에서 춤을 추고 있다고 말할 수 있다.

14 파티가 너무 즐거워서 누구도 파티를 떠나고 싶어 하지 않았다는 문장을 쓸 수 있다.

15 원인과 결과를 나타내는 'so ~ that' 구문을 이용하여 문장을 만든다.

교과서 Reading

확인문제
p.132

1 T 2 F 3 T

확인문제
p.133

1 F 2 F 3 T 4 T

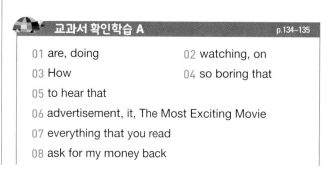

교과서 확인학습 A
p.134~135

01 are, doing
02 watching, on
03 How
04 so boring that
05 to hear that
06 advertisement, it, The Most Exciting Movie
07 everything that you read
08 ask for my money back

09 Hold on, lie because　　10 not following you

11 express people's feelings　12 that, can be proven

13 For example, check that on the map

14 the connection with

15 Let me explain　　16 It's

17 look for its advertisement

18 It says　　19 uses facts unlike

20 the difference　　21 exactly, says, says

22 Aren't, both opinions

23 words like, usually expressing opinions

24 which the movie won　　25 that on the Internet

26 From now on, trust, with

27 that simple, mix, with

28 make a smart choice, both　29 to watch

30 the rest of

1 Emma: What are you doing, Kyle?

2 Kyle: Oh, Emma. I'm watching the movie, *Y−Men 7* on my computer.

3 Emma: How is it?

4 Kyle: Don't ask. It's so boring that I want to cry.

5 Emma: I'm sorry to hear that.

6 Kyle: I'm so mad. The movie advertisement said it was "The Most Exciting Movie of the Year."

7 Emma: Well, you can't believe everything that you read.

8 Kyle: They lied on the advertisement. I'm going to ask for my money back.

9 Emma: Hold on, Kyle! They didn't really lie because they used opinions, not facts.

10 Kyle: Huh? I'm not following you.

11 Emma: Opinions express people's feelings like, "The desert is beautiful."

12 You can't say that it's true or not. But, facts can be proven.

13 For example, "The Atacama Desert is in Chile," is a fact. You can check that on the map.

14 Kyle: Okay.... But what's the connection with movies?

15 Emma: Let me explain. What's your favorite movie?

16 Kyle: It's *Forrest Gump.*

17 Emma: Okay. Let's look for its advertisement. What does it say?

18 Kyle: It says, "Winner of 6 Academy Awards including Best Picture."

19 Emma: See? It uses facts unlike the *Y−Men 7* advertisement.

20 Do you see the difference?

21 Kyle: Not exactly. The *Y−Men 7* ad says "Most Exciting Movie" and the *Forrest Gump* ad says "Best Picture."

22 Aren't they both opinions?

23 Emma: That's a great question, Kyle. When people use words like "best" or "most," they are usually expressing opinions.

24 But in the *Forrest Gump* ad, "Best Picture" is the award which the movie won.

25 We can check that on the Internet. That's a fact.

26 Kyle: Aha! From now on I'm only going to trust ads with facts.

27 Emma: It's not that simple. Most ads mix facts with opinions.

28 So you have to make a smart choice based on both of them.

29 Kyle: Got it! Emma, do you want to watch the rest of *Y−Men 7* with me?

30 Emma: Thanks, but no thanks. Enjoy the rest of the movie!

01 ①, ②　　02 ③　　03 opinions

04 It's because the movie is so boring.

05 ②　　06 ④　　07 아타카마 사막이 칠레에 있는 것　　08 ③　　09 ⑤　　10 a fact

11 ③　　12 facts and opinions　　13 ①

14 People usually express their opinions with words like "best" or "most."

15 ④　　16 ⑤　　17 ④

18 He is watching the movie, Y−Men 7 on his computer.　　19 ④

20 The movie advertisement said it was "The Most Exciting Movie of the Year."

21 ④　　22 ②　　23 an opinion, a fact

24 ④　　25 ⑤

26 (D) → (A) → (C) → (B)　　27 ③

28 영화 "Forest Gump"가 "Best Picture" 상을 받은 것

29 facts and opinions

01 사물을 선행사로 취하는 목적격 관계대명사가 들어가는 것이 옳다.

02 ③ Kyle은 영화에 만족하지 않는다. be fooled by: ~에 의해 속다

03 어떤 것에 대한 감정이나 생각은 '의견'이다.

04 Kyle이 울고 싶은 이유는 영화가 너무 지루하기 때문이다.

05 기다리라는 의미이다. 따라서 wait이 옳다. way to go: 잘 했어

06 앞 문장의 내용을 예를 들어 설명하고 있다.

07 "Atacama Desert is in Chile."를 가리키는 말이다.

08 Emma가 가장 좋아하는 영화는 글을 읽고 알 수 없다.

09 증명될 수 있는 것이 사실이다. 따라서 ⑤번이 사실이다.

10 의견과 사실의 차이점을 설명하는 글이다. 의견이 어떤 것인지를 설명한 후 사실에 관하여 설명하고 있다.

11 ① 오랫동안 ② 당분간 ③ 지금부터 ④, ⑤ 가끔

12 사실과 의견 둘 다 가리키는 말이다.

13 both 뒤에는 복수명사가 쓰인다.

14 사람들은 "best" 또는 "most"와 같은 말을 사용하여 그들의 의견을 표현한다.

15 ④ 대부분의 광고는 사실과 의견이 섞여 있다고 하였다.

16 ⓐ는 감정의 원인을 나타내는 to부정사이다. 따라서 ⑤번이 옳다.

17 그들이 거짓말을 한 것이 아니라는 이유를 설명하고 있으므로 because가 옳다.

18 Kyle은 컴퓨터로 영화 "Y-Men 7"을 보고 있다.

19 (A) 답변으로 미루어 보아 영화가 어떤지를 물었다고 볼 수 있으므로 how, (B) 지루함을 유발할 때에는 boring, (C) be going to V: V할 예정이다.

20 영화 광고에는 그 영화가 "올해의 가장 흥미진진한 영화"라고 쓰여 있었다.

21 that은 아타카마 사막이 칠레에 있다는 것을 받는다.

22 (A) 사실은 증명이 되는 것이므로 수동태, (B) 사역동사+목적어+원형부정사: 목적어가 V하게 하다 (C) '~을 포함하여'라는 의미의 전치사가 쓰여야 하므로 including

23 글의 내용에 따르면, 그 아기가 가장 예쁘다는 것은 의견이고, 에베레스트 산이 세계에서 가장 높은 산이라는 것은 사실이라고 할 수 있다.

24 모두 확인 가능한 사실이지만 '혼자 해변 가에 가는 것은 안전하지 않다'는 것은 의견이다.

25 "Forest Gump"는 "Best Picture'를 포함하여 여섯 개의 아카데미상을 받았다고 하였다.

26 (D) 둘 다 의견이 아니냐는 질문 → (A) 의견과 사실의 차이를 설명 → (C) 이해한 후 사실만 있는 광고를 믿겠다고 말함 → (B) 보통 광고에는 사실과 의견이 섞여 있다고 말해 줌.

27 mix A with B: A와 B를 섞다. with: ~을 가진, ~을 포함한

28 영화가 상을 받은 사실을 인터넷을 통해 확인할 수 있다는 것이다.

29 대부분의 광고에는 사실과 의견 모두 있다고 하였다.

서술형 시험대비
p.142~143

01 I am going to ask for my money back.

02 It's so boring that I want to cry.

03 They used not facts but opinions, so they didn't really lie.

04 It is *Y-Men 7*.   05 excited

06 be proven   07 We can check that on the map.

08 doesn't use facts

09 Did you see the movie that won 6 Academy Awards?

10 Kyle's favorite movie is *Forrest Gump*.

11 Aren't they both opinions?

12 "Best Picture" is the award. The movie won the award.

13 People who use words like 'best' or 'most' are usually expressing opinions.

14 base, facts and opinions

01 ask for ~ back: ~을 돌려달라고 청하다

02 원인과 결과를 나타내는 'so ~ that' 구문을 이용하여 문장을 만들 수 있다.

03 그들은 사실이 아니라 의견을 사용했으므로 꼭 거짓말을 한 것은 아니다. so는 결과를 이끄는 접속사이다. not A but B: A가 아니라 B(= B, not A)

04 Kyle이 보고 있는 영화의 제목은 "Y-Men 7"이다.

05 가장 흥미진진한 영화라는 광고와는 달리 Kyle은 흥미진진함을 느끼지 못했다고 말하는 것이 옳다.

06 사실은 '증명이 되는 것'이므로 수동태를 쓰는 것이 옳다. 조동사 뒤에 동사원형을 쓰는 것에 유의한다.

07 밑줄 친 문장이 사실이라는 것은 지도를 확인하여 알 수 있다.

08 "Y-Men 7" 광고와는 달리 사실을 사용하고 있다고 하였으므로 "Y-Men 7" 광고는 사실을 사용하지 않는다는 것을 알 수 있다.

09 관계대명사 that을 대신하여 which를 써도 무방하다.

10 Kyle이 가장 좋아하는 영화는 "Forest Gump"라고 하였다.

11 답변으로 미루어 보아 '둘 다 의견이 아니니?'라고 질문했음을 알 수 있다.

12 관계대명사를 이용하여 두 문장을 하나의 문장으로 쓴 것이다. 선행사를 이용하여 두 개의 문장으로 쓸 수 있다.

13 'best'나 'most'와 같은 말을 사용하는 사람이라고 하였으므로 관계사절이 people을 수식하도록 문장을 만든다.

14 대부분의 광고에는 사실과 의견이 섞여 있기 때문에 결정을 내릴 때 사실과 의견을 바탕으로 선택해야 한다.

영역별 핵심문제
p.145~149

01 full   02 ④   03 ④

04 (1) How do you like the present?

(2) There is no evidence to prove his claim.

05 (1) make a choice   (2) check out   (3) full of

06 ③   07 ①   08 ②   09 ③

10 ②   11 ②   12 ⑤

13 How did you like your trip to Gyeongju?

14 worth   15 ⑤   16 ⑤   17 ⑤

18 ②   19 ①, ②, ⑤

20 It was so hot that we went swimming yesterday.

21 ②   22 ⑤

23 The drug that[which] the man stole was for his
son.   24 ③

25 We eat the carrots which my grandfather grew on
the farm.

26 There are so many leaves on a single tree that it
is impossible to count them.

27 Tell me about the museum that you visited last
week.

28 The movie that[which] Kyle chose used opinions
in the advertisement.

29 ③, ⑤   30 ⑤   31 ①   32 ⑤

33 It's because most ads mix facts with opinions.

01 주어진 단어의 관계는 반의어 관계를 나타낸다. empty: 텅 빈,
full: 가득 찬

02 사실이 아닌 무언가를 말하거나 쓰는 것을 가리키는 말은 lie(거
짓말하다)이다.

03 worth: 가치가 있는

04 How do you like ~?: ~가 마음에 드니?, claim: 주장

05 make a choice: 선택하다, check out: 확인하다, be full of:
~로 가득 차다

06 주어진 문장에서 lie는 '거짓말하다'를 뜻하며 이와 같은 의미로
쓰인 것은 ③번이다. 나머지는 모두 '눕다'를 뜻한다.

07 worth: 가치가 있는, be worth ~ing: ~할 가치가 있다

10 여자와 소년은 점원과 손님의 관계임을 알 수 있다.

11 these days: 요즘에 = nowadays

14 무언가에 대해 충분히 중요하거나 좋거나 즐길 만한 것을 나타
내는 말은 worth(가치가 있는)이다.

16 ⑤ 배낭의 무엇이 가장 마음에 드는지에 대한 구체적인 답변이
이어져야 한다.

17 관계대명사 that과 접속사 that을 구별하는 문제이다. 관계대명
사는 불완전한 절을 이끌고 접속사는 완전한 절을 이끈다는 사
실에 유의하자.

18 날씨가 나빴기 때문에 우리 여행을 미루었다는 의미이다. 따라서
'날씨가 너무 나빠서 여행을 미루었다'는 ②번이 가장 적절하다.

19 목적격 관계대명사가 들어가야 한다. 사람이 선행사이므로
who, whom, that이 쓰일 수 있으며 생략도 가능하다.

20 너무 더워서 수영하러 갔다는 문장으로 쓸 수 있다. go Ving:
V하러 가다

21 원인과 결과를 나타내는 문장이므로 because가 옳다.

22 모두 Maya가 비행을 너무 무서워해서 비행기로 여행할 수 없
다는 의미이지만, ⑤번은 비행이 무섭다 할지라도 비행기로 여
행한다는 의미이다.

23 that[which]은 생략할 수 있다.

24 목적격 관계대명사나 '주격 관계대명사+be동사'는 생략 가능하다.

25 which 대신 that을 쓰거나 생략해도 좋다.

26 한 그루의 나무에 잎이 너무 많아서 그것을 세는 것이 불가능하
다는 문장으로 쓸 수 있다.

27 that을 대신하여 which를 쓰거나 목적격 관계대명사이므로 생
략해도 무방하다.

28 'Kyle이 선택한 영화'라고 하였으므로 관계사절이 the movie
를 수식하도록 문장을 만든다.

29 (A)는 인칭대명사로 the movie를 가리키는 말이다. it은 가주
어, 비인칭 주어, 인칭대명사로 쓰일 수 있다.

30 Emma가 Kyle에 관해 어떻게 생각하는지는 알 수 없다.

31 모두 관계대명사 that이 들어갈 수 있으니 ①번에는 의문대명사
who나 what이 들어간다.

32 사실과 의견을 바탕으로 현명한 선택을 해야 한다고 하였으므로
⑤번이 가장 적절하다.

33 대부분의 광고들은 사실과 의견을 섞기 때문에 사실로 이루어진
광고만 믿는다는 것은 간단한 일이 될 수 없다

단원별 예상문제   p.150~153

01 ⑤   02 (1) wisely   (2) recommend
(3) strongly   03 (1) number one   (2) look for
(3) right now   (4) Hold on   (5) worth it

04 (E) → (A) → (C) → (D) → (B)   05 ⑤

06 I was very happy with it.   07 ④

08 Cheomseongdae, Bulguksa

09 ⑤   10 ⑤   11 ③   12 ④

13 Can you give me back the pen that you
borrowed from me?

14 ②   15 ⑤

16 The barbell was so light that I could lift it up.

17 ②   18 ④   19 facts, opinions

20 They are mainly talking about the difference
between facts and opinions.   21 ③

22 The book was so touching that I read it many
times.   23 ⑤

24 Charlotte's Web is a children's novel which
E. B. White wrote.

01 무언가를 다른 무언가에 더하는 것을 가리키는 말은 mix(섞다)

이다.

03 (4) hold on: 기다리다 (5) worth it: 그만한 가치가 있는

04 (E) 도움 요청 → (A) 가방 추천 → (C) 거절 및 이유 설명 → (D) 다른 가방 추천 → (B) 반응 및 구매

05 이어지는 대화에서 자전거가 마음에 들지 않는 이유를 설명하고 있으므로 ⑤번처럼 무엇이 마음에 드는지 묻는 표현은 어색하다.

07 (A) How do you like ~?:~가 마음에 드니? (B)에는 주어 That이 생략되어 있으므로 sounds, (C)에는 동명사 주어 walking이 적절하다.

09 주어진 빈칸에 들어갈 말로 추천하는 이유를 설명하는 표현이 적절하다.

10 Brian이 Antonio's에 가격이 좋은지 아닌지 확인하려고 갈 것이라는 설명은 대화의 내용과 일치하지 않는다.

11 관계대명사와 의문대명사를 구별하는 문제이다. 관계대명사는 해석되지 않으나 의문대명사는 '누구'라고 해석된다.

12 일을 열심히 한 것이 원인이고 그 결과로 그가 아프게 된 것이므로 ④번이 옳다.

13 '네가 나에게 빌려간 펜'이므로 the pen that you borrowed from me라고 쓰는 것이 옳다.

14 '의자에 앉다' 표현은 sit on이다. 따라서 on which라고 쓰는 것이 적절하며 관계대명사 that은 전치사의 목적어로 쓰이지 않는 것에 유의하자.

15 전치사의 목적어로 관계대명사 that은 쓰일 수 없다. 따라서 to whom으로 쓰는 것이 적절하다.

16 가벼운 것이 원인이고 내가 들어 올릴 수 있었다는 것이 결과이므로 'so light that ~'을 쓴다.

17 Emma가 하는 말을 이해할 수 없다는 의미이다.

18 (B)는 명사절을 이끄는 접속사로 완전한 절을 이끈다. ④번은 불완전한 절을 이끄는 관계대명사 that이다.

19 사실은 증명될 수 있는 것이라고 하였다. 따라서 '사실과는 다르게 의견은 증명될 수 없다'라고 쓰는 것이 옳다.

20 사실과 의견의 차이에 관하여 주로 이야기하고 있다.

21 모두 확인할 수 있는 사실이지만 ③번은 의견이다.

22 '이 책은 너무 감동적이어서 나는 이 책을 여러 번 읽었다'는 의미이다.

23 Wilbur가 몇 명의 친구를 가지고 있는지는 알 수 없다.

24 which를 대신하여 that을 써도 무방하다.

서술형 실전문제

p.154~155

01 Her favorite restaurant is Antonio's.

02 She recommends the bulgogi pizza.

03 She thinks it is a little slow on the weekends.

04 (C) → (B) → (A) → (D)

---

05 I can't find the cup which my husband likes to use.

06 (1) The wind blew my hat off my head because it was strong.

(2) The wind was so strong that it blew my hat off my head.

07 who[whom] Peter fell in love with left him / with whom Peter fell in love left him

08 that you baked / so delicious that

09 The jewel is so precious that it is priceless.

10 It says, "Winner of 6 Academy Awards including Best Picture."

11 She is using the advertisement of Forrest Gump.

12 의견은 진짜인지 아닌지 말할 수 없지만 사실은 확인할 수 있다.

13 opinions, facts

14 The book was so interesting that I couldn't put it down.

15 The genre of the book is fantasy.

01 미나가 가장 좋아하는 식당은 Antonio's이다.

02 미나는 불고기 피자를 추천하였다.

03 미나는 주말에는 서비스가 좀 느리다고 생각했다.

04 (C) 새 스마트폰을 갖게 된 것을 언급 → (B) 대답 및 만족 표현 → (A) 가장 마음에 드는 점 질문 → (D) 가장 마음에 드는 특징 설명

05 목적격 관계대명사이므로 생략해도 무방하며 that으로 써도 좋다.

06 원인은 바람이 강한 것이고, 그 결과로 내 머리에서 모자가 벗겨진 것이다.

07 'Peter가 사랑에 빠졌던 그 여자는 몇 주 전 그를 떠났다'는 문장을 쓸 수 있다. who[whom] 대신 that을 쓰거나 생략해도 좋다.

08 관계대명사 that은 생략하거나 which로 바꾸어 써도 좋다.

09 priceless: 값을 매길 수 없는, 대단히 귀중한

10 "Forest Gump" 영화 광고에는 "Winner of 6 Academy Awards including Best Picture."라고 쓰여 있다.

11 Emma는 Kyle이 가장 좋아하는 영화의 광고를 사용하여 사실과 의견의 차이점을 설명하고 있다.

12 의견은 사람의 감정을 나타내어 어떠한 것이 사실인지 아닌지 말할 수 없지만, 사실은 확인할 수 있는 차이가 있다고 하였다.

13 해석: 광고에는 우리가 믿을 수 없는 많은 의견들이 있다. 우리는 많은 사실을 가진 광고가 필요해.

14 원인과 결과를 이끄는 'so ~ that' 구문을 이용하여 문장을 만들 수 있다. 재미있는 것이 원인이고, 책을 놓을 수 없었던 것이 결과임에 유의한다.

15 책의 장르는 공상 소설(a fantasy novel)이라고 하였다.

창의사고력 서술형 문제

|모범답안|

01 (A) the bulgogi pizza (B) prices (C) a little slow

02 (1) Tom was so busy that he couldn't answer the phone.

(2) The waves were so high that we couldn't swim in the sea.

03 **Facts**

It is located in Yongin.

/ There are Korean traditional houses.

/ Visitors can watch nongak and jultagi.

Opinions

It's a fun place in Yongin.

/ They are beautiful.

/ Nongak and jultagi are very exciting to see.

01 제가 가장 좋아하는 식당, Antonio's를 소개하고자 합니다. 이곳은 괜찮은 피자 식당이에요. 저는 불고기 피자를 추천합니다. 이것은 진짜 맛있어요. 만약 여러분이 주말에 이곳에 방문한다면, 서비스는 조금 느릴 수 있어요. Antonio's를 방문해 보는 게 어떨까요?

단원별 모의고사

01 ⑤   02 ②

03 It was difficult for her.   04 ③   05 ⑤

06 (A) red (B) a different color

(C) the navy backpack (D) side pockets

07 They are talking about Tom's new smartphone.

08 He is really happy with it.

09 He likes the camera most about his smartphone.

10 ⓓ → check it out   11 ⑤

12 (1) Mix the butter with the sugar.

(2) Jack lifted the chair.

(3) Are you telling the truth?

13 ④   14 ②

15 His speech was so famous that everyone knew about it.   16 ⑤

17 It is so cold that my mouth is frozen. 18 ③

19 ④   20 ⑤   21 ④

22 ⓕ → unlike   23 fact, an opinion

24 ④   25 that I read is so touching that / recommend it to you

02 경주 여행에 매우 만족함을 알 수 있다.

03 Suji에게 석굴암까지 올라가는 것은 어려웠다.

04 이어지는 대화에서 추천하는 표현이 이어지므로 빈칸에 추천하는 표현이 적절하다. recommend: 추천하다

05 ⑤번을 제외한 나머지는 모두 추천을 하는 표현이다.

06 나는 오늘 새로운 배낭을 사서 기분이 좋았다. 나는 빨간색 배낭을 메곤 했었다. 그래서 나는 다른 색을 사고 싶었다. 점원은 내게 남색 배낭을 추천하였는데 이것은 양쪽에 주머니를 갖고 있었다. 나는 이것이 매우 마음에 들어서 샀다. 나는 내일 새 배낭을 메는 것을 기대하고 있다.

07 Tom과 Sue는 Tom의 새 스마트폰에 대해 이야기하고 있다.

08 Tom은 그의 스마트폰을 정말 만족스러워하고 있다.

09 Tom은 그의 스마트폰에서 카메라를 가장 좋아한다.

10 check out과 같이 '동사+부사'로 이루어진 구동사의 목적어가 인칭대명사일 때는 동사와 부사 사이에 목적어가 위치한다.

11 위 대화에서 Antonio's에서 불고기 피자가 얼마인지는 알 수 없다.

12 mix: 섞다, lift: 들어 올리다. tell the truth: 진실을 말하다

13 모두 날씨가 너무 좋아서 우리가 밖으로 나갔다는 의미이지만 ④번은 날씨가 너무 좋아서 밖으로 나갈 수 없었다는 의미이다.

14 모두 불완전한 절을 이끄는 관계대명사 that이지만 ②번은 접속사 that으로 완전한 절을 이끈다.

15 유명한 것이 원인이고 모두가 아는 것은 결과이다. 따라서 so famous that everyone knew about it이라고 쓰는 것이 옳다.

16 주어가 복수 명사인 The women이므로 are friendly라고 쓰는 것이 옳다.

17 너무 추워서 내 입이 얼었다는 문장으로 쓸 수 있다.

18 무엇을 하고 있는지 묻는 말에 ⓒ 대답 → ⓐ 영화가 어떠냐는 질문에 → ⓓ 너무 지루하다는 대답 → ⓑ 이 대답에 유감이라고 답하는 순서가 자연스럽다.

19 hold on: 기다리다

20 광고에는 사실과 의견이 모두 있다고 하였으므로 ⑤번이 글의 내용과 일치한다.

21 ④ "Forest Gump"의 광고를 가리키는 대명사이다.

22 "Y-Men 7" 광고에는 의견이 사용되었고 "Forest Gump" 광고에는 사실이 사용되었다고 하였으므로 unlike를 쓰는 것이 옳다.

23 어떠한 것이 증명될 수 있으면 사실이지만, 진실인지 아닌지 확인할 수 없는 것은 의견이라고 말할 수 있다.

24 ignore: 무시하다, 못 본 체하다

25 '내가 읽은 책'이라고 하였으므로 관계사절이 the book을 수식하도록 문장을 만든다.

교과서 파헤치기

단어 TEST Step 1   p.02

01 화살	02 근처, 이웃, 인근	03 나타나다
04 어두운	05 해결하다	06 장식하다
07 먼, 멀리	08 폭죽, 불꽃놀이	09 따르다
10 모이다, 모으다	11 형태, ~ 모양으로 만들다	
12 놀라운	13 거대한	14 지속하다
15 광고하다	16 대회, 시합, 경쟁	17 축제
18 썰매	19 거의	20 완전히
21 게시하다	22 음악가	23 축하하다, 기념하다
24 야외의	25 뒤쫓다	26 더미
27 예술 작품	28 가루	29 성인, 어른
30 형형색색의	31 개최하다	32 던지다
33 고향	34 빵집, 제과점	35 서로
36 손을 쓸 수 없는	37 처음부터 끝까지	38 A와 B 사이에
39 지속되다, 계속되다		40 ~ 때문에
41 더욱 더	42 ~의 오른편에	43 ~ 앞에

단어 TEST Step 2   p.03

01 bakery	02 celebrate	03 colorful
04 parade	05 take	06 during
07 sail	08 artwork	09 chase
10 hold	11 hometown	12 boat
13 cross	14 live	15 near
16 powder	17 outdoor	18 block
19 pile	20 adult	21 throw
22 decorate	23 gather	24 advertise
25 solve	26 last	27 appear
28 neighborhood	29 competition	30 firework
31 huge	32 arrow	33 completely
34 follow	35 more and more	
36 get off	37 each other	38 in front of
39 because of	40 next to	41 go on
42 between A and B		
43 from beginning to end		

단어 TEST Step 3   p.04

1 lift, 들어올리다   2 adult, 어른   3 chase, 뒤쫓다
4 artwork, 예술 작품   5 competition, 대회, 경쟁
6 festival, 축제   7 sled, 썰매   8 last, 지속하다
9 hometown, 고향   10 gather, 모이다   11 hold, 개최하다

12 pile, 더미   13 advertise, 광고하다
14 shape, ~ 모양으로 만들다   15 celebrate, 축하하다
16 decorate, 장식하다

대화문 TEST Step 1   p.05~06

Listen and Speak 1-A
How can I get to the library / Cross, go straight, make a left / Thank you

Listen and Speak 1-B
What's up / Are, free this Saturday / Why do, ask / about having lunch / Let's try, Chinese restaurant, near / How can I get there from the school / Come out, go straight, Make a left, be on your left / All right. Let's meet at / See you then

Listen and Speak 1-C
Excuse me, can, get to / Go straight, make a right, will be on your right / Is, far from / No, not / Thank you

Listen and Speak 2-A
hurry up, going to be late for / How long will it take to get to the theater / take about, by bus / almost ready

Listen and Speak 2-B
excited about, this Friday / Me, too, can, do to advertise / about making / can post them, neighborhood / How long will it take to / take about three hours / I hope, come to the festival

Real Life Talk
Excuse, How can, get to / easy, over there / I do / Take, get off / How long will it take to get there / take about 20 minutes / very much / problem, Are, going, the festival / its's a lot of fun / I hope, have a great time

대화문 TEST Step 2   p.07~08

Listen and Speak 1-A
Sora: Excuse me. How can I get to the library?
Tom: Oh, the library? Cross the street and go straight two blocks. Then make a left.
Sora: Thank you very much.

Listen and Speak 1-B
Minsu: Hi, Emma. What's up?
Emma: Hey, Minsu. Are you free this Saturday?
Minsu: Yes. Why do you ask?
Emma: Well, how about having lunch together?
Minsu: Sure.
Emma: Let's try the new Chinese restaurant, Ming's.

It's near the school.

Minsu: Okay. How can I get there from the school?

Emma: Come out from the school and go straight to Green Street. Make a left, and the restaurant will be on your left.

Minsu: All right. Let's meet at 12 o'clock.

Emma: Wonderful. See you then.

Listen and Speak 1-C

A: Excuse me. How can I get to the post office?

B: Go straight to 1st Street and make a right. It will be on your right.

A: Is it far from here?

B: No, it's not.

A: Thank you very much.

Listen and Speak 2-A

Amy: Jinho, hurry up. We're going to be late for the movie.

Jinho: Okay. How long will it take to get to the theater?

Amy: It will take about 15 minutes by bus.

Jinho: All right. I'm almost ready.

Listen and Speak 2-B

Andy: I'm so excited about the school festival this Friday.

Mike: Me, too. What can we do to advertise it, Andy?

Andy: How about making posters?

Mike: Great idea. We can post them in our neighborhood.

Andy: Right. How long will it take to make them?

Mike: Well, it will take about three hours.

Andy: Okay, I hope many people come to the festival.

Real Life Talk

Man: Excuse me. How can I get to Suwon Hwaseong from here?

Mina: It's easy. Do you see the bus stop over there?

Man: Yes, I do.

Mina: Take the No. 11 bus and get off at the sixth stop.

Man: How long will it take to get there?

Mina: It will take about 20 minutes.

Man: Thank you very much.

Mina: No problem. Are you going there for the festival?

Man: Yes. I heard it's a lot of fun.

Mina: I hope you have a great time.

01 Festival, Colors
02 from Delhi
03 most popular, my
04 is usually in
05 During, say, hello
06 celebrate, everywhere for
07 On, gather around, at
08 main, begins, next
09 chase each other
10 What, green, powder
11 run around, throw, at
12 also join, parades
13 White Nights
14 from, Petersburg, Russia
15 Have, heard of
16 Every, amazing, happens
17 get completely dark
18 During, hold
19 in, lasts, about
20 there, almost every
21 most popular, celebration
22 with, appears on
23 begin, follows
24 also hear, playing
25 Kiruna, Festival
26 from Kiruna
27 favorite, because of
28 starts, last, goes on
29 largest event, competition
30 shape, into, other
31 watch, shaping, from, to
32 activity, sled ride
33 to, through, on

01 Festival of Colors
02 from Delhi, India
03 the most popular festival
04 is usually in March
05 During, say goodbye, hello, warm spring
06 celebrate, for two days
07 On, gather around, at night, sing and dance
08 main, begins the next day
09 chase each other with
10 What, powder 11 to run around, throw, at everyone
12 also join street parades
13 White Nights
14 from, Russia
15 Have you heard of
16 amazing, happens
17 does not get completely dark
18 During, hold
19 usually starts in, lasts for about
20 During, there is, almost every night
21 most popular, celebration

22 appears on the river

23 fireworks begin, follows

24 also hear, playing   25 Snow Festival

26 from Kiruna, Sweden

27 my favorite season because of

28 starts in the last week, goes on for

29 The largest event, competition

30 shape huge piles, into, other

31 watch, shaping, from beginning to end

32 favorite activity, dog sled ride

33 It, amazing to fly through, on

---

29 가장 큰 행사는 '눈 디자인 대회'예요.

30 미술가들이 거대한 눈 덩어리를 동물, 건물, 다른 아름다운 작품의 모양으로 만들어요.

31 사람들은 미술가들이 그들의 작품을 만드는 것을 처음부터 끝까지 지켜봐요.

32 내가 가장 좋아하는 활동은 개썰매 타기예요.

33 개썰매를 타고 눈 세상을 날아가는 것은 정말 놀라워요.

---

1 홀리, 색의 축제

2 인도, 델리의 Amala

3 '홀리'는 우리나라에서 가장 인기 있는 축제예요.

4 그것은 보통 3월에 있어요.

5 축제 기간 동안에, 우리는 추운 겨울에게 작별 인사를 하고 따뜻한 봄을 맞는 인사를 해요.

6 우리는 이틀 동안 어디서든 축제를 기념해요.

7 첫째 날, 사람들은 밤에 큰 모닥불 주변에 모여 노래하고 춤을 춰요.

8 주요 행사는 다음 날에 시작돼요.

9 어린이들과 어른들이 'gulal'을 지니고 서로를 쫓아다녀요.

10 'gulal'이 무엇이냐고요? 그것은 파랑, 노랑, 초록, 분홍의 가루예요.

11 주변을 뛰어다니며 형형색색의 가루를 모든 사람들에게 던지는 것은 정말 재미있어요.

12 우리는 거리 행진에도 참가해요!

13 백야 축제

14 러시아, 상트페테르부르크의 Victor

15 '백야'에 대해 들어 봤나요?

16 매년 여름, 이 놀라운 일이 나의 고향에서 벌어져요.

17 밤하늘이 완전히 어두워지지 않아요.

18 그 시기 동안, 우리는 백야 축제를 열어요.

19 축제는 보통 5월에 시작되고 약 한 달 동안 지속돼요.

20 축제 기간 동안 거의 매일 밤 발레나 오페라 공연이 있어요.

21 가장 인기 있는 행사는 '붉은 돛 축하 행사'예요.

22 빨간 돛을 단 배가 강 위에 서서히 나타나요.

23 곧 불꽃놀이가 시작되고 물 쇼가 이어져요.

24 또한 여러분은 음악가들이 아름다운 라이브 음악을 연주하는 것을 들을 수 있어요.

25 키루나 눈 축제

26 스웨덴, 키루나의 Ebba

27 겨울은 키루나 눈 축제 때문에 내가 가장 좋아하는 계절이에요.

28 축제는 1월 마지막 주에 시작해서 5일이나 6일 동안 계속돼요.

---

1 Holi, the Festival of Colors

2 Amala from Delhi, India

3 Holi is the most popular festival in my country.

4 It is usually in March.

5 During the festival, we say goodbye to cold winter and hello to warm spring.

6 We celebrate the festival everywhere for two days.

7 On the first day, people gather around a big fire at night and sing and dance.

8 The main event begins the next day.

9 Children and adults chase each other with *gulal*.

10 What is *gulal*? It is blue, yellow, green and pink powder.

11 It's a lot of fun to run around and throw colorful powder at everyone.

12 We also join street parades!

13 White Nights Festival

14 Victor from St. Petersburg, Russia

15 Have you heard of the White Nights?

16 Every summer, this amazing thing happens in my hometown.

17 The night sky does not get completely dark.

18 During that time, we hold the White Nights Festival.

19 It usually starts in May and lasts for about a month.

20 During the festival, there is a ballet or an opera almost every night.

21 The most popular event is the Scarlet Sails celebration.

22 A boat with red sails slowly appears on the river.

23 Soon, fireworks begin and a water show follows.

24 You can also hear musicians playing beautiful live music.

25 Kiruna Snow Festival

26 Ebba from Kiruna, Sweden

27 Winter is my favorite season because of the Kiruna Snow Festival.

28 The festival starts in the last week of January and goes on for five or six days.

29 The largest event is the snow design competition.

30 The artists shape huge piles of snow into animals, buildings, and other beautiful artworks.

31 People watch the artists shaping their works from beginning to end.

32 My favorite activity is the dog sled ride.

33 It is amazing to fly through a world of snow on a dog sled.

구석구석지문 TEST Step 1 p.19

Listen and Speak 2 - C

1. will, do, class party
2. make sandwiches
3. How long, take to
4. Maybe, take about an hour

Think and Write

1. Love
2. live in
3. There are, neighborhood
4. a lot of, to swim
5. famous *hanok* in
6. is called, was born
7. The most famous food
8. Come and enjoy

Project Culture

1. to introduce
2. is held in, in July
3. many interesting events
4. see people do
5. it, to do, painting
6. Lastly, outdoor concert
7. hear musicians play

구석구석지문 TEST Step 2 p.20

Listen and Speak 2 - C

1. A: Chris, what will you do for the class party?
2. B: I'll make sandwiches.
3. A: Great idea. How long will it take to make them?
4. B: Maybe it'll take about an hour.

Think and Write

1. I Love Gangneung
2. I live in Gangneung.
3. There are beautiful beaches in my neighborhood.

4. It's a lot of fun to swim at the beach.

5. There is a famous hanok in Gangneung.

6. It is called Ojukheon. Yulgok was born there.

7. The most famous food in Gangneung is potato tteok.

8. It is soft and sweet. Come and enjoy Gangneung!

Project Culture

1. I want to introduce Boryeong Mud Festival.

2. It is held in Daecheon Beach in July.

3. There are many interesting events in the festival.

4. First, you can see people do Ssireum in mud.

5. Also it is fun to do colorful mud body painting on your body.

6. Lastly, there is an outdoor concert.

7. You can hear musicians play beautiful musics.

단어 TEST Step 1 　　　　　　　　　　　　　　p.21

01 발명가	02 마지막으로	03 지원하다
04 환경, 주위의 상황	05 시각 장애가 있는, 눈이 먼	
06 약속하다	07 의사소통하다	08 비슷한
09 청각 장애가 있는, 귀가 먹은		10 평균
11 장식하다	12 우주, 공간	13 활발한
14 용감한	15 전시회	16 (비록)~이긴 하지만
17 더 먼, 더 멀리	18 친절한, 상냥한	19 포함하다
20 바르다, 펼치다	21 발명	22 다음에 나오는
23 몇몇의	24 기간, 길이	25 적응하다
26 필요한, 없어서는 안 될		27 조직, 단체
28 호기심이 많은, 궁금한		29 껍질을 벗기다
30 임무	31 차이	32 (얇게) 썰다, 자르다
33 전기	34 게다가	35 놓치다
36 평균적으로	37 지금부터	38 ~로 만들어지다,
~로 구성되다	39 ~와 잘 지내다	
40 기운을 내다, ~을 격려하다		41 발명하다
42 ~에 대해 궁금해 하다		43 ~을 잘하다

단어 TEST Step 2 　　　　　　　　　　　　　　p.22

01 invention	02 blind	03 similar
04 electricity	05 deaf	06 average
07 decorate	08 promise	09 inventor
10 lastly	11 necessary	12 organization
13 slice	14 environment	15 curious
16 communicate	17 friendly	18 reason
19 solar system	20 peel	21 outgoing
22 stick	23 exhibition	24 brave
25 produce	26 mission	27 although
28 include	29 apply	30 following
31 several	32 length	33 adapt
34 difference	35 miss out	36 from now on
37 get along with	38 on average	39 in addition
40 be made of	41 be curious about	
42 cheer up	43 have a great time	

단어 TEST Step 3 　　　　　　　　　　　　　　p.23

1 blind, 시각 장애가 있는, 눈이 먼　2 length, 기간
3 mission, 임무　4 slice, (얇게) 썰다, 자르다
5 deaf, 청각 장애가 있는, 귀가 먹은　6 spread, 바르다
7 similar, 비슷한　8 peel, 껍질을 벗기다　9 difference, 차이

---

11 half, 절반　12 inventor, 발명가　13 adapt, 적응하다
14 stick, 나뭇가지, 막대　15 apply, 지원하다
16 organization, 조직, 단체

대화문 TEST Step 1 　　　　　　　　　　　　p.24~25

Listen & Speak 1-A

what this is / looks like / butter stick / is there butter in it / can spread butter, with

Listen & Speak 1-B

show and tell / who this man is / inventor, was interested in, What, invent, deaf, made some inventions, deaf people, opened

Listen & Speak 2-A

looks interesting, What, for / for slicing eggs / try / here is an egg

Listen & Speak 2-B

look at, in science class / Why, make / not just for wearing / what, for / put them on, clean the floor / will clean, from now on / Don't worry about

Listen & Speak 2-C

look at / have never seen, before, What, for / for making ink / interesting

Real Life Talk – Step 1

How was / had a great time, science exhibition with / heard there were / Look at, what it is / not sure / What is it for / wear, can experience another world / Sounds, try / Her, go

대화문 TEST Step 2 　　　　　　　　　　　　p.26~27

Listen & Speak 1-A

Brian: Do you know what this is?
Amy: Um, it looks like a glue stick.
Brian: No, it's a butter stick.
Amy: Oh, is there butter in it?
Brian: Yes, you can spread butter on the bread with it.

Listen & Speak 1-B

Ms. Lee: Hello, class! Jisu is today's speaker for show and tell. Jisu?
Jisu: Hi, class! Do you know who this man is? His name is Alexander Graham Bell. Bell was an inventor. He was interested in sound. What did he invent? Yes, the telephone! His mother and wife were deaf. So he also made some inventions for deaf people and opened a school for them.

Jane: This looks interesting. What is it for?

Mike: It's for slicing eggs.

Jane: Really? May I try it?

Mike: Sure, here is an egg.

Tom: Mom, look at these slippers. I made them in science class.

Mom: Why did you make slippers in science class?

Tom: They are not just for wearing.

Mom: Then, what are they for?

Tom: You can put them on and clean the floor.

Mom: Oh, so you will clean your room from now on?

Tom: Sure. Don't worry about my room, Mom.

A: Jane, look at this. It's a meok.

B: I have never seen it before. What is it for?

A: It's for making ink.

B: Oh, really? That's interesting.

Judy: How was your weekend, Hojin?

Hojin: I had a great time. I went to a science exhibition with my brother.

Judy: Did you? I heard there were so many interesting things.

Hojin: Yes. Look at this. I bought it there. Do you know what it is?

Judy: Well, I'm not sure. What is it?

Hojin: It's a VR headset.

Judy: A VR headset? What is it for?

Hojin: If you wear it, you can experience another world.

Judy: Sounds cool. May I try it?

Hojin: Sure. Here you go.

본문 TEST Step 1 · p.28~29

01 Live on
02 live on another
03 looking for, to
04 to build, on
05 healthy / curious / along / adapt
06 To apply, send
07 must include, to following
08 Why, want, go / good sense, humor / perfect, for, mission
09 chance, so, miss out
10 the Second Earth
11 Although, one, been, yet
12 These, looking at, as
13 In fact, trying, right
14 big, live on
15 believe so, several reasons

16 think, that, water
17 because, necessary for
18 hard land, build, on
19 lengt, similar to that
20 In addition, has, seasons
21 So, lead , lives
22 Lastly, very far
23 the second closest
24 however, differences from
25 about half, size
26 second smallest, solar system
27 year, about twice, as
28 much colder than
29 On average, about
30 because, farther away, than
31 Although, answer, exciting, imagine
32 be the, Korean on

본문 TEST Step 2 · p.30~31

01 Live on
02 to live on another
03 Korea Space Organization, looking for people to go
04 Our misson, to build, on
05 are looking for / who, healthy / who, creative, curious / who, get along with / who, adapt to new environment
06 To apply, send us
07 must include, to, following questions
08 want to go / a good sense of humor / perfect person for this mission
09 a chance of, don't miss
10 the Second Earth
11 Although, many books, movies, has been, yet
12 These days, looking at, as
13 In fact, are trying to send, right now
14 Can people live on
15 believe so, several seasons
16 that, water on
17 because, necessary for
18 hard land to build, on
19 length, is similar to that
20 In addition, has four seasons
21 can lead similar lives
22 not very far
23 the second closest planet
24 however, some differences from
25 about half
26 the second smallest, solar
27 about twice as long as
28 much colder than
29 On average, about
30 because, farther away from
31 Although, answer, right now, exciting to imagine
32 the first Korean on

1 화성에서 살아요!

2 다른 행성에서 살고 싶은가요?

3 한국 우주 기구(KSO)는 화성에 갈 사람들을 찾고 있습니다!

4 우리의 임무는 화성에 도시를 세우는 것입니다.

5 우리는 다음과 같은 사람을 찾고 있습니다. 건강한 사람. 창의적이고 호기심이 많은 사람. 다른 사람들과 잘 지낼 수 있는 사람. 새로운 환경에 빨리 적응할 수 있는 사람.

6 지원하려면 우리에게 짧은 동영상을 보내세요.

7 동영상은 다음의 질문에 관한 답을 포함해야 합니다.

8 1. 당신은 왜 화성에 가고 싶은가요?

   2. 당신은 유머 감각이 있나요?

   3. 왜 당신이 이 임무에 적합한 사람인가요?

9 이것은 일생에 단 한 번뿐인 기회이므로 놓치지 마세요!

10 화성, 제 2의 지구?

11 화성에 관한 많은 책과 영화가 있긴 하지만, 아직 화성에 가 본 사람은 아무도 없다.

12 요즘, 과학자들은 화성을 새로운 거주지로 보고 있다.

13 사실, NASA와 몇몇 회사들은 그곳에 사람들을 보내기 위해 바로 지금도 노력하고 있다.

14 중요한 질문은 "화성에서 사람들이 살 수 있는가?"이다.

15 많은 과학자들은 몇몇 이유로 그렇게 믿고 있다.

16 첫째, 그들은 화성에 물이 있다고 생각한다.

17 물은 모든 생명체에 필수적이기 때문에 이것은 중요하다.

18 둘째, 화성은 집과 건물을 지을 수 있는 단단한 땅을 가지고 있다.

19 셋째, 화성의 낮과 밤의 길이는 지구의 낮과 밤의 길이와 비슷하다.

20 게다가, 화성은 사계절도 있다.

21 그래서 사람들이 비슷한 생활을 할 수 있다.

22 마지막으로, 화성은 그렇게 멀지 않다.

23 화성은 지구에서 두 번째로 가까운 행성이다.

24 그러나 화성은 지구와 다른 점이 몇 개 있다.

25 첫째, 화성은 지구의 약 절반 크기이다.

26 화성은 태양계에서 두 번째로 작은 행성이다.

27 둘째, 화성에서의 일 년은 지구에서의 일 년보다 약 두 배 길다.

28 셋째, 화성은 지구보다 훨씬 더 춥다.

29 평균적으로, 화성의 기온은 약 섭씨 영하 60도이다.

30 이것은 화성이 지구보다 태양에서 더 멀리 떨어져 있기 때문이다.

31 비록 누구도 그 중요한 질문에 지금 당장 답할 수는 없지만, 이 새로운 세상을 상상하는 것은 신이 난다.

32 누가 알겠는가? 당신이 화성에 발을 디디는 첫 번째 한국인이 될 수도 있다!

1 Live on MARS!

2 Do you want to live on another planet?

3 The Korea Space Organization (KSO) is looking for people to go to MARS!.

4 Our mission is to build a city on Mars.

5 We are looking for someone… who is healthy, who is creative and curious, who can get along with others, who can adapt to a new environment quickly.

6 To apply, send us a short video.

7 The video must include the answers to the following questions:

8 Why do you want to go to Mars? / Do you have a good sense of humor? / Why are you the perfect person for this mission?

9 This is a chance of a lifetime, so don't miss out!

10 Mars, the Second Earth?

11 Although there are many books and movies about Mars, no one has been there yet.

12 These days, scientists are looking at Mars as a new home.

13 In fact, NASA and some companies are trying to send people there right now.

14 The big question is, "Can people live on Mars?"

15 Many scientists believe so for several reasons.

16 First, they think that there is water on Mars.

17 This is great because water is necessary for all life.

18 Second, Mars has hard land to build houses and buildings on.

19 Third, the length of day and night on Mars is similar to that on Earth.

20 In addition, Mars also has four seasons.

21 So, people can lead similar lives.

22 Lastly, Mars is not very far.

23 It is the second closest planet to Earth.

24 Mars, however, has some differences from Earth.

25 First, Mars is about half the size of Earth.

26 It is the second smallest planet in the solar system.

27 Second, a year on Mars is about twice as long as a year on Earth.

28 Third, Mars is much colder than Earth.

29 On average, it is about $-60℃$ on Mars.

30 This is because Mars is farther away from the Sun than Earth.

31 Although no one can answer the big question right now, it is exciting to imagine this new world.

32 Who knows? You could be the first Korean on Mars!

Real Life Talk - Step 2

1. what this is
2. No, don't, What, it
3. Clean Straw
4. What is it for
5. while you drink
6. that's great

Think and Write

1. from Korea, years old
2. want to, because, been curious about
3. friendly, enjoy making friends
4. good at taking
5. perfect person, adapt, new environment
6. Although, communicate well with others
7. the chance to live

Project

1. Neptune
2. moons, cold planet
3. named after, god of the sea
4. the farthest planet, the solar system

Real Life Talk - Step 2

1. A: Do you know what this is?
2. B: No , I don't . What is it?
3. A: It's a Clean Straw.
4. B: A Clean Straw? What is it for?
5. A: It cleans water while you drink.
6. B: Wow, that's great!

Think and Write

1. My name is Suji Lee from Korea. I'm 15 years old.
2. I want to go to Mars because I've been curious about space.
3. I'm friendly and I enjoy making friends.
4. I'm good at taking photos.
5. I'm the perfect person for this mission because I can adapt to a new environment quickly.
6. Although I'm young, I can communicate well with others.
7. Give me the chance to live on Mars!

Project

1. Neptune
2. It has 14 moons. It's a very cold planet.
3. It's named after the god of the sea.
4. It's the farthest planet from the Sun in the solar system.

Lesson 7

01 작가	02 배낭	03 완벽한
04 관련성, 연관성	05 여행	06 상
07 차이점	08 섞다	09 믿다, 신뢰하다
10 모험	11 전통적인	12 설명하다
13 간단한, 단순한	14 우정	15 특히
16 ~와 달리	17 진실, 사실	18 거짓말하다
19 광고	20 가치가 있는	21 공상
22 신념, 생각	23 강력하게	24 들어 올리다
25 현명하게	26 식사	27 증명하다
28 나타내다, 표현하다		29 해결하다, 풀다
30 남색	31 추천하다	32 지루한
33 감동적인	34 의견	35 예를 들면
36 ~로 가득한	37 ~을 바탕으로	38 지금부터
39 기다려, 멈춰	40 선택하다	41 지금
42 ~을 확인하다	43 그만한 가치가 있는	

01 trust	02 author	03 perfect
04 touching	05 express	06 boring
07 trip	08 navy	09 adventure
10 purple	11 novel	12 opinion
13 advertisement	14 pocket	15 simple
16 award	17 worth	18 especially
19 meal	20 friendship	21 strongly
22 lift	23 solve	24 prove
25 explain	26 traditional	27 difference
28 mix	29 fantasy	30 recommend
31 belief	32 unlike	33 wisely
34 truth	35 check out	36 look for
37 from now on	38 make a choice	
39 for example	40 full of	41 based on
42 right now	43 hold on	

1 trust, 신뢰하다, 믿다   2 opinion, 의견   3 mix, 섞다
4 lift, 들어 올리다   5 truth, 진실, 사실   6 meal, 식사
7 express, 나타내다, 표현하다   8 lie, 거짓말하다
9 pocket, 주머니   10 recommend, 추천하다
11 advertisement, 광고   12 connection, 관련성
13 explain, 설명하다   14 prove, 증명하다

15 award, 상   16 desert, 사막

Listen & Speak 1-A

recommend a good movie / really liked / haven't seen, yet / number one, right now

Listen & Speak 1-B

help / looking for, backpack, recommend one / How about, the most popular color these days / My old backpack, different color / How about, navy, has side pockets, looks good, take

Listen & Speak 2-A

got, new smartphone / really happy with / What, like most about it / takes great pictures

Listen & Speak 2-B

How did, like, trip / happy with / Where, visit / visited / Where else did, go / wonderful place / Sounds like, perfect trip / walking up, was difficult / I'm sure, worth it

Real Life Talk – Step 1

can you recommend / Why don't, my favorite / What, like about / delicious, recommend / How, the prices / think, too / Sounds like, How, like the service / little slow / check it out / problem, Enjoy

Real Life Talk – Step 2

recommend a book for me / How about / What do you like / main character, special / Sounds, read

Listen & Speak 1-A

Brian: Can you recommend a good movie?

Emily: Try Star Wars. I really liked it.

Brian: Oh, I haven't seen it yet.

Emily: It's the number one movie right now.

Listen & Speak 1-B

W: May I help you?

B: Yes. I'm looking for a backpack. Can you recommend one?

W: How about this red one? Red is the most popular color these days.

B: My old backpack was red, so I want a different color.

W: How about this navy one? It has side pockets.

B: Oh, that looks good. I'll take it.

Listen & Speak 2-A

Sue: Tom, you got a new smartphone.

Tom: Yes, I did. I'm really happy with it.

Sue: What do you like most about it?

Tom: I love the camera. It takes great pictures.

Listen & Speak 2-B

Jack: Hi, Suji. How did you like your trip to Gyeongju?

Suji: I was very happy with it.

Jack: Where did you visit?

Suji: I visited Cheomseongdae. It was great.

Jack: Where else did you go?

Suji: Bulguksa. It was a wonderful place.

Jack: Sounds like the perfect trip.

Suji: Yeah, but walking up to Seokguram was difficult.

Jack: But I'm sure it was worth it.

Real Life Talk – Step 1

Brian: Mina, can you recommend a good pizza restaurant?

Mina: Why don't you try Antonio's? It's my favorite.

Brian: What do you like about it?

Mina: The food is delicious. I recommend the bulgogi pizza.

Brian: How are the prices?

Mina: I think the prices are good, too.

Brian: Sounds like a good restaurant. How do you like the service?

Mina: It's a little slow on the weekends.

Brian: Okay. I'll check it out. Thanks.

Mina: No problem. Enjoy your meal!

Real Life Talk – Step 2

Amy: Yujin, can you recommend a book for me?

Yujin: How about The Little Prince?

Amy: What do you like about the book?

Yujin: I like the main character. He is very special.

Amy: Sounds good. I'll read it.

01 are, doing

02 watching, on, computer

03 How, it

04 Don't, so boring that

05 sorry to hear

06 mad, advertisement said

07 believe everything that, read

08 lied on, for, back

09 Hold, lie because, opinions

10 not following you

11 express, feelings like

12 that, not, facts, proven

13 For example, check, on

14 the connection with

15 Let, explain, favorite　　16 It's, *Gump*

17 Let's, its advertisement, say

18 says, Awards including　　19 uses facts unlike

20 Do, see, difference　　21 exactly, says, ad

22 Aren't, both opinions

23 question, like, expressing opinions

24 ad, award, movie won　　25 check, on, fact

26 From, on, trust, with

27 that simple, mix, with

28 have, make, choice, both

29 Got, watch, rest, with

30 no thanks, rest

01 What are, doing

02 watching the movie, on

03 How, it

04 Don't, so boring that, to cry

05 sorry to hear that

06 mad, advertisement, it, The Most Exciting Movie

07 can't believe everything that you read

08 lied on, ask for my money back

09 Hold on, lie because, used opinions, facts

10 not following you

11 express people's feelings

12 that, true or not, can be proven

13 For example, check that on the map

14 the connection with

15 Let me explain　　16 It's

17 Let's look for its advertisement

18 It says, including　　19 uses facts unlike

20 the difference　　21 exactly, says, says

22 Aren't, both opinions

23 words like, usually expressing opinions

24 award which the movie won

25 check that on the Internet

26 From now on, trust, with

27 that simple, mix facts with opinions

28 make a smart choice based on both

29 to watch the rest

30 no thanks, the rest of

1 Emma: Kyle, 뭐 하고 있니?

2 Kyle: Emma. 나는 컴퓨터로 영화 "Y-Men 7"을 보고 있어.

3 Emma: 어때?

4 Kyle: 묻지 마. 너무 지루해서 울고 싶어.

5 Emma: 유감이야.

6 Klye: 난 정말 화가 나. 영화 광고에는 이것이 "올해의 가장 흥미진진한 영화"라고 쓰여 있었어.

7 Emma: 음, 넌 네가 읽는 것을 모두 믿을 수는 없어.

8 Kyle: 그들은 광고에 거짓말을 한 거야. 돈을 환불해 달라고 해야겠어.

9 Emma: 기다려, Kyle! 그들은 사실이 아닌 의견을 사용했기 때문에 꼭 거짓말을 한 것은 아니야.

10 Kyle: 뭐라고? 네 말을 이해하지 못하겠어.

11 Emma: 의견은 "사막은 아름다워."와 같이 사람들의 감정을 표현하는 것이야.

12 그것이 사실인지 아닌지 말할 수는 없어. 하지만 사실은 증명할 수 있어.

13 예를 들면, "아타카마 사막은 칠레에 있다."는 사실이야. 넌 그것을 지도에서 확인할 수 있어.

14 Kyle: 알겠어⋯. 하지만 그게 영화와 무슨 관련이 있니?

15 Emma: 설명해 줄게. 네가 가장 좋아하는 영화가 뭐니?

16 Kyle: "Forest Gump"야.

17 Emma: 좋아. 그 영화의 광고를 찾아보자. 뭐라고 쓰여 있니?

18 Kyle: "Best Picture를 포함하여 아카데미 6개 부문 수상작"이라고 쓰여 있어.

19 Emma: 알겠니? "Y-Men 7" 광고와는 달리 사실을 사용하고 있어.

20 차이를 알겠니?

21 Kyle: 잘 모르겠어. "Y-Men 7" 광고는 "Most Exciting Movie"라고 쓰여 있고 "Forest Gump" 광고는 "Best Picture"라고 쓰여 있잖아.

22 둘 다 의견 아니니?

23 Emma: 좋은 질문이야, Kyle. 사람들이 'best'나 'most'와 같은 말을 사용할 때, 그들은 대개 의견을 표현하는 거야.

24 하지만 "Forest Gump" 광고에서 "Best Picture"는 영화가 받은 상이야.

25 우리는 인터넷에서 그것을 확인할 수 있어. 그건 사실이야.

26 Kyle: 아하! 지금부터 사실로 이루어진 광고만 믿겠어.

27 Emma: 그렇게 간단하지는 않아. 대부분의 광고는 사실과 의견이 섞여 있어.

28 그러니 그 둘을 바탕으로 현명한 선택을 해야 해.

29 Kyle: 알겠어! Emma, "Y-Men 7"의 남은 부분을 나와 함께 볼래?

30 Emma: 고맙지만 사양할게. 영화의 남은 부분 잘 봐!

1 Emma: What are you doing, Kyle?

2 Kyle: Oh, Emma. I'm watching the movie, *Y–Men 7* on my computer.

3 Emma: How is it?

4 Kyle: Don't ask. It's so boring that I want to cry.

5 Emma: I'm sorry to hear that.

6 Kyle: I'm so mad. The movie advertisement said it was "The Most Exciting Movie of the Year."

7 Emma: Well, you can't believe everything that you read.

8 Kyle: They lied on the advertisement. I'm going to ask for my money back.

9 Emma: Hold on, Kyle! They didn't really lie because they used opinions, not facts.

10 Kyle: Huh? I'm not following you.

11 Emma: Opinions express people's feelings like, "The desert is beautiful."

12 You can't say that it's true or not. But, facts can be proven.

13 For example, "The Atacama Desert is in Chile," is a fact. You can check that on the map.

14 Kyle: Okay.... But what's the connection with movies?

15 Emma: Let me explain. What's your favorite movie?

16 Kyle: It's *Forrest Gump*.

17 Emma: Okay. Let's look for its advertisement. What does it say?

18 Kyle: It says, "Winner of 6 Academy Awards including Best Picture."

19 Emma: See? It uses facts unlike the *Y–Men 7* advertisement.

20 Do you see the difference?

21 Kyle: Not exactly. The *Y–Men 7* ad says "Most Exciting Movie" and the *Forrest Gump* ad says "Best Picture."

22 Aren't they both opinions?

23 Emma: That's a great question, Kyle. When people use words like "best" or "most," they are usually expressing opinions.

24 But in the *Forrest Gump* ad, "Best Picture" is the award which the movie won.

25 We can check that on the Internet. That's a fact.

26 Kyle: Aha! From now on I'm only going to trust ads with facts.

27 Emma: It's not that simple. Most ads mix facts with opinions.

28 So you have to make a smart choice based on both of them.

29 Kyle: Got it! Emma, do you want to watch the rest of *Y–Men 7* with me?

30 Emma: Thanks, but no thanks. Enjoy the rest of the movie!

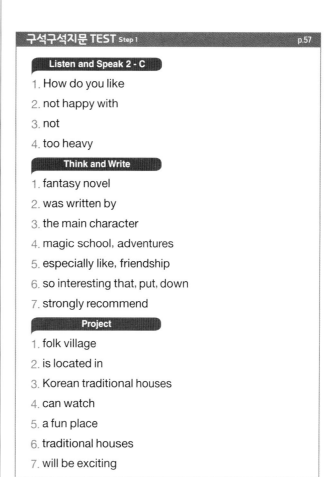

Listen and Speak 2 - C

1. How do you like

2. not happy with

3. not

4. too heavy

Think and Write

1. fantasy novel

2. was written by

3. the main character

4. magic school, adventures

5. especially like, friendship

6. so interesting that, put, down

7. strongly recommend

Project

1. folk village

2. is located in

3. Korean traditional houses

4. can watch

5. a fun place

6. traditional houses

7. will be exciting

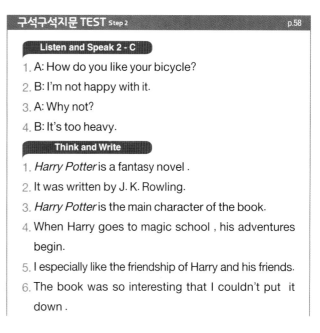

Listen and Speak 2 - C

1. A: How do you like your bicycle?

2. B: I'm not happy with it.

3. A: Why not?

4. B: It's too heavy.

Think and Write

1. *Harry Potter* is a fantasy novel .

2. It was written by J. K. Rowling.

3. *Harry Potter* is the main character of the book.

4. When Harry goes to magic school , his adventures begin.

5. I especially like the friendship of Harry and his friends.

6. The book was so interesting that I couldn't put it down .

7. I strongly recommend it to everyone.

Project

1. Korean folk village

2. Facts: It is located in Yongin.

3. There are Korean traditional houses.

4. Visitors can watch nongak and jultagi.

5. Opinions: It's a fun place in Yongin.

6. Korean traditional houses are beautiful.

7. Nongak and jultagi will be exciting.

MEMO

적중100

영어 기출 문제집

정답 및 해설

동아 | 이병민